Reading Writing

An Argument Rhetoric and Reader

George Y. Trail

HEINLE & HEINLE

THOMSON LEARNING™

Australia • Canada • Mexico • Singapore • Spain
United Kingdom • United States

HEINLE & HEINLE

™

THOMSON LEARNING

Publisher: Earl McPeek
Acquisitions Editor: Julie McBurney
Market Strategist: John Meyers

Project Manager: Angela Williams Urquhart
Compositor: TechBooks
Printer: Malloy Lithographing

Asia
Thomson Learning
60 Albert Complex, #15-01
Albert Complex
Singapore 189969

Australia
Nelson Thomson Learning
102 Dodds Street
South Melbourne, Victoria 3205
Australia

Canada
Nelson Thomson Learning
1120 Birchmount Road
Toronto, Ontario M1K 5G4
Canada

For more information about our products,
contact us at:
Thomson Learning Academic Resource Center
1-800-423-0563

For permission to use material from this text,
contact us by:
Phone: 1-800-730-2214
Fax: 1-800-730-2215
Web: http://www.thomsonrights.com

Europe/Middle East/Africa
Thomson Learning
Berkshire House
168-173 High Holborn
London WC1 V7AA
United Kingdom

Latin America
Thomson Learning
Seneca, 53
Colonia Polanco
11560 Mexico D.F.
Mexico

Library of Congress Catalog Card Number:
00-105742

ISBN: 0-15-507234-X

Spain
Paraninfo Thomson Learning
Calle/Magallanes, 25
28015 Madrid, Spain

CONTENTS

A NOTE TO THE INSTRUCTOR

As the introduction reports, this rhetoric/reader is keyed to its companion volume, *Rhetorical Terms and Concepts: A Contemporary Glossary,* and depends throughout on the definitions and discussions presented in that book. *Reading Writing* is only available with the *Glossary* and is conceptually inseparable from it. The *Glossary,* however, can be used with other texts and is accordingly available as a separate item.

Originally developed as a text for use in composition classes that met in large lecture combined sections which were rotated with small-section instructor-led discussion meetings, the text presents examples and analyses intended to be followed up with specific assignments of exercises for analysis either from the readings or from materials taken from the press of the moment. Local issues, political scandals, presidential and senatorial campaigns, current controversies on issues juridical, medical, ethical, educational, and social are all grist for the mill of rhetorical analysis. Nearly any current Op/Ed piece is suitable material for analysis. And so is any piece of prose from any discipline, insofar as it is advocating a position.

Reading Writing tries to make the point that we all perform rhetorical analysis whenever we interact with language, that whether we are conscious of it or not, our linguistic exchange with the world around us is comprised of a sort of continual process of rhetorical analysis. What this text presents, then, is how to do skillfully what one must do anyway to live in sociolinguistic interaction with that world, and most specifically in its written form.

TEACHING APPROACH

Words on a hard copy page have to take certain forms for certain times (those times between editions), but even bearing this in mind, *Reading Writing* and *Rhetorical Terms and Concepts* were never intended to proscribe the approach to the material that the instructor using them might take.

There are, for example, exercises dispersed throughout the introduction and following chapters as well as exercises accompanying the readings. It is intended that these present the instructor with a variety of materials from which to choose, or upon which to base wholly different exercises. The specific exercises are all presented as writing assignments, but are designed to be immediately convertible to class discussion subjects if so desired. They are also suitable to adapt for use with any up-to-the-minute material you may wish to present to your class, whether that be as substitute for or supplement to the materials included.

The instructor, in other words, can use any of the materials, all of them, or none of them.

Some instructors prefer multiple revisions of a small number of writing assignments. Others like a larger number of short "disposable" assignments from which student writers constantly move toward a polished, selected portfolio. Still others like a lot of discussion preceding cooperative writing efforts.

I have attempted to produce a text that could be used with any of these approaches with only small interpretive adjustments. Its emphasis on writing rather than discussion assignments was determined by my wanting to build it as suitable for use in an exclusively web-based course (in addition, of course, to partially web-based courses, or in the traditional face-to-face classroom). The virtual and especially the asynchronous virtual classroom lacks (outside the very limited resources of the chatroom) the luxury of the real-time discussion section. Rather then, than to provide some written and some discussion exercises, I constructed written exercises any or all of which could be easily converted to discussion topics.

It does need to be noted that this is a text in argument. It is not adapted to the short story, the lyric poem, or the personal memoir. Or at least it is not adapted to any of these as such. However, if a shift in point of view to approach any of these genres as argument as opposed to privileging them as "art" is considerable, accommodation is possible. The instructor who is sympathetic to this view and disposed toward these forms may find comfort in the **persuasive writing** entry in the *Glossary* and be able to find justification for including items from the genre or genres of choice.

Finally, poetry or prose, fiction or nonfiction, it all comes down to words, it all comes down to choice, and I would argue that inescapably it all comes down to rhetoric. Shelley, we need remember, referred to the distinction between poetry and prose as a vulgar error, and Whitman promised the origin of all poems in respiration, and inspiration, the simple breathing in required for the respiration, the controlled breathing out, attendant upon articulation.

Let me know what you think. Let me know how you use this book. Let me know how to make it a better book.

GYT: gtrail@uh.edu
gytrail@mac.com

INTRODUCTION

This rhetoric/reader is keyed to its companion volume, *Rhetorical Terms and Concepts: A Contemporary Glossary.* The text throughout depends on the definitions and discussions presented in the *Glossary,* and at least initially the reader is urged to look up each of the bold-faced terms appearing in the introduction and throughout.

While this text is flexible enough to accommodate a number of different approaches to the writing of argument, it emphasizes learning to *generate* argument through the *analysis* of contemporary "real-world" written argument.

Generating argument through the analysis of argument.

The text and the glossary were originally designed for the second in a series of courses: The first was devoted to exposition and largely concerned issues of clarity, organization, and development. The second was devoted to rhetoric, understood as writing with persuasion as its aim.

The assumption which stood and stands beneath these courses was and is that the writer who has acquired a firm grounding in the fundamentals of clarity, organization, and development will best enhance her writing ability and sophistication by becoming

Sophisticated reading leads to sophisticated writing.

a more skillful and sophisticated reader who will finally be able to translate those skills into her own work.

Much of what has been called the writing "process" is editing, *and editing is, at base, a reading skill.* The "three R's" of tradition, not only remain basic, but remain, as in the lyrics of the song, in the order of their most efficient acquisition—"Reading, and [W]riting, and [A]rithmetic." Quite simply, the better we understand the ways in which English (or any language) is in fact written in the world outside the classroom, the better one will be at writing it, in the classroom or out.

Editing is a reading skill.

ANALYTIC READING

For many who have not had much experience with careful and attentive reading, with "analytic" reading, this approach can be difficult at first. To read and write actively (paying attention not only to *what* is being presented but to *how* it is being presented) requires constant attention and constant inquiry into and development of the writing skills which follow from increased familiarity with the uses of the written word.

Reading for "how" as opposed to "what."

AVOIDING JUDGMENT

In this approach you do most of your writing about other writers' attempts to persuade. The intent of this writing, however, is not to render the usual judgment, to "prove" the other writers wrong, or, conversely, to endorse their views—not, in other words, to agree or disagree. It is instead an attempt to understand *why* the subject essays were written as they were—*why* the writer of the subject argument made the linguistic choices she did in presenting her argument to the audience she wished to convince.

Focusing on analysis rather than judgment.

This approach differs so radically from what some of you are used to that you may react as if it was somehow dishonest. *Deliberately* avoiding judgment can seem like lying about how you *really* feel. But rhetoric is not just about saying how you feel, it is about the attempt to get other people to feel the same way. Moreover, concentration on what *you* want to say, on how you *personally* react often stands in the way of understanding what you are reading. And finally you can only accept or reject in any real sense, what you understand.

Personal reaction can cloud understanding.

I want to stress that to *understand* is not the same thing as to *accept.* I am convinced that the better I understand what any writer is doing, the *less* vulnerable I am to being convinced by her approach, and the *more* capable I am of making a free judgment about the argument. And I would maintain that in the capacity to make free and informed judgments lies real empowerment. If you are accustomed to reacting to a piece of writing with a statement like, "Well, what *I* got out of it was . . ." you may initially be uncomfortable with the approach used here. But after working with it I hope you will come to the conclusion that understanding is at least as important as expression.

Understanding versus agreement.

Too frequently readers are like listeners who listen *only* until they hear what they want to hear, or what they do not want to hear, and then interrupt (and I'm sure you know some of these). The judgmental *reader* who reads until she encounters one or another of those points cannot, of course, interrupt. The essay writer, unlike the person speaking, is after all, not there. So the reader typically puts the text down, or, if the reading is an assignment, begins to skim. The result is that nothing is learned. The reader departs from the text holding precisely the attitude she began it with.

Judgmental listening and reading: how *not* to learn.

The *analytic* reader, however, is not there to agree or disagree. The analytic reader is there to determine

- what the writer is trying to sell,
- to whom the writer is trying to sell it, and
- by what means.

Whether, after she has determined this, she wants to become a customer, whether she wants to buy the conclusion herself, is another question. But it is now a question that she can answer in an informed way.

Judgmental reading is further complicated by the chance (even the likelihood) that whoever you in particular happen to be in terms of age, race, gender, economic circumstances, religion (or the lack thereof), politics, philosophical orientation, nationality, and so on, you may very well *not be* within the **target audience** of a given essay. You may very well not be a representative of the audience of this or that particular "attempt" (which is the most important of the meanings of "essay") at persuasion.

Analysis as deliberately prior to judgment. Personal reaction versus analytic rhetoric.

Acting in your capacity as an analyst you need, in other words, to consciously try to abstract yourself from, to move outside of, dealing with the subject of the argument on a personal level.

The purpose of this text, then, is two-fold:

1. to train you in the recognition of the resources of the language as a persuasive device (and both the uses and abuses of these resources); and

2. through exposure to and writing about the uses of these resources of language, to help you to gain understanding of the many ways to write arguments and the capacity to use them in your own attempts at persuasion.

From one perspective, all written communication, from the personal diary to the note on the refrigerator, can be seen as an attempt to persuade. But from the more specific view taken here, we study discursive prose (as opposed to poetry, or fiction, or the "personal essay"), which makes no pretense of any other motive than persuasion as its particular goal.

The type of analysis presented in this text then, is specifically, "rhetorical" analysis (analysis of the ways in which writers use language in an attempt to persuade). You will be constantly dealing with and speculating about why a given writer has written something in one way as opposed to another—why she has chosen this particular sentence structure, this particular word—what she was attempting to accomplish through the language choices made.

Your own writing, in turn, is made up of attempts (essays) to persuade your readers of the accuracy of your analysis. Thus, to keep the direction of your thinking focused on analysis, you should be particularly concerned with *avoiding* a number of very tempting areas of response to a given essay, the most frequently encountered of which are as follows.

1. Unless specifically instructed otherwise (as for instance would be appropriate in a lesson in writing summary, or demonstrating understanding of the subject essay by writing an abstract of it) assume that the person or persons reading your essay are familiar with the piece that you are writing about. Consequently they do not need to be told *what* the writer is saying. Presumably, we all can read (but as you will discover, we do not all read with the same capacity of attention to detail or sensitivity to the writer's choices). An analysis should not, in other words, say, "in his first paragraph the writer says X, and in the second paragraph he expands on this by saying Y." Remember, our concern is not with *what* the writer is saying. That is a given—that, it can be assumed, we

The consideration of written language as a persuasive device.

Speculation is basic to analysis. The hypothesis is central to analytic rhetoric.

Do not assume that summary is analysis.

already know. Instead you should remember that your reader is concerned with your presentation of *how* the writer is saying something. In rhetorical analysis, we are interested in everything *but* the "bottom line." *How* is this writer using the introduction, argument, data, in her attempt to persuade? To put it as briefly as possible, when you are writing analysis, don't summarize, analyze.

2. Do not argue with the position that the writer is defending. Your task, in rhetorical *analysis,* is to present an argument defending *your identification* of the specific rhetorical strategies the writer is using, and what evidence from the text itself you can offer to support your hypothesis concerning why the writer made the particular rhetorical choices she did—not whether she was right or wrong. If the writer you are analyzing is, for instance, defending abortion, and you are absolutely convinced that abortion is totally wrong, *your position on the question has no place in a rhetorical analysis.* Simply put, your task is only to analyze the writer's use of rhetoric in her attempt to persuade.

   > In analysis, do not take a position regarding the subject matter of the argument being analyzed.

3. Closely related to the temptation to indulge in arguing with the writer's thesis is the temptation to pronounce on the essay's, or a particular rhetorical device's, "effectiveness." Clearly a writer will use the resources of rhetoric in an attempt to persuade her audience. Whether the writer *succeeds* in that attempt, however, is a question that is beyond our capacities to judge. You could, of course, say that the writer succeeded in convincing *you,* but that is not the question you should be concerned with—indeed it is irrelevant to the question of *analysis.* We can write about what a writer attempts to do, and how she attempts to do it, but we cannot say what a writer has actually accomplished. Finally, leave questions of "effectiveness" to the market researchers of the advertising media.

   > Do not make judgments on the subject writer's effectiveness. (See Chapter 1 for fully developed discussion.)

4. The study of rhetoric and logic over the last twenty-four centuries has produced, and continues to produce, a specialized nomenclature used to refer to a writer's use of particular rhetorical devices. These you will hear referred to as "rhetorical terms," and such terms are likely to be very useful to you as a brief description of a given rhetorical strategy. It is important, however, that you not confuse a simple knowledge of these terms, or using them *in* an analysis, with rhetorical analysis itself. It is not sufficient to say that in the second paragraph the writer is using such and such a rhetorical device. What is important is your presentation of the evidence on which you have based your decision that the device

is being used. In other words, simply assigning names to strategies does not fulfill the requirements of rhetorical analysis. In the long run *what* you call a particular use of language in an argument is much less important than *why* you think this particular use of language should be so labeled.

What to, and what not to do.

These instructions deal primarily with what *not* to do. The hard part, of course, is to learn what you can do as a rhetorical analyst.

A SAMPLE ANALYSIS

To provide an example of rhetorical *analysis,* I have chosen a brief but rhetorically dense public relations piece from R. J. Reynolds Tobacco Company which occupied a full page in the June 14th, 1994, *New York Times.* There is a reproduction of the page in the appendix, but I request that the reader *not* refer to it until after working through the analysis of the written text. *Reading Writing* is centrally concerned with the rhetorical analysis of written texts, as opposed to spoken or illustrated texts. Then why have I chosen a text which includes a picture? My thinking was that you are mostly familiar with multi-media attempts at persuasion (text, typography, two-dimensional representations of three-dimensional visuals, and for the computer-hip, all of the above plus motion). On that basis, I am more likely to be able to make my case for the analysis of *writing* if I can present an argument for an analysis of the *written* text in isolation from the picture. So I have used the picture as support for the analysis rather than as the source of it. Again, don't peek. We will get to the picture soon enough

RJR ad text representation.

The text begins with a photograph caption, moves to a headline-like centered, all-caps and boldfaced introductory paragraph, then to eight normal-faced paragraphs of quoted material, followed by a concluding acknowledgment paragraph (in the same type-face, and a last line in reversed type (white type on a gray banner) also in all caps. The text reads as follows:

Written descriptive presentation of a text which is typographically complex.

> "[all caps, boldfaced centered large type] I'm one of America's 45 million smokers. I'm not a moaner or a whiner. But I'm getting fed up. I'd like to get the government off my back."

> "[two columns, regular type] If you're a smoker you'll know exactly what I'm talking about. If you're a non-smoker you may think the current attempts to ban smoking in America have nothing to do with you. But, if you

give me two minutes, I'll tell you why I think it's important that you know what's going on and how it's going to affect you.

I choose to smoke. It's my decision. As an adult in a free country, it's my right. That doesn't mean that I believe I have the right to blow smoke in your face. I think smoking and no-smoking sections in restaurants and public places are a good way of keeping everybody happy.

But when it comes to smoking in other places, in my own home, in my car or truck, and with my friends, that's a different story. That's my right. You've probably now heard about the proposed workplace ban. They want smoking to be banned anywhere where ten or more people visit in a one-week period. This means that smoking will be illegal in almost every workplace in the country unless an incredibly expensive, specially ventilated room is provided. And who can afford that?

Did you know the government also intends for the ban to extend to trucks, vans and even private cars if they're used by workers? Did you know that your right to smoke at home will be threatened every time a repairman visits, or any other worker?

You may also have heard about the proposed 800% tax increase on cigarettes some congressmen are talking about. That's discrimination against smokers, nothing less. And it will affect non-smokers too when the bootleggers start to get involved.

There is no question in my mind that the government is seeking an all-out prohibition on cigarettes. And once we've let them achieve their goal they'll be free to pursue other targets. They'll go for liquor and fast food and buttermilk and who knows what else. There's a line of dominoes a mile long.

"You" becomes part of "we."

We can work these issues out together without the government telling us how to do it. If we let it become law then we've got a serious problem. Because then people are no longer allowed to work it out themselves. We have to talk."

The "I" of the first paragraph is identified in the caption of the photograph at the top of the page as Archie Anderson, "a Minnesotan born and bred. In the past he tolerated the attacks made against smokers. But now he wants to speak up."
The piece closes with this paragraph:

This opinion is brought to you in the interests of an informed debate by the R. J. Reynolds Tobacco Company. We believe that the solution to most smoking issues can be found in <u>accommodation</u> [underlined thus, not in italics], in finding ways in which smokers and non-smokers

Ad text presented as "public service announcement."

can co-exist peacefully. And we encourage dialogue and discussion that will help solve the issue without government intervention. For further information please call [1-800 phone number].

"We" have "issues," but no "problems."

Then in boldfaced white on gray in all caps we have:

TOGETHER, WE CAN WORK IT OUT

I will not try to offer any sort of complete definition of the rhetorical terms that I will be using in the discussion that follows. Here, as elsewhere in the text, specifically rhetorical terms should be looked up in the *Glossary*. For other terms a good standard English dictionary will do. If, for instance, you did not understand the terms "caps" and "boldfaced" in the preceding, a standard dictionary would supply the appropriate definitions. Any word for which there is a discussion in the *Glossary* will be in boldface type (as was **target audience** earlier in this introduction).

How to Read the Reading

Writing analysis *is* writing argument. *My* argument here is a defense of my reading, my hypothesis concerning the RJR piece. It is presented in the hope that you will accept it as *your* reading as well.

Bear in mind that what I am writing in the following analysis *is itself an argument*—an argument in support of the analysis I am presenting. The analysis is no different from any other attempt at persuasion and is in itself an exercise in rhetoric. What I will present is *an* analysis, a *reading* of the rhetorical intentions of the R. J. Reynolds document. From here on I will refer to this particular untitled piece as "I'm One."

> **Exercise Introduction: 1.** Note the ways in which my analysis attempts to establish *its* points, and whenever you are not convinced by my presentation formulate an alternative reading of your own. Remember that to reject a rhetorical explanation you are obligated to provide one of your own which explains the choices made by the writer of the subject text better than the explanation you reject. The goal of this exercise is not to coerce you into accepting my reading, but to help you to recognize that the most satisfactory analysis is the one that most coherently explains the largest number of the rhetorical choices made by the author(s) of the subject essay.

Exercise Introduction: 2. In what follows the initial use of rhetorical terms which are treated at some length in the glossary will be presented in bold face. As you proceed through the analysis make a list of those terms and write a brief definition of each in your own words.

Of specific importance here are the *Glossary* and a dictionary. See especially the entry for "The Dictionary" in the *Glossary*.

Identifying the Thesis

The first question to be answered in any rhetorical analysis is "What is the writer's **thesis**?" To put the question within the structure of an economic **metaphor,** I ask "What is the writer trying to sell?" Here answering the question is more complicated than usual because to answer that question I need to first try to determine who the writer is. An obvious answer is Archie Anderson. But if there is such a person, and he did write the piece it is still only a partial answer. It doesn't take into account the last paragraph which is presented as the product of the R. J. Reynolds Tobacco Company (henceforth referred to as RJR). So also the picture caption (and to the extent that we wish to consider it a part of the argument, the picture itself) would be an RJR product.

We could conclude, then, that "I'm One" has a corporate authorship. *If* we presume that there is a real Archie Anderson he *may* have provided the idea behind some of the statements, but the whole (very expensive) page was clearly assembled and edited by some sort of staff before space for it was bought by RJR.

Real or not, however, Anderson is rhetorically *represented* as the author of the material which appears in quotes. It would appear that RJR wishes the **target audience** to believe that a real biographical person from Minnesota named Archie (Archibald?) Anderson is the writer of the material in quotes.

Corporate authorship and "Archie Anderson."

There can be, through this mechanism, a **thesis** *and* a subthesis—RJR's thesis and Anderson's. The *overt* and *declared* thesis is that RJR wants to "solve" smoking "issues" without government intervention. RJR states specifically that "this *opinion*" (my italics) is brought to you "in the interests of an informed debate." This implies that this opinion is one of a number of opinions and that RJR does not *necessarily* endorse it. So when RJR writes that "we" seek "<u>accommodation</u>" (sic) as the solution to "issues," they write as if Anderson has *offered* some **accommodation,** and that his "opinion" has been "brought to you" for this reason.

Anderson's "accommodation" appears in the third sentence of the second paragraph. He writes, "I think smoking and

Accommodation

no-smoking sections in restaurants and public places are a good way of keeping everybody happy."

What, then, is Anderson's thesis? I suggest it is not **accommodation,** but is rather to be found in his opening and penultimate paragraphs where he **asserts** that there are "current attempts to ban smoking in America" and that "the government is seeking an all-out prohibition on cigarettes" as the first step on the **slippery slope** of the prohibition of "who knows what else" which "we" must not "let them achieve." The items Anderson specifically mentions as targets are "liquor and fast food and buttermilk." Presumably what ties all of these together is that each has been labeled as unhealthy.

I would argue further that the entire piece has a **covert thesis**—an attempt to establish **existential import** for the notion of a "right to smoke" and the related concept of "smokers' rights." In paragraph two Anderson writes "As an adult in a free country, it's [smoking] my right." In the next paragraph, in reference to smoking "in my own home, in my car or truck, and with my friends" Anderson comments "That's my right." Then in paragraph five Anderson asks, "Did you know that *your right to smoke at home* will be threatened every time a repairman visits, or any other worker?" (my emphasis). In the first two instances of references to rights, Anderson advances the notion of *his* right to smoke as an **assertion,** a point that needs to be established. The phrase in which Anderson talks about the **target audience's** rights *assumes* that there is such a right without asserting it. In other words, given that the question is if there *is* such a thing as a right to smoke, and consequently such a thing as "smokers' rights," this statement **begs the question.**

(margin notes)
The overt and declared thesis.

The sub-thesis.

Creating a reference for a term while **begging the question.**

Exercise Introduction: 3. Begging the question is a complex conception and needs to be clearly understood from early on in the process of rhetorical analysis. Study the glossary entry and identify what questions are begged in each of the following items.

1. Current research shows that homosexuality can be cured.

2. A woman's place is at her husband's side.

3. What church do you go to?

Write your answers as if they were addressed to a person making each statement. Write your answers to minimize offending the person addressed.

And the question which is begged here is vital to RJR's interests. If the target audience can be convinced overtly *or* covertly that there *is* such a thing as "smokers' rights," then the largest part of the battle has been won. Legislation against tobacco could then be characterized as an attempt to limit or eliminate an established right and would thus be uncharacteristic of a "free" country (it would be, in an expression that has not been used in a good while, "un-American").

Assuming without asserting: **Begging the Question.**

Identifying the Target Audience

Another "issue" here is the question of who constitutes the **target audience.** A quick and easy answer would be "readers of the national edition of *The New York Times,*" but this assumes that "I'm One" appeared only in the *Times,* and it assumes further that it is aimed at the demographics of the entire *Times* readership.

The RJR person at the other end of the 1-800 phone number was unwilling or unable to tell me what other newspapers "I'm One" ran in but did say that it was run in other papers. I had suspected this because even if *Times* readers could generally be assumed to be old enough to recognize the **allusion** to the Beatles' song of the same name in the concluding "WE CAN WORK IT OUT," they would be less likely to sympathize with the fiftyish, flannel-shirted, Levi-clad smoker leaning with one hand on the open tailgate of his pickup with the alternate thumb (of the hand with the cigarette in it) hooked in a wide belt with a flying eagle trophy buckle (to say nothing of the "Minnesota" printed on the front of the gimme cap and the "blue-dot" taillight lenses on the pickup) in the photograph (of, presumably, Archie Anderson) which takes up a little more than the top third of the page.

Target Audience more specific than "readers of the publication."

The initial and major appeal is to those who think of "the government" as "on my back" (in reference to the **cliché** phrase "get off my back") in terms of regulations, requirements, restrictions, taxes, and so on. These would be people who think of themselves as hard-working (the truck, the work clothes, and what might be OSHA-approved safety glasses), patriotic (the eagle trophy buckle—American Rifle Association?) Americans (Minnesota) who enjoy a drink (liquor), a burger (fast food), and, I guess, an occasional glass of buttermilk, or maybe even lots of glasses of buttermilk.

The apparent target audience.

The buttermilk, whether you like the stuff or not, ties in nicely with the gimme cap and the pickup.

RJR headquarters is in Winston-Salem, North Carolina— a staple crop is tobacco, and a good many of the population are heavily economically involved with the related agriculture and processing. Minnesota, my encyclopedia tells me, is a "leader" in the production of creamery butter, dry milk, and cheese. Buttermilk is what's left over when the butterfat used to make butter has been removed from cream or whole milk. I propose that buttermilk is intended to invoke whatever the local version is of the relationship between prohibition in the name of health concerns and the facts of local economies. Think, for instance, of Baytown, Texas, a refinery town, and air pollution, or of the whole economy of Texas in relation to the burning of fossil fuels in relationship to "government" regulations.

Localizing the economic "issue": a specific and local appeal considered in terms of an intended generality of "local" concerns.

Exercise Introduction: 4. As presented here, dairy (buttermilk) and beef (burger) products, like tobacco, are items on the production of which significant numbers of people are economically dependent. As such each product can function as a sort of locally defined, or geographically specific, buzz word. After examining the glossary on this topic, write a definition which deals with buzz words based on an appeal to an age or gender or race specific population.

Exercise Introduction: 5. After completing the above exercise, as a clincher on the concept of **buzz words**, return to the text of the advertisement and 1) categorize and 2) list all other buzz words you find.

If it is credible to the **target audience** that the thinking expressed in "I'm One" could come from an actual Archie Anderson, then other readers would not even *need* to be smokers to sympathize with him or identify with him. That audience could recognize that Archie Anderson is like *many* citizens. He is like citizens in a number large enough, were they to come to see cigarette regulation *as related to economic circumstances like their own,* as directly related to how they earned their living, to make up a significant voting power.

And when we look at the details, we see that Archie says, in the all-caps boldface, "I'M ONE OF AMERICA'S 45 MILLION SMOKERS." If the current population of the United

States is about 250 million, of whom maybe a third are registered voters, *or could become registered voters,* this "opinion" would probably be of considerable interest to at least the "some congressmen" who are "talking about" the "proposed 800% tax increase on cigarettes." And if there is *a* newspaper that national politicians read, it is *The New York Times.*

The real **target audience.**

As such, what is presented is an **Ad Baculum** argument in which right and wrong are of no final consequence. One cannot, after all, defend the right and proper, let alone truth, justice, and the American way, if one has been voted out of office.

We need to note, also, that "the government" as here used, is a **synecdoche,** the use of a part for the whole. The phrase is so commonly used in this way that it is easy to think of "the government" as some sort of monolithic and single-minded entity. The device is often used to **demonize** a given group, race, population, and so on. The interests of Italy, Japan, and Germany were quite different from each other in World War II, but "the Allies" referred to the combination as "The Axis."

A consideration of the rhetorical appeal of **synecdoche,** using a part for the whole, or the whole for a part. Archie Anderson as representative of many citizens, not just smokers.

In universities we often encounter the same kind of thinking employed in relation to "the administration," a simplification of a complex structure invoked for the purpose of making positive or negative generalizations. To say something like "the administration will never abolish the football program" not only assumes that those people who populate the structure that comprises the administration are in total agreement, but that they will always remain so, and beyond that, that it will remain made up of the same people.

"The government" demonized.

"The Supreme Court" is perhaps a more accessible model. If we thought of the Court as monolithic we wouldn't be concerned with the politics of appointees—and clearly we are concerned. At the time of this writing, for instance, there are indications that the presidential candidate's position on abortion is likely to be highly significant given the number of appointees to the Supreme Court that the next president will be able to place.

In "I'm One," "the government," is presented as a monolithic structure devoted to the suppression of the rights of individuals which the true American must be willing to resist. The essay begins with it ("I'D LIKE TO GET THE GOVERNMENT OFF MY BACK"), but it also uses a subtle structure of pronoun development to reinforce the idea.

Arguing with Pronouns

Six of the first paragraph's 28 words are "I'm," "I'd," and "my," two of which hold the important places of the first and penultimate words. In the 60 words of the second paragraph, four are first person and nine are *second* person ("you," "you're" and "you'll"). The third person occurs only four times in the essay and three of those occur in the seventh paragraph, the same paragraph where "we" ("we've") first occurs. In the next paragraph, Anderson's last, "we" occurs three times, and "we've" and "us" once each.

Like **begging the question,** the introduction of "we," especially when such pains have been taken to clarify the relationship between the "I" and the "you," is important. The writer waits to use the familiar "we" until he (who could very well be a she, or what I think is even more likely, a mixed gender committee) has clearly established the "they"—the "other," which is the government. It is as if the "I" and the "you" must respect each other's autonomy until the enemy is defined, at which time you and I can become "we" in the face of the threat to us both (the enemy of my enemy is my friend). If this sounds improbable, look back at the essay and mark the occurrence of the "I" and "you" forms and note then how late the "we" is introduced.

Pronouns: As trivial as it may sound at the outset, an examination of the pronouns in a specific argument will frequently reveal a strategy in terms of an "us/them" **either/or** approach.

At the end of paragraph eight, (the supposed) Anderson stops and RJR begins. **Typographically,** however, no shift is signaled to the reader. The typeface and spacing remain the same as that in Anderson's purported text. Here, I suggest, is where the pronoun "we" is brought to its most subtle use. RJR writes "We believe that the solution to most smoking issues can be found in <u>accommodation</u>. . . . And we encourage dialogue and discussion that will help solve the issue without government intervention." Notice *here* that the "we" is quite clearly the R. J. Reynolds Tobacco Company, which is bringing "you" the "opinion." But notice further that the typographically isolated last line reads "TOGETHER WE CAN WORK IT OUT." Who is "WE" now? If it includes "you," it also includes Archie Anderson and RJR, and it very clearly does *not* include "them," the government who, as the seventh paragraph tells us "once *we've* let achieve *their* goal *they'll* be free to pursue other targets" (my emphasis).

Exercise Introduction: 6.   As is the case with begging the question, **synecdoche** is conceptually very important to argument. After studying the glossary entry, try to present the concept to an interested friend in no more than five sentences using at least three examples other than those provided in the text. Bear in mind that synecdoche need not only be used to **demonize.**

> **Exercise Introduction: 7. Typography** as method of argument: With this specifically in mind, look at three magazines that you could find in the check-out line at any grocery store. Formulate an explanation for the distribution of boldface and hot boxes that you encounter and consider how these devices influence the formation of what is frequently called "public opinion."

Analyzing Examples of Diction

Many other details of the essay could be discussed in terms of its rhetorical strategies. I will end this exercise with one example of an attempt to defuse the language of those campaigning for additional restrictions on access to and consumption of *them* (tobacco products). I have already commented on Anderson's "accommodation" ("smoking and no-smoking sections in restaurants and public places"), the term that RJR tries to make its **buzz word.**

Accommodation is, in general, a good thing. But only in general. It is not a good idea to "accommodate," say, carriers of a highly contagious disease or child molesters or ax murderers. At best, one should isolate them. *At issue is the contention that smoking causes injury to non-smokers.* Without trying to make any statement about whether this is or is not accurate, consider only the language in which it is stated—specifically the phrase "at issue." Here is RJR's version from the last paragraph: "We believe that the solution to most smoking issues can be found in accommodation . . . we encourage dialogue and discussion that will help solve the issues without government intervention" (and it may now be appropriate to point out that "accommodation" is the *only* word which is underlined in the entire text).

Notice that there are no "problems" in this paragraph. There are only "issues." One doesn't "solve" issues, one addresses them, deals with them, discusses them. One "solves" problems. But in the RJR paragraph there *are* no problems. Where do we have "problems"? We have problems in the previous paragraph, Anderson's last, where "he" writes "We can work these *issues* out together without the government telling us how to do it. If we let it become law then we've got a serious *problem* [my emphasis]." The "problem" from the perspective of RJR, is not tobacco. Tobacco is an "issue." The "problem" is the government.

Accommodation as rhetorical tool: After you have consulted the glossary on this term, consider the conversational function of tag terms like "yeah, but," "ok, and," and "another thing."

"Problems" and "Issues": Using any "news" magazine as a sample, *Time, Newsweek,* etc., see how frequently the word "issue" could be replaced with "problem." It is hard to say where it began, but it was clearly institutionalized by Microsoft and has since even been adopted by Apple techs. There are, apparently, no longer any "problems."

What I have tried to present is an analysis which accounts for the details, the specifics of this essay (buttermilk, for instance, and the patterns of pronouns), each of which represents a *choice* made by the corporate "author" of "I'm One" to contribute to its attempt to persuade.

I will emphasize again that this analysis is a *reading*. It is active rather than passive. It always assumes that the details of the text are part of a deliberate construction and that its authors intend with the text to influence opinion—to reinforce it or to change it, and that the reader who is not attentive to the ways in which language is used to persuade will be its victim rather than its beneficiary.

Notice that there has been no discussion concerning whether the position taken is "reasonable," or "correct," or "fair." No attempt has been made to "evaluate" the argument. Finally, as analysts we (now notice *my* "we") are concerned with how the writer is trying to persuade the **target audience,** *not whether that* **target audience** *should or should not be persuaded.* The assumption is that if, and only if, we understand how an argument is intended to work can we make a knowledgeable decision concerning whatever it is that it is trying to sell.

The tobacco portion of the R. J. Reynolds corporation is fighting for its economic life against anticipated congressional action. What it seeks are those who will make common cause with it—in short, allies. What it hopes is that legislators will recognize the potential voting power of not just 45 million

---

Exercise Introduction: 8. An interesting parallel to the efforts of tobacco companies interested in profits, is the apparently more purely ideological effort of the National Rifle Association to resist state and federal governmental efforts to restrict gun ownership. Find an ad for the NRA and analyze it from the same perspective as the R. J. Reynolds piece.

smokers, *but whoever else can be induced to think that the slippery slope runs from tobacco to whatever the local version of buttermilk is.*

The text you are embarking upon makes a great many demands of you as a reader and a writer. It can help you to appreciate skilled argument when you encounter it and to recognize the ways in which that argument attempts to persuade its targeted audience. Moreover, because you will be capable of recognizing these approaches when you encounter them, you will be able to produce them yourself when it seems to you appropriate given who it is you want to convince of whatever you want to convince them of.

It offers an approach to both reading and writing which can be the beginning of a rewarding, life-long, and continually developing active relation to the written language. Welcome.

Slippery slope: You should be able to think of at least three standard slippery slope arguments almost immediately. I have already discussed what I referred to as "the local version of buttermilk," that is, something that is bad for one's health but good for the local economy. What would be your local application?

Remember that an analysis is a *reading* rather than an *evaluation*.

C H A P T E R 1

EFFECTIVE ARGUMENT

The British comedy troupe Monty Python has a sketch in which the British military during World War I discover a joke so funny that everyone who hears it dies laughing. In the sketch a number of scholars, each one of whom can only translate one word more than the previous scholar before dying of laughter, sacrifice their lives to translate the joke into German. British troops, selected on the basis of their knowing no German, advance on the German lines whilst (as the British would say) reading the joke aloud in German from copies they carry. The German troops, upon hearing the joke, crawl out of their trenches laughing convulsively and drop dead. England wins the war, and the joke is destroyed, or locked up, or something.

Then there is Homer's ancient Greek tale of the sirens who lure mariners into fatal shipwrecks with the beauty of their songs. Ulysses, going for the gusto, plugs his rowers' ears with wax and has himself tied to his ship's mast before voyaging within earshot of the sirens. Deaf to his pleas for release and unable to hear the songs themselves, his mariners row him safely past. Ulysses thus becomes the first to hear the sirens' songs and live. (Although the sound track of the 1955 Italian film *Ulysses* carries the siren's song, there have been no reported incidents of audiences throwing themselves through the screen to reach the speakers or VCR/DVD viewers trashing their equipment for similar reasons.)

A joke so funny that it kills you. A song so seductive that the listener will die to approach the singer. Each of these is an example of an extreme of "effectiveness." However, outside of the worlds of Monty Python and ancient myth, in the world as we know it, and regardless of the skill of the comedian or the songwriter, we do not expect to find a joke or a song that would have such an irresistible effect. Nevertheless teachers in the area of writing instruction called "argument," or rhetoric, continue to present methods for producing "effective" argument.

This book cannot, in any of these senses, teach you to write "effective" argument. It can, however, teach you a great deal about argument itself, and a great deal about writing, and in the process, help you to recognize the choices that are made in the process of producing written argument. And in *that* process, this book can familiarize you with the skills necessary to make such choices to guide you in your own writing.

If someone could teach you how to write truly "effective" arguments, with that skill you could, conceivably, convince anyone of anything. You could, to make an analogy, sell anything to anyone. But what happens when your teacher instructs another student? Since each of you learned how to argue effectively, each of you would presumably be able to protect yourself against the arguments of the other.

And if that were the case, would not each of you know only how to write arguments that are "effective" *on those who do not know how to write effective arguments? That is to say, would not the "effectiveness" of the argument depend directly on the ignorance of the person to whom it is directed?* Similarly, does not the effectiveness of *any* argument depend on the readers' susceptibility to the specific methods of argument? How, for instance, does a salesperson go about selling to another salesperson? So while neither this book nor any other will be able to teach you how to write effective arguments, it can enable you to judge the value of arguments presented to you.

The argument as a selling machine.

But even that is not the direct focus. What this book directly proposes to do is to give you the tools with which to take written arguments apart into their constituent pieces to see how they may be intended to function.

Analysis is disassembly, taking arguments apart.

What do we mean by an "effective" argument? Presumably we would mean an arrangement of words that would lead the chosen audience to an acceptance of the desired conclusion.

[A critique of my own argument in the interests of a working definition of "effectiveness."]

If this is our definition, then the penultimate paragraph about the two students is a **straw man** argument. A flashy attack is made and victory is claimed (in **rhetorical questions,** no less) over an opponent who is not real. The opponent is not real because no one ever claimed that an effective argument would convince *everyone*. After all, the deadly joke only kills those people who understand the language that it is presented in. And the sirens' song only destroys those who can both hear it *and* are free to approach it. So let us refine the argument, and define the terms more precisely.

Effective argument in relation to **sound** argument.

First let us limit the discussion by specifying that we are not dealing with questions having to do with the soundness of an argument (see **sound (adjective)** in the glossary). Both sound and unsound arguments are equally dependent for their acceptance on the effectiveness of their presentation. So, in the following discussion we are not dealing with the question of whether the position being argued is good or bad, or right or wrong. We are dealing solely with how that position, whatever its final value, is being presented.

EFFECTIVENESS

A Working Definition

What is "effective" is what "works," in the sense that we use the word in the question "Did it work?" or "Is she going for it?" That which is effective is that which "gets the job done." It may not get the job done in the best way, or the quickest way, or the cheapest way, but it gets it done.

Thus there can be degrees of effectiveness. One thing can be more effective than another thing, and a third more effective than the second. In an argument or in relationship to selling, "more effective" would have to mean "influencing more of the audience" rather than influencing any individual member more "strongly." That argument, then, is the *most* effective which

"Selling an argument."

leads the largest number of its chosen audience to the desired conclusion. That sales method is the best that induces the largest number of customers to buy the product. (Notice here how closely arguing and selling are associated in informal American English—we "buy" or "don't buy" an argument, we call the conclusion the "bottom line," as on a financial statement.)

Given the examples of the funniest joke and the sirens' song, we may conclude that no argument works with everyone, nor will it work all of the time. Since there is no such argument, there cannot be any principles derived from it which we can take to be characteristic of effective argument. We must, thus, discuss particular arguments rather than abstract principles. In order, then, to discuss the effectiveness of any particular, any given argument, we need to know a number of things:

Definition: That argument, then, is the *most* effective which leads the largest number of its chosen audience to the desired conclusion.

1. What is the point the writer intends the reader to be convinced of? (In the jargon of composition classes this would be asked as "What is the *thesis* of the argument?")
2. To whom is the argument addressed? (Again, in the jargon of the composition class, who is the *intended audience,* or the *target audience?*)
3. What are the circumstances of the intended audience?
4. When is (or was) the argument presented?

Basics for analysis:
1. what is being sold
2. to whom
3. in what circumstances
4. when.

Argument for Grownups

If we know all of these things, we can say something like the following: *Given* our assumptions about human nature and psychology, and *given* that we have correctly estimated the level of understanding and sophistication of the target audience, it would seem likely that that group would (or would not) find this argument convincing.

I can be more specific by turning to the previously mentioned analogy of selling. In this analogy, the *product* is the thesis and the packaging and advertising of the product is the argument. Businesses use "test markets" in statistical approaches to investigating questions of "effectiveness," for testing the "appeal" of a specific product in relation to how it is advertised. The investigation of test markets is a method of examining what factors may constitute the causes that lead particular consumers to buy the merchandise in question. Let's look at a specific example of how this works.

Thesis as "product."

Buying (and Selling) Bug Spray

A couple of years ago I went to a grocery store and looked specifically at the "insecticides," and particularly those that made a claim to kill cockroaches. What I saw on the shelves was a great many red aerosol cans. One can stood out because it was black. But Raid (which came in a red can) was what I had previously bought and what I bought again. I looked for it by name among the red cans. I had no evidence that it worked any better than, or indeed was any different from any other brand, but I knew that I had seen dead roaches after using it previously, and the television ads that I had seen were sufficiently flashy to be memorable. But then, after the purchase, and as a result of the grocery store experience, I had another name in my head, Black Flag, presumably because it "stood out," because it was in a black rather than a red can.

Last week, however, I bought an entirely different brand in a *green* can. The can beside *it* in the shelf display said "contains pyrethrum, made from flowers." This, I supposed, was to let me know that it didn't contain any of those "artificial" (whatever that might mean) chemicals. Flowers=Nature=Good. Kill insects ecologically. Spray some stuff made from flowers on them out of an aerosol can. But I didn't buy that one. I bought the green can.

Why? I'll never "know," but I *think* it was because I thought it was funny. Green suggests "Nature" suggests "Peace," etc., etc., etc., but this bug spray was named HOT SHOT. I associate hot with red, orange, yellow, white even, but not with green. I could have it both ways. I could be ecologically correct *and* violent and "strong." I didn't want to spray any flower stuff on roaches. That might give them the wrong idea. I wanted it clear to the roaches that I was kicking butt, not indulging in some kind of wimpy euthanasia.

But, at the same time I could "love" the earth and sort of pretend that cockroaches aren't "natural" beings. One usage of the term "hot shot" was (is?) underworld slang for uncut heroin given to an addict who has become a police informer, a "rat." This uncut heroin, injected in the dosage typical for the many times "stepped on" drugs ordinarily available, would result in the addict overdosing and dying in convulsions. A "hot shot" is also what someone is called who *thinks* she is more important than she is, as in "Listen, hot shot, I wouldn't do that if I were you." But I liked the first association. Roaches dying in convulsions, and *deservedly,* for ratting. The metaphoric implications of a roach "ratting" were pleasingly disgusting.

What is the most effective color for an aerosol can of roach spray?

So here's the question. What is the most effective color for an aerosol can of roach spray? Well, for certain people who feel it is all right to indulge power fantasies while "exterminating" roaches but who feel concerned about the environment, green. *But,* only with a power brand name. For most people, right now, *probably* red. Changing the color of Raid to green might make brand-name loyal buyers nervous. But on the other hand, that black can does stand out. Still, it doesn't stand out as much as that weird green. Let's go for the green. Later on at Acme Insecticides we can say that Acme was among the pioneers in green poisons, and if that pyrethrum flower stuff looks like it's selling we can put some of that in.

In order to determine the most effective way to sell something (and in terms of the analogy to determine the most effective way to persuade someone of something) one needs to take into consideration *to whom* one wishes to sell it and what the contemporary conditions are. That is, one must take into consideration *when* and even *where* one wants to do the selling (Cockroaches, for instance, are a much larger problem in southern states than in northern).

[Selling metaphor continued as analogue for persuasion.]

Exercise 1:1. The previous example is presented from the point of view of the consumer, a person shopping for a particular product. When the consumer's wants match the features of the product, and the product is presented in such a way that the consumer is aware that her wants have been met, presumably she will buy. Using another product, write three paragraphs describing the process you would go through in selecting one from a number of offerings.

Exercise 1:2. The "argument" I presented as an illustration for the thesis that the concept "most effective" is conditional and relative was presented in the form of a narration, an **anecdote.** It was a "story" about bug spray. Thinking specifically about making a point by telling a (hopefully) entertaining story, rewrite the narrative from another point of view. If you remember the "local version of buttermilk" discussion from the introduction, you might want to change the geography or the gender of the buyer. What else might be changed?

"Effectiveness" Is Relative

Writing texts frequently (in fact I know of no exceptions—that I have found none is one of the reasons for this book) present an essay and then ask "Why is X aspect of this essay effective?" or, "What is effective about X aspect of this essay?" It isn't necessary to know what X refers to recognize an example of **begging the question,** or even a **loaded question,** or, to use the more technical designation, a **complex question.** Asking, "What is effective about X?" *presumes* that X is effective (here, as elsewhere, if you are not completely comfortable with the rhetorical terms being used you should consult the glossary).

It would be similar to my asking "Why is green an effective color for roach spray?" (leaving completely aside the obvious point that roaches will die just as quickly from the spray no matter what color the can). So we've added another question. Not only does one need to know *to whom* and *when,* one needs to know how "effectiveness" is being defined, and then, in terms of that definition, *how* effective is it?

"Well," you could reply, "you bought the roach spray didn't you? Doesn't that prove that green is effective?" In one sense, yes. But I don't believe that that is what a market researcher would assume. That *one* person bought a can of roach spray because *he* thought it was funny does not mean that 1) he will buy it again, or 2) that he will recommend it to others. "Effectiveness," in terms of *selling* roach spray, would need to be understood not as a positive answer to the question "Would *a* person buy it?" but "Would a certain percentage of the population that buys roach spray buy it?" (i.e., what market "share" would it command)? One might want to consider, for instance, that if we assume that most roach spray is bought in grocery stores, it would seem likely that that roach spray would sell the best which would appeal to women.

"Degrees" of effectiveness.

Taking these things into consideration then, we could talk about *degrees* of effectiveness depending on what share of the market was being addressed, or even if the market itself increased. For instance, might the market share constituted by those people who had stopped buying *aerosol* roach spray because of fear of threat to the ozone layer be induced to come back to the market by a green can?

Now if all this is clear, let's complicate it some more. The analogy of selling is useful because in some senses its results are clearer than the results of persuasion attempted *only* by means of the written word. In selling one can count units purchased, and one can calculate that amount over a measured period of

Measuring effectiveness.

time. We know what "purchased" means in this area. So we could say, "We sold a 24-percent market share with a green can. We only had a 10-percent share with a red can, so green must be effective."

But was the color the *only* thing changed about the can? Do we know that it is *just* the green, or is it the green and the name, and that the can is more slender than most, and that yellow was used as well? In other words, we can *know* that the spray is a success in terms of sales, but we can only *guess* at why. Every estimation we make would have to be with "all other factors considered equal." And we know well that "all other factors" are never equal. If it were true that green *was* the only thing changed about the can, we would need also to take into consideration that more people *appear* to respond well to advertising that fronts a concern with ecology than the number who did so, say, ten years ago.

Problem with the concept of "all other factors being equal."

So we must take into account, or attempt to take into account, that the *bases* of an appeal are in a constant state of change. If we decide that it is a pretty good bet that a green can sells more roach spray, it does *not* follow that we can derive from that any universal principles concerning "buyer response" to particular colors.

The color green *now* is likely to be associated by some people in a positive way with ecology. In ten years it may be associated in a positive way with ecology by a much larger number of people. But, in ten years it may be that nineteen out of twenty cans of roach spray are green, so that the color will not help increase the market share of any particular spray.

Exercise 1:3.   One of the problems faced by the marketer is trying to decide what aspect of the many factors involved in marketing a particular product has the largest effect on the increase or decrease of market share of the product in question. I have discussed color and name. Write an analysis suggesting that the reason for the sales increase/decrease could be influenced by other factors (suggestion, regional preferences, needs).

In other words, in the *relatively* clear-cut world of selling merchandise, no simple answer is possible to the question "Is X effective in selling Y?" To begin to formulate an answer to that question we would have to ask:

No clear-cut measure of "effectiveness."

1. Absent all other factors?

2. To whom?

3. Where? and

4. When? (Now? On a continuing basis? For what period of the history of the product?)

Complex as that is, matters are *more* complex in considerations of effectiveness for written argument. In addition to the difficulty of identifying the element or elements that caused the "positive" response, in terms of written argument it is very difficult to know what is the equivalent of "purchased." In the case of the roach spray, I hand someone some money or a check or a credit card and they hand me, in exchange, a can of roach spray.

But, to continue to develop the analogy, in what sense do we "buy" arguments? Consider the following: I handed out an essay called "Why I Want a Wife" to 100 people enrolled in a first-year-level university writing class in the fall of 1996. The only information supplied with the essay was that under the title the name Judy Syfers appeared. I asked the class to read the essay, and when the class members were looking up at me again instead of down at the essay (which I was willing to assume meant that they had finished reading it) I asked them to hand the essay in. That having been done, I then asked each person to answer the following questions and to hand in their answers on a piece of paper but not to put their names on the paper.

How are arguments "bought"? How can we know?

A. Is this an effective essay?

B. If you thought it was, what did you find particularly effective about it or if you did not think it was effective can you say why?

C. What is Syfer's thesis?

Here is the essay as it was presented to the class.

Why I Want a Wife
Analyst's notes:

Why I Want a Wife

Judy Syfers

1   I belong to that classification of people known as wives. I am A Wife. And, not altogether incidentally, I am a mother.

2   Not too long ago a male friend of mine appeared on the scene fresh from a recent divorce. He had one child, who is, of course, with the ex-wife. He is looking for another wife. As I thought about him while I was ironing one evening, it suddenly occurred to me that I, too, would like to have a wife. Why do I want a wife?

3   I would like to go back to school so that I can become economically independent, support myself, and, if need be, support those dependent upon me. I want a wife who will work and send me to school. And while I am going to school I want a

Analyst's notes:

wife to take care of my children. I want a wife to keep track of the children's doctor and dentist appointments. And to keep track of mine too. I want a wife to make sure my children eat properly and are kept clean. I want a wife who will wash the children's clothes and keep them mended. I want a wife who is a good nurturant attendant to my children, who arranges for their schooling, makes sure that they have an adequate social life with their peers, takes them to the park, the zoo, etc. I want a wife who takes care of the children when they are sick, a wife who arranges to be around when the children need special care, because, of course, I cannot miss classes at school. My wife must arrange to lose time at work and not lose the job. It may mean a small cut in my wife's income from time to time, but I guess I can tolerate that. Needless to say, my wife will arrange and pay for the care of the children while my wife is working.

4 I want a wife who will take care of my physical needs. I want a wife who will keep my house clean. A wife who will pick up after my children, a wife who will pick up after me. I want a wife who will keep my clothes clean, ironed, mended, replaced when need be, and who will see to it that my personal things are kept in their proper place so that I can find what I need the minute I need it. I want a wife who cooks the meals, a wife who is a good cook. I want a wife who will plan the menus, do the necessary grocery shopping, prepare the meals, serve them pleasantly, and then do the cleaning up while I do my studying. I want a wife who will care for me when I am sick and sympathize with my pain and loss of time from school. I want a wife to go along when our family takes a vacation so that someone can continue to care for me and my children when I need a rest and a change of scene.

5 I want a wife who will not bother me with rambling complaints about a wife's duties. But I want a wife who will listen to me when I feel the need to explain a rather difficult point I have come across in the course of my studies. And I want a wife who will type my papers for me when I have written them.

6 I want a wife who will take care of the details of my social life. When my wife and I are invited out by my friends, I want a wife who will take care of the baby-sitting arrangements. When I meet people at school that I like and want to entertain, I want a wife who will have the house clean, will prepare a special meal, serve it to me and my friends, and not interrupt when I talk about things that interest me and my friends. I want a wife who will have arranged that the children are fed and ready for bed before my guests arrive so that the children do not bother us. I want a wife who takes care of the needs of my guests so that they feel comfortable, who makes sure that they

have an ashtray, that they are passed the hors d'oeuvres, that they are offered a second helping of the food, that their wine glasses are replenished when necessary, that their coffee is served to them as they like it. And I want a wife who knows that sometimes I need a night out by myself.

7   I want a wife who is sensitive to my sexual needs, a wife who makes love passionately and eagerly when I feel like it, a wife who makes sure that I am satisfied. And, of course, I want a wife who will not demand sexual attention when I am not in the mood for it. I want a wife who assumes the complete responsibility for birth control, because I do not want more children. I want a wife who will remain sexually faithful to me so that I do not have to clutter up my intellectual life with jealousies. And I want a wife who understands that my sexual needs may entail more than strict adherence to monogamy. I must, after all, be able to relate to people as fully as possible.

8   If, by chance, I find another person more suitable as a wife than the wife I already have, I want the liberty to replace my present wife with another one. Naturally, I will expect a fresh, new life; my wife will take the children and be solely responsible for them so that I am left free.

9   When I am through with school and have a job, I want my wife to quit working and remain at home so that my wife can more fully and completely take care of a wife's duties.

10   My God, who *wouldn't* want a wife?

You might note here that I did not ask you to try to answer the same questions that I asked the '96 class to answer, so you might or might not have read the essay with those questions specifically in mind. However, to check on the processes involved with a consumer of a writing product (rather than bug spray), respond to the next exercise (which is composed of the same questions asked of the '96 class) by writing a paragraph in response to each of the three questions. At least initially try to answer the questions without looking back at the essay.

Exercise 1:4.
b) Is this an effective essay?
c) If you thought it was, what did you find particularly effective about it or if you di not think it was effective can you say why?
d) What is Syfer's thesis?

When I did this in class I was, in a sense, performing a market survey. Could I, from this test, determine if "I Want a Wife" is an effective essay?

[Market survey as analogy.]

A careful reader could here respond, "Bad question. You can only say if a given item is effective if you can answer the question 'effective to whom and when?'" And of course I would agree. So, what if we made the question more specific and asked, "Can we determine if the essay was effective to this group of 100 college students in the fall semester of 1996?" And then of course there's not just the "time," there is the "place/time." So I should modify the question again and ask "Can we determine if this essay was effective to this group of 100 college students in the fall of 1996 at the University of Houston?"

Number, place, and time as factors in assessment.

What I am trying to accomplish by asking you to answer the same questions, even though you do so with the advantage of knowing about the questions before reading the essay (which the class did not), is to let you see if the discussion of effectiveness which preceded the exercise was helpful in terms of what you paid attention to in your reading.

Consider, as we explore possible answers to this question, what happened in the actual class. 100 sheets of paper were turned in. Six of them were totally blank. What could I conclude from those blank sheets in terms of the essay's effectiveness? I had asked that the answers have no names on them so that students would not try to anticipate what answer they might feel that I was looking for. I wanted people to feel that they could answer honestly because (since the answers were anonymous) no one could be held responsible (or get special credit) for any particular answer.

1996 results.

Apparently, however, for six members of the group, no names meant that since they could not be identified they would suffer no negative consequences from not taking the trouble to answer and so could "get away with" not doing the assignment that, for one reason or another, they rejected. It seemed clear that they did not want to do the assignment but were uninterested in *overtly* refusing to do so (since they *handed in* blank pages, and in so doing behaved in the ways that could be *observed* like those people who did answer the questions].

Difficulties in interpretation of the data.

If that conclusion was correct, I could *probably* only count the 94 who did respond as significant. (Even if my suppositions were correct, and the motives of each of the six were the same, I could not be sure they would do the same with a different essay, on a different day, with a different course load, with a good night's sleep, etc.). Remember, now, I am doing a market survey. I am trying to determine if the essay is "effective," if it succeeds in "selling" its point.

Necessary speculation as complication.

Trying to focus responses.

Out of that 94 then remaining, sixty-three answered the first question (Is this an effective essay?) with a "yes." That's 68.8 percent. If we go back to our selling analogy, that's a pretty good market share. Better than two thirds.

But for the time being let's skip the next question and look at the answers to number three. What I had intended to accomplish with question two was to lead the members of the class to think about the essay in specific terms, in part to see what portions of it they could remember, in part to get beyond the possible response "Nothing in particular, I just didn't like (or I just liked) it." The reason I wanted the class to go through that thought process rather than just a "reaction" process was that I wanted the mental review to provide as much information as possible for the class to utilize in answering the last, and presumably easiest, question, "What is Syfers' thesis?"

What is Syfers' thesis?

And since this is an example, let me ask you as the present reader, before going on, to look again at your own answer to the question, and if you have not yet written it down, to do so. Your response could be as short as a sentence or as long as a paragraph but should be as specific as possible. At this point you can approach it either by trying to remember without looking back at the essay or by re-reading the essay. Or (best from a learning perspective) you could do both—write down the thesis from memory and then go back and re-read the essay to confirm or correct what you wrote down.

Of the sixty-three who thought the essay was effective, twenty-four said that the thesis is that Syfers wanted someone to do all of the things for her that "a wife does." In so identifying the thesis, these people took the essay as expressing what Syfers wanted rather than as attempting to argue a point or to persuade anyone of a particular point. They thus took the essay as expository/expressive rather than "persuasive." They took the title literally, saying that what the essay *expressed* (rather than argued) was that Syfers "wants a wife." Eighteen of those who did *not* think the essay was effective agreed that this was the thesis but thought that the essay was stupid because Judy Syfers (presumably) was a woman, "and women don't have wives."

Range of disagreement.

Twelve of those who thought the essay was effective thought that Syfers was saying that wives do a great deal and are not recognized for it. They took the essay for an argument intended to persuade the reader that wives should be more appreciated.

Fifteen people thought that the essay was about how selfish "men are," a response that can be seen as a variation or perhaps a sub-category of number two with the emphasis on how little husbands recognize rather than how much wives do. Nine of this fifteen thought the essay was not effective because they saw it as an exaggeration "to prove a point." That is to say this group was not convinced that husbands were as selfish as they understood Syfers to portray them as being.

And there were a variety of other identifications of the thesis. What seemed to me to emerge was that people either did or did not *like* the essay depending on what they thought that its point was. After deciding on what the point was, readers then proceeded to agree or disagree with it.

Evaluation based on the "point" each reader saw.

All of this is interesting for a number of reasons, but it appears to have very little to tell us about what does or does not constitute effective argument. In part I hope by this example to have illustrated how problematic it is to make any *general* statement concerning the effectiveness of a piece of writing and how individual response is conditioned by *who* is reading the essay and what their circumstances are in relation to it. *General* statements about effectiveness, in other words, not only tend to be artificially formulaic but are misleading in terms of what they can contribute to a person who wishes to improve her ability to write argument.

Difficulty with general statements about effectiveness.

My thesis is that learning how arguments are written, and coming to appreciate what they are intended to accomplish with the specific audiences they are written for, gives you a set of tools. These tools, these rhetorical devices, can then be directly applied in support of accomplishing your persuasive purpose, to gaining your point, to speaking, as the case may call for, directly or indirectly to the circumstances of the target audience.

Acquiring the tools to use to gain your point with the target audience.

It is important at the outset to reinforce that for the purposes of the study of rhetoric and argument, the thesis of a given essay cannot be considered simply in terms of what a particular individual "got out of it." Further, it must be understood that there is no particular location where an essay's thesis is to be found, nor is there a particular place where that thesis *should* be.

*The **thesis** versus what the reader "got out of" the essay.*

The Five Paragraph Theme and the Thesis in Argument

You may be familiar with a teaching tool called "the five paragraph theme." In this structure the first paragraph directly states the thesis, the second through fourth paragraphs present support for that thesis, usually in the form of examples, and the fifth paragraph restates the thesis "in conclusion." There is a development from this that adds paragraphs usually equal in number to the "support" paragraphs, or "example" paragraphs. These added paragraphs reply to "the other side" of "the question" (a particularly widespread use of the **either/or** fallacy).

A problem central to this structure is that although it can be useful in producing clear organization and reinforcing ideas concerning what constitutes support, it has very little to do with how arguments are written in the world outside of the classroom.

It is probably most useful considered as an expository form where the purpose is to convey information to a captive audience rather than as a mode of persuasion. A reported method for conveying information in the military, "First you tell 'em what you're gonna tell 'em, then you tell 'em, and then you tell 'em what you told 'em," closely resembles it. The "telling what you are gonna tell 'em" is the thesis paragraph, the "telling 'em" is the body paragraphs, and the "tell 'em what you told 'em" is the conclusion. The form presumes an audience that is not terribly bright, not much interested, and totally captive.

Real-world written argument seldom begins with the thesis, and quite frequently does not end with it. In fact, real-world written argument often does not *directly state* the thesis *at all,* but instead *implies* it (and that, I will argue, is the case with the Syfers article). In relation to this, consider the following:

1. Argument, to *be* argument, must be addressed to those who, at the beginning of the presentation, disagree with the conclusion (thesis) or don't feel strongly enough about it to act on it, or are in danger of coming to disagree. They do not, of course, have to hold an opinion *opposite* to the conclusion, and may simply have *no* opinion in regard to it (see **target audience** and **preaching to the converted**).

Audiences for argument, at the outset may
1. disagree with,
2. agree with but be unwilling to support,
3. be beginning to doubt,
4. be unconcerned about, or
5. have no opinion concerning the thesis.

2. Leaving entirely aside the question of "effectiveness," it does not make sense to expect anyone but a masochist (or a student—see 3. below) to sit still and be instructed in why she is wrong. Who, after all, *likes* to be told that she *is* wrong, let alone that she is *going* to be told why she is wrong?

3. On the basis of the previous two items we can expect that when a real-world essay leads with the thesis it indicates one or more of a particular set of relationships between the writer and her audience:

Essays which begin with the thesis.

   a) The writer is a recognizable "name," the direction of whose views is known to the reading audience, or

   b) The reader (like the military audience mentioned two paragraphs ago) is in some sense captive to the writer and has come to her to find out what to think rather than to evaluate the presentation.

In the case of a), there is no particular point, for instance, in William F. Buckley, or Charles Krauthammer, the Pope, or Molly Ivins leading with anything less than their thesis. For frequent readers, the overall position of each of these people is well known. Those who read them do so more to see *how* they will approach a particular question than to determine what their position will be.

The situation described in b) is the position of the person who has bought a "how-to book." It is also the position of the student in relation to a *required* text. Both writers exist in a position of more or less **authority** in the relationship. The buyer of the "how-to book" exists in that relationship *prior to any attempt in the actual text by the writer to acquire that authority for herself* on the basis of the reader having granted the writer authority by laying down money for the book in the first place.

"Authority" in relation to the buyer of the "how-to" book and the student.

The student, in a similar although not identical way, has, by enrolling in the course, accepted the authority of the institution and the text *prior to any attempt in the actual text by the writer to acquire that authority for herself.* In this case *belief in the conclusion* is often less of an issue than the ability to act *as if* one accepted the argument. Consequently the *practical* student is usually more interested in understanding the position than in disputing it.

With the foregoing in mind, let's turn to Syfers' text. As rhetorical analysts our first question is "What is Syfers trying to sell?" (What, in other words, is her **thesis?**). I hope that the presentation above has made clear that this is no open-and-shut question—that is, that there can be considerable disagreement concerning the best answer to the question.

What I am going to do is present an argument, grounded in evidence taken from the text itself, for what Syfers' thesis is. I have asked you to write down your idea of what that thesis is, but I will never see that, so whatever that decision was has no "public" personal investment. You can change your mind, in other words, as I develop my argument, and no one will ever know that you didn't think whatever your final position is from the first.

Defining a thesis is frequently problematic, in that it depends on the writer's strategy as concerns her target audience. Everyone may be entitled to "his" opinion, but no one is obligated to be interested.

I ask you simply this—*rather than reject an interpretation that I will propose, see if you can come up with a better explanation than I have supplied to explain the writer's (Syfers') particular choices.* Note here as principles:

The responsibility of the analyst toward a proposed analysis.

1. There are no "right" answers in analysis. All answers are hypothetical—based on particular explanations for the arrangement of and choices made in the text. But there are principles:

2. Because no interpretation can be finally confirmed as "the" interpretation, it does not follow that one answer is as good as any other. It will seldom, if ever, be found that one explanation of the arrangement and choices made in the text will be as satisfactory as another will. The explanation that accounts for, or explains in the most complete way, the greatest number of choices will be accepted as the superior analysis—at least until a better analysis (according to the same criteria) is presented.

3. It follows that if one wishes to reject an explanation it is incumbent upon the reader doing the rejecting to supply a more satisfactory explanation according to the criteria presented in 2. above.

That analysis is best which explains the greatest number of textual details.

JUST YOUR OPINION

The point of the foregoing is to take this process of analysis outside of the "that's just your opinion" categorization. The analyst *inevitably* presents her opinion, but it is not *just* her opinion. It is presented against all competitors with the intention that it be accepted as the best opinion available *at this time*. Given the opportunity it seems likely that each of us would like to hold the strongest and most consistent opinions possible.

Since this is a textbook (or a "how-to book"), I am going to lead with my thesis. I am presuming that I can count on sufficient investment on the reader's part to continue reading whether or not she and I initially disagree about what the thesis is.

RHETORICAL ANALYSIS OF "WHY I WANT A WIFE"

The essay for analysis is short, but the implied (rather than stated, or overt) thesis cannot be stated in any brief form. I will argue that Syfers' thesis is as follows: Were we to strip all gender associations from the category "wife" (i.e. "wives are women") and view that category as a job description, no "person" would apply for or accept the job. To put that another way—I will argue that her thesis is that the job description "wife" should be abolished or revised.

The technique that Syfers uses to present this thesis is simple—those paragraphs that detail why a wife would be a

Assuming a captive reader (the student, or the person who has bought this book as a "how-to" text), I begin with the thesis. The reader is invested in continuing to read even if she disagrees.

good thing to "have" (two through nine) contain no gender-identifiable pronouns. It isn't just a reversal of the "traditional" roles by saying "he" in place of the usual "she." Instead it is saying *neither* he nor she and so presenting the expectations from a wife as if they could be expected from a "person" rather than a woman or a man.

"Person" as genderless, human, not man, or woman.

Notice the steps she follows to set this up, beginning in paragraph one. The first sentence of the essay does not say, as we might expect it to, "I belong to that classification of women known as wives." Instead it says, "I belong to that classification of *people* known as wives."

Ordinarily considered, "wife" is a subset of the larger category "women," rather than the much larger category "people." To skip the intermediary set is something like saying that an apple is a plant rather than saying it is a fruit. The statement is accurate, but it is not presented in the way we usually think about it. Indeed I would suggest that this unusual presentation (an unwillingness to see "wife" as a subset of "women" rather than a subset of "people") that makes the kind of thinking Syfers is introducing possible. What she is attacking, albeit indirectly (she never *says* she is attacking it), is the idea that wives are "naturally" women.

Syfers' second sentence is "I am A Wife." Her capitalization goes further than a simple assertion that "wife is my primary category of identification" as one might reply to the question "What do you do?" One might reply to that question, for instance, with "I am a student," or "I am an accountant," or "I am a teacher," or "musician," but none of these would be presented in caps. Further, it would be unusual for anyone to so categorize themselves even without the caps. Imagine the pause in the conversation if someone answered the question "What do you do" with "I am a wife," as opposed to the usual reply, "I'm a housewife."

Interpretation of the rhetorical use of capital letters.

Exercise 1:5. Assume a reader who does not understand the sentence immediately above that begins "Imagine the pause." Write a narrative of an **anecdotal** conversation that begins "Why did you pause?" Your goal in this narrative is to clarify the point of the distinction being made between "wife" and "housewife."

The poet who wrote his name e. e. cummings explained once that he did so because he reserved the use of capital letters for EMPHASIS. An initial reaction to Syfers' use of caps might be similar—that it is a way to lend emphasis and hence importance to the classification "wife." That is to say, one way to think about the capitalization is that it is intended to imply "I am a wife and that is important."

But consider that this is not done for other classifications that are often held to carry considerable importance. One does not say, for instance, "I am a Senator," let alone "I am A Senator." What one does conventionally capitalize, however, are the so-called proper nouns, the names of specific persons or places, and the classification name is capitalized when it is treated as a title attached to a particular person. At this writing, for instance, the president (notice the lower case) of the United States is "Bill" Clinton. His name, with the title, is President Clinton. When he is spoken to he is often addressed as Mr. President, in which case the title is treated as a proper noun—it is the name of the office used as the name of the individual *who holds* the office. Further, as with "Mr. President," a speaker may seek permission to address the "Chair," or one may call a Ph.D. or an M.D. "Doctor," or a ranked academic "Professor," in all of which cases the title is treated *as if* it were a name (and hence it is capitalized).

Ironic use of **synecdoche** involving the problematics of **naming**.

It is this last treatment of capitals that I think Syfers is playing on. "A Wife" has *become* her name. Formerly an individual named Judy Syfers, she has now been subsumed by the category and her "name" is "A Wife."

Even so, you could ask, isn't it being treated as an honorific, a title of respect, as Doctor and Professor are? To answer that I need to go into the third and last sentence of the first paragraph, "And, not altogether incidentally, I am a mother." And at this point the date of publication of the article becomes relevant. I will postpone consideration of the *place* of publication until a more particular discussion of the target audience.

[Analyst's argument for an interpretation of the text based on the date of publication.]

[Average age of target audience (first-to-third-year college students) presumed by analyst to necessitate presentation of significant historical data.]

"Why I Want a Wife" first appeared in 1971, and as such it would probably be classified by many parties interested in the politics and developments of the time as part of an effort called "consciousness raising." Consciousness raising was (and still is) a name applied to deliberate efforts to bring to the foreground of consideration assumptions that (in the view of those trying to raise consciousness about whatever the particular issue was) were built into the vocabulary and ideas surrounding particular concepts. These concepts were felt to be built in in such a way that most people (that is to say, those whose consciousness had not been "raised") were not aware of them *as* assumptions.

The associations were unquestioned in part because they were invisible (unconscious) and in part because they were assumed to be "natural" (see **Nature, argument from** and **Authorizing trope**).

Nature as Authorizing Trope.

The concept is difficult to explain in that once such an assumption is pointed out it can become fairly rapidly and widely recognized and that it not only existed in a previous state, but was the dominant opinion, becomes progressively more difficult to accept. (More often, however, the assumption is so deeply ingrained that the point remains unrecognized). From this point of view "consciousness raising" is a program of continuously drawing attention to the undesirable (again, from the perspective of those involved in the "raising") assumptions.

I will present three examples in chronological order as far as the date of their composition, and follow them with a third that remains, for many people, at least arguable.

The first example is taken from Mark Twain's 1884 *The Adventures of Huckleberry Finn*. Huck, at the point we enter the story, is a fugitive looking for something to eat when dogs surround him. The dogs' owners mistake him for a late guest who was to have arrived by Mississippi riverboat. The time of the action is the 1840s. The place is northern Louisiana (Twain himself, like Huck, was a Missourian).

> "We been expecting you a couple of days and more. What's kep' you?—boat get aground?"
>
> "Yes'm—she—"
>
> "Don't say yes'm—say Aunt Sally. Where'd she get aground?"
>
> I didn't rightly know what to say, because I didn't know whether the boat would be coming up the river or down. But I go a good deal on instinct; and my instinct said [his 'instinct' incidentally is wrong] she would be coming up—from down towards Orleans. That didn't help me much, though; for I didn't know the names of [sand]bars down that way. I see I'd got to invent a bar, or forget the name of the one we got aground on—or—Now I struck an idea and fetched it out:
>
> "It warn't the grounding—that didn't keep us back but a little. We blowed out a cylinder-head."
>
> "Good gracious! Anybody hurt?"
>
> "No'm. Killed a nigger."
>
> "Well, it's lucky; because sometimes people do get hurt. Two years ago last Christmas your uncle Silas was coming up from Newrleans on the old *Lally Rook,* and she blowed out a cylinder-head and crippled a man. And I think he died afterwards. . . ."

Racism as assumed standard.

Twain's structural repetition shows that he is himself concerned with some consciousness raising. Twain renders Huck here as making up details so his story will give him some more time to figure out who it is that he has been mistaken for. Twain hits the point twice—Huck replies to Aunt Sally's "Anybody hurt" with a negative and adds "Killed a nigger." *Without missing a beat* Aunt Sally replies "Well its lucky; because sometimes *people* do get hurt [my emphasis]."

Assumed here, implicit in this if we are to assume it is supposed to make sense, is that *for the speakers* (two pre-Civil-War whites) "niggers" (a term that, for them, includes all blacks) are *not* people. Indeed a central point of the book is Huck's discovery that this is not the case as a result of his relationship with the escaped slave Jim.

It is not that the whites in the book (no matter what their social or economic class) have *consciously* decided this. Twain does *not* imply that either Huck or Aunt Sally is cruel or thoughtless. Instead he tries to show that the classification of blacks as sub-human (the point that the book as a whole is working to subvert, to undermine) is, for *them,* automatic. For them, as representing the average American white idea structure of the time, it is built *into* that idea structure. Hence it is *below* the level of their consciousness. I wish to emphasize, however, that this is distinctly not to say that all white people held that idea at the time—Twain himself, for example, clearly does not.

Let me anticipate the example that I use in Chapter 3. Syfers' thesis works in the same way as the suggestion that the only people who object to slavery are those who do not own slaves. If *everyone* could own a slave, (and hence the objection to slavery disappear), from what population would the slaves be taken?

Thus also for Syfer's thesis. She states "My God, who *wouldn't* want a wife?" It should be clear that not every*one,* however, *could* have a wife. If every*one* did, there would be no population from which the wives could be taken.

The answer is the same as in the slavery notion, except here the population to be drawn from becomes the category of women, who for the notion "everyone" to work would have to be considered sub-human. And since Syfers has described the "job" of wife in non-gender-identifiable terms, the only possibility is that the population would be drawn from inferior "beings," (albeit still humans). Yoko Ono, as a Japanese taking the discussion outside of colonial American and British concerns to make a statement about how women are regarded world-wide, put the point much more directly in her '70s statement that John Lennon put into his song "Women are the Niggers of the World."

My second example concerns a plaque I saw at the University of Kansas Museum of Natural History in the 1970s. It was attached to a floor-to-ceiling glass show-case that contained a

---

Representation as mode of countering received opinion.

Note the use of verticality as a metaphor for states of knowledge.

The opinion of the writer never bound to the opinion of the citation.

Wife as job description.

John Lennon's use of Yoko Ono's pairing of racism and sexism as rhetorical device.

stuffed horse, a reddish bay with black mane and tail, wearing a U.S. Cavalry saddle blanket and saddle. The plaque said "Comanche, lone survivor of Little Bighorn." This example is perhaps even more compelling than the Twain example in that it is not one person representing how another thinks, as in the work of fiction, but an actual instance of real-world provincialism.

The plaque, of course, is no longer there, although I believe the (stuffed) horse is. But it is/was clear testimony that in the consideration of someone connected with the museum, the "tragedy" of Custer's final defeat (or "last stand" if you would rather) was so complete as to ignore the several thousand Sioux who survived the encounter. But further, and more importantly, it is testimony that if anyone noticed the "survivor" problem at all he or she either said nothing or was unable for some considerable amount of time to have it changed to recognize that the population now referred to as "Native Americans" won the battle.

[Personal narrative as rhetorical device: A horse as "The only survivor of Little Bighorn." Where are the Sioux?]

All that is otherwise noted is that Custer and the third of the command he had earlier divided were killed to a man (but, apparently, not to a horse). I emphasize here as I tried to do earlier that there was nothing malicious or cruel in the inscription. Malice and cruelty are conscious, and the thinking that allowed this wording, and allowed the thousands who viewed it to do so without protest, lay beneath the level of consciousness. The horse (that even more ironically carried the name of a Native American tribe) ranked higher in the consideration of the makers of the memorial than the native population that lived (and died) in the same encounter.

[Note that "person" was *not* used here.]

My third example of this sort of thinking is the title of a two-part course called "The Human Situation, Antiquity" and "The Human Situation, Modernity."

Neither of these titles is in the least objectionable until one discovers that what is taught is southern European literature and philosophy (in Antiquity) and southern and northern European and British literature and philosophy in Modernity.

The conclusion would appear to be inescapable. In these two courses the "human" is defined as that which can be thought of as culturally significant for what this community calls (for some fairly interesting un-geographic reasons) the "west." Like the "only survivor" of Little Bighorn, who, despite being only a horse, was on the side of the right, the only "humanity" is "western." But the "human situation," according the honors program containing the courses, does not include the Vedas, the Upanishads, the Sutras, the Buddha, Lao-tzu, or, for that matter, Mao Tse Dong. (Currently it includes Confucius and the *Bhagavad Gita* despite the fact that the course description contains

The "Human" Situation as the "western" world.

the statement "we begin the study of our cultural heritage by examining the Greco-Roman and Judeo-Christian cultures of antiquity."

Again, I wish to stress that I am not arguing that there is anything malicious or cruel here—rather that the threshold of their provincialism is revealed in the wide applicability of the terminology employed. There were, and indeed are, many courses like this. Most of them are called "Western Civilization." The first part, however is usually called "the Ancient World" and the second "the Modern World." So while the overall course title recognizes that the west constitutes only one civilization, the subtitles take that back with the global claims inherent in "world."

Members of the presenting program would almost certainly deny that they think Buddhists, Muslims, Taoists, Hindus, and the rest are less than human, but there is nothing in the naming of the courses or the selection of texts that so indicates.

In terms of "consciousness raising" one of the things that was going on in the late '60s and early '70s had to do with the *pre-conscious,* or unconscious association between marriage and child bearing, and/or (for that matter) the association between women and child bearing. We have discussed previously the "naming involved in the capitalization of "A Wife." Less evident, because of our historical distance from the circumstances of the argument, from the circumstances of the condition in which American women of the time lived, is the subtlety of the point Syfers is attempting to make with her third sentence.

Starting a sentence with "And."

"Normally" our expectation for the third sentence would be that "properly" it is a part of the second sentence. Each of us has probably been told a number of times never to start sentences with "and" (which we probably ought to ignore along with any other instruction containing an *absolute*).

Consider, then, the differences between "I am a wife and, not altogether incidentally, a mother" and the material as Syfers wrote it: "I am A Wife. And, not altogether incidentally, I am a mother." Consider what a writing teacher who was not paying particular attention to the rhetorical strategies involved would do when "marking" (or, what used to be called "correcting") Syfers' paragraph. A writing teacher might "correct" the entire paragraph into the single sentence "I am a wife and a mother."

What, after all, the writing teacher might argue, does this omit? Wives, it could be argued are women, not "people" (i.e. "women" is the more specific term and one should be as specific as possible), and "I belong to a classification" is a long way of saying "I am." The phrase "not altogether incidentally" is unclear with a qualified (altogether) negative (not). "A Wife" should not be capitalized, and if it is for the purpose of emphasis, so also should "mother" be capitalized (to make it parallel).

So much for writing teachers. So much for the concept of "correct."

Precisely counter to this, *each of those things the writing teacher would want changed in order to make the paragraph "better writing"* removes the rhetorical intention of the parts of the paragraph. The paragraph has not been "corrected." Instead it has been *modified* in such a way as to remove all of the rhetorical intentions inherent in its original form.

As a rhetorical analyst one must continually resist the urge to "correct" or rewrite, or even express "in other words."

Avoid thinking in terms of "in other words."

Let's concentrate for a moment on the "ambiguous" or even "unclear" phrase, "not altogether incidentally." The "incidental" is that which occurs merely by chance and is of secondary importance to what it is incidental to, or a minor consequence of.

The deliberate use of ambiguity as a rhetorical device.

What is initially vague in this structure is which of these two things is being suggested is not *altogether* a minor consequence of the other, and, further, to what extent the word "altogether" is being used ironically (see **irony**).

"Not altogether" is typically understood to mean "not completely, " that is to say, "almost completely, but not quite." If the term is being used ironically then the meaning becomes "it is possible that there is a tiny part of one of these that is not a direct consequence of the other."

What looks like a lack of clarity, then, can be seen as an attempt to slow the reader down in order to allow her the time to try to understand what meaning is intended. What, I argue, is intended would, although it would remain ambiguous, be clearer in 1971 when the article was first published than it is today, or if it is assumed that the essay in some way presents a "timeless" argument.

Necessity to consider the argument "in time."

The capitalization indicates that the "Wife" identity comes first, and the (small "m") "mother" identity comes second. But if the phrase is read ironically (and I would argue that the function of the word "altogether" is to signal that irony to the reader), the "priority" (in time) of the "mother" aspect is suggested.

"wife" and "mother"

That is, the irony implies that the "motherly" condition (pregnancy) either preceded what we might call the "wifely" condition, or that the two conditions were *assumed* to be so closely connected that there was no real choice in the matter.

Ironic qualification used as rhetorical device.

In a phrase not uncommon after W.W.II and only beginning to fade in the seventies, children were spoken of as "coming along," as when, in a marriage, children "come along."

It was assumed more often than not that married people who did not have children "couldn't" for some biological reason. And it was assumed that a pregnancy outside of wedlock indicated that the couple "had" to get married. In 1971 abortion was not legal except in cases of medical danger to the mother, and oral contraceptives (birth control pills), available (depending on various state laws) in some form since the early sixties, were in the midst of medical controversy.

The connection, in other words, between "wife" and "mother" was much stronger than it is now, and further, in that the pill was not as uncontroversial as it is now, so was the connection between "woman" and "mother." Roe versus Wade, the United States Supreme Court case that ruled a state law (Texas) in violation of constitutional right to a first-trimester abortion would not be decided until 1973.

Hence the joke, that the first pregnancy (in a marriage) was typically of uncertain term—anywhere from four to eight months, while succeeding pregnancies were always nine months to the day.

In 1971 four cases came before the United States Supreme Court involving women's rights. One of these resulted in the ruling that it was unconstitutional to deny a woman a job on the basis of her being the mother of small children unless the same rule was applicable to the fathers of small children. In 1970 Richard Brautigan published a novel titled *The Abortion: An Historical Romance 1966* that closed with a trip to Mexico for an abortion that was legally unavailable in California.

One might, at the time, have heard a woman reply to a question concerning what she "did" (although women were not as frequently asked that as they might be now) with a statement like "I'm a wife and the mother of three (or you pick the number as long as its more than one) growing children." It was extremely unlikely that one would hear, as one hears it in Syfer's essay, the answer "I am a wife" (let alone "I am A Wife").

CORRECTNESS AND RHETORICAL INTENT

Rhetoric is the result of deliberate choices made by the writer.

That the paragraph is three sentences long, and that it contains the apparent redundancies and errors of classification that it does, in other words, are not mistakes. Those things that the bored writing teacher might "correct" are deliberate aspects of the rhetorical strategy.

Wife is presented as a classification of "people" instead of "women." There is nothing in the "wife" job description, as it were, that is gender restricted. There is nothing that a wife does, in other words, that cannot be done by either sex.

"A Wife" is capitalized to present the classification as if it were the "name" of the individual concerned (something like the construction "Come by and meet the wife sometime" or "The wife and I just got back from Las Vegas").

The sentence is short so that it will be difficult for the reader to combine it with the sentence following. Hence it is intended to call attention to the possibility of *separating* the roles of wife and mother. The longer third sentence, which begins with "And," emphasizes this separation further, as with "And another thing," but undercuts that separation at the same time with the ironically qualified, negated, "incidentally."

Explaining the text.

Biologically, women bear children. *That they often do so in the circumstances of a marriage is not necessarily related to the job description entailed by the term "wife."* The intention is to weaken, if not deny, the notion that the terms wife and mother go "naturally" or "automatically" together. The first sentence ends with the word "wives," the second with "Wife," and the third with "mother."

READING OUT OF, READING INTO

I anticipate at this point the remark, "You sure are reading a lot into one word ('people') and two capital letters." My reply is that I am doing my best to avoid reading *anything* "into" Syfers' text. What I am trying to do is read "out" of Syfers' text in an attempt to derive an explanation for those things in that text that are unusual, that deviate from the expected, or the "normal" way something would be put.

Syfers' use of the word "person" rather than "woman" is not an accident, nor is her capitalization in the next sentence. These represent deliberate choices on her part toward the goal of persuading her target audience of her thesis.

Another frequently encountered response from beginning analysts is "I don't see how you get all that out of there. I didn't see that at all." I will resist the urge to reply "Trust me, I'm a professional." My point, however, is not to convince you as a reader of a *particular* rhetorical analysis of a *particular* piece of writing. Instead, my point is to illustrate *how written arguments are put together and how they are intended to work and upon whom.*

This reading as one reading of one paragraph.

The hope is that as a reading writer (and the reading comes first, always) you will be able to apply the methods you have learned here to your own writing, not in any formulaic sense, but with a knowledgeable attitude toward the analysis and generation of argument.

Nothing that I have done in the foregoing called for any specialized sort of knowledge. It did, however, call for very close attention to detail and for emphasizing rhetorical choices by contrasting them with the results of *different* choices (emphasizing, in other words, what the writer did say by contrasting it with what she did *not,* but *might have* said).

As analysts, and as writers, we must assume the following:

1. What exists on the page is the result of a series of conscious and deliberate decisions by the writer. What the writer hopes to accomplish by means of these choices can only be determined by trying to account for these choices as represented by the text.

2. The impulse to "correct" an argument or to "improve" the writing assumes that the reader knows better than the writer what it was that the writer wanted to say. This cannot be, however, because the only evidence the reader has for what the writer wanted to say is contained in what she did say.

3. The analysis of argument, therefore, presents arguments which attempt to account for what is present, rather than what "should be" present.

4. It is frequently the case that what seems incongruous to us in a particular argument may be accounted for by the time and circumstances in which the argument was constructed and the nature of the target audience as that differs from us as individual readers.

Summation of essential assumptions.

Informed writing makes choices.

Analysis does not "correct," it explains.

Analysis accounts for the text as it exists.

Analysis pays attention to and tries to take into account the date of composition of the analyzed material.

So much, then, from the perspective of this reading, for the first paragraph. I invite the reader to continue the analysis on her own, paying particular attention to how the subject area of each paragraph prepares for the following subject area, and further, how the character that Syfers creates for herself becomes such an exaggeration of blind ego that by the end of the essay the "I" has become monstrous to the point of being comic. It might be helpful to notice that all of this thinking is represented as going on while she is ironing, an activity that is so mindless as to encourage fantasizing.

Notice also how the avoidance of using a gender-identifiable pronoun begins to call more and more attention to itself as the essay proceeds. It can be recognized, I suggest, as not simply awkward, but necessary for the point to be made that those activities associated with the role "wife" have no necessary connection to the gender "female."

Exercise 1:6. In the invitation to the reader in the paragraph immediately above I ask that you complete the analysis. As a part of that project, select a paragraph or a "theme" (pronouns, promiscuity, fantasy, etc.) and write a 500-word explanation of the rhetorical intent of the author.

CHAPTER 2

NEVER SIMPLIFY (OR SIMPLIFY AT YOUR OWN RISK)

This is a book about written argument, but as the introduction and first chapter point out, it is not a book which tells you in a *direct* way how to write arguments. Because there are an infinite number of ways to combine the words of our language, into sentences and paragraphs, there are an infinite number of ways in which to write argument. But what about the ways to write "effective" argument?

There are all kinds of formulas for "effective" argument. One, for instance, says that the first thing an effective argument has to do is "grab" the reader's attention, an approach I hope that the first chapter has shown to be simultaneously obvious and useless as a guide to writing argument. The insecticide discussion in that chapter made clear, I hope, that what constitutes a "grabber" is always a matter of speculation. It should also be clear that writing (as opposed to the graphic representation of writing in flashing signs or in PowerPoint slide presentations) can't "grab" its audience except in a very sloppily considered, metaphoric way.

What one person finds exciting and interesting may very well bore or even disgust someone else. What is appealing to

"Grabbing" the reader's attention is a simplistic and finally indefensible formula for "effective" argument.

one taste is banal to another. Analyze the metaphor itself. To "grab" someone is to suddenly detain her physically without consideration of her own wishes relevant to that detention. Indeed, the person "grabbed" has no say in the matter. In the physical world it is clear that such action *is* possible. In the world of the written word acting upon a reader or readers, it is difficult to argue that any particular set of words would result in the same arresting of thought as being physically, forcibly retained results in an arresting of continued motion.

The reaction of any given reader is always something that the writer can only guess at, and which should (and for the trained rhetorician will) be conditioned by her estimation of the of the target audience's susceptibility to being "grabbed."

But there is also the complication of determining what it is that the writer wants to sell to that target audience (what, in the terms of the typical composition class, the "thesis" is). In the previous chapter I discussed this in terms of what a classroom of readers took to be the thesis of "Why I Want a Wife." This was complicated by the problematics of that particular class's (or any particular class's) relation to the intended target audience. How many members of the class actually belonged to the group of people the writer of the essay had aimed at?

> The **target audience** of the subject essay is unlikely to be the rhetorical analyst, and only *may* be you in the real world.

In this chapter, among other things, I want to particularly discuss what we could call the "layerings" of theses, and especially how those relate to the temporal relationship of the target audience to the subject essay itself. I mean the word "temporal" both in the sense of the "date" of the encounter, and in the sense of the potential clock time spent with the argument. And there is another complication with the question of targeted audience in relation to the text as a speech, a speech written down, and/or a speech recorded and filmed.

As noted earlier it is common to write that a given writer "says" so and so in her (say) fourth paragraph, but the careful rhetorical analyst must pay particular attention to whether the term is being used metaphorically or not. Properly speaking a writer *writes*, and a reader *reads* what the writer writes (as distinguished from what the writer might "say" in a filmed interview, or at a reading, which an auditor/viewer could "hear").

> Writing that a writer "says" x is metaphoric. The frequency of this usage can sometimes obscure very real distinctions between writing and speaking.

Gilbert Highet has written an essay which might be called an "appreciation" of one of the briefest and most famous American arguments. (His essay can be found in the "Readings" section of this text which is arranged alphabetically by author.) That argument is "The Gettysburg Address," and can seen in its entirety carved into an inner wall of the Lincoln Memorial in Washington D. C.[1] Highet argues that the "Address," far from having been dashed off on the back of an envelope in the train on the way to Gettysburg, as popular legend would have it, is the careful production of a writer who was familiar with great literature, and that it fully deserves consideration as a work of art, as a "prose poem" which "belongs to the same world as the great elegies, and the adagios of Beethoven."

At a number of points in his essay Highet refers to the address as oratory, and writes that Lincoln's "serious speeches" are "important parts of the long and noble classical tradition of oratory which begins in Greece, runs through Rome to the modern world, and is still capable (if we do not neglect it) of producing masterpieces." He writes that the address has the structure of "a skillfully contrived speech," and that the "oratorical pattern is perfectly clear."

Well, of course, we might want to say, "It *is* a skillful speech, so it *must* have a clear oratorical pattern." I suspect, however, that Highet has a message that is less than obvious. I suspect that Highet is telling us that while the "Gettysburg Address" "acts" like a speech, and "looks" like a speech (oratory), it isn't just a speech. It is a great deal more than that. But he doesn't want to say this in a direct way. Why he would not want to state this sub-thesis, or as I will discuss it, the "covert" thesis, I hope will become clear in the process of my presenting an argument for its existence.

If it quacks like a duck, and walks like a duck, it still may not be a duck. Considering the "speech" as written text.

*Thinking about the **covert thesis** and the sub-thesis.*

SPOKEN TEXT AND WRITTEN TEXT

Current practice is to print the "Address" in collections of "readings" selected for writing classes alongside of a transcription of Martin Luther King's "I Have a Dream" speech, or if not directly alongside it, at least within easy hailing distance and with notes directing the reader from one to the other.

The "Address" is 268 words long. It takes less than two minutes to read it aloud, slowly. Lincoln, Highet reports from eyewitness accounts, read, as opposed to "delivered" the address, and did so "very slowly, in a thin high voice, with a marked Kentucky accent, pronouncing 'to' as 'toe' and dropping his final r's." King's speech, usually called "I Have a

---

[1] I am indebted in this chapter and throughout this text to Dorothy U. Syler's *Read, Reason, Write,* a book from three editions of which I have taught rhetoric, and that I would recommend to those who like the "read first then write" approach, but find this text too narrowly focused.

Dream," takes easily ten times as long to read. And we know (without having to consult "eyewitness accounts" as Highet did) from film of the delivery, that it was neither "read" in a monotone, nor in a thin high voice.

I find reading King's speech an interesting experience, and one that I automatically compare with the experience of hearing it. Like most Americans of my age, I've "heard" it, or portions of it, through the medium of film, at least several dozen times. Perhaps as a result I find it disappointing on the printed page. When I read it I try to "hear" it in order to make it as moving as it is in my memory. I find that I want to supply King's gospel preacher intonations and timing to the words on the page, and that I want to "read" the speech with increasing volume and intensity. I want to "act" it, in other words.

But that doesn't happen when I read the "Gettysburg Address." I have no idea what the "Address" is supposed to "sound like," and thinking about it leads to some pretty curious speculations, such as that Lincoln was a great speech writer but not much of an orator, or that what Lincoln needed was a really good public address system and a terrifically photogenic backdrop (such as King had with the Lincoln Memorial behind him). But a PA system would have magnified Lincoln's already unimpressive voice, and it would have made little sense to deliver the speech in front of, say, a statue of the slave holding plantation owner George Washington. In fact the notion of what it was "supposed" to sound like presumes that what it sounded like the only time that Lincoln delivered it was *not* what it was "supposed" to sound like.

Comparing "The Gettysburg Address" and "I Have a Dream": a text to be read and a text to be heard.

Reading vs. Hearing

The more I think about it the stranger the notion of what it was (is) "supposed" to sound like becomes. And then it occurs to me that this isn't a speech, it isn't an "oration," it isn't even an "address"—it is a piece of *writing*. I want to go further—it is different in kind from King's speech. King's speech, if it was originally written, was not written to be read, but rather to be heard. Lincoln's "speech," on the other hand, I will argue was written to be read, rather than with the intention that it have its wished-for rhetorical effect as a speech.

Consideration of the rhetoric of a given text should take into account the medium in which it was designed to be delivered.

I suspect that Highet would agree, and would like for *his* readers to understand this, but he leaves the point implicit rather than explicit. I suspect that he does this because to discuss that point explicitly might distract his readers from what for him is a much more important point—that Lincoln is a literary genius.

[Personal narrative employed rhetorically to support an analytic point.]

I have stood inside the Lincoln memorial facing the statue of the seated Lincoln and read the "Address" from the wall to my right, and in those circumstances and at that time it brought tears to my eyes. It is important, however, to say here there are a good number of things that that experience does *not* allow me to conclude. I may not conclude therefrom that *any* sensitive reader will be brought to tears by the "Gettysburg Address." Nor may I conclude that the "Gettysburg Address" is moving enough to bring tears to *the* reader's eyes. My circumstances were, at that moment, unique, *as are the circumstances of every person who reads the "Address."* Everyone reads it, in other words, at some time, and in some place, and in some physical and emotional state occupied by no one else.

Shared experience as a basis for communication is always problematic.

Before you could know what I felt you would have had to have shared my education and my life experience, the weather, and my physical and emotional state. And no one could do that. From the simplest perspective, no one could stand where I stood when I stood there for the mere reason that I was already standing there.

On a less personal level, it should be evident that there is bound to be some difference in response between reading the address from a marble wall in Washington D. C. as an adult, and reading it from a text book on United States history in (say) the fifth grade. But my point is that *like* others in the presence of the "Address," I did not *hear* it. I *read* it. And while reading it *I had no desire to speak it aloud.*

The sound of King in contrast to the silence of Lincoln may be considered as rhetorically significant.

My experience was that except for small children, people tended to be very quiet inside of the memorial. One may, as King did, decide to speak from the *steps* of the Lincoln memorial, but facing the Washington monument, so that one has at one's *back* the huge seated statue. King's speech was delivered from that position, and *that* speech I cannot read without "hearing." It evokes on the page the memory of its recorded, televised, and frequently replayed sound. Lincoln's "speech" I resist imagining being read aloud. (Martin Sheen reads Lincoln? The late Richard Burton? Jack Nicholson? The late Jimmy Stewart might have been able to do it, but he'd need the whole 80 or so minutes of a film to build up his ethos.)

When we talk about rhetoric we usually have in mind a tradition of descriptions of the tools of the speech maker. That was certainly what Aristotle had in mind when he wrote his *Rhetoric*. The writing that he does discuss is writing done in preparation for a speech. The "Gettysburg Address" failed (Highet provides substantial evidence that it was initially ill received) as a delivered speech not only because of Lincoln's voice, "country" pronunciation, and lack of a public address system, but because it didn't (and doesn't) have time to build up, to establish its rhythms, to cement its metaphors, its tropes, in the consciousness of the hearer.

The Mind's Ear

And, as I suggested above, it was never intended to. I suggest that Lincoln knew too much about oratory to have delivered a speech, which, from the perspective of the audience (especially given the oratorical styles of the day), would end before they were warmed up to listen. Lincoln knew that his speech would appear as a written document, knew that at some time after its initial delivery it would be consumed as a written document— that it would appear in print, and if that appearance was successful, would appear in print again and again and again. He anticipated that it would be *read*, and then that it would be studied, and that only then would it be "heard," as we "hear" it today, if you can stand *this* metaphor, in the mind's ear.

> Lincoln recognized that the address would be known and appreciated as a print argument.

In 1872 (the "Gettysburg Address" was written nine years earlier) Friedrich Nietzsche wrote in his lecture notes on ancient Greek eloquence that Greek rhetors and stylists felt that they controlled "'opinion about things' and hence the *effect of things upon men*. . . . Basically, even today 'classical' higher education still preserves a good portion of this antique view, except that *it is no longer oral speech but its faded image, writing* that emerges as goal" (my italics). There are a number of ideas here that need to be examined before we can begin a discussion of rhetorical analysis, (much less say anything about "effective" rhetoric).

In our age of sophisticated and high-speed media, part of Nietzsche's point, seems naive. But we need to remember that "news," prior to the printing press, photography, radio, film, or television, was in the hands of "rhetors," or "speakers," and only in a minor sense in the hands of the writer (as writer of print text, as opposed to writer of speeches).

Rhetoricians we understand here as persons who teach rhetoric and analyze the productions of rhetors. A written version of a speech could be disseminated in ways that a painting, or a sculpture, or a performance, could not. Materials for the study of rhetoric, in the absence of other recording technology, had to be written records of or drafts for speeches, themselves (which would be *only*, as Nietzsche writes, the "faded image" of the oration). The central mode of communication, of persuasion in the era he discusses, was *speech*. Writing was understood primarily as a record and/or an imitation of speech.

> Confusing written argument with spoken is the heritage of our slowness to appreciate changes in media.

Without printing, wide dissemination of written materials, "popular" dissemination, as we understand it, was not possible.

The ancient rhetors' claim, that they controlled opinion and thus the effect of "things" (events) upon humankind, could not be made today solely by the writer or orator, nor, as long as the media are not monolithic, could it be claimed by any single power in mass media. But the argument could certainly be made that if any one group *did* control the dissemination of words and images, that group could define what constituted reality. (Indeed this is precisely the argument that George Orwell makes in *1984*.)

Nevertheless, that component of what we call "reality" as we define it, or as we wish it to be understood, which is constituted by the written word is very large, and perhaps larger than that commanded by any other medium. We can be thankful that this medium, the written word, is not monolithically controlled—that while there are people who will attempt to say how things *should* be written, there is no one with the power to control how things *are* written.

I need to note here that although this is a text on writing and is specifically designed to help the reader to become a better writer, it will postpone suggesting to you *how* to write as long as possible, and then will do so only in general terms. Persuasion, in the metaphor I frequently use for it in this text, can be understood as *selling* (this is, of course, to use a metaphor for a metaphor in that the word "persuasion" is itself metaphoric, involving, in its Latin root, "bringing over").

Selling involves inducing readers to "buy." It could be argued, then, that this is, part, a course in consumer education, and from one perspective it is. But that is not the focus of the text. Rather than saying this is how one tells good products from bad, or how one decides if one wishes to buy or not, or if one would be better off possessing the product (or being possessed by it), this text presents analyses of how writers have attempted to persuade. Further, because the book is intended to be completely practical (rather than historical, or theoretical), the arguments examined will be "contemporary" (that is to say, written at least after the turn of the century, and for the largest part, well after World War II).

You will not be asked, in other words, to rhetorically analyze the "Gettysburg Address." But you *will* be taken through Highet's contemporary rhetorical analysis of the "Gettysburg Address." In that exercise I will present a rhetorical analysis of an argument which is itself a rhetorical analysis. The writing that this text will ask you to do will be analytic. You will be asked to analyze (in writing) written arguments. You will be

Big Brother and the nature of "reality."

The written word is important in defining how we understand what we think of as "reality."

The "practicality" of rhetorical analysis.

asked to examine the means that writers have used in an attempt to persuade their chosen audience, and to present the results of that examination in your own argument.

RHETORICAL ANALYSIS AND THE REAL WORLD

You might ask, at this point, how is that "practical"? Who but a person being trained to teach rhetoric would ever be asked to write a rhetorical analysis of an argument? My answer is that on the range between passively to actively, naively to skillfully, ignorantly to knowledgeably, inexpertly to expertly, insofar as we are literate and conscious at all *we all perform rhetorical analyses of every piece of writing that comes before us.*

We seldom write those analyses down. Most often we pay little attention to arguments that appear to have no direct relationship to us, or on subjects about which we have, or think we have, fixed opinions. But we pay enough attention to those arguments, and analyze them to a point sufficient to assure ourselves that we already know *that*, or we already know *better* than *that*, or we aren't interested in *that*. That is to say we react to arguments in a direct relationship to how those arguments relate to us. *But every time we see writing on paper we know that someone is trying to sell something to someone.*

We perform rhetorical analyses of every speech and text we encounter. Studying the process aims at improving our skills rather that creating them.

Our initial reaction, as I suggested, may well be that that someone is someone *else*, and so we stop reading, and hence, reacting. In making that decision we have performed, whether we know it as such or not, an act of rhetorical analysis. We have looked at the words and on the basis of what we have seen decided that the message is not intended for us. If we were asked to articulate on what basis we made that decision, after a little thought, we would almost certainly be able to do so. The practicality comes from learning how to do better what we do already, but perhaps not very well, or with less skill in one application than in another.

Learning rhetorical analysis is learning to do better what we already do, and must do, in our interactions with language, be they personal, political, or professional.

Practical Application: The Note on the Refrigerator

I have mentioned the note on the refrigerator as an example of one extreme of writing used for persuasion. This might be an opportune moment to defend that supposition, particularly in the presence of what is likely to seem to be one of the *least* defensible examples of the practicality of acquiring skills in rhetorical analysis (a rhetorical analysis of a rhetorical analysis of an argument presented by a politician at the dedication of a cemetery in the mid-nineteenth century).

The Post-it note goes anywhere. You can put one on your forehead, or someone else's, but outside of office applications we are highly likely to find it on the refrigerator. Why? Because we go there a lot—more frequently, probably, than we go to the bathroom or the back door (my candidates for popular post-it locations numbers two and three). So, we've got a general idea of where, and not quite a "when." This one could be number twenty of the post-its on the refrigerator. So I've got to make a decision. How urgent is it? If I read the whole bunch, say, once a week and it has no more urgency than that, I can put it any-where. Otherwise I'll put it on top of others, or higher up, or whatever my schema is.

> We leave arguments to ourselves in places we go often.

I have become, by this decision, a member of a **discourse community**. It has only one member, but "me now" is talking to "me sometime in the future." I have to try to decide what I am most likely to respond to at the time I want to respond by, so I adopt a "strategy," and that strategy could be described as (and, within the "community" of this textbook, *would* be de-scribed as) "rhetorical."

Exercise 2:1.   Find an example of the kind of thing I am describing above as an argument with yourself and write a paragraph-length analysis of why you composed it as you did and placed it where you placed it.

But what if the note you leave isn't to you? Now we really have a discourse community, and you need to decide how you best get the attention of whatever member of the household you are leaving the note for, and further, you need to decide what the fewest number of words are that you can use which will make your attempt "effective," that is, allow it to accomplish what you want to accomplish with it. It may just be a phone number, but it's an argument at the same time, and the situa-tion is the same if the message is only for you.

At this *relatively* uncomplex level of the household served by this particular refrigerator, you've got a lot of information about your target audience, but as you move up in levels of complexity you have less and less. And in the post-it situation as it has been developed to here, we only have half of the relationship. We are dealing only with notes that *you* write. So what happens when we move on to the complexities added when someone else leaves a note on the refrigerator for you? Or *is it* for you? And how do you decide?

The complexity of the rhetorical approach is directly related to the size and complexity of the **discourse community** addressed.

We now return to the complexities of selling bug spray, and attitudes toward race, and gender, and sexual preference, and questions of who will lead the free world, and what is to be done about nuclear missles, and gun control. The practicality involved in attempting to understand arguments not specifically designed to influence us in particular, is that we will better learn how arguments have been made, and from that knowledge we build for ourselves a mental reference bank that we might call "methods of argument." This would be something like what a computer manual might call a "custom menu" (or, for you Mac people out there, the Apple menu) from which we can select whatever tool we find useful, depending on our project,

Everyone who writes, writes argument. Everyone who reads, reads argument. The question is do we do either one well? Or to put it in terms of what this text is for, what argument could be advanced *against* being able to do both things better? Now, if you are in college in preparation for getting a job where you will not have to write, or, in which you will not have to read, you don't need this course. Of course that's presuming as well that someone else does your shopping for you, and votes for you, and talks to other people for you.

Interaction with writing is inescapable. There is no one who does not "need" rhetorical skills.

The Overheard Effect

I hope that one of the lessons you will take from this book is that there is no single way to write argument, no formula for "effective" persuasion, and that when an "effective" mode of persuasion emerges it is exactly that, a "mode," in the sense that we say something is "modish," or "fashionable," or "in style." And we know also that unless the word "style" changes meaning, that the concept "timeless style" is not only provincial, it is an **oxymoron**.

The concept of a "timeless style" is an **oxymoron**.

Let us return to the above discussion about what I could not conclude from my response to the "Address" on the wall of the Lincoln Memorial, and the problem that that creates in terms of prescriptions or directions for the creation of "effective" arguments. I could *not* conclude that because (reportedly) the speech failed with its hearers, with the people to whom it was delivered at Gettysburg, that it was, therefore, a failed piece of rhetoric.

But if I took the longer view which I have been presenting, and presumed that Lincoln was not particularly, or at least centrally, interested in the response of the *immediate* ("temporality" concern) audience, but was instead interested in the response of a reading audience who would come to be familiar with the "Address" *over time and with the opportunity to read and re-read it*, I will understand the rhetorical approach in a very different way. From this perspective Lincoln sacrifices the response of the immediate audience in favor of the hoped-for gains in respect to the long-term audience, the *readers*.

This is a strategy that those who follow television news reporting see with some regularity. Bill Clinton, for example, attacked a black rap singer's response to the LA riots (the community's response to the video-recorded LA police's beating of Rodney King) while he was addressing Jesse Jackson's Rainbow Coalition. Since the rap singer in question was a participant in the conference, Clinton's attack on her would seem to be ill advised in that it would be unlikely to win friends among the members and supporters of the Rainbow Coalition.

*The audience directly addressed is not always the **target audience**.*

I suggest, however, that Clinton was only peripherally interested in his immediate audience, the Rainbow Coalition itself. His "real" audience, provided the networks carried his remarks, his attack, on their news shows (and they did), was the much broader group who would see the incident on the news, and if the attack strategy succeeded in becoming "news," who would read about it in later analyses of the event. Clinton, in other words, was not particularly trying to win friends among members of the Rainbow Coalition, but he was taking the opportunity, while addressing them, to sound tough on the subject of the destruction of property and unlawful conduct.

Clinton's reply to the immediate audience intended for appeal to the audience that news coverage would supply.

Exercise 2:2.   Watch CNN or the national news on one of the network channels for reporting of prominent public figures making statements at meetings of various coalitions or special interest groups. Analyze the content of one or more of these statements in terms of the intended rather than the immediate audience. This exercise can be brief or extended, depending on the material presented and the complexity of the issue.

Lincoln delivers a speech designed to be read.

So also Lincoln was familiar enough with the oratory of the period to know that it was unlikely that he would have a great deal of effect on the audience at Gettysburg itself, but if he succeeded in getting the speech into print (as, in a quite different way, Clinton hoped to get his response to the rap singer onto the evening news), he could hope to reach an audience with the time and opportunity to appreciate the subtlety and thoughtfulness of the piece. The "Address," in print, can be read and re-read. It was only *delivered* once, and there were no sound equipment or video cameras present. Clinton, on the other hand, was not looking for an audience that would "read" the response, but instead an audience that would "hear" his response which was much larger and differently constituted than the group to whom the response was actually physically delivered.

GILBERT HIGHET'S GETTYSBURG ADDRESS

I have chosen Highet's essay for this sample analysis for a number of reasons.

1. The essay itself is a rhetorical analysis of Lincoln's "Gettysburg Address" and is consequently valuable to the student of argument simply in terms of its content, that is, simply for what it has to say about Lincoln's rhetoric.

2. One of Highet's rhetorical strategies is to use the rhetoric and rhetorical devices he finds in the "Address" in his own appreciation of, or tribute to, that address. We have as a result a clear-cut example of deliberate rhetorical complexity used to complement (and compliment) Lincoln's complexity.

3. As a rhetorical analysis it presents an argument which contains both overt and covert aspects—it has a declared thesis and another related thesis which is only implied.

4. Another of Highet's strategies is to treat his own writing as if it were a recording, or a transcription, of a more or less extemporaneous talk rather than a highly wrought, carefully worked out and revised piece of writing. Consequently the essay can be seen in itself as a sort of commentary on the differences between the spoken and the written as modes of persuasion.

5. The essay takes as among its direct subjects the placement of Lincoln's speech in history, in its own time, and deals with (although less directly) what the "Address" can mean in the present.

Highet's essay is a complex, carefully constructed, completely thought out document intended to celebrate, even by imitation, a complex, carefully constructed, completely thought out document.

By What Means: Highet's Rhetorical Devices

I will begin close to the end of Highet's essay with paragraphs 15, 16, and 17. These contain Highet's examples of and elaboration on Lincoln's use of the classical rhetorical figure which he tells the reader "is technically called *tricolon*—the division of an idea into three harmonious parts, usually of increasing power." Highet then cites what he calls "the most famous phrase of the Address"

[Summary and quotation presented to focus your attention on specific portions of the essay under rhetorical analysis.]

> government of the people
> by the people
> and   for the people.

He next cites, in its own paragraph, what he calls "the most solemn sentence."

> we cannot dedicate
> we cannot consecrate
> we cannot hallow   this ground.

And then, using an elaborate metaphor, he introduces (in the third and last paragraph dealing with tricolon), "above all," the final sentence, which he describes as "essentially two parallel phrases, with a tricolon growing out of the second and then producing another tricolon: a trunk, three branches, and a cluster of flowers." He refers to the triad

> that these dead shall not have died in vain
> that this nation . . . shall have a new birth of freedom
> and   that government of the people, by the people, and for
>   the people. . . .

Without beginning a new paragraph he concludes the third paragraph with "Now,[!] the tricolon is the figure which, through division, emphasizes basic harmony and unity. Lincoln used antithesis because he was speaking to a people at war. He used the tricolon because he was [1] hoping, [2] planning, [3] praying for peace." (Material in brackets mine.)

What I am trying to illustrate here is that Highet's structure incorporates the device he is discussing as part of its strategy of presentation—that he uses the rising "hoping, planning, praying" as his three-part, flowered cap for the three paragraphs in which he deals with Lincoln's thrice-repeated three-part rhetorical device. Highet, in other words, is deliberately imitating Lincoln's use of tricolon, and in the process he is attempting to educate the reader to be able to recognize not only Lincoln's skill, but also Highet's.

With the foregoing in mind, let me focus on Highet's first paragraph. I will quote it in its entirety, including what is nearly, but not quite, the essay's title.

Fourscore and seven years ago. . .

These five words stand at the entrance to the best known monument of American prose, one of the finest utterances in the entire language, and surely one of the greatest speeches in all history. Greatness is like granite: it is molded in fire and lasts for many centuries.

Again we have an elaborate metaphor, but with the knowledge gained in the last three paragraphs the attentive reader can also see ("These five words stand at the entrance to [1] the best known monument of American prose, [2] one of the finest utterances in the entire language, and surely [3] one of the greatest speeches in all history.") the tricolon. Moreover, the reader can also notice the "increasing power." Highet begins the tricolon by placing the "Address" within American prose, then moves to the larger claim concerning "the entire language" (that is, everything that has ever been written in English, of whatever English-speaking nationality), and concludes the structure with the huge claim that the address is one of the greatest speeches in any language (and therefore in all language) for as long as there has been (and I wish to emphasize this) *writing*. We may not pay particular attention to it in this way, but that period which we call the "pre-historic" is understood as that which pre-dates writing—thus the greatest speech in all *history* is the greatest speech in all the time in all languages, in which there has been (and I again emphasize) *writing*.

> Highet uses tricolon in his discussion of Lincoln's use of the same figure of speech.

> Writing in relationship to the existence of "history."

The Use of Metaphor

Let me turn now to a consideration of Highet's use of metaphor in these four paragraphs. Note first Highet's treatment of *Lincoln's* use of metaphor (although Highet never uses the word). In his 10th paragraph he writes that Lincoln "did not say there was a chance that democracy might die out: he recalled the somber phrasing of the Book of Job—where Bildad speaks of the destruction of one who shall vanish without a trace, and says that 'his branch shall be cut off; his remembrance shall perish from the earth.'"

The way Lincoln "recalled" this was to say (*write*) that "government . . . shall not perish from the earth." The recall that Highet speaks of is apparently total—the words are *exactly* those of the King James Bible. But note that while the biblical Bildad uses a metaphor, Lincoln does not. Lincoln uses that section from the citation which does not contain a metaphor ("perish from the earth") rather than the reference to a branch being cut off as a metaphor for the death of a portion of a family "tree."

It is Highet who brings that branch back in by referring to the last sentence of the "Address" as "two parallel phrases with a tricolon *growing* out of the second and then *producing* another tricolon: a *trunk*, three *branches*, and a *cluster of flowers*." Highet, in other words, "recalls" what Lincoln does not, and indeed could not at the time of the "Address," that the branch of democracy was *not* cut off, and the remembrance did *not* "perish from the earth." Lincoln's hope, that is to say, that the Union, the "United" States, would survive was realized.

[Specific words (like "recalled") are quoted from the text in the discussion of the text in the hope that the reader (you) will note an attempt to focus closely on details.]

My own metaphor at this point may strike you as excessive, but I want to suggest that what Highet is doing here in this third of the tricolon paragraphs (paragraph 16), is bringing flowers to Lincoln's monument—that monument he presented in his first paragraph at the *"entrance"* to which "five words *stand"*; the monument that is carved in "granite," the rock "molded in fire" (igneous) as was Lincoln molded in the fire of the Civil War, which does not "perish," which indeed "lasts for many centuries." I cannot, of course, be positive about this, but Highet may be suggesting the ultimate instantiation of the "Address," before which I and thousands of others have stood, on the wall of the Lincoln Memorial.

[The analyst's discussion calls attention to its own use of metaphor in the treatment of Highet's use.]

Lincoln's metaphor (as opposed to Highet's) has to do with birth, has indeed to do with two births. The first birth occurs when "Our" fathers *"brought forth"* a new nation *"conceived"* in liberty. The second is the *"new birth"* of freedom in that new nation which brings into being that condition that was only implicit in the phrase "all men are created equal" until it was extended with the Emancipation Proclamation.

This is a point with which Highet does not deal. Instead he offers that Lincoln was working with ideas of the relationship of life to death and the two as the "triumph over death" (paragraph 10). Highet apparently does not wish to deal with the question of what might be meant by a *new* birth of freedom rather than a *rebirth* of freedom. He cites "the great task remaining" but does not elaborate concerning specifically what that is.

We need to remember that Highet is writing in 1954, and would probably have thought that, for Lincoln, "the great task remaining" would be seeing the North through to winning the Civil War. An opposing view is taken by Garry Wills in his 1992 *Lincoln at Gettysburg: The Words that Remade America*. Wills argues that Lincoln was in the process of doing nothing less than altering the Constitution as it applied to racial issues "from within, by appeal from its letter to the spirit." The Constitution, after all, has nothing to say concerning equality, and, as a document, was tolerant of slavery. The "created equal" phrase comes from the Declaration, not the Constitution. But issues of civil rights were much more in the forefront in 1992, when Wills published his book, than the relatively placid 1954 (the second year of Eisenhower's first term as President of the United States).

When the subject essay was written is important to an understanding of its rhetorical choices.

Highet's rhetorical devices, or at least some of them, are produced in imitation of Lincoln's. And that imitation is deliberate—I do not wish to imply that Highet's essay is thus some kind of a copy and therefore a flawed piece of writing. To whom, then, is Highet writing? Having determined that, we can then move on to try to determine what Highet's thesis is, of what point, or points, is he trying to convince his target audience.

To Whom: Highet's Target Audience

Remember here that you cannot assume that a writer is writing to you simply because you are sitting in front of one of the pages upon which the work in question has been reproduced. As I suggested earlier, Lincoln's primary audience was not those present at Gettysburg that day, nor was Clinton's intended audience Jackson's Rainbow Coalition. In order to come to rhetorical grips with any piece of writing, it is incumbent upon the analyst to try to remove herself from a reactive position and to take on instead an analytic view. In other words, the rhetorical analyst should try to set aside judging from the position of gender, race, social class, educational attainment, personal expertise, and so on. The analyst, as analyst, should try to determine, from the evidence presented in the essay, what group the writer was trying to influence. As always, and for all rhetorical points, the evidence is in the words.

It is important to distinguish between a reactive and an analytic approach to a written argument.

In the abstract, what will, or can, the words tell us about the identity of the target audience, and how can they do so? The reader here needs to turn to the *Glossary.* The necessary term is **warrant**. As an analyst, you must ask yourself, "What group would accept the assumptions which lie behind this statement? What group would be unlikely to accept these assumptions?" Or, in the terms of rhetorical analysis, "What group would 'warrant' these assumptions?"

An examination of "warrants" should replace value judgments in the process of analysis.

Because the analyst's task is to attempt to discover by what means the subject writer is trying to convince the target audience of the thesis or theses, it is not relevant to ask if a given audience *should* accept a particular statement. It is exactly relevant, however, to ask *if* a specific group would accept a particular statement. Let me try an example. Take the statement

> There is no longer a need for a "feminist agenda." Women achieved their long awaited equality a decade ago. In fact if they don't back off from their "demands" for "women's rights," they may well lose the human rights they spent so long in earning.

Role-playing, trying to think as a member of a particular group would, is important to the task of analysis.

You may or may not be a feminist, but think of yourself as one for the purposes of examining the rhetorical intent of this passage. Would a person who finds a need to think of herself (or himself) as a feminist find the second sentence acceptable?

If you define a feminist as a person who supports and participates in activities aimed at securing the equal treatment of women (equal "rights") then it would seem there are (at least) two possibilities here:

1) the statement is incorrect and indicative of the writer's ignorance of the current condition of women and/or it demonstrates hostility to feminism or

2) the statement is correct, but the price of that equality is eternal vigilance (i.e. the "achieved equality" is under attack and needs defense).

In other words, in the very unlikely circumstance that a feminist was willing to **warrant** the *second* sentence she would *not* **warrant** the first. At this point, we would have to postulate that the paragraph (and presumably the essay of which it is a part) is not addressed to feminists—that feminists are not among those people who constitute the target audience.

Approaching analysis through exploring a hypothesis.

We look then to the rest of the paragraph to see if it will support this hypothesis. We find the terms "demands" and "women's rights" placed in quotation marks. Since they are not particularly unusual words, nor is any specific source being cited, presumably the quote marks are intended to convey the comment, "so called." They are meant to express something like "what *they* call, but *we* know better than to call 'rights,' what *they* think *they* have the power to 'demand' but *we* know better that *they* have not." The later part of the sentence, by saying that women "earned" "human rights" implies that "they" had to achieve a position from which it could be seen that "they" ought to be considered (now) as human.

Always consider when a population is referred to as "they," who the implied "we" would be.

But here we find another possibility. This last sentence can be read as a threat, in which case it *might* be addressed to feminists (however ill advisedly). It might be intended to invoke fear. And that fear might be intended to cause a cessation of the activity that provoked the threat. It could then be read as something like, "If you feminists don't quit your agitating we will see to it that you are put back where you belong" (presumably barefoot and pregnant). On the basis of giving the writer the benefit of the doubt in such cases, this reading doesn't seem very likely in that it is this sort of attitude that feminism has historically dealt with since there has been feminism.

Who, then, *can* we say constitutes the target audience? It seems unlikely that it is addressed to feminists, or even that the target audience includes women (feminist or not). The statement suggests, after all, that only after a long struggle have women "earned" the position from which "they" can be considered human. Moreover, except in the case of the **overheard argument**, "they" is not a term writers use to refer to those being addressing. (The **overheard argument** is supposed to work on the basis of the reader's anonymity, something like a mother seeing her small children hiding saying so that they can hear her, "If I wanted to stay up and watch television tonight I think I would pick up my clothes.")

> If you find yourself rejecting an argument, can you determine if you are part of the intended audience?

In the Highet essay, we find the matter of **warrants** a little more clear cut, if only because they are less complex. Figuring out what the warrants are in a given argument is not usually difficult, but the process may seem difficult initially because looking for them is not something most people do in their everyday interaction with discourse and argument. If we happen to actually be members of the target audience, looking for warrants will probably seem silly because we often reflexively (and, obviously, wrongly) think that "everyone" thinks *that*.

Exercise 2:3.   Return to the indented paragraph and develop an argument to support a hypothesis about who you believe the target audience for the statement to be. At least in part support your hypothesis with an analysis of warrants.

In theory Highet's first paragraph could be addressed to anyone. It makes a series of assertions, but these assertions are not based on any clear set of divisive, categorizing assumptions. We might want to say that the target audience is here limited to people who read English. But there is no particular justification for even that assumption in that we can imagine the paragraph translated into any language without it encountering any

The question, "If this were translated, would any referents need to be changed to make it understandable?" can be useful to the analyst.

particular problems. (See the discussion of Orwell's "Politics and the English Language" in the next chapter for an example of a case where the native language of the target audience *is* important.) Since the claim is made for the greatness of the "Address" in relationship to all languages and over all recorded time, one could argue that the first paragraph does not limit the target audience to any group except those who can read.

The second paragraph, however, attempts more particularity, and a more intimate tone. Highet writes "he and his speech are now further removed from *us* than he himself was from George Washington and the Declaration of Independence" (my italics). Highet thus specifically makes himself a member of whatever group the reader finds herself a member of, or, conversely, makes the reader into a member of whatever group Highet is a member of. The specifics of that group are defined in the paragraph's closing sentence (and in another tricolon)— "that date is already receding rapidly into our troubled, adventurous, and valiant past." Since "[f]ourscore and seven years before the Gettysburg Address, a small group of patriots signed the Declaration . . . ," the target audience is clearly citizens of the United States. Lincoln, although of worldwide significance, is *our* president, and a part of *our* history. It may seem obvious, but those who are "patriots" to Americans are, to the British, revolutionaries, rebels, or even traitors. So also the "valiant past" is *ours* in a way different from its being a part of the past of *the* rest of the world.

In discussing arguments, pay attention to built-in assumptions concerning the reader's nationality, race, and gender. Who makes up the "they" is a very good indicator of who the target audience is by indicating who is *not* part of that audience.

How does this relate to warrants? How do warrants help us to identify the **target audience**? If we look, for instance, at the word "patriot," it should be clear that Americans would assume the historical interpretation on which the word "patriot" depends in a way that other nations, and specifically other English-speaking nations, would not. As indicated above, if you think about it in this way, those people America now thinks of as patriots would have been, had the Revolution been lost, almost certainly hanged as traitors by the British. There would have been no "Americans" to warrant the phrase "our . . .

Exercise 2:4.   Note here that the word "patriot" presumes that the reader is a U.S. citizen. Write a paragraph in which you try to explain to someone who has not studied argument what my use of the word "Americans" to describe U.S. citizens presumes that the target audience would not include, say, Colombians, or Chileans.

past." To the world it is "the" American revolution. To Americans it can be "our" revolution.

The Importance of Pronoun Analysis

Before moving to the thesis a few things about how Highet deals with his relationship with the target audience should be considered. Highet does not use "I." This makes perfect sense in his employing "us" and "our" in the second paragraph. He would like the American reader to know that he, the writer, is a fellow-American. In paragraph eight, however, Highet uses the pronoun in another way than that which encourages the reader to think of herself as a participant in the "appreciation." In the convention utilized here, and with only one exception, up until the last paragraph the writer refers to *himself* as "we." If you look at the paragraph preceding this one you will notice that I use a different convention in the third sentence ("If we look, for instance, at the word 'patriot,' . . ."). As I use it the "we" is something like saying to an audience, "Come with me to page 13 where we will find X." I am using it not only to promote the idea that I am with you and vice versa, but that the act of paying particular attention to this detail is not something that requires special training. That is, it is not just that "I" can do it; you can do it as well. Hence "we" can do it.

You must be careful about assigning a particular referent to a pronoun in that pronouns can, and frequently do, shift references, especially as used by highly skilled writers.

Highet closes paragraph eight with "But we can say something about the Gettysburg Address as a work of art. . . ." This might appear to employ the same device, but we would have to give up that idea when we look at the sentence opening the next paragraph.

Highet writes "A work of art. Yes. . . ." The implication is that the reader has responded to the previous sentence with something like "Aw, come on, Gilbert. Good speech, maybe, but 'work of art'? That's going a little far." In other words, the "we" which referred to "our country" and "our history" has now become what is called the "editorial" we—it refers to the writer and any organization she might be writing as a representative of (i.e. "we" at *The New York Times*).

But by the end of paragraph nine Highet has switched back to the "we" which can be understood as "constituted by," made up of, the writer *and* the reader. He writes, in a very long sentence, "Therefore, his serious speeches are important parts of the long and noble classic tradition of oratory which begins in Greece, runs through Rome to the modern word, and is still capable (if *we* do not neglect it) of producing masterpieces [my italics]." How does the *we* which is made up of you and I as students of rhetoric go about finding if there is an explanation for this?

The complexities of "we."

In analysis, as opposed to evaluation, the writer is always right. And if she doesn't appear to be it is most likely because the wrong reader has been posited. Writers, of course, make mistakes all the time, but from the analyst's perspective this is only asserted when all other explanations have been explored.

The Benefit of the Doubt in Rhetorical Analysis

In rhetorical analysis we are obligated to assume that until we have exhausted other possible explanations, the work in question, the work being examined (essay, advertisement, book, etc.), is the production of a writer who is exercising conscious and deliberate choice in her selection of language. We are obligated to reject, at least for the time being, at least initially or until we have satisfied ourselves that we have done a thorough job of looking for alternative explanations, that what we find on the page is an example of carelessness or inattention to detail. In this particular example, for instance, we must reject assuming (at least initially) that the apparent vacillation between the two uses of "we" is either an accident or an example of sloppy writing. We must instead assume that what is on the page is there because Highet had a reason for putting it there.

Methods of Rhetorical Investigation

How do we investigate this question? As in any other task of investigation we first gather the data. My procedure was to go back through the essay with a highlighter and mark every occurrence of "we" and the related words "our," "us," and "they."

Isolating elements of a text with markers, etc., can often show patterns of the writer's rhetorical development.

Initially I omitted occurrences in material in quotes. What I found seemed (and seems) to me to almost graphically reinforce what I suspected Highet was trying to do.

Exercise 2:5. At this point turn to the Highet essay in the readings and while slowly going through it, mark each of the occurrences of these words. Then on the basis of what you found, formulate your own theory concerning what Highet is doing with these words before going on with my discussion. This practice will be useful to you as a rhetorical analyst because what I propose as an explanation can be checked against your own theory. If they do not agree, which of the two most satisfactorily explains the evidence in the text, or what combination of the two most satisfactorily explains the text? If you still like yours better than mine, send it to me, and if I find it more satisfactory I'll put it in the next edition.

Rhetorical Analysis and the Argument from Ignorance

I need to try to anticipate here some of your possible responses. My hope is that if you know why you are being asked to do these things with the text you may be able to consciously make quick connections. These would otherwise accumulate, if they did, only as a by-product of the analytic process.

One response I have encountered to similar analyses is that they are too complicated. The writer, this person assumes, just sat down and wrote, and what we see is just how it came out. To find a reason or reasons for the way things are written, this person continues, unnecessarily complicates the process of reading and does not reflect what actually goes on in the process of writing.

Writing doesn't just happen. It is a deliberate and self-conscious activity.

A second response, which is related, although not directly, is that the person being asked to perform the analysis will reply that she "just doesn't see those things" until they are pointed out.

Reading In and Reading Out

Note here the difference between the two responses. The first says, in effect, that the explanations are not "in" the text, or are not derived "from" the text, but are rather superimposed on it, are, in the often-used phrase, "read in" to the text. The reader, or the "analyst," brings the explanations *to* the text rather than discovering them *in* it.

What I have often found in cases of this response is that the writer is honestly reporting her own experience with writing, with the production of text. Usually the idea of revision or rewriting is not seen as an ordinary part of the writing process.

While sometimes this writer will go back and cross out a paragraph and write another one in place of it, she seldom, if ever, thinks in terms of deliberate strategies for relating to the intended reader, or even that there is an intended reader. This type of writer will often think that there are many ways in which to say "the same thing" and that the differences among them are negligible.

No two ways of saying something are the same. Indeed, two different statements cannot say a single "something."

Admittedly a great deal of writing, and especially classroom writing, is produced this way, but this is not the way that writing which is recognized as excellent is produced. Because excellent writing is produced in many ways, there can be no such thing as "*the* writing process," but there are certainly writing *processes*, and no good writing is done outside of one or another of them.

For some very experienced writers their process has become sufficiently internalized and familiar that many, indeed most, of the adjustments and decisions are made before pen, pencil, or keyboard, is taken to paper or monitor display. These are usually writers, however, who earn the major part of their living through writing and are, hence, in almost constant practice.

(Two prolific prose writers who here come to mind are Garry Wills and Stanley Fish, both of whom profess that writing comes easily to them, and that they revise little. I would suggest, however, that each of these writers has forgotten how much he has absorbed and internalized over the large amounts of time that he has spent writing. Both of them live, as it were, surrounded by, immersed in, writing, both their own and that of others.)

The second response, that of the person who "just doesn't see these things" shows a considerable advance over the first. This writer, in effect, has said that although *she can recognize the strategies as such once they are pointed out*, she cannot recognize them on her own. Note here that the first response is an **argument from ignorance**, as I indicated in the section head. It says "because I do not utilize such things, and because I cannot see them in the writing of others, they are not there." The second response accepts that the devices are there once an argument has been presented for their presence.

What you don't see cannot be thought to be "therefore" not there.

I hope it is clear that one cannot reject an argument for the presence of a device simply by saying "I don't see it and therefore it isn't there." The assumption basic to the study of rhetoric, let alone rhetorical analysis, is that words not only can be arranged in a specific way in order to accomplish a particular purpose but in the work of skilled writers are arranged in that way.

Further, the study of rhetoric supposes (or pre-supposes, if you would rather) that the practices of so arranging words fall into various patterns which can be studied, described, and learned from (to employ a tricolon).

This text is based on those assumptions. It does not assume that language usage is accidental, nor does it assume that some people simply have a "gift" for utilizing it. This text assumes that in order to use language, to employ it, to deploy it, in the service of whatever cause you wish to promote, whether that promotion be through presenting a case to the Supreme Court, to your best friend, or to your worst enemy, knowledge of the ways in which language has been, is, and can be employed are the necessary starting points. (Did you catch both of those tricolons?)

The study of rhetoric is the study of how language is used to serve a cause.

In paragraph two, as has been previously discussed, Highet uses "us" twice. Both uses refer to Highet *and* the reader, and the second refers specifically to Highet and the reader as Americans. The next occurrence is in paragraph eight where we find a "they" (referring to "most people" who don't realize Lincoln's true greatness). The reader, because she is known to be a member of the group "us," is understood not to be a member of this

Distinguishing the editorial "we" from the "companionate we."

group. Then we find a "we" which refers to Highet, who now begins to argue for the "Gettysburg Address" as a work of art.

In paragraph 10 we find an "our" qualifying "State," which harks back to the earlier identification of Highet and the reader as Americans, followed by a "we" a few lines later which refers to Highet. I quote the last sentence of paragraph 11 and the first two sentences of paragraph 12.

> Lincoln took the important phrase "under God" (which he interpolated at the last moment) from Weems, the biographer of Washington; and *we* know it had been used at least once by Washington himself.
>
> Analyzing the Address further we find it is based on a native theme, or group of themes. The subject is—how can *we* put it so as not to disfigure it?—the subject is the kinship of life and death, that mysterious linkage which we see sometimes as the physical succession of birth and death in *our* world, sometimes as the contrast, which is perhaps a unity, between death and immortality. [Italics mine]

It is terribly unlikely that "we" (meaning Highet and the reader) "know that it [the phrase 'under God'] had been used at least once by Washington himself." This is hardly an item of common knowledge, or debate, even for Washington-loving Americans. It sounds like an aspect of some discussion about the founding fathers (as Deists) belief in "providence" and how that does or does not resemble what Americans (as opposed to eighteenth-century rationalists) for the most part now think of as "God." That is, Highet is back to the editorial "we," the voice of the specialist or the member of a particular interested group (American historians, classical rhetoricians, specialists in eighteenth-century thought, and so forth).

The second "we," in "how can we put it so as not to disfigure it" clearly belongs to this same category—the specialist sharing information. The "our," however, takes us out of this rarified air into what is common to all—life and death.

The "we" occurs once more before the climactic final paragraph. The last sentence of the relatively brief paragraph 10: "But within that [the structure of the traditional memorial speech], *we* can trace his constant use of at least two important rhetorical devices." There follow two quotations in which the reader, no matter how inexpert in the specialized language of rhetorical analysis, *can*, as Highet says, easily discern the rhetorical devices. And she doesn't need to know the specific rhetorical nomenclature for them. Highet explains, or provides, the terms *after the presentation of the examples*, as "antithesis" and "tricolon."

My argument here is that Highet has attempted the merging of the voice of the expert and the voice of the reader/writer/American composite. He has not, after all, supplied the analysis—rather he has supplied the nomenclature, the terminology by which the items of the analysis can be labeled. I here ask you, reader, with Highet's text in front of you, to follow the illustrations through to the final paragraph which I will quote in its entirety.

The separation of the American "we" and the editorial/specialist "we" earlier makes possible their combination at the unifying close of the essay.

> No one thinks that when he was drafting the Gettysburg Address Lincoln deliberately looked up these quotations and consciously chose these particular patterns of thought. No, he chose the theme. From its development and from the emotional tone of the entire occasion, all the rest followed, or grew—by that marvelous process of choice and rejection which is essential to artistic creation. It does not spoil such a work of art to analyze it as closely as *we* have done; it is altogether fitting and proper that we should do this; for it helps *us* to penetrate more deeply into the rich meaning of the Gettysburg Address, and it allows *us* the very rare privilege of watching the workings of a great man's mind. (italics mine)

For Highet, as for Lincoln, I am arguing, it is here that all the strategies come together. *One* of these strategies involves the use of pronouns. We (you and I) have heretofore seen Highet use "we" in two different senses: 1) Americans, and 2) rhetorical/historical specialists. In this paragraph the two come together (the possibility has been presented at the end of paragraph 10). The reader is accepted into the group of specialists (she, after all, has experienced the essay itself—she has followed and presumably confirmed its assertions through her own judgment). Finally, as Americans *and* rhetoricians "we" can appreciate the "Gettysburg Address."

Why such emphasis on a use of pronouns? Here, in this particular example, "we" (would you have paid attention to that word if it wasn't in quotes?) are starting small. We are starting with pronouns, which are, physically anyway, the smallest words in the language (there are smaller units of communication—the period, for instance is tough to beat). You can't get shorter, at the word level, than "I." Not much is shorter than "we," or "us." The third level, "you" and "they" are, by comparison, extravagantly long. But why devote so much time (metaphoric for "space," since the text is printed, and hence does not exist in the same relationship to "time" as speech does) on such a set of "small" items?

Rhetoric Is Details

Because all that writing involves are words (would you have been grammatically happier if I had written "is" words?), *all* that rhetoric involves is the study of the supposed or hoped for effect of a particular arrangement of words upon a chosen, or targeted, or designated audience.

And it is important to observe and understand that the words do not exist in any kind of a magic way "inside" of a writer and just hang out waiting an occasion to emerge. Rather they accumulate and accrete from the would-be writer's experience in the world of language. (You don't have to memorize word lists, or read a dictionary, although it certainly won't hurt you. Malcolm X felt that a dictionary gave him freedom). No one, after all, is born knowing any words at all.

The study of rhetoric is the study of choice. The power of choice lies in the number and variety of items we have from which to choose.

All the words, without exception, which are at our disposal have come to us from our experience with our particular language. That experience involves language in all of its parts, of which none is more humble, more lowly, than another. It should be evident that pronouns are utterly basic to language—"we" cannot do without "them." "It" does not follow, however, that because "they" are basic, "they" are not subject to rhetorical consideration as tools to be utilized in the processes of attempted persuasion. And all of these things are clearly "there," in writing. All that you have to do is notice them rather than simply take them for granted.

If one understands how other writers use rhetoric, those same tools are available to you as a producer of rhetoric yourself. And the process of revision can become an extension of the analysis of your own writing.

Exercise 2:6.   Go to the *Glossary* and look up **absolute**. Mark the absolutes in the preceding paragraph and write a paragraph of your own presenting a rhetorical explanation for why I might have used so many of them.

WRITING THE ANALYSIS

From my experience with training reading writers to become analysts of rhetoric, I have delineated three stages of development:

1) "That's not really there. You are making it up and reading it into the text."

2) "Now that it has been pointed out to me I can see it, but I wouldn't be able to find it on my own." And

3) "I have an idea about what is going on here, but I don't know how to explain it. "

Approaching the Rhetorical Explanation

I respond to this by asking what it is about the text that makes the analyst think that x is going on. In other words, why do you think that? What the developing analyst typically does not, at this stage, grasp is that the presentation of a rhetorical analysis is nothing more or less than an attempt to communicate to another "reader" what you think is going on in the text. And one way to communicate this is to explain why it is that you think what is going on is going on.

For instance, consider this dialogue:

A: I think Highet is trying to get his reader to feel more comfortable with his analysis so she will be more likely to accept it.

B: What makes you think so?

A: Well, the way he keeps saying "us."

B: What about it?

A: He says "we". . .

B: Just a second. You said "us" before.

A: It's the same thing.

B: Look again.

A: OK, he uses "us" at the beginning and the end and "we" in the middle.

B: Does that jibe with what you first said?

A: Well, yeah.

B: How?

A: When he was using the "we"s in the middle it was mostly him.

B: For example?

A: In paragraph 12 he says, "We can trace his constant use of at least two important rhetorical devices."

B: So?

A: Highet is doing that. At least he's doing it more than "we" are.

B: So he should have said "I" instead of "we"?

A: No, that's the point—when he says "we" he lets the reader have a part of the analysis. If he said "I" the reader would just be watching, but when he says "we" the reader can think she is, like, being asked to help.

B: For instance?

> The presentation of an analysis is the presentation to your reader of the reasons you have for thinking what you think.

> Thinking of presenting an analysis as if it was an answer to a series of questions may be helpful.

A: Look at paragraph 11. He says, "How can *we* put it so as not to disfigure it?"

B: Is that a real question? Does the reader know?

A: Well, no. But the reader is being asked as *if* she did, and that can be pleasant. It's like "we're in this together."

B: Can you find more evidence for that?

And of course A could, once A had started looking for the reasons that led to her initial impression that Highet was trying to make his reader, who is a less expert rhetorician than Highet is, feel more like a participant in the analysis than the recipient of a lecture.

Remember here that the basic question the analyst is always answering is "What makes you think so?"

Bear in mind, again, that this whole discussion is about the desired effect of *pronoun choice*, something that readers typically pay very little attention to, but that, whether the reader is paying attention to them or not, are very likely to have an effect on how the reader "feels" about the content of a given argument. If Highet's device works, the naive reader will be more likely to accept Highet's argument. The rhetorician, on the other hand, because she can say *how* Highet is attempting to influence the reader, can make a knowledgeable choice.

Nothing is too small to be rhetorically important.

Before I go on let me note that as Highet is using something as apparently trivial as pronoun choice, Judy Brady in "Why I Want a Wife" (see Chapter One) was using nothing larger than capitalization and the *absence* of gender identifiable pronouns.

Brady's rhetorical tools are more basic and even simpler than Highet's (caps vs. pronouns).

Tone: Conversational

The use of pronouns in an attempt to involve the reader in the process of the analysis then points to another of Highet's devices—his conversational **tone**. A piece of writing is essentially a **monologue**; it is one person talking. Unlike the *speaker*, as was earlier pointed out, the *writer* has no immediate feedback from the audience to use in order to adjust her tone, or speed of delivery, or vocabulary to the tastes and abilities of those present.

As a result writing is usually very different from speech, and that which is written to be read rather than to be delivered aloud by a speaker reflects that difference. (Just look back, for instance, at the piece of writing a page ago which was an imitation of a dialogue between two speakers). A writer, for instance, does not have to concern herself to the same degree that a speechmaker does that all the words she uses are currently part of the vocabulary of the reader.

The conventions of speech and of writing are very different.

It is important to a speaker that her audience knows the vocabulary. It is less important to the writer.

In writing this chapter, for instance, I am not paying particular attention to whether the words I am using are within the average verbal repertoire of my reader (as, for instance, with the word "repertoire"). I assume that if my reader (you) is (are) not familiar with a word I am using she (you) will look it up. Were I *speaking,* were this the content, say, of a lecture, it would be completely inappropriate to make this same assumption. The reader's relationship with the spoken text is such that were she to consult a dictionary during the speech she would miss the next part of the speech. The best multiprocessor alive cannot listen and read at the same time. This is not the case with the word in print. It just sits there on the page and waits for you to come back.

Further, I can assume that if you do not understand a particular section on the first reading you have the opportunity to return to it at another time and perhaps in another context. This is not the case with an audience listening to a speaker.

Exercise 2:7.   A clear example of this will emerge from a comparison of the text of the "Gettysburg Address" with the text of King's "I Have a Dream" speech. An even clearer example will emerge from a further comparison of King's speech to his "Letter From a Birmingham Jail." Choose one of these two sets of linguistic presentations and write a full-length comparison of them.

Highet's attempts to give an air of spontaneity and immediacy to his writing imitate the patterns of interactive speaking.

Highet's rhetorical approach imitates a number of the characteristics of an interactive verbal encounter involving some give and take (that is a statement and a reaction, to which the next statement is yet another reaction). I have already presented one example of this in the discussion of the way he opens paragraph 10 *as if* it was an answer to an expression of disbelief from an audience member. He uses the technique of the imitation of a speaker at other places in the essay as well.

I will present them chronologically. The first instance is in paragraph five, where he writes, "There are many descriptions of Lincoln, all showing the same curious blend of grandeur and awkwardness, or lack of dignity, or—it would be best to call it humility."

Notice here that Highet is trying to give the effect of someone casting about to find the exact word to express what he wants to say, trying out three before settling on the "right" word—"humility." This sort of "trying out" if I can call it that, is characteristic of extemporaneous or conversational speech. It is not something that we usually expect to find in a piece of writing. We would usually expect the revision of the piece would remove the "fumbling."

Remember that writing doesn't "just happen." It doesn't just spill out onto the page in the way that words can and do when we are talking and, as it were, thinking on our feet. If the right word really was (is) "humility" then we would expect the writer to use it, and not use the words which are *not* the right word. (I believe there is something else going on here as well, which I will develop in a bit. For the moment I want to emphasize the air of "immediacy," the "I'm thinking right here, right now" attitude that I think Highet wants to convey as part of his reader-involvement strategy.)

The next instance is the previously presented opening of paragraph nine. The "A work of art. Yes. . . ," which is followed by the second sentence of paragraph 11, "The subject is—how can we put it so as not to disfigure it?—the subject is the kinship of life and death." The same principle operates here, I would argue, as we saw in the "getting to humility" episode in paragraph five. Again we see Highet attempting to give the effect of casting about for the proper phrasing and even implying that the reader might be able to help him in this effort.

Exercise 2:8. You will notice here that I am using the pronoun "we" rather than my usual "you." Write a paragraph hypothesizing about my reasons for doing so.

The next example is very clear-cut if the previous ones were not. Paragraph 13 opens with

The first of these is *antithesis* : opposition, contrast. The speech is full of it. Listen:

> The world will little *note*
>   nor long *remember*   what *we say* here
>   but   it can never *forget*   what *they did* here.

[Italics Highet's]

Highet uses italics for the emphasis characteristic of speech.

The reader of course remembers that the language of writing draws metaphorically on the language of speaking with great frequency. In the dialogue that I presented between A and B, for instance, there is considerable use of the word "says" when, if one were not speaking metaphorically, the "proper" word would be "writes."

But Highet's use here, I suggest, goes further than that almost traditional metaphoric invocation. Notice first that he italicizes "antithesis" (which is an English word and does not need the italics traditionally given to foreign words) to put a conversational or spoken stress on it, to tell the reader that he wants it read (heard) as stressed. He then follows that, not with "Look" to call attention to his graphical representation of Lincoln's use of antithesis, but with "Listen." The word is "spoken" if you will, directly to the reader with the intention, I am arguing, of invoking an air of immediacy and intensity. The italics in the spatially presented quotation which follows the "Listen" are instructions on how to *hear* the lines, as opposed to how to read them.

Asking the reader to "listen to" written text is an attempt to create the "immediacy" of speech.

These are additional devices to reinforce the reader involvement Highet hopes to achieve with his use of pronouns. And both of them are designed to try to bring the reader into the process of examining the rhetorical construction of the "Address."

If we can agree (that is, if you will agree with me) that the target audience is composed of American citizens who are not particularly rhetorically sophisticated but who can be expected to take pride in the "Gettysburg Address" as a piece of the "valiant" past of American history, it is to this audience that Highet makes his appeal; it is to this audience that Highet addresses his thesis. What is that thesis, and what else can we say (can be said) about how Highet tries to sell it?

Exercise 2:9. I have inserted two sets of parentheses in the immediately preceding paragraph. Write a two- or three-paragraph explanation of what I might have been trying to accomplish with those parentheses.

The Thesis (or Theses), Overt and Covert

When I first began to work with Highet's essay I found it odd that he spent as much time as he does with what he is at great pains *not* to call "the plagiarism issue" in the "Address."

Paragraph 10 begins, "The first proof of this [that the "Address" is part of a tradition of oratory which begins in Greece and runs to the present] is that the Gettysburg Address is full of quotations—or rather of adaptations—which give it strength." The "Address," Highet tells us, is "interwoven" with "memories" of the Bible and of American history. Hence the Biblical quality of the "Fourscore and seven" and a suggested origin for "shall not perish from the earth" in the book of Job's "his remembrance shall perish from the earth."

But then Highet changes his tactics. Lincoln is no longer "remembering," but instead his phrase "government of the people, by the people, and for the people" was "adumbrated" by Daniel Webster in 1830 (thirty-three years before the "Address") and then "elaborated" by Theodore Parker in 1854 (nine years before the "Address").

> Highet's use of "adumbrated" illustrates the importance of obscure words used as part of an argument.

If we are paying close attention here, (and I missed this point for three years while *teaching* the essay) Highet is making an astonishing claim. He is claiming that somehow Webster's "the people's government, made for the people, made by the people, and answerable to the people" was a *foreshadowing* of another phrase finally spoken more than three decades later. Webster, Highet implies, *foretold* what Lincoln was going to say, anticipated it, but didn't get it quite right. Parker, in his "elaboration," "government of all the people, by all the people, for all the people," didn't get it quite right either.

It is, of course, quite impossible to elaborate on something that does not yet exist. As a rhetorical analyst, I was left, seemingly, with two options:

1. Highet used the word "adumbrate" without knowing what it meant (which ran afoul of the "always give the writer the benefit of the doubt" rule) or

2. Highet actually meant that Lincoln's words were somehow "present" before they were written—that far from him having plagiarized, or "quoted" (although without quotation marks) or "adapted" these earlier works, the earlier works prophesied Lincoln's production. The speech, somehow, was already written, was fated to be, in the same sense that we can say, "It is written that after the opening of the sixth seal there will be a great earthquake, the sun will become black and the moon become as blood."

I remembered, however, that I had taught the piece numerous times earlier and had not noticed this. Indeed I had never looked up "adumbrate" which, at the time, was not within my lexicon. And I noticed further that Highet returns in his next example to the earlier adaptation and quotation explanation. He writes, to close the paragraph,

There is good reason to think that Lincoln took the important phrase "under God" (which he interpolated at the last moment) from Weems, the biographer of Washington; and we know that it had been used at least once by Washington himself.

Highet's "Lincoln took" is as unequivocal as the slightly earlier "adumbrate." I was convinced that something was going on here rhetorically, but I didn't know what it was.

> **Exercise 2:10.** There are two words in the preceding paragraph that would most likely not show up in a lecture. What are those words, and within the discussion of the difference between written and spoken text, how might their presence here be explained? What might I be trying to do with them as a writer that I would not as a speaker?

Analytic explanations do not occur all at once in chronological order. Confirming analytic hypotheses involves backward and forward movement in the text.

Then I remembered the elaborate path Highet had taken to get to the word "humility" in paragraph five, and it occurred to me that here was another case of multiple "sources" (which is what I would have called the Webster and Parker citations). And on looking at it again I came to the conclusion that there could very well be a reason beyond the desire to have the reader feel involved in the process of analyzing the speech.

Highet didn't use the word "humility" initially because it was not one of the words he found in his sources (the "many accounts of the day itself," the "many descriptions of Lincoln"). By writing, "It would be best to call it humility," Highet is in effect saying, "I have an advantage that none of these witnesses had. Each of them is limited to his or her own impression. I, by contrast, am seeing the totality of them, and from seeing the composite, can determine what it is that they all have in common. I can see that quality that from their limited viewpoints none of them could. And what I can see is that they were trying to describe humility."

I then look at what Highet says they "all" show, the "same curious blend of grandeur and awkwardness, or lack of dignity. . . ." From my perspective, Highet is playing fast and loose with the data, which I only have in the versions he has given me. Try as I might, I cannot make the leap from "grandeur and awkwardness" to "humility." It is even less possible for me with "lack of dignity," out of which I can get "undignified," but, again, not "humility."

And then I look at the physical description of a tall man entering a town in a ceremonial procession on a too-small animal "with his feet too near the ground" who is patient and whose virtue, Highet has told me, is humility. And now I have an explanation to supplement the effort to involve the reader for the fumbling around before coming up with the term.

Highet needed the term "humility" to complete his **implicit**, his suggested, not stated, drawing of a parallel between Lincoln and Christ, and specifically Christ's entry into Jerusalem on what Christians now observe as Palm Sunday. This may, at first, strike you as fanciful and over-elaborate, but consider the parallels, and consider what they explain about Highet's essay. I am, finally, trying to do no more than to explain the details of the essay. Why did Highet provide the detail of that too-small animal, those feet too near the ground?

The story is that the death of Christ, the sacrifice of a divine figure, made possible salvation from original sin—i.e. made possible for humankind, otherwise damned because of Adam's sin, to achieve the eternal reward of heaven. Lincoln's death, via assassination, could, in a parallel way, be said to assure the "immortality" of "government of the people, by the people, and for the people," assure, in other words, that that government "shall not perish from this earth."

It was presumably the proposition that "all men are created equal" that Booth killed Lincoln for. But that death achieved, by its fame, and by the respect showed by the nation for the dead president, exactly the opposite effect from that which Booth sought. It became, henceforward, unthinkable to attack that "proposition," which became, instead, not a proposition but a principle. And finally it explains Highet's use of the term "adumbrate" in reference to the apparent historical sources for Lincoln's tricolon. The implication is that Lincoln was born to his destiny, was fated to accomplish it.

For Highet to say any of this straight out would amount, for many potential readers, to blasphemy. But if he can *suggest* it without saying it, he can, in effect, have his cake and eat it too. If he can suggest, as a **covert thesis**, that Lincoln died for our sins, and by doing so made possible our potential salvation as a form of government and as a people, then the **overt** thesis, that the "Gettysburg Address" is a work of art of high achievement in the history of all such works, is minor by comparison.

Let's look, then, in closing, at what I would argue ties Highet's whole essay together—its relation to the "Address" itself. Highet begins by telling us that we stand to Lincoln, in terms of the passage of time, as Lincoln stood to Washington. We stand to the "Gettysburg Address" as Lincoln stood to the

Description is always significant in that any given thing can be described in multiple ways. Thus, what way is chosen is rhetorically significant.

When a thesis is covert rather than overt there are reasons for it so appearing.

"Declaration of Independence." As Lincoln wrote a commentary on and interpretation of that "Declaration" in his "Address," so Highet, in his analytic and adulatory essay, writes a commentary and interpretation of the "Address." Highet's essay, I am suggesting, is intended to stand in relation to the "Gettysburg Address" as the "Address" stands to the "Declaration of Independence." Much of what I have said previously bears upon this, but I will cite two further examples in support of it.

At the close of paragraph nine, Highet writes "his serious speeches are important parts of the long and noble classic tradition of oratory which begins in Greece, runs through Rome to the modern world, and is still capable (if we do not neglect it) of producing masterpieces." The "still" that Highet is referring to is the time of the composition of his own essay. The "not neglecting it" is precisely what he is doing with his own rhetorical exercise, is precisely what he is doing in what I suggest he hopes we recognize as a tricolon in praise of and example of that "long and noble tradition."

My final example is from Highet's closing paragraph where he utilizes a quotation, plagiarizes if you will, because he omits the quotation marks. So also, I think we must conclude, did Lincoln. Highet, however, does so in such an obvious way that I think it is clear that he wants to be caught. The words I have placed in italics are taken directly from the "Address." He writes

Signaling deliberate quotation without quotation marks.

> It does not spoil such a work of art to analyze it as closely as we have done; *it is altogether fitting and proper that we should do this*; for it helps us to penetrate more deeply into the rich meaning of the Gettysburg Address, and it allows us the very rare privilege of watching the workings of a great man's mind. (Italics mine)

If any doubt remains, look back at the "Address" itself. Of its two-hundred and sixty-eight words, ten are "we," three are "us," and two are "our." Like tricolon, the pronoun is also one of Lincoln's central rhetorical devices.

Exercise 2:11. In the readings section of this text is an essay by William Raspberry titled, "When it All Started." Like Highet and Brady, Raspberry has a covert thesis, and, like Highet, works in interesting ways with pronouns. Write a full-length analysis of Raspberry's essay centered around his imitation of a spoken communication and his use of the second- and third-person pronouns. Look out for irony.

C H A P T E R 3

EMOTION'S REASON: PSYCHOLOGY IN RHETORIC

Principles essential to the analysis of argument:

The following principles form one of the bases from which argument is approached in this text. Remember that at the moment we are talking about the analysis of rhetoric rather than its production. I am asking, thus, that you postpone asking what this has to do with *your* arguments, written in the here and now.

1. It is inescapable that all arguments are located in an historical place/time. They are in *a* language, and at *a* time. Audience response to an argument will be conditioned by, in very obvious ways, "who" the audience is.

    1. Argument must be located geographically as well as in time.

    For instance, a translator of George Orwell's "Politics and the English Language" (the primary essay I will be discussing in this chapter) into French, could not simply assume that "English" is only important as a sort of place-marker or indicator for "the language of those being written to." The translation of the title could not, in other words, be "Politics and the French Language," or "Le Politique et La Langue Français." The essay, we must remember, is not titled "Politics and Language" but specifically "Politics and the *English* Language" (my emphasis).

Think of this as an element of an understanding of target audience, a specific extension of the concept of the target audience into time, or, put another way, the target audience considered historically. Orwell's essay needs to be considered as addressed to those English speakers who made up the "Allies" at the close of World War II.

2. Considering an argument in terms of its psychological appeal is more useful than considering its "emotional" appeal.

2. The appeal an argument, or aspects of it, can often be most usefully considered in psychological terms. I am using the word "psychological" here as distinct from (although not antithetical to) "emotional."

I suggest considering an appeal to community, or to suspending differences in the face of threat, as "psychological" rather than "emotional" because the word "psychological" does *not* carry the same baggage, the same set of associations, that the word "emotional" does. It makes sense to say "Calm down and think about this reasonably. You're being too emotional." It does *not* make sense to say, "Calm down and think about this reasonably—you're being too psychological."

The "reasonable" and the "emotional" are often thought of as in binary opposition. The "reasonable" and the "psychological" do not pair in any similar way, nor do they even oppose each other. They are typically taken to describe two *different*, rather than *opposite*, domains. The next postulate follows from this distinction as a corollary.

3. The terminology associated with "logic" and "reason" is analytically most useful as descriptive rather than evaluative.

3. Description of an argument or reference to part of an argument as "irrational" or "unreasonable" constitutes a rhetorical appeal to a privileged principle and is tactical rather than definitive. This postulate demands an extended discussion, but you are again asked to consider it for the moment before I present a full discussion of it.

Many textbooks on argument will have a chapter on "reason," and its systematic investigation, "logic." Usually, however, it will be presented in a single chapter in which formal logic is discussed briefly and informal logic, usually called the "informal fallacies," is given some space. In this text the discussion of fallacies, as such, is relegated to the *Glossary* and not separated out from the other entries in any specific way.

The reason for this should become apparent as you go through the following discussion of Orwell's essay, but to put it formulaically, *the analyst most usefully describes any informal fallacy in terms of its intended effect rather than merely, or even dismissively, as a fallacy.*

Pathos and Logos, Emotion and Reason

It is important to discuss the **either/or** aspect of reason and emotion at some greater length before going into the analysis of Orwell's most famous essay. The traditional distinction is made between reason and emotion, and this distinction is deeply embedded in the history of rhetoric as it has developed from Aristotle onward in terms of the so-called "modes" of appeal, **Ethos**, **Pathos**, and **Logos**, or character, emotion, and reason.

The "traditional" rhetorical "modes."

While it is Aristotle who brings us these distinctions, it is the spirit of Plato that looms largest over the application and definition of them. And it is Plato's *Republic* from which we are the clearest inheritors of one of the most pervasive of the binaries, which inform the western intellectual tradition—that split which is postulated between the "reason" and the "passions."

The western historical tradition has defined the two more particularly as in a struggle with each other, with passion trying always to overcome reason (reason, of course, does not try to overcome passion, probably because reason is "good" and passion is "selfish"). In a vast oversimplification, these polytheistic or "pagan" distinctions were taken up into monotheistic concerns. They found their most distinctive embodiment in the Christian distinction between the body (tied to the passions) and the soul (naturally in affinity with the Logos, the first principle, the godhead), the salvation of which depended upon the overcoming of the passions.

The reason and emotion of the ancients have their analogues in western conceptions of body and soul.

I cannot, in a few paragraphs, nor for that matter could I in several books, delineate how important this primary distinction has been in the history of how we think. But of central concern to us here is that for at least the last century and a half, and probably for the last three centuries, we have in one way or another been assimilating or incorporating (and resisting) a competing idea in the unruly, untidy, but difficult to deny, concept of psychology.

Rhetoricians have not yet, but could, were we given to such formulations, add psychology to the rhetorical modes. Although this has not yet happened, we are accustomed to hearing the phrase "psychological appeal" presented in much the same way as we have heard the term "emotional appeal."

Yet, as I have tried to indicate, the two are not synonyms for one another, although we usually pair them in opposition to the still important concept of reason. But this oppositional pairing is not entirely comfortable because, although we recognize psychology as *other* than reason, we do not automatically see it

Psychology can be considered as a rhetorical mode that combines the ancient conceptions of pathos and logos.

as in *opposition* to reason, or indeed as without a "reasonable" system of its own, as without, that is, its own "logic."

Exercise 3:1. Write three to five paragraphs, including at least one example, in which you explain to another student of rhetoric what distinctions are being made here between an "emotional appeal" and a "psychological appeal."

Rogers and Toulmin, the Psychologist and the Logician

The importance of Stephen Toulmin, a professional philosopher (an academic), and Carl Rogers, a practicing psychologist (a member of the medical profession), can hardly be overemphasized. That they are seen as so important may be indicative of the surviving tensions between attempts to revive and adapt classical rhetoric to contemporary concerns and the out-and-out psychologizing of the advertising industry. Advertising is unarguably in the business of persuasion and thus, like it or not, a rhetorical pursuit.

> Advertising is a rhetorical pursuit.

Why the philosopher Toulmin when we have Aristotle's logic? Perhaps because, even as a philosopher, Toulmin's methodology is modeled on the court of law, the relation between which and "truth," as traditionally defined by philosophy, is totally conditional. Toulmin, thus, lives in the real world, to which traditional philosophy is frequently seen as having little relevance.

Rogers, like Toulmin, wants to foster communication, to facilitate linguistic interaction. And almost incidentally, in that there is nothing specifically virtuous about the practice of rhetoric, neither Rogers nor Toulmin wants what is to be learned from them turned to selling things that are bad for you (like cigarettes). However, I only wish to introduce these figures at this point (you are, of course, invited to jump ahead, if you wish, to the larger discussions of them in Chapter 5).

PLACING "POLITICS AND THE ENGLISH LANGUAGE"

In April of 1946 the British magazine *Horizon* published what has become almost certainly the single most reprinted article in

English on the effects of writing. Even a cursory reading of the piece will reveal a number of aspects which, taken in combination, may begin to account for at least its initial popularity.

In April of 1946 World War II had been concluded for a scant seven months. The English-speaking portion of the world, having defeated fascism, found itself in a very uneasy relationship with its ally in that victory, the USSR. That the emerging dictatorships in Italy and Germany were both strongly opposed to Communism is commonly accepted as a largely contributing factor to the (as it turned out very costly) delays in British and American reactions to those countries' expansionist policies. The USSR, however, ally or not, was Communist.

"Politics" in relation to WWII.

The now famous "Politics and the English Language" (see **Readings** section) would have then been seen by a great many speakers of English as urging all the "right" things. It was (naturally) anti-fascist. And it was (commendably, from any *establishment* view) anti-Communist. In other words the "Politics" part was suited to what many (and especially those in positions of power and influence) saw as the needs of the English-speaking world at that time.

Opposing fascism in 1946 would have had, at the very least, the appeal that opposing "crime" does currently. One could hardly *oppose* opposing fascism in any public way. People now, for instance, who find crack prosecution racist have a difficult time establishing their point in that they can be simply dismissed as pro-criminal, which, of course, sidesteps the whole issue of how an activity comes to be considered a "crime" in the first place.

The "English Language" part of the title may have carried an even stronger appeal to the target audience. After all, hundreds, if not thousands, of print essayists opposed fascism and Communism after WWII without coming close to Mr. Blair's (George Orwell's real name was Eric Blair) reprint count. I suggest it is because Americans, much as we might like to think so, don't speak American, nor do Britons speak British, or Australians speak Australian. We all speak English—and we all, more particularly to my point here, *read* English.

The "English Language" unifies Britons, U.S. citizens, Australians.

Americans (when they pay attention) can usually understand Britons and Australians in person or on film without major difficulty. But on the printed page, an American reader might well not notice a difference (not "hear" what is often unthinkingly called a "British accent") until she ran into, say, "lift" for "elevator" or a spelling like "aluminium" (or Orwell's "aeroplane").

The phrase "the English Language," then, can serve to unify the English-speaking Allies (the Britons, the Canadians, the Australians, and the Americans) while simultaneously distinguishing them from the (communist) Soviets and the (Vichy collaborationist) French. I'm going to argue that this unification/separation us/them mechanism is among Orwell's major rhetorical strategies in the presentation of his argument.

What I have so far presented should be thought of as psycho-historical, or even lingua-psycho-historical. I am proposing that Orwell's essay presents an appeal based on 1) a particular set of historical circumstances, 2) a set of psychological tendencies, and 3) a shared language among peoples who might otherwise see themselves as quite distinct from one another. Remember, for instance, that those people who designate themselves as the English, the Scots, and the Irish, have invested a good bit of their historical time in killing each other.

My analysis, to this point, has dealt with the potential appeal of Orwell's title. I have suggested that, given the place/time of the original argument, it was intended to make an appeal on the basis of a kind of post-war celebratory linguistic solidarity and the perception of a need for unity in the face of the potential threat of "International Communism."

The "argument" of the title is thus *ad populum,* and I will try to make the case that the *ad populum* appeal is Orwell's core rhetorical strategy for the entire essay.

The *argumentum ad populum* is, by definition, an appeal to the populace, the people, rather than to an elite. It is based in the idea that "the people," or "a" people (from the Latin origin of the term, say, "Romans") hold a certain body of beliefs in common on which they, as a people, pride themselves. An appeal *ad populum,* is then, to the pride of a group in what it thinks of as its best features, its primary virtues.

> Orwell's appeal to "the people" *(ad populum)* is a central rhetorical strategy.

Exercise 3:2. Speakers of English currently reside in very different circumstances than those Orwell was writing in. Write five or more paragraphs on the way the "English only" movement in the United States relates to Orwell's rhetorical treatment of the language as a unifying device.

In his first paragraph Orwell establishes the major value to which he will appeal and simultaneously urges his readers to act according to their better characters. In this they are further invited to feel superior to those unlike them who have (theoretically) stopped reading the essay and are therefore not behaving according to their better characters.

He begins, "Most people who bother with the matter at all would admit that. . . ." The periodicity of this segment of the first sentence (which amounts to just over a third of the full sentence by syllable count) delays naming the actual subject (the English language) until the reader has had a number of opportunities to identify herself with a particular set of *ad populum* values through a series of binary choices. And all of these choices will presumably be made prior to any actual commitment to the proposition that the sentence ends with, namely that the subject (the English language) "is in a bad way."

Exercise 3:3. If you didn't recognize what was being referred to by the word "periodicity" in the second sentence of the paragraph immediately preceding, look up "periodic sentence" in a dictionary. Write, or find, three examples of a periodic sentence. Write a paragraph about each of them in which you explain the rhetorical goal of such a construction (if the sentences are yours), or speculate about why the author produced them (if they are not yours).

I would characterize those opportunities as first being given a choice between "most people" and the implied "the rest of the people." The preferred choice here, by *ad populum* values, is, however, not at all clear.

What is at issue is the very **paradox** that democratic governments are founded upon—the will of "the people" is defined by the ballot as that of "most people." Democracies hold with "majority" (most) rule.

Ad populum invocations may involve paradox.

Simultaneously, however, democracies profess to value actions taken by their citizens as *individuals*. So, majority rule is tempered by a supposed "respect for the rights of the minority" (which rights are typically spelled out in some central document, as in the *Constitution*, for Americans). Citizens are expected to decide as *individuals* what it is that makes up (or "constitutes") the decision of the majority. This is the reason, for instance, for insisting on the privacy of the ballot, the curtain on the voting booth. In other words, confronted with the statement "most people think X," the *democratic* thinker, while inclined to respect the choice, is under no compulsion to be of the same opinion herself.

In the second of these binary choices that Orwell presents, however, that majority which constitutes his "most" is qualified

Ad populum argument frequently invokes binary choices, either/or choices directed toward identifying one pole as moral and the

as being made up of people who "bother." The other pole in this binary is people who "don't bother." Here there is no reason to hesitate. "Bothering" is good. Even when we say, "don't bother," we say it in appreciation of the act of bothering, acknowledgement of the act coupled with modesty (don't go to all that trouble for *me*).

The sentence continues with the words "with the [as yet unidentified] matter *at all* [my emphasis]." If *not* bothering is *not* good, then not bothering *at all* is not just worse, but bad. The virtuous choice, no matter *what* the subject of the sentence turns out to be, is clear. The virtuous choice is to be one of those "most" people who bother, as opposed to being one of those *other* people (whose number may be legion) who not only don't bother, but who don't bother "at all."

Exercise 3:4. Following the point presented in the preceding paragraph is basic to understanding the development of the rest of the analysis. Write from one to three paragraphs explaining that point "in other words" to someone who claims not to understand what is being argued.

Begging the Question is used as a deliberate rhetorical tool.

The next binary choice, then, is not between "would admit" and "would deny," but between "would admit" and "would not admit," which subtly begs the question of the truth of the as yet unstated proposition concerning the English language. That is, what has been said so far, or implied so far, is "It makes no difference whether you admit it, or you do not admit it, the case with the language is X, *and those who refuse to admit it know that it is, nevertheless, the case.*"

The Informal Fallacy in Rhetorical Analysis

The device that I have been referring to in terms of Orwell presenting his readers with "binary choices" is rhetorically classifiable as utilizing an either/or argument. The either/or is, beyond any question, fallacious. My point earlier in this chapter that "any informal fallacy can be most usefully described, from the perspective of analytic rhetoric, in terms of its intended effect rather than merely, or even dismissively, as a fallacy" is applicable here.

It does us no good, as analysts, to dismiss Orwell's first paragraph on the basis of his use of this device. It does us no good in the same way that it is not particularly valuable to point out that the "argument" of the "Gettysburg Address" relies totally on begging the question. We have accurately named the rhetorical device in question, but having done so and having recognized that it is among those devices classified as fallacies does little to advance our understanding of how these devices are intended to work to achieve the intended affect with the targeted audience.

To claim, rightly or not, that an argument is fallacious is finally not relevant to understanding it as an act of rhetoric.

To return to the discussion of Orwell's first sentence, let me suggest that very few people, *at any time*, think about the "condition" of their language. English, for most speakers of English most of the time, is something that they live with and in and pay as little conscious attention to as breathing. Further, for one to notice that the language is in a "bad way," one would have to be able to note a change from a prior and better state.

Some people have, of course, deplored the presence of "four-letter words" or what "they" have done to the "perfectly good word 'gay'," or some such statement that implies that somewhere at some time there was a "pure" English where words were used in their "real" meanings. But, if we can now *print* the "four-letter words" with relative impunity, it does *not* follow that they have only recently become a part of the language. Indeed, it does not follow that writers of English have only recently been "allowed" to use the "four-letter words" in print.

There was never a time when words were used in their "real" meanings.

Chaucer has no problem at all with "shit," and Shakespeare has Hamlet pun on "the c-word used to refer to female genitalia." (Hamlet asks Ophelia did she think he meant "country matters," and when she replies that she meant "nothing" he follows with "That's a fair thought, to lie between maids' legs.")

What is "acceptable" does not move in a single direction. The "printable" of one time can become the "unprintable" of a later time.

In a more contemporary vein, we should remember that this is the kind of "thinking" about language that gave rise to the joke about the state legislator rising to speak against bilingual education with the declaration that "If English was good enough for Jesus Christ, it's good enough for our kids." Leaving aside all of these points, however, it is not likely that anyone, even if these views were defensible, would, for these reasons, find the *entire language* "decadent."

Orwell takes as one of his rhetorical goals to raise concern about the abstraction that constitutes the "use" of "the English language." (It should be noted here that the decay of "the language" has been a popular theme of essayists for at least the last two centuries.)

Consider here that, if Orwell's rhetorical strategy succeeds, readers are given the opportunity not just to *bother*, to "care" about the language, but to count themselves among the *honest* people who will *admit* that the language is in a bad way (as opposed, by implication, to those slothful prevaricators [lazy liars] who won't admit it).

Orwell doesn't *argue* that the language is in a bad way, he *assumes* it, and then redoubles the *petitio principii* with the passive construction of the second half of the sentence, "but it is generally assumed that we cannot by conscious action do anything about it." The "it" (that English is in a bad way), if there had been any question about its existence previously, has now acquired **existential import**.

Why the **passive voice**? As those who urge its avoidance will point out, the passive is a "weak" construction. Instead of "it is generally assumed" Orwell could have written, "most people assume." This would be "stronger." But it would also, in that the reader has already been asked to identify with the virtue of those "[m]ost people who bother with the matter at all," be confusing because *Orwell distinctly wants to avoid giving the reader another group with which to identify.* For his purposes it is better to emphasize the assumption itself rather than to emphasize or even identify who is doing the assuming.

This is precisely what the passive construction here allows. (So one should rewrite the traditional "rule" about avoiding the passive voice as "don't use the passive voice unless you have a reason to." Or, to put it another way "If you were asked why you used the passive voice, could you explain?")

> **Exercise 3:5.**   Write four sentences in which you deliberately employ the passive voice. Then write a paragraph for each in which you present a rhetorical circumstance in which the passive voice would be appropriate. For me to write, here, for instance, "The passive voice should never be used," would be a joke. Right?

Note further that Orwell is returning to his *ad populum* invocation of the virtue of "bothering." What began as "bothering" is here strengthened to "action," and within two lines will become "struggle." Also he plants, as it were, the thematically vital concept of "conscious" action—that is, action taken in a thoughtful and deliberate way—in attributing its negation to "the argument" which he will oppose. Ending the sentence with "but it is generally assumed that we cannot do anything about it" would have forced Orwell to *assert* the "conscious action." Here he can let it emerge as the contrary to the position held by the "argument" of the doomsayers (and I do not present this designation as hyperbole).

It is vital to understand the "givens," the assumptions of a piece of persuasion.

Use the passive voice when there is a reason to.

Orwell uses the passive voice to "float" the question of responsibility.

Orwell begins "Politics and the English Language" talking about nothing less than the death of a civilization. In his first paragraph he implies that such death is possible if we do not take appropriate steps with regard not only to how we write (and read) but to change how we think about the relationship between civilization and language.

This depends on what Orwell would have us think of as the power of language itself. If we accept the metaphor of language and civilization as parts of an organism and hence subject to decay ("decadence") then the collapse is "inevitable" (as is death for all organisms). Decadence, if we consciously or half-consciously take the metaphor literally (and Orwell suggests that if we do it half-consciously we cannot do *other* than to take it literally), leads inevitably to death. One may be in a period of decay for an extended or a brief time, but decay can only lead to one state—death.

Orwell then proposes in the last sentence of his first paragraph a substitute metaphor. Instead of thinking about language and civilization as an *organism*, which one must do if one accepts the implications of "decadence," consider language and civilization as "instruments."

> The implications of Orwell's use of "decadence" present the death of English-speaking civilizations as a result of a conscious use of language.

Exercise 3:6.   The *ad populum* is frequently employed by politicians who are trying to represent themselves as speaking for the values of "the people," who, supposedly, are the same population as comprises the "voters." Without doing a complete analysis, find a political sound-bite from an office seeker that can be described this way and discuss its intended effect by an examination of its specific language.

George W. Bush sought his party's presidential candidacy with the sound-bite label of "compassionate conservatism." Consider the implications of this label in relationship to the *ad populum*. Of central concern ought to be who is being compassionate to whom and the difficulties Republicans have had in presenting themselves as the party of "the people."

One can slow, but not *halt* the decay of an organism. An *instrument*, by contrast, can be continually renewed, rebuilt, replaced. (Take, for example, the story of the 400-year-old ax that was used to chop wood for an hour of each day of its life. It had worn out 25 heads and 100 handles, but still, somehow, it was the same ax.) In other words, Orwell implies that our civilization will live or die depending on what language, what metaphoric structure, we use to think about it in, that we use to "understand" it.

Careful reading leaves no doubt that Orwell here intends the full implications of the word "decadent" (although he is less careful about treating the metaphor literally later in the essay). The last sentence of the paragraph insists that "*Underneath* this lies the *half-conscious* belief that language is a *natural growth* and not an *instrument* which *we shape* for our own purposes [my emphasis]." That is, if we are *fully conscious* as opposed to "half-conscious," we can reject the passivity of the half-conscious for the deliberate action of shaping.

Metaphors frequently carry implications which can be exploited by the user.

Expanding the *Ad Populum* Appeal: The Extended Metaphor

I have argued that "Politics and the English Language" depends rhetorically on the *ad populum*, and specifically the appeal to *work*, to "taking pains," to action rather than passivity. (Moreover, although it is not directly stated, the appeal is to practice this in reading or listening as well as in writing.) It begins with this appeal, inviting the reader to identify herself with those who "bother," those who are honest and will "admit," those who are ready to "struggle," and continues to invoke this "action" throughout.

Orwell's use of the extended metaphor related to a popular value is a central aspect of his strategy.

This may seem to be a small thing, but as with **existential import**, if the *implicit* value (working hard, taking pride in one's work, valuing that which shows painstaking effort and attention) is continually invoked, it may become, in the mind of the reader, a measure of value. It may become a way in which value can be determined.

We are dealing here with the very sensitive issue of the investment of the personal in the particular and valuing the particular for the reason of that investment. It may be an appeal, for instance, that for us, in our current place/time, has lost its value/worth appeal.

Orwell, in 1946, lived in a pre-technological world, in even a pre-robotic world. For us, for instance, "home-made" can mean (at least) two different things: made-up, patched together, crude, unreliable, or, on the other hand, expressing care and love, personal, one of a kind. We need only to move a short way to get to "custom made," a vastly different thing. "Custom made" or "hand made" implies exclusive, expensive, of limited availability. By comparison to it, the "assembly line," the "machine made," the "manufactured" is, well, just "ok."

Argument is tied to historical period.

But for Orwell the "manufactured" was to that extent "in-human" and empty of implicit human value. It was "cheap," in the way that means shoddy rather than "inexpensive." We have a notion, which would be completely foreign to Orwell, of "human error," which says, if you let the machine run on its own it will do it right, its product will be precise and dependable. If, on the other hand, you get some hourly wage operator involved in the production process, you are likely to get a flaw. The hourly wage operator, however, is what makes the product "home made," or even "hand made."

> Orwell stood in a different relation to the mechanical than we do.

Given all of this, then, we may be able to appreciate what Orwell was trying to do in relation to his audience at the time— he was trying to say that to the extent a construction is me-chanical, predictable, uniform, it is inhuman and destructive. To the extent a construction is hand-made, home-made, custom, and varied, it is expressive of freedom and positive value.

With the foregoing as qualification, let's examine this metaphoric referentiality to the "home-made." In terms of rhetorical analysis, I am now "interrogating" the essay for evi-dence with which to support my assertion that the machine-made is to be associated with the uncaring, passive, victimized, and ultimately, doomed.

Exercise 3:7. Go directly to the essay and mark each in-stance where you find the overall metaphor of the hand-made compared to the machine made. For this exercise to be useful you will need to do it before reading further.

At the end of the first paragraph Orwell writes that lan-guage might be considered as "an instrument which we shape for our own purposes." Here is the first reference to the "mak-ing" of a thing. Notice that "we" shape it. It is not, in other words, shaped for us. The next instance that I find is in para-graph four, and the usage moves into the explicitly metaphori-cal. Orwell writes "prose consists less and less of *words* chosen for the sake of their meaning, and more and more of *phrases* tacked together like the sections of a prefabricated hen house" (emphasis Orwell's). He continues, "I list below, with notes and examples, various of the tricks by means of which the work of prose-construction is habitually dodged. . . ."

A hen house, outside of a chicken ranch, at least in post-war England where food shortages were very real, is no item of contempt. But what about a "prefabricated" hen house? What about one which is (not screwed, not nailed, not bolted but) "tacked" together? Pretty "tacky," right? I think that Orwell's point is, not that there is anything wrong with hen houses, but that there are hen houses, and then there are hen houses. And a hen house pretty clearly is not a structure of high significance from which we expect design excellence or in which we invest national pride.

"Dodging" in British English and American English

"Work," nevertheless, is good, and what someone who has tacked together a hen house has done is "dodged" it. And a "dodge" at least for a Brit, is a fraud, an evasion, a pretense. For Americans it used to be a car. The British, post-Dickens, had the "Artful Dodger," the best of the pickpockets. Americans had the Dodge Dart, and the Brooklyn and later Los Angeles Dodgers baseball team.

Exercise 3:8.   Using Orwell's hen house as a model, construct three sentences in which you use a metaphor to describe careless, sloppy work of some sort. Be sure that the metaphors you use cannot be classified as clichés.

Looking on this metaphoric foundation for metaphors of "action" and "construction," I find, in paragraph five, reference to a "newly *invented* metaphor." Any question I might have about Orwell using "inventing" as referring to conscious action is answered by the phrase, later in the same paragraph "merely used because they *save people the trouble* of inventing phrases for themselves (my italics)." We have returned to "work," effort, taking the time, putting in the effort, as a virtue. At the end of paragraph five I find "A writer who stopped to think what he was saying would be aware of this. . . ." I am not as confident about "stopping to think" as constituting work, but it does suggest something other than passivity and so it will, for the time being anyway, remain on the list.

In paragraph six we are told that verbal false limbs "save the trouble of picking out appropriate verbs and nouns. . . ." Again, "honest" work is avoided. In paragraph seven I find "It is often easier to make up words of this kind . . . than to think up the English words that will cover one's meaning." "Making up" is here distinguished from "thinking up" on the basis of how much "work" is involved ("it is . . . easier").

Paragraph 11 contains, for me, the clincher, the sentence that tells me that searching for rhetorical instances concerning the *ad populum* appeal to "work," and the "hand-made," or the "home-made" as the authentic and valuable are on the right track. I will need to quote at length, with supplied emphasis, but as an exercise the reader could now go to paragraph 11 and highlight (hi-lite?) the words and phrases she thinks are illustrative before looking at my rendition.

I am going to remove Orwell's italics in the citation. He uses italics to indicate material that he is citing as example. I will substitute for his italics with quotation marks. My italics, in other words, are to emphasize words that Orwell uses to invoke what is by now within the essay an existentially established virtue—words that invoke "work," "effort," "activity," and, finally, what they all amount to, "caring."

Graphic rendition of a text is often helpful. Highlighters, etc., can be used to mark words within a specific metaphoric construction.

> As I have *tried to show*, modern writing at its worst does not consist in *picking out words* for the sake of their meaning and *inventing images* in order to make the meaning clearer. It consists in *gumming together* long sets of words already *set in order by someone else*, and making the result presentable by sheer humbug. The attraction of this way of writing is that *it is easy. It is easier—even quicker*, once you have the habit—to say "In my opinion it is not an unjustifiable assumption that" than to say "I think." If you use *ready-made phrases*, you not only *don't have to hunt* for words; you also *don't have to bother* with the rhythms of your sentences. . . . By using stale metaphors, similes and idioms, *you save much mental effort*, at the cost of leaving your meaning vague. . . . [And here Orwell becomes as specific as he will be about this example of bad writing, and closes the paragraph with the following.] But you are not obliged to *go to all this trouble*. You can *shirk it by simply throwing your mind open and letting the ready-made phrases come crowding in. They will construct your sentences for you—even think your thoughts for you, to a certain extent*—and at need they will perform the important service of partially concealing your meaning even from yourself.

Analyses of rhetorical constructions need to be constantly measured against the evidence of the text itself.

In the next paragraph I find "the speeches of under-secretaries do, of course, vary from party to party, but they are all alike in that one almost never finds in them *a fresh, vivid, home-made* turn of speech." We might think of that phrase as the metaphoric extension at full-length development. As Americans we might want to compare this with something like what would be intended by someone who referred to a home-made cherry pie made from "scratch" with fresh fruit and hand-rolled dough as evidence of a cook who really cares. In either British or American English, I think the valuation is clear. Work is equal to virtue, taking the easy way is equivalent to vice.

"But you are *not obliged* to go to *all this trouble.* You can *shirk* it by *simply throwing your mind open and letting the ready-made phrases come crowding in*" (emphasis mine), shows again how Orwell is using the passive construction. In this case it is intended to echo the passivity that he attacks in "letting the ready-made phrases come crowding in."

Another example of rhetorical use of the passive voice.

Interestingly, the culmination of Orwell's metaphors of passivity occur in narratives of outside activity, where the passivity, at least as expressed, of the writer, makes "him" victim to the forces of political conformity, whatever the source of that politics might be. I cite the close of paragraph 15.

> You see, he "feels impelled" to write—feels, presumably that he has something new to say—and yet his words, like cavalry horses answering the bugle, group themselves automatically into the familiar dreary pattern. This invasion of one's mind by *ready made phrases* ("lay the foundations, achieve a radical transformation") can only be prevented *if one is constantly on guard against them,* and every such phrase anesthetizes a portion of one's brain.

Exercise 3:9. Examine the preceeding quoted paragraph in terms of the organizing metaphor that Orwell uses to describe reader/writer interaction. Write a paragraph of explanation of the device explaining why "on guard against," in this context, is not a cliché.

Reader Participation

A large part of Orwell's rhetorical approach is to attempt at every opportunity to *acquire reader participation, to involve the reader as an active and engaged consumer of the essay.*

The rhetorical use of numbered lists is typically to demonstrate to the reader that the writer is in "control" of the material, and thus in a position of authority in relation to it.

Popular journalism is full of what may be the inheritance of Orwell's reader involvement devices. We have all seen pieces like "15 ways to rate your lover" (or cholesterol, job appeal, exercise program, interior decorating skills). "How do *you* rate as a daughter-in-law [or friend, lover, hostess, houseguest]: eight ways to tell." What the inevitably included number is is not as important as that there *is* a number, the presence of which suggests organization, order, scoring, "chances."

The seminal Victorian social critic John Ruskin wryly commented on his similar use of number in his own early work. A "young friend" had been to a botanical lecture in which she had found out that there were seven sorts of leaves. Ruskin comments, "Now I have always a great suspicion of the number seven; because when I wrote the *Seven Lamps of Architecture*, [a very famous and influential work arguing that architecture has a moral content] it required all the ingenuity I was master of to prevent them from becoming Eight, or even Nine, on my hands. So I thought to myself that it would be very charming if there were only seven sorts of leaves; but that, perhaps, if one looked the woods and forests of the world carefully through, it was just possible that one might discover as many as eight sorts; and then where would my friend's new knowledge of Botany be?"

Many such pieces provide, in addition to their numbers, a scoring scale sometimes reversed on the page or on a later page to (presumably) ensure that the reader doesn't peek at the answers before finishing the test and thus call the "accuracy" of the offered diagnosis into question. It is doubtful, of course that many readers take such rating devices very seriously, but it is fairly certain that a great many readers, and even sophisticated readers, "take" the tests. They do so probably as much in the spirit of a game, or of testing the test, as to acquire necessary or even helpful information. Consider, in this light, what Orwell is attempting rhetorically with the following:

> . . .the fight against bad English is not frivolous and is not the exclusive concern of professional writers. I will come back to this presently, and I hope that by that time the meaning of what I have said here will become clearer. Meanwhile here are five specimens of the English language as it is now habitually written.
>
> These five passages have not been picked out because they are especially bad—I could have quoted far worse if I had chosen—but because they illustrate various of the mental vices from which we now suffer. They are a little below the average, but are fairly representative samples. I number them so that I can refer back to them when necessary.

He tells the reader twice that there will be *five* specimens, and he notes again immediately before presenting them that he has *numbered* them. Note also that he tells the reader that these are *bad*, but not especially so. What he is doing, I suggest, is inviting the reader to play a game with him. On the model of contemporary popular magazine journalism we might think it as something like "How many bad things can you find in the following passages—rate your skill as an active reader."

The sophisticated rhetorician attempts to influence how the reader will approach the essay.

But of course what the reader who plays such a game is also doing is judging how good the writer (Orwell) is at his own game. So, if the reader responds, she reads carefully and critically, looking for the errors that Orwell has already said are there, and perhaps for some that Orwell himself has not noticed.

Now if we count the examples themselves as part of the third paragraph of the essay, we find that none of them is specifically discussed until a brief mention of number three in paragraph 10. Then a quarter of paragraph 11 devotes one sentence to each of the five examples. The last two of these sentences are "In (4), the writer knows more or less what he wants to say, but an accumulation of stale phrases chokes him like tea leaves blocking a sink," and "In (5), words and meaning have almost parted company."

This is in an essay that is, in total, 19 paragraphs long. It would appear, then, that the "examples" are part of a reader participation strategy. The reader begins "playing" knowing nothing more specific than that she seeks the "bad." To find confirmation from Orwell of whatever judgements she makes must wait until she has read more than two-thirds of the essay.

Exercise 3:10.   Either find or create a piece of writing which uses a numbered list as an approach to presenting an argument to a reader in the form of an explanation rather than as an overt argument. Write a paragraph explaining how the list is intended to work rhetorically.

But, if Orwell has succeeded in his strategy, that reader is reading *carefully*, is reading *critically*, and is reading "*consciously*," from at least paragraph three onward.

In the final analysis this major rhetorical appeal is to the vanity of the reader willing to pit her critical skills against those of Orwell, the professional writer. Much as in the first paragraph, Orwell relies on the reader priding herself on being one of those *superior* people who "bother," who do not "dodge" the "work" of "prose construction." Here he relies on that democratic pride in the "one" which British English specifies more clearly than American does. Notice the play of "you" against "one" toward the end of the closing paragraph of the essay:

> If *you* simplify *your* English, *you* are freed from the worst follies of Orthodoxy. *You* cannot speak any of the necessary dialects, and when *you* make a stupid remark its stupidity will be obvious, even to *yourself.* Political language . . . is designed to make lies sound truthful and murder respectable, and to give an appearance of solidity to pure wind. *One* cannot change this all in a moment, but *one*

Once again, a writer's selection and use of pronouns is an active part of the rhetorical strategy.

can at least change *one's* own habits, and from time to time *one* can even, if *one* jeers loudly enough, send some worn-out and useless phrase—some *jackboot, Achilles' heel, hotbed, melting pot, acid test, veritable inferno* or other lump of verbal refuse—into the dustbin where it belongs [pronoun emphasis mine, and a "dustbin" is our "garbage can"].

If Orwell has succeeded and we have played his question begging "guess why these are bad English" game in paragraph three, and as *active* readers at this point, we are attending to his lesson, we may here notice a patch of writing that, by Orwellian standards, is terrible. Consider the struck-through passages in the following quotation as examples of "ready-made phrases," and consider the words I have inserted in brackets as Orwellianly appropriate substitutions:

> They will construct your sentences for you—even [partly] think your thoughts for you, ~~to a certain extent~~—and at need they will perform the important service of partially concealing your meaning even from yourself. ~~It is at this point that~~ [Here] the special connection between politics and the debasement of language becomes clear. ~~In our time~~ it is broadly true that political writing is bad writing. Where it is not ~~true, it will~~ generally ~~be found that~~ the writer is some kind of rebel, expressing his private opinions, and not a "party line." Orthodoxy, of whatever colour, seems to demand a lifeless, imitative style. The political dialects ~~to be found~~ in pamphlets, leading articles, manifestos, White Papers, and the speeches of Under-Secretaries do, of course, vary from party to party, but they are ~~all~~ alike in that one ~~almost never~~ [seldom] finds in them a fresh, vivid, home-made turn of speech.

This editing of Orwell by his own standards for "home-made" language is another example of a type of graphic representation as an aid to rhetorical diagnosis.

Exercise 3:11. Rewrite the paragraph above inserting the words in brackets and omitting the words with the strikethroughs. Then perform the exercise that I performed in my edit of Orwell's text on the edit itself—that is, without sacrifice of clarity, see if you can find ways to eliminate even

---

And this mess is followed in the latter half of the paragraph and the next two by some of Orwell's most chilling and memorable writing. Paragraph 14, especially by comparison, is a *tour de force* of the Orwellianly prescribed "concrete images." The following begins *immediately* after the above citation, introduced, indeed, by the previously discussed phrase "a fresh, vivid, home-made turn of speech."

When one watches some tired hack on the platform mechanically repeating the familiar phrases—*bestial atrocities, iron heel, bloodstained tyranny, free peoples of the world, stand shoulder to shoulder*—one often has a curious feeling that one is not watching a live human being but some kind of a dummy: a feeling which suddenly becomes stronger at moments when the light catches the speaker's spectacles and turns them into blank disks which seem to have no eyes behind them. . . .

Abstract terminology followed by images of nearly extreme specificity exemplifies Orwell's writing ideal.

. . . . Defenceless villages are bombarded from the air, the inhabitants driven out into the countryside, the cattle machine-gunned, the huts set on fire with incendiary bullets: this is called *pacification*. Millions of peasants are robbed of their farms and sent trudging along the roads with no more than they can carry: this is called *transfer of population* or *rectification of frontiers*. People are imprisoned for years without trial, or shot in the back of the neck or sent to die of scurvy in Arctic lumber camps: this is called *elimination of unreliable elements*. (Emphasis Orwell's)

Not only is the contrast between these passages striking, but also if we have attended to Orwell's instruction, if we have paid attention and become active readers, we search the rest of the essay for such "ready-made" patches in vain. (The "In our time" which begins paragraph 14 is contextually very different from the same phrase beginning paragraph 13.)

Orwell even congratulates us for having caught him in paragraph 16 with the coy (if we have caught him) or admonitory (if we have not) "Look back through this essay, and *for certain* you will find that I have again and again committed the very faults I am protesting against" (emphasis mine). It is "for certain" because it is *intentional*, because the *active* reader is intended to catch it, just as the active reader is intended to try to anticipate Orwell's diagnosis of his five examples of not "especially bad" writing in paragraph three.

The Fully Active Reader

The final example of this invitation to active reading occurs in the famous list of rules in the penultimate paragraph. Number iii reads: "If it is possible to cut a word out, always cut it out." I find inescapable the conclusion that Orwell was fully aware that the word "always" is rendered redundant by the conditional "If it is possible." That is, Orwell is here inviting the following:

The deliberate use of redundancy as a rhetorical device.

"If it is possible to cut a word out, ~~always~~ cut it out."

He is still playing the game begun with the five examples of "not especially bad writing." Here, though, he is asking the by now hopefully fully active reader for constant attention to *all* written English, and most especially the most dangerous of written English, that which lays down "rules," that which presumes to prescribe.

My central concern with this essay from the perspective of this text is not that the reader becomes convinced that all issues are political issues (although I believe that they are) nor for the reader to follow any of Orwell's "rules," or prefer the word deriving from Anglo-Saxon to the word which has its origin in Latin or Greek. Indeed, I believe that what Orwell is doing with this is making a further appeal to "patriotism," or "solidarity" at least, among English-speaking peoples.

Orwell and English First

The preference for the Anglo-Saxon that Orwell expresses, I think is meant to make English-speaking peoples conscious of representing a valuable order of civilization whose traditions and very existence were threatened by Soviet Communism. The idea of this sort of "nativism" thus lies in direct opposition to the view that was prevalent in British and much American education of the time, that western civilization not only began in but will never live up to the glories of ancient Athens and Rome.

Linguistically and historically, however, the proposition is pretty silly. Orwell was a sufficiently linguistically sophisticated writer to know that the number of words which English has assimilated from Greek and Latin roots is so large, and so pervasive as to be unavoidable. What, for instance could he suggest as a substitute for "linguistic," or indeed "the Language" of his title, which comes from the Latin? This is not to say, however, that there are no longer teachers of "English" who try to enforce as "correct English" a grammar based, not on English as it is in fact spoken and written, but on a grammar derived from Latin, on what is seen as a prescriptive, rather than as current linguistic research supports, a "descriptive" grammar.

The applications of what Orwell is saying in "Politics and the English Language" go far beyond what is conventionally thought of as "political writing." Indeed you will find that they are pertinent to your interaction with all writing, both as a producer and a consumer of that writing.

I hope I have been able to make clear that this essay was chosen for analysis rather than to promote any specific political agenda. I have tried to treat it as an arena for the discussion of conscious and critical response asking for "active" analysis of *argumentative writing in general*, especially as concerns vagueness and exhausted idioms, but most especially in terms of trying to aid in your development of a conscious analytic response to the written word.

Important among the points that I have tried to make is that an argument cannot be separated from the time in which it was written. The difficult point concerned in absorbing this point as a guide for your own writing is that it is difficult to the point of impossibility to understand the conditions, the assumptions under which you and I write in the present.

It is, in a sense, easy enough to look back on an essay written immediately after WWII and say that the attitude expressed differs from our own concerning the mechanically produced artifact. What is more difficult is to recognize that our attitude toward the mechanically produced artifact is not, because it is current, therefore permanent, or correct, is not, because it is current, the *only* way to think.

The rhetorical analyst, from one perspective, attempts the impossible. She tries to see her own work as an analyst who may well be from another time period would see it. She hopes, in that effort, that she will not be smug about her assumptions concerning what is "self-evident," or "undeniable," given her knowledge that, over time, no claim to such has ever held up.

The rhetorical analyst must act in the same way in relationship to a text as Orwell's ideal of the fully active reader.

Exercise 3:12.   Self-evidence is a difficult concept to deal with in the setting of rhetorical analysis. Each of us carries a set of assumptions that we do not think of as assumptions, which rather we think of as constituting simply "the truth," or "reality," or some similar conceptual construction. Those of us who have "moved away," "gone to college," or hung out with a "different" group, have frequently found that some "principle" which was, before the experience simply assumed, is now no longer tenable, believable, acceptable.

Unless we are so trained, unless we have had the specific experience, it is very difficult to consider that no idea has been able to sustain itself on the basis of its "self-evidence," and that therefore those things that we believe are "obvious," as individuals, are not so seen by people whom we would be willing, for the most part, to consider as "reasonable."

Write an essay in which you describe the process of what might be called "changing your mind," the process which you went through when you abandoned one idea in favor of another which seemed superior.

As a condition of the exercise, write it as if you accepted that your current position is as susceptible to change as your former position.

C H A P T E R

THE COMPLEXITIES OF AUDIENCE: ARGUMENT AND CHANGE

riting With a Purpose, The Critical Edge, Strate-gies for Argument, The Power to Persuade. Each of these is a writing text, and each is based on the principle which the title to the first book presents perhaps the most clearly and simply. I will put that point more complexly, but I hope as clearly:

> *From the point of view of its producer, writing which has persuasion as its goal is best con-sidered as the product of deliberate activity which takes constant consideration of the writ-ing's hoped-for effect on its intended audience.*

Writing argument is a deliberate activity directed to a specific audience.

I have put the preceding sentence in bold italics because I intend it as a sort of formula basic to all consideration of pro-ducing persuasive writing. It directs the writer to ask herself, at every turn, at every word, sentence, and paragraph:

1. What is the point (or are the points) of which I wish to per-suade my audience?

2. What population comprises that audience?

3. What means are best suited to accomplish my goal, and have I throughout constructed my writing according to the choices which I believe are best suited to accomplishing that goal?

Let's briefly return to a consideration of "The Gettysburg Address" in terms of these three questions. In relation to question 1, let us begin by assuming that Lincoln wished to persuade his audience (and as the second chapter discusses, Lincoln thought of this audience as much larger than simply those in attendance at the dedication of the Gettysburg cemetery) that the outcome of the Civil War would determine whether the United States of America would fulfill, in its *Constitution*, what he saw as the promise of the *Declaration of Independence* that "all men are created equal."

Let's assume, in terms of question 2, that Lincoln's intended audience was those inhabitants of the at that time contested "United" States of America, North and South alike, free person and slave.

VERIFYING THE TARGET AUDIENCE

An "assumption" in rhetorical analysis constitutes a hypothesis and consequently must be defended by evidence from the text.

How then do we go about verifying the accuracy of the above two assumptions? To do so we must ask if all parts of the essay are understandable as attempts to persuade the group postulated as the target audience in response to question 2 of that point (the thesis) which was postulated in response to question 1. Simply put, if the hypothesis about the audience allows you to explain the details of the essay, you've got the evidence to support the hypothesis.

If the details can be explained, you can assume that appropriate identifications have been made in each case. Notice here, however, that I *began* with an assumption concerning Lincoln's thesis, and then, for the purposes of verification, tested it against the third question. As analyst, how do you come up with the postulated thesis from which to begin?

Chapter 2 discussed Gilbert Highet's essay on the "Address" at considerable length, but little time was devoted to discussing *Highet's* presumption of what the thesis of that document is. Instead the discussion was focused on the question of what Highet's thesis is. The presentation above postulates, not the thesis that Highet assumes for the address, but a different one presented by Garry Wills in his Pulitzer Prize-winning 1992 *Lincoln at Gettysburg.*

When we look to Highet's essay for his statement of Lincoln's thesis we find a great deal about his *subject*, but very little on the thesis. Presumably Highet assumes that his audience *knows* that Lincoln is trying to persuade his audience that government of, by, and for the people should not perish. The only thing Highet says on this topic is that Lincoln "used the tricolon because he was hoping, planning, praying for peace." This tells us very little if we stop to consider that peace could be obtained either by allowing the secession or by the Union surrendering, just for starters.

Indeed there are sections in Highet's essay where he seems to deny that the address *has* a thesis, as such. He seems to imply that if the work had a direct intent, a "thesis" as we consider it, that it would be somehow degrading to it considered, as Highet says he wants to do, as a work of art.

It is always important to consider what the writer implies as well as what the writer says.

Listen again, from the perspective of this view, to Highet's last paragraph.

> No one thinks that when he was drafting the Gettysburg Address, Lincoln deliberately looked up these quotations and consciously chose these particular patterns of thought. No, he chose the theme. From its development and from the emotional tone of the entire occasion, all the rest followed, or grew—by that marvelous process of choice and rejection which is essential to artistic creation. It does not spoil such a work of art to analyze it as closely as we have done; it is altogether fitting and proper that we should do this: for it helps us to penetrate more deeply into the rich meaning of the Gettysburg Address, and it allows us the very rare privilege of watching the workings of a great man's mind.

Notice that in his first sentence he says no one thinks Lincoln "consciously chose" these thought patterns (and think about this in terms of Orwell's insistence on consciousness). But in the next sentence, after saying Lincoln *did* choose the theme (consciously, presumably) the rest "followed, or grew" by that "process of choice and rejection which is essential to artistic creation." The choice and rejection mentioned here must, in some way, be *unconscious* choices, and *unconscious* rejections guided by some sort of an instinct. This conscious/unconscious conflict might explain why Highet does not deal with Lincoln's rhetorical purpose. As Highet presents it, the address does not have a purpose—it has instead a subject, a theme (like, say, a dance or a festival can have a "theme") and it contains "rich meaning" which the reader can "penetrate."

Neither I nor Garry Wills, nor for that matter Orwell, holds with the theory of "marvelous process" by the invocation of which Highet seems to think that he is praising Lincoln and Lincoln's prose. Indeed Will's statement stands in striking contrast to Highet's reverential treatment.

"Marvelous process" has nothing to do with the creation of rhetoric.

This is Wills.

> He [Lincoln] would cleanse the Constitution—not as William Lloyd Garrison had, by burning an instrument that countenanced slavery. He altered the document from within by appeal from its letter to the spirit, subtly changing the recalcitrant stuff of that legal compromise, bringing it to its own indictment. By implicitly doing this he performed one of the most daring acts of open-air sleight-of-hand ever witnessed by the unsuspecting. Everyone in that vast throng of thousands was having his or her intellectual pocket picked [!]. The crowd departed with a new thing in its intellectual luggage, that new constitution Lincoln had substituted for the one they brought there with them.

Notice here that Wills writes that Lincoln "implicitly" does this, and calls it "sleight-of-hand," or trickery, performed by a pickpocket who substitutes one piece of property for another. In what sense can we understand it as having been done "implicitly"? I would argue that Wills is saying that Lincoln treated his reading of the constitution's "spirit" *as a given.*

It was a reading, an interpretation, of the Constitution and the Declaration that he did not argue, for which he presented not one iota of evidence, but which he flatly and *immediately* (in the first sentence) asserted. In other words, according to the vocabulary of logic and rhetoric, he begged the question. And he got away with it.

If you look carefully at the address you will notice that there is *no argument in it.* And yet it is regarded as a powerfully persuasive piece of writing. Nor has anyone before Wills called it the work of a pickpocket (which Wills intends, unquestionably, as high praise to a highly skilled politician, especially in terms of what Lincoln wished to accomplish by the act).

My point here is much like a similar point that I tried to make in regard to "Politics and the English Language"—that rhetoric cannot be usefully analyzed if one looks to it for the presentation of arguments founded on sound logical bases. Rhetors, and anyone who uses language in an attempt to persuade can be considered a rhetor, *use* logic, *use* reason, as one, but only one, of their tools. There is nothing "logical," for instance, about the phrase "all men are created equal." It is a bald assertion made in the face of all evidence to the contrary (think, for instance of the difference between that statement and the statement "All men will be treated as equals under the law"). No logic will support it. Nevertheless, it is a *principle* (as opposed to a **fact**) concerning which many people have died. It is

---

Will's Lincoln is a trickster, a rhetorical manipulator of the highest order.

The Gettysburg Address contains no argument.

The phrase "all men are created equal" is not subject to "logical" investigation.

important here to note that having had the extra-logical nature of a given statement pointed out does not constitute a "reason" to reject it. *All* arguments begin from a-rational, extra-logical bases.

Exercise 4:1. Write a three- to four-paragraph explanation of how a writer can use a word (like "pickpocket" for instance) associated with dishonesty in praise of the productions of another writer. Use Wills, as an example, or invent a hypothetical writer.

Where Arguments Begin

In the *Glossary's* definition of **surd** I wrote the following sentence: "If a participant in the argument objects to the beginning proposition it ceases to be a surd and the logical process moves backward until a proposition is found upon which the participants can agree." Because the basic assumptions involved here are so important to the whole idea of argument, and to the place of "logic" in it, I will expand on that discussion with the suggestion that you follow the instructions in the *Glossary* to see the entries for **proof, faith,** and **belief.**

I wrote of "the beginning proposition" and "a proposition upon which the participants can agree" in an attempt at a simplification which may be misleading. What I refer to as "real-world" arguments are seldom based on "a" statement, nor, finally, is there such a thing as "the" beginning proposition from which all other propositions derive. What must be emphasized is that the disputants must agree on "a" beginning proposition.

In the first place, arguments must involve questions concerning the relationships among a minimum of three terms in categorical syllogisms, or two in hypothetical or disjunctive syllogisms (see **syllogism**). Thus in order for the disputants (the parties to the argument) to use "logic" in an attempt to resolve their disagreement, they must agree on a minimum of *two* terms, must, in other words, agree on accepting not simply one, but two statements from which they can then reason.

Arguments deal with the relationships among terms, usually three.

To stay within the example, take the statement "All men are created equal." To present that in the form of a **premise** in a **categorical syllogism** we would render it as "All members of the set men" are members of the set "beings who have been created equal." We would designate the set "men" as A, and the set "beings who have been created equal" as B. The statement could then be presented in the form "All A is B."

This apparently single statement is, as considered in logic, a statement of a relationship between two "terms" (here "men" and "equal"), each of which depends on the acceptance of prior terms. We cannot say, for instance, that in the Declaration the term "men" referred to "all members of the species Homo sapiens without regard to 'race.'" Nor can we say that the term was intended to be understood as applying to women. (The 19th amendment guaranteeing women's right to vote was not passed until 1920.)

What was intended by the term "men" is *not* "self-evident."

Exercise 4:2. Create the logical "terms" for the statement "The only good cat is a flat cat" for translating that statement into the form "All A is B."

The meaning of the term "men," then, is something that the disputants *must agree on before the argument can begin,* and what the term is taken to mean will involve another pair of terms, each of which can be similarly questioned. On the other side of the original statement we have the B term, "beings who have been created equal." Here, because we have a complex term, the statement can be questioned in terms of what is meant by "being," "created," and "equal."

Notice that we started out with one statement (all men are created equal). Then, in order to define that statement we divided it into two terms (men and beings who have been created equal). In order to define those two terms we proposed a definition for one which involved at least three terms ("species," "Homo sapiens," and "race") and the other which involved three terms from the outset ("being," "created," and "equal") and at least six to define those three.

Exercise 4:3. Given the terms created for 4:2 above, write a definition for "cat," and a definition for "flat cat."

In other words, as we "back up" to try to find a set of terms upon which the disputants will agree, the question becomes *more*, not less, complex, and involves *more*, not fewer, terms that increase in a progression that doubles with each move "backwards."

Why Arguments Must Begin in Hypotheticals

When, then, do we arrive at the bedrock-certain statements from which we can argue? Never. We don't. The further "back" we go, the more complex the question becomes. The very best that we can do is to agree to accept *as given* a set of statements from which we may then proceed.

Exercise 4:4. The paragraphs preceding present a complex argument concerning the proposition that no argument begins from anything other than agreed-upon terms. Working from the principle that the best way to learn something is to teach it to someone else, find a "basic" argument and write an explanation of how the argument depends on agreement about the "terms." Examples: "X is only natural"; "Science has demonstrated Y"; "History has shown us that Z."

Arguments Must Begin from "Acceptable" Premises, Not "Sound Logical Bases"

From the perspective of the creation of a piece of persuasive writing, there is never a question of whether your, or another's, argument begins from sound logical bases for the basic (no pun intended) reason that there *are* no such things. The question is, instead, from what statements does the argument begin? These statements then, would be ones the writer of the argument would need to believe that the target audience will find acceptable.

> The phrase "sound logical basis" is a rhetorical gesture with no defensible foundation lying outside of a specific group's assumptions.

The essay this chapter will be centered on has been selected for multiple reasons, but most important is its particular relation to the question of target audience. Target audience is always relevant, but is often defined in such broad terms that it does not seem to be an important part of a rhetorical consideration. Usually this is because of the myopia of the reader who assumes that because she is included (or not excluded) that the essay is therefore addressed to that convenient fiction frequently called "the general reader."

> The "general reader" is a convenient fiction.

There Is No General Reader

Last week, at a conference about books and computers attended by several hundred people not all of whom were academics I was engaged in conversation by a person who had read the "English" on my name tag. He told me that his father was a professor, and that there were a lot of academics in his family, but that it was his experience (by inference much larger than that of the "ordinary" person who lacked academics in their families) that these academics were not in touch with what he referred to as what was "going on."

[Argument is presented in the form of an **anecdote**.]

I asked what this meant (I was asking him, in other words, to define his terms). He said that "they" (and by using this term he presumably paid me the compliment of assuming that I could think in some way "outside" of my "academic" identity) were out of touch with "reality."

I replied that it had been my impression that "reality" was precisely what these people thought they were studying; historians, sociologists, linguists, political scientists, and so on, were concerned precisely with "reality," indeed, professionally speaking, they had no interests *other* than reality.

He replied that I didn't understand him. I agreed, but suggested that I was trying to and was prevented from doing so by my impression that his terms had no referents on which I could base such an understanding—that indeed he seemed to me to be talking nonsense.

He paused. He said that what he meant by reality was what "the man in the street" perceived. I told him that I had considerable difficulty with this concept. I could not, for instance, since the population of the world was better than half female, figure out what the gender of "the man in the street" was, nor could I know, for instance, provided that this was an *American* "man in the street," if he was a woman (presuming that the term man was being used in a generic rather than a gender sense), and whether he was one of those who votes. I didn't know what race or combination of races he would identify himself as affiliated with, nor did I know how much money he made, what books he had read, if he read books, what radio station he listened to, what television station he watched, and when, and so on. I offered that I found the whole concept of "the man in the street" to be so fraught with problems that it had never been useful to me as a concept to apply to any idea of what it was that constituted "reality."

The "average person" is an insupportable concept.

The next speaker came on and our conversation stopped, but I wondered, given this brief encounter, whether my interlocutor would understand my point—that the notions of a "general reader," or an "ordinary person," or the "typical person," or, especially the "man in the street" were not only unacceptably crude in terms of determining characteristics, but were finally fictions created so that one could talk *as if* such a being existed.

Exercise 4:5. Notice in the development of the above illustrative anecdote I used indirect citation—I did not, that is, directly quote myself, but presented instead paraphrase of the content of my supposed statements. Write a three-to five-paragraph ancedote to illustrate a point in which you refer to your own contributions to a conversation indirectly.

That is to say, reference to such a construct was a rhetorical device to which I did not choose to respond.

If such a person did exist she would be about 52% female, 8% voting, 11% black, 46% a city dweller, and so on. This would be further complicated by the figures that the projection was based on being the result of a two-year-old census which was not replied to by "illegal aliens" (among others) and so was, on the face of it, inaccurate. It could hardly have much to do with the "reality" that my conversational partner was so interested in. Moreover, he seemed to presume that the "street" in question existed in the United States, and that somehow that country had some strange ability to define "reality" on the basis of popular opinion.

How Is the Targeted Audience to Be Identified?

People cannot, in other words, be sensibly categorized by the rhetor as being "ordinary," or "the common reader," or "average." How then, since arguments are constructed in relation to the targeted reader, can they be categorized? From the perspective of the creator of a piece of persuasive writing, the answer can be fairly simple.

A great deal of persuasive (or would-be-persuasive) writing is very task- and audience-specific. In many cases the writer actually knows the person or many of the people who will receive the document she is creating. When the specific recipients are known the item can be tailored to take into account those things which set the audience members apart as individuals and as a group from some other group.

But more often the writer only knows a little about the members of a given small audience and so has to guess at what will appeal to and what will offend the members of that audience. In the case of essayists writing for any of the varieties of what are considered media the choice would apparently become much larger. What is often not considered, however, in relation to such publication is that a given writer need not, and often does not, attempt to appeal to the total readership of the medium in question. In the case of the essay we will next examine, "readers of *The New York Times*" is a much larger target audience than, I will argue, the author is addressing.

Place of publication says a limited amount about target audience.

In the cases of the writers we are dealing with in this text, we have to reason backwards from what we are presented with to our construction of whom it is addressed to, to the point of what group constitutes the target audience. Like the whole process of rhetorical analysis, the exercise is useful to the creator of argument as well because it sensitizes us to the choices made in purposeful, conscious, deliberate attempts to persuade.

There is usually some area of disagreement between the target audience and the author, but only usually.

The analytic process can be very frustrating if you're not a member of the group the essay is targeted to. However, it is still important to be able to articulate the bases upon which such a judgment is made. How, that is, do you know you are not a member of the target audience *and* what do you believe the characteristics of the audience that the essay intends to appeal are?

> **Exercise 4:6.** Using any article in the *Readings* section of this text, write at least four paragraphs in which you explain what leads you to think that you are or that you are not a member of the writer's target audience.

Only in some cases are you talking to people who think as you do. Why talk to them if they already agree? The rhetor, consequently, who is best prepared to participate in argument, or present an argument, is that writer who can anticipate the reactions of those who think differently from the way she does.

One hoped for consequence of studying the concept of target audience is that you will become sensitized to the issues involved and consequently improve your capacity to make informed, knowledgeable choices regarding the presentation of an argument as well as the reception of one.

An exercise which you can conduct throughout your relationship with this book is to try put yourself in my position. To whom am *I* writing? What constitutes the list of things that *I* assume my audience will find acceptable as a basis for the argument that I present? What does the vocabulary and sentence complexity indicate about the relationship I seek with my audience? Does the rhetorical concept of argument from authority come into consideration?

The rhetorical analyst should try to place herself in the position of the writer being analyzed.

The author of the exercise essay for this section, Lester C. Thurow was, at the time of its publication in the op-ed (opinion-editorial) section of *The New York Times* (8 March 1981), a professor at the MIT Sloan School of Management. He was born in 1938.

You are asked, as always, to read carefully and slowly, asking yourself the questions: What is the writer trying to sell? To whom is the writer trying to sell it? By what means is the writer trying to sell it? In the case of this essay particular attention should be paid to the second of the three questions (although it remains the case that no one of the questions can be answered in isolation from answering the others).

Viewing the rhetoric of the entire text as an exercise for analysis

Why Women Are Paid Less Than Men

Lester C. Thurow

1 In the 40 years from 1939 to 1979 white women who work full time have with monotonous regularity made slightly less than 60 percent as much as white men. Why?

2 Over the same time period, minorities have made substantial progress in catching up with whites, with minority women making even more progress than minority men.

3 Black men now earn 72 percent as much as white men (up 16 percentage points since the mid-1950s) but black women earn 92 percent as much as white women. Hispanic men make 71 percent of what their white counterparts do, but Hispanic women make 82 percent as much as white women. As a result of their faster progress, fully employed black women make 75 percent as much as fully employed black men while Hispanic women earn 68 percent as much as Hispanic men.

4 This faster progress may, however, end when minority women finally catch up with white women. In the bible of the New Right, George Gilder's *Wealth and Poverty*, the 60 percent is just one of Mother Nature's constants like the speed of light or the force of gravity.

5   Men are programmed to provide for their families economically while women are programmed to take care of their families emotionally and physically. As a result men put more effort into their jobs than women. The net result is a difference in work intensity that leads to that 40 percent gap in earnings. But there is no discrimination against women—only the biological facts of life.

6   The problem with this assertion is just that. It is an assertion with no evidence for it other than the fact that white women have made 60 percent as much as men for a long period of time.

7   "Discrimination against women" is an easy answer but it also has its problems as an adequate explanation. Why is discrimination against women not declining under the same social forces that are leading to a lessening of discrimination against minorities? In recent years women have made more use of the enforcement provisions of the Equal Employment Opportunities Commission and the courts than minorities. Why do the laws that prohibit discrimination against women and minorities work for minorities but not for women?

Note that Thurow is using large generalizations concerning large sets: men, women, whites, blacks, etc. Consider this in terms of the "man in the street" discussion, and in terms of Thurow's target audience.

8   When men discriminate against women, they run into a problem. To discriminate against women is to discriminate against your own wife and to lower your own family income. To prevent women from working is to force men to work more.

9   When whites discriminate against blacks, they can at least think that they are raising their own incomes. When men discriminate against women they have to know that they are lowering their own family income and increasing their own work effort.

10   While discrimination undoubtedly explains part of the male-female earnings differential, one has to believe that men are monumentally stupid or irrational to explain all of the earnings gap in terms of discrimination. There must be something else going on.

11   Back in 1939 it was possible to attribute the earnings gap to large differences in educational attainments. But the educational gap between men and women has been eliminated since World War II. It is no longer possible to use education as an explanation for the lower earnings of women.

12   Some observers have argued that women earn less money since they are less reliable workers who are more apt to leave the labor force. But it is difficult to maintain this position since women are less apt to quit one job to take another and as a result they tend to work as long, or longer, for any one employer. From any employer's perspective they are more reliable, not less reliable, than men.

13   Part of the answer is visible if you look at the lifetime earnings profile of men. Suppose that you were asked to predict

which men in a group of 25-year-olds would become economically successful. At age 25 it is difficult to tell who will be economically successful and your predictions are apt to be highly inaccurate.

4 But suppose that you were asked to predict which men in a group of 35-year-olds would become economically successful. If you are successful at age 35, you are very likely to remain successful for the rest of your life. If you have not become economically successful by age 35, you are very unlikely to do so later.

5 The decade between 25 and 35 is when men either succeed or fail. It is the decade when lawyers become partners in the good firms, when business managers make it onto the "fast track," when academics get tenure at good universities, and when blue collar workers find the job opportunities that will lead to training opportunities and the skills that will generate high earnings.

6 If there is any one decade when it pays to work hard and to be consistently in the labor force, it is the decade between 25 and 35. For those who succeed, earnings will rise rapidly. For those who fail, earnings will remain flat for the rest of their lives.

7 But the decade between 25 and 35 is precisely the decade when women are most apt to leave the labor force or become part-time workers to have children. When they do, the current system of promotion and skill acquisition will extract an enormous lifetime price.

8 This leaves essentially two avenues for equalizing male and female earnings.

9 Families where women who wish to have successful careers, compete with men, and achieve the same earnings should alter their family plans and have their children either before 25 or after 35. Or society can attempt to alter the existing promotion and skill acquisition system so that there is a longer time period in which both men and women can attempt to successfully enter the labor force.

20 Without some combination of these two factors, a substantial fraction of the male-female earnings differentials are apt to persist for the next 40 years, even if discrimination against women is eliminated.

Consider which statements can be considered "argued" and which "asserted," and the extent to which Thurow's occupation may influence this.

ROGERIAN ARGUMENT AS ORGANIZING STRUCTURE

A primary text in the literature of persuasion is Carl Rogers' 1961 *Dealing With Breakdowns in Communication* which is reproduced in the Readings section. Please go to it now, and then return to this point in the text. This is, of course, completely voluntary—it is simply that it will be a more efficient expenditure of your time if you are familiar with Rogers' approach as he presents it himself before you are confronted with it as **Rogerian Argument**. I'll wait.

["I'll wait" is an attempted rhetorical joke employed by the writer acting as if he and the reader were occupying the same time/space location.]

The virtuous among you are now back. The rest of you (who just skipped on to this paragraph) will have to fend for yourselves—the remainder of this chapter is written to an audience that is presumed to be familiar with Rogers' essay.

Since the type in which Rogerian argument appeared in the penultimate paragraph is bold-faced I will further assume that you have consulted the *Glossary*. What the glossary does not make clear is that Rogerian argument describes a tendency, an attitude, an approach, rather than a clearly defined hard-and-fast set of rules for the presentation of a point. As the *Glossary* tries to make clear, rhetors since Rogers have rendered his concept into more formal and formulaic terms than his own idea provided. One could argue, even, that Rogers would not accept those things that have been done in argument theory and pedagogy in his name.

A definition of Rogerian argument

ROGERIAN ARGUMENT: A WORKING DEFINITION

For our purposes, however, simply assume the following:

1. Rogerian argument (thought of as a form of writing) begins with a statement which presents a definition of a (the) problem.

2. It then moves to a presentation of alternative views regarding the problem.

3. It considers, in the interests of a solution to the problem presented in 1 above, the strengths and weaknesses of the alternative views.

4. It then comes to a tentative conclusion based on the information presented in the alternative views previously examined.

There are all sorts of wonderful possibilities that open up from presenting an argument in a Rogerian mode. I will list a few of them, but you should bear in mind that the subject is complex and the list by no means exhausts the possibilities of the form.

1. The writer appears to have no particular ax to grind, or a specific cause to support. Rather she presents herself as

seeing a problem, attempting to define it, and trying to find a solution to it. This is intended to prevent the reader from approaching the essay with a mind-set which tries to classify the writer as "with me" or "against me" (see **either/or**).

Some of the advantages of the Rogerian form of argument

2. It is also well suited to that portion of the target audience occupying the center section of the audience spectrum (see the illustration which accompanies the **target audience** discussion) who have not identified with a particular cause, or, for that matter, are not particularly knowledgeable about the issue itself. Like them, the writer presents herself as only interested in the best available answer. (Look back to the chapter on Orwell's "Politics and the English Language" for an example of the creation of a "problem" as a rhetorical device).

Viewing a subject as a "problem."

3. Sometimes the writer can elicit a collegial (i.e. "we're colleagues working together on this problem") attitude in the reader which can allow that reader to be less defensive concerning ideas with which she is unfamiliar or previously uncomfortable. This is particularly reinforced by the conclusion of a Rogerian argument being presented as *tentative*. Because the writer is not insisting that the conclusion presented is the one and only and final answer, it is less likely to be perceived as a threat. The reader may be able to "hear" positions to which previously she might have been resistant to to the point of (metaphoric) deafness concerning them. This is the attitude we encounter when someone says, "Don't tell me that; I don't want to hear that; I won't listen to that," etc.

However, you should remember that because someone acts sincere, it does not follow that she is, therefore, sincere. Because you behave as if you are only interested in the best solution of the problem for all concerned does not mean that that is your actual motivation. Because you act as if you wish to examine all alternative positions in an objective way does not mean that you have done so. Carl Rogers, a practicing psychotherapist, was interested in fostering communication. Rhetoricians are interested in winning arguments. The two are not identical. They need not be, however, mutually exclusive.

It must constantly be borne in mind that Rogerian argument is a strategy, a way the writer has of presenting herself to accomplish her rhetorical purpose.

Morality and Rhetoric

There are dozens of books on this subject, in at least a dozen languages. No discussion of it within these covers can begin to be satisfactory. I will, nevertheless, offer the following considerations:

1. The exercise of rhetoric, given that there are no assured truths from which one can *begin* to reason, is at *best* a practice in which the participants act from their own convictions (that is, not in the service of another's convictions, not, as it were, hired guns).

2. At its worst, of course, it is the opposite, it is what is represented by such books as *Secrets of Power Persuasion: Everything You'll Ever Need to Get Anything You'll Ever Want* (this is a real book, published by Prentice Hall in 1992). From the long perspective the claim is silly. (It resembles the *Mad Magazine* take-off on all of the ads which promise instant popularity and relief from acne, "Limited Time Offer! Get our Atom Bomb Kit! Be the first kid on your block to RULE THE WORLD!") But from the short view it offers, like the study of rhetoric, a series of methods for persuading an audience to take a certain course of action. It says nothing about the worth of what any given course of action is, any more than the rhetorician can say "these techniques should only be used to persuade people of things that are good for them."

Rhetoric is selling. The rhetorically informed are the smartest consumers.

3. But, if you know rhetoric, or if you know the techniques of the sales people who are rhetoricians, (and rhetoric, you should not forget, is the set of tools for selling your conclusion) you are in a position to evaluate an argument or a sales pitch with knowledge of the skill exercised by its presentor. And, in terms of the presentation of your own positions, you will be able to anticipate and counter the techniques which your skilled opponent may use against you.

This returns us, in a sense, to the first chapter, and the discussion on effectiveness as a conceivable criterion for judging, learning, or interacting with written argument. How possibly could two people, each of whom has assimilated (I don't want to use the word mastered) the *Secrets of Power Persuasion* book, presuming that they have different goals, act in relation to one another?

I have sometimes entertained rhetorical fantasies relative to this in which (a la every martial arts movie in the world) the super good guy and the super bad guy confront one another in some sort of rhetorical pyrotechnics to the death (if the good guy doesn't win, it is only temporary, but by the same token the bad guy is never completely, totally, destroyed—as they said in *Halloween* [the first one], you can't kill the bogeyman).

Given all of the above, rhetoric is a tool. Unfortunately it is a tool the characteristics of which are like a gun. It can be used to kill, and it can be used to defend yourself (to anyone who wants to add that it can also be used for "target practice" I would only ask, "practice for what?"). From the point of view of morality, rhetoric itself is totally neutral.

My metaphor, I hope, illustrates the potential of rhetoric. It can kill. That it has done so and that it continues to do so is indisputable. But by the same token, one who is familiar with its tools and devices can make a judgment about the message being transmitted—can choose not to become one of the killers, or choose not to acquiesce in becoming a victim.

Rhetoric cannot be defined as a tool to deceive people, even though it is frequently used for exactly that purpose. It is a tool, and in the final analysis, and even by definition, the *only* tool, which can be utilized in the service of disseminating what is right.

> That a metaphor is not a very good fit can sometimes be used to make a point on that basis. Unlike guns, for instance, the only way to "ban" rhetoric would be to ban language.

All Statements, Like All Arguments, Are Rhetorical

I can use an ax to make a house, or to cleave someone's skull. The ax is a tool. Such is rhetoric. To make a statement, particularly a written statement, *without* rhetorical purpose is, from the perspective of this book, impossible, even self-refuting—it is something like Orwell says in "Politics and the English Language" when he writes, "In our age there is no such thing as 'keeping out of politics.' All issues are political issues. . . ."

> Rhetoric is a tool.

All issues, we could say, are argued, are presented, are discussed, are disseminated *rhetorically*. The question becomes, then, how well can you utilize the tool, and how knowledgeable are you about the use that is made of it by others.

Exercise 4:7. In the preceding discussion I have employed a number of analogies to describe the uses of rhetoric. Given your understanding of rhetoric, write three or more paragraphs in which you use your own analogies in an attempt to explain how you see that rhetoric relates to morality.

Thurow and the Rogerian Argument

Thurow's presentation, in "Why Women are Paid Less than Men," has many of the characteristics of the Rogerian argument.

It begins with a question to which it claims to seek an answer: why have white women for the last forty years made "slightly less" than 60 percent of the pay of white men? To be truly Rogerian it would have to begin not simply with a question, but with a problem. Is this conceived of as a problem?

Something that needs an *explanation* does not *necessarily* need a solution. There are any number of questions to which the answer, presumably, shows that there is no solution to the problem, or that there is no problem.

"Where are you going at this hour of the night?"

"Down to the store to buy milk so the baby will have some in the morning."

"Oh. OK. No problem."

When we look at Thurow's last two paragraphs it may initially appear that he is offering a solution. So, preliminarily, we might want to consider that the material in the first paragraph is being presented as a problem, and that the *form* of the Rogerian argument is still applicable here.

The other criteria of the Rogerian argument are that alternative solutions to the problem are presented and evaluated during the movement toward a tentative conclusion. Again, when we look at the body of the essay, this criterion seems to have been met. In paragraph four Thurow mentions Gilder's hypothesis and in paragraph six he seems to find it problematic. In paragraph seven he begins to look at the "discrimination" argument and discusses the problems he finds with that until paragraph 10. Paragraphs 11 and 12 are devoted to looking at education and dependability, respectively, both of which are found to offer unsatisfactory explanations.

Thurow's movement toward his conclusion begins in paragraph 13, and it is here we encounter our first overt conflict with the Rogerian model—Thurow uses an absolute. He writes "Part of *the* answer is visible if you look at the lifetime earnings profile of men" (my italics). The true Rogerian argument would have said instead "Part of the answer *may* be provided by . . . ," or "The data *which we presently hold* indicate that . . . ," or "We are left, *at least for now*, with the conclusion that . . . ," or the like. I have italicized the words intended to convey tentativeness, a lack of *absolute* conviction.

It is vitally important in analyzing Rogerian argument to determine what the central question is.

Alternatives and the Rogerian argument

The importance of the "tentative" to Rogerian argument

The Rogerian Argument and the Argument from Authority

This may be clearer if we think about it in relation to the argument from authority. In the argument from authority the writer will cite "expert" opinion, or speak from her own expertise. Obviously in order to do this the expertise has to be recognized (accepted) by the reader. If the reader is in any way dubious concerning the extent of the authority of the writer, an appearance of tentativeness may well be taken as an indication of weakness, of lack of information, of self-doubt.

Arguments from authority tend to present their positions boldly, and flatly, as if argument on the point is not possible. The authority implies "I have spent years gaining a deserved reputation in the field and have all of the information pertinent to the point. Trust me."

Authority and the Rogerian argument

The Rogerian arguer, by contrast, implies "I am an honest person, who is genuinely concerned with finding the best solution to this problem. I have looked at the 'experts' (the authorities) and find that they disagree with each other. The best I can make out of it, at the moment, is X." The Rogerian writer's seeming weakness, in other words, is her strength. If I do not threaten you you are much more likely to listen to what I have to say. Why not? If I am not a threat, what do you have to lose?

Ethos and the Rogerian argument

The authorities go boldly about declaring each other wrong, while the humble searcher for a solution, who informs herself about the issues as the "experts" see them, offers her conclusions tentatively to an audience treated as peers. Implied is that, "You, reader, could have done the same thing if you had had the time."

The end of a Rogerian argument implies something like "Well, I gave it my best. Now what do *you* think? I think my answer is a good one, but you may have a better idea and we really need to get this worked out." (In the *College English* version of material that appears in the previous chapter I tried to make explicit what the typical journal article only implies. I tried to reinforce to my reader that I seek disagreement in order to improve my interpretation of the subject under analysis by providing my email address and inviting responses to the analysis.)

When we then look back on Thurow's argument we find that the ersatz (imitation) Rogerian approach is dropped at the end of paragraph eight. There he writes, "Why do the laws that prohibit discrimination against women and minorities work for minorities and not for women?" This is the last question in the essay. It occurs in paragraph seven of a 21-paragraph essay. From here forward Thurow will give his audience *the* answers those questions and give them in sentences that are designed to squelch any "yeah, but" responses. Thurow, in other words, stops being the person in search of a solution and becomes the professor who is giving the answer. He is, after all, an "expert." He has written books.

The Rogerian "form" bears no relation to the necessary content.

Keeping in abeyance for the moment exactly what the answer *is* that Thurow delivers to the target audience from his assumed position of authority, we need to examine what Thurow assumes, what he takes for granted, what are the "givens" in the argument that he presents.

I quote the only sentence of paragraph 18 and the first sentence of the two-sentence-long paragraph 19.

Authority vs. inquiry—"knowing" as contrasted to seeking as a rhetorical projection. Few knowledgeable reviewers refer to any reference text as "authoritative," or, especially, "definitive." Reviewers a decade ago, however, used those terms frequently.

> This leaves essentially two avenues for equalizing male and female earnings.
>
> Families where women who wish to have successful careers, compete with men, and achieve the same earnings should alter their family plans and have their children either before 25 or after 35.

Thurow seems to assume that working white women are married, or will be.

The question that Thurow sets himself up to answer in the beginning of the essay is why, for the last 40 years, "white women who work full time have . . . made slightly less than 60 percent as much as white men." The question, it should be noted, is not why married white women make less, nor is it why married or formerly married white women with or without children make less.

In his answer, however, Thurow begins, not with women, but with "families." Further, he does not assume that a family is comprised of a wife and husband, but instead he assumes that a family is composed of "man," wife, and (plural) children. The question, as he puts it, is not whether the wife and husband will have no children, one child, or more than one, it is only a question of *when* the *family* is going to have *their* children. Note that the "wife" does not decide this (although there is nothing to make us presume that she doesn't have a voice in the matter).

Defining "family"

Thurow's Givens

What is assumed? It is assumed that white women who work full time are 1) married and 2) either have or are going to have more than one child. What is further assumed (remembering that we are staying, at the moment, within one sentence) is that there are families in which women who work full time do *not* wish to have successful careers, and/or do *not* wish to compete with men. Look back at the essay and look again at the paragraph under discussion.

Are there other assumptions? I am not asking if there are other components to Thurow's argument, but simply if there are ideas or bases of thinking which Thurow neither presents directly or argues for but *assumes* (and consequently must feel that his target audience is willing to assume as well).

Paragraph 17 begins with the sentence "But the decade between 25 and 35 is precisely the decade when women are most apt to leave the labor force or become part-time workers to have children." The assumption which lies behind this statement is not clear until we join it with the previously quoted first sentence of paragraph 19, "Families where women who wish to have successful careers, compete with men, and achieve the same earnings should alter their family plans and have their children either before 25 or after 35."

The assumption is that "having children" takes ten years. Since actually physically giving birth takes from ten minutes to twenty-some hours, something different must be meant. Apparently what is meant is that being a mother occupies ten years of practically full-time effort.

Again, what is assumed? It is assumed that the woman of the family bears, nurtures, and is the primary to sole caregiver until the child in question is 10 years old.

Examine the givens. What is assumed?

But we must remember additionally that for Thurow a family involves more than one child. Consequently it may be that the age of the youngest child at which a mother could consider returning to or entering full time employment could be, say, eight (although "having a child" by Thurow's definition would still take ten years).

The women of whom Thurow speaks do not absent themselves from the work force for the six months of a maternity leave, they absent themselves, in Thurow's calculations, for a decade. And this decade just *happens* to be precisely the period during which men "succeed or fail."

Exercise 4:8. In no more than three paragraphs, define the term "economically successful." Do so taking into consideration who constitutes your target audience, and write another two paragraphs defining them. Do not, in other words write simply "What economic success means to me," a conception, after all, against which no one could argue.

At this point I need to move into Thurow's assertions before returning to the gamut of his assumptions. Here are two assertions from paragraph 14. "If you are successful at age 35, you are very likely to remain successful for the rest of your life. If you have not become economically successful by age 35, you are very unlikely to do so later." How is it that we are to understand "successful" as Thurow uses it, or how should we understand "economically successful"?

How does what the writer means by "The woman of the family" to how Brady defines a "Wife" compare?

Here is Thurow on the subject, and notice that it is presented in an either/or framework. One either succeeds, as defined, or one fails. There is no middle ground. Notice further that while he has previously said "If you are successful at age 35, you are likely to remain successful. . . ," he now writes that "The decade between 25 and 35 is when *men* (not "people") either succeed or fail."

He writes that between 25 and 35 is when "lawyers become partners in the good firms, when business managers make it into the 'fast track,' when academics get tenure at good universities, and when blue-collar workers find the job opportunities that will lead to training opportunities and the skills that will generate high earnings." The next paragraph tells us that for "those who succeed, earnings will rise rapidly. For those who fail, earnings will remain flat for the rest of their lives."

What, to Thurow, is a failure? A failure is a lawyer who, while *he* may be a partner, is not a partner in a *good* firm. Being a lawyer is not enough to be a success, nor is being a lawyer who is a partner in a firm. One must be a partner in a *good* firm. One can be a business manager, but one is a failure if one does not, from that position, make it onto the "fast track" which will lead to one's becoming an executive. One can have earned a Ph.D., and be tenured, but unless one has been awarded that tenure at a *good* university, one is a failure. The blue-collar example caps the definition off with the blue-collar workers who can achieve, through skills and training opportunities, "high earnings."

Terms, and how they are defined, remain vital to understanding and analysis. Here "success" is the vital term.

What, by contrast then, is success? "High earnings" which continue to rise rapidly. What is high? Given the lawyers and academics who are considered failures, I would want to say that as Thurow considers it, it isn't a specific amount; it is instead that amount which qualifies one for membership in the most highly paid 5%, 10%, or whatever, of one's already (by ordinary standards) very highly paid or prestigious job.

The reason, he argues, that women do not occupy these jobs in sufficient numbers to bring their earnings to par with the earnings of men is that they absent themselves from the "work force" for a decade or portion thereof, while they "have children."

The audience has been told how men succeed, or, better, how men can recognize if they fit into the category "successful." Readers (who, as rhetoricians we can understand are not necessarily members of the intended audience) have been told on what basis they can consider themselves to be "failures."

What have the women who might find themselves among the readers been told? Let me pull out three paragraphs from which to formulate an answer to this question, paragraphs eight through 10.

Thurow's definition of success

> When men discriminate against women, they run into a problem. To discriminate against women is to discriminate against your own wife and to lower your own family income. To prevent women from working is to force men to work more.
>
> When whites discriminate against blacks, they can at least think that they are raising their own incomes. When men discriminate against women they have to know that they are lowering their own family income and increasing their own work effort.
>
> While discrimination undoubtedly explains part of the male-female earnings differential, one has to believe that men are monumentally stupid or irrational to explain all of the earnings gap in terms of discrimination. . . .

I now ask a question which I hope is a rhetorical question: "Would women, considered as a group, have any particular difficulty accepting the notion that men, as a group, are "irrational" *or* (you can make a choice, you don't have to go for *both* as you had to go for *all three* in the "women who wish to have successful careers, compete with men, *and* achieve the same earnings . . ." [italics mine] from paragraph 19) "monumentally stupid"?

If you would answer something like "No, most women would regard the history of the world as a record of the stupidity and irrationality of men," then you should have no difficulty with the proposition that Thurow is not addressing women. He is not talking *to* women, he is talking *about* women.

Thurow's audience

This explains why the "you" and "your" usages in the essay have either ambiguous or exclusively male referents. In other words it is possible to understand some of the uses of "you" as addressed to men *and* women. But that it is *possible* to so read them is no indication that that is their intent. Other of the uses are clearly addressed only to men (second sentence, paragraph eight). None of the uses are addressed only to women. Further, as the first sentence of paragraph 15 tells us, between

Thurow and how to understand "you"

25 and 35 is when *men* succeed or fail, not when *people* succeed or fail. I have already mentioned the precedence of "families" over women in paragraph 19.

I conclude thus that none of Thurow's rhetoric is directed to women. On the contrary, it is rhetoric that many women would find repellent, condescending, and an example of the kind of biological determinism that led Napoleon to say (of women) "Anatomy is destiny." That statement has usually been understood to mean that because women *can* bear children they will make themselves vulnerable and in need of protection supplied by men by doing so. Since Napoleon was something over five feet tall and had conquered Europe and North Africa it seems unlikely that he was using "anatomy" to refer to relative size.

If this is correct, then it follows that Thurow is talking to men. But is he talking to men in general? Look at the way he has defined success, and further the vast number of people who might think pretty well of themselves and their careers who are classified, in his terms, as "those who fail." I find it hard to argue that he is addressing any group of men outside of a distinct and exclusive minority—that is men who make a great deal more money than a very large percentage of their male contemporaries.

If this is so, what is his thesis? I would suggest that there are two. The first of these is the "literal" or stated thesis, what I would here call the "overt" thesis, which advances two possible solutions to the "problem" of the disparity in earnings between men and women, neither of which would be taken seriously by the target audience.

The "covert" thesis is unstated. I would argue that it is as follows: Because neither of the "essentially" two avenues for equalizing female earnings is practical (let alone practicable) there is no reason to inquire for other means of equalization. It comes down to what was first presented in paragraph five which then was only an assertion, as Thurow states evidence was lacking to support it. But now that evidence has been supplied (as Thurow sees it, and as he thinks his audience will agree). That is:

> Men are programmed to provide for their families economically while women are programmed to take care of their families emotionally and physically. As a result men put more effort into their jobs than women. The net result is a difference in work intensity that leads to that 40 percent gap in earnings. But there is no discrimination against women—only the biological facts of life.

Think about what target group would **warrant** these statements. Could Thurow's appeal be something like "I am talking

How we know that Thurow isn't writing to women.

Thurow's pronoun referents are either ambiguous or male.

Thurow's rhetoric would repel many women.

to you successful men, who *know* that you are neither 'irrational' nor 'monumentally stupid' (and indeed you *have* to know—Thurow the economist from MIT said so in paragraph nine). I am talking to you successful men who recognize that men who hold down the salaries of women deprive *their own families* of income, but are happy that *your* wives do not need to "have successful careers [and] compete with men. I am talking to you successful men who know that nevertheless if your wives *did* need to work you would never do anything to hold their salaries down."

"So you successful men need not feel badly about the disparity between male and female earnings, and you need not listen to those who would tell you that it is you and people like you who are responsible for that disparity. It is not your fault. So carry on."

The argument in favor of doing nothing. The argument intended to tell the audience to stay put.

Exercise 4:9. Much of the material in the preceding two paragraphs (as well as a number of others) is presented as indirect paraphrase—it is presented as if Thurow was writing them himself. Rewrite the preceding two paragraphs in the form of direct discourse.

Thurow's argument, thus, is directed to the people who have profited from the status quo and who are now responsible for maintaining that status quo. *It urges that nothing be changed.*

The argument for the status quo

Note thus that an argument does not *have* to attempt to move anyone from one position to another. It may be designed and focused on reinforcing and defending a position already held by the target audience. As rhetoricians, how do we go about deciding what group constitutes the target audience of a particular argument? We ask

1. what group will warrant the assertions made in the argument and, as a check on the viability of the first hypothesis,

2. what group or groups would not.

An assertion is a statement that is not argued for, that is not defended, but is simply stated. It depends, thus, on one of two things in order to function in an argument:

1. the agreement of the target audience with the assertion on the basis of their sharing the values of the presenter of the argument and/or

2. the willingness of the target audience to accept the assertion of the speaker on the grounds of their honoring that speaker's credentials, their willingness, that is, to recognize the speaker as an authority.

ASSERTIONS IN ARGUMENT

Assertions need only be supported if the target audience would not accept them.

As I have tried to show earlier in this chapter and at other points in the text, all arguments begin with assertions, with statements that the writer assumes will be accepted by the target audience. Those who do not find the base assertions from which the argument is built acceptable are not members of the target audience. The argument is always addressed to those who will accept the bases from which the argument is made.

Earlier these bases have been discussed as "givens," and as "surds." Behind these concepts is the essential understanding that no argument begins from a position of certainty—rather it begins from a position or positions of mutual acceptance. If you or another do not find these beginning assumptions acceptable as a rhetorician you are not allowed to conclude that the argument is flawed (although as a person you certainly may) but rather that *you* are not a part of the target audience.

"Kill the Borg" statements are usually not addressed to the Borg.

If you saw on a wall the statement "Kill the Borg," and you were (a) Borg, you could be fairly certain that you were not the target audience (you could not be completely certain, however, on the basis that part of purpose of the message might be to convince the Borg that they should leave in the interests of their own survival).

Assumptions and Assertions

Assertions are stated. Assumptions are unstated, but implicit.

Materials that I have been referring to as "assumed" do not constitute assertions (the assertion is stated, the assumption is not stated). Like assertions, however, those points which are assumed must also be acceptable to the target audience. As with an assertion, if you do not find the assumptions underlying an argument acceptable (hoping, of course, that you can detect what assumptions an argument is based on) you are again safe to conclude that you are not included in the target audience.

Here again, however, there is a wrinkle. The argument may be constructed in such a way as to obscure from clear consideration the concepts it is based on. If this is the case it may be that those who would disagree with the basic argument, but who are likely to fail to see upon what basic concepts the argument is built, may be included in the audience.

Assertions and Warrants

On this basis, let's look at a few more of Thurow's assertions in terms of the question of who might find them acceptable. In paragraph 11 Thurow writes "Back in 1939 it was possible to attribute the earnings gap to large differences in educational attainments." The "back in" with which Thurow introduces the subject is meant to suggest that 1939 was a long time ago (as in one of my favorite joke constructions "back in the winter of ought twelve"—a date which would have to be in the 11th century), or what we will be able to have fun with for a few years, "back in the 20th century."

Notice also that Thurow says educational "attainments," not educational "opportunities." Implicit here is that had women *applied* themselves at that time, or "back then," the gap would not have existed. Notice further that Thurow says "it was possible" to attribute the gap to this lack, but he does not say that this attribution would be accurate, would be correct.

Indeed he does not mean this. He means that it was *then*, as it has *now* been demonstrated to be, inaccurate. How do we know this? The second sentence of the paragraph says "the educational gap between men and women has been eliminated since World War II." That, we must presume, is how "we know this."

How "we" know, as Thurow defines the "we"

I would ask, does Shannon Faulkner, the woman hazed out of The Citadel, know this? Professor Thurow taught at MIT. I would ask if the graduate enrollment at MIT reflects the frequency with which women occur in the general population. I would ask if the Harvard law school graduates more women than men. I would ask if the contingent of Ph.D.s produced at the "best" schools of which Thurow speaks is more than 50 percent female.

[I hope that you notice that all of the questions being asked are rhetorical, that is, that I am assuming we agree on the answers.]

This is, of course, different than noticing how many women now "go to college," but just "going to college," and even graduating, does not put one in line for the "success" that Thurow speaks of. I would ask all of these questions as rhetorical questions because I know that the answers would not support Thurow's assertion. But what I have demonstrated, in terms of Thurow's rhetoric, is *that I am not a member of his target audience.* (Moreover, the school at which I am tenured would not rank among Thurow's "best.")

Who, then, would warrant Thurow's assertion that the "educational gap" has been eliminated? In that I have no evidence to the contrary, I am willing to assume that there is some educational statistic relative to, say, number of baccalaureate degrees earned that would support an equal distribution between men and women. And I could see that someone who was interested in finding a different cause for earning differential could use this to dismiss the education relative to earnings argument.

That a statistic may be accurate does not indicate that it is relevant to the subject. Its use, thus, needs to be assessed according to the rhetorical goals of the writer.

I would not accept, however, that the *number*, as such, had particular relevance to earnings potential. It is not a question of the number of degrees, it is a question of what the degrees are in. It is further a question of where the degrees are from. Those who "attain" degrees in education (predominantly women) are not big earners, and can only become big earners (or bigger earners) if they go into administration (occupied predominantly by men). How many female heart surgeons are there? Why?

So I ask again, who would warrant Thurow's statement? *My* answer is, "highly paid males who like things the way they are."

Who would warrant the statement from paragraph eight, "To discriminate against women is to discriminate against your own wife and to lower your own family income"? My answer to that would be "someone who needs to believe that he doesn't discriminate against women, but instead pays the market standard for the services which they provide." I am led to this conclusion because otherwise I must think that the reader is in the habit of accepting such undistributed terminology.

For the sake of clarity, let it be understood that the "I" in my discussion following is *consciously* identified as male. This is to say that unlike Thurow's essay it is not simply a given in this discussion that when "you" is used it refers to a male reader nor is it assumed that the position here articulated is the only possible position. (A sort of interesting light is shed on the power relationships that are part of Thurow's vision if we reverse the gender identifications. Take, as an example, the sentence "To discriminate against men is to discriminate against your own husband and to lower your own family income.")

Let us say then that were I married and my wife working full-time Thurow allows one of two possibilities: either she can work for me, or she can work for someone else. There is no possibility, in Thurow's vision, for me to work for her nor does there seem to be any possibility that she could be self-employed.

Again, the gender of the pronoun is important to an understanding of the rhetorical intent.

If she works for someone else, and I have female employees, I have no particular motivation *not* to discriminate against them. After all, in order to maximize my (and consequently my "family" income) I should only pay the market rate, which is some 40 percent less than a man would make in the same job. In other words, discriminating against women *only* lessens my "family" income if I am my wife's employer.

Let's see what happens, however, if I *am* my wife's employer. In that case, in terms of a family, what is hers is mine and vice versa. So it makes very little difference what I pay her—the "family" income remains the same (the total of her salary and mine—on the presumption that if I gave her more it would come out of the resources available for my pay).

Thurow's assumptions concerning women as employees, but not employers

What then if my wife was one of a number of women who worked for me? Would I then therefore, as Thurow, the economist, says, *not* discriminate against women? But consider, if I paid *her* more than the going rate (40 percent less than men), and this became known among my other female employees, it would seem likely to create morale problems.

So, since it doesn't make any "family" income difference anyway (my salary is higher to the exact extent hers is lower), my motivation would be *not* to increase her salary, and let whatever she did not get accrue to the "family" income through my salary. That way I could continue to pay low salaries to my other female employees without their noting that my wife was paid more than they, because, indeed, she would not be.

In the abstract the statement "to discriminate against women is to discriminate against your own wife . . ." will not hold water either as logic (where it would be dismissed as invalid) or in practical real-world experience. Abstractly, my wife is a woman, but I did not presumably marry her *because* she was a woman. Rather (understanding, of course, that marriage involves two consenting people) I married her because she was, or I thought of her as, a *special* woman.

The relation between "women" and "my wife"

Hence my act in marrying a given person is, in itself, an act of discrimination. I may very well, then, think that my wife deserves to make as much or more than any man in the same position. But I will be conscious of this only if she works for someone else. *He* (note the gender) has no motivation to give her a raise any more than I have that motivation for my own female employees (that is because to do so is to lower my own "family" income).

Let's look at this in terms of syllogistic logic. Let the terms of the syllogism be as follows:

The statement "To discriminate against women is to discriminate against your own wife" is logically insupportable and must therefore have a rhetorical purpose.

A = My Wife

B = Women

C = People Against Whom I Discriminate

The syllogism itself then would then be written,

All A is B (all members of the set "My Wife" are members of the set "Women")

No A is C (no member of the set "My Wife" is a member of the set "People Against Whom I Discriminate")

Therefore: No B is C (no member of the set "Women" is a member of the set "People Against Whom I Discriminate")

In ordinary language this would appear as: "My wife is a woman. I wouldn't discriminate against my wife. Therefore, I wouldn't discriminate against women." The conclusion to this syllogism, the argument, may or may not be true. But *if it is* true, that truth is not demonstrated by this argument. It does not follow that because I do not discriminate against my wife (or perhaps only think that I don't). I do not discriminate against women.

Try it another way. Because I find my Pekingese (Labrador, St. Bernard, Pit Bull, Weimaraner, whatever), charming does not mean that therefore I find all dogs charming. For instance: My Pekinese is charming; my Pekingese is a dog; therefore dogs are charming, is invalid. Dogs may *be* charming, but they are not charming *because* my Pekingese is charming. Translating the Thurow assertion into this form we get: My wife is not a person against whom I discriminate. My wife is a woman. Therefore I do not discriminate against women. In this case we have the following terms:

A = My Wife

B = People Against Whom I Do Not Discriminate

C = Women

The syllogism for this rendering is:

All A is B (all members of the set "My Wife" are members of the set "People Against Whom I Do Not Discriminate")

All A is C (all members of the set "My Wife" are members of the set "Women")

Therefore: All C is B (all members of the set "Women" are members of the set "People Against Whom I Do Not Discriminate")

An argument may be valid and its conclusion false, but by the same token, it may be invalid and its conclusion true. Invalidity demonstrates only that the conclusion is not true *because* of the argument, although it *may be* true for other reasons.

Neither of these syllogisms is valid. Their conclusions do not follow from the premises, so it makes no difference if the premises themselves are true or false. The truth of both conclusions remains indeterminate. The conclusions *may* be true or they *may* be false, but they are not *demonstrated* to be either by the arguments from which they are purported to follow.

To return to the original question, "Who would warrant such a statement," I would now reiterate my earlier assertion, "someone who needs to believe that he doesn't discriminate against women, but instead pays the market standard for the services which they provide." It would be, in other words, a person whose need to affirm his own behavior is strong enough to make him susceptible to accepting statements which do not bear, which cannot stand up to, examination.

Since it is the analyst's rule to give the writer the benefit of every doubt, we are bound in this case to assume that Thurow's own commitment to the conclusion he wished to reach was strong enough to blind him to the fact that the statements would not stand up. Otherwise we are driven to the conclusion that he is simply dishonest. This explanation would also account for the reading he applies to the information he presents in paragraph 12. Thurow writes:

> Some observers have argued that women earn less money since they are less reliable workers who are more apt to leave the labor force. But it is difficult to maintain this position since women are less apt to quit one job to take another and as a result they tend to work as long or longer, for any one employer. From any employer's perspective they are more reliable, not less reliable, than men.

We must remember that Thurow is not presenting this information in order to explain the differences in earnings between men and women. He is presenting it in an attempt to discredit one of the explanations which has supposedly been offered. His thinking appears to be that if he can eliminate all competing explanations, his own will remain as the only possible accurate diagnosis. Additionally, since it would appear to praise women's dependability it could be hoped that such a presentation would protect him from the charge of anti-female bias.

Who would warrant these statements and the conclusions that Thurow draws from them? I would suggest that it would be men whose experience in the workplace would bear this out—men in management positions who had worked with specific women in lower-paid positions for long periods of time.

Again, in their desire to affirm the conclusion that Thurow reaches (that the lower salaries of women is not the fault of men—that men are not responsible for the state of the market) they would be willing to ignore another conclusion which can be drawn from the very same data, and forget simultaneously that for Thurow's explanation to apply these must be the same women who (according to Thurow) absent themselves from the workplace during the vital 25- to 35-year age bracket, and who are hence all married and all mothers.

The alternative explanation that he does not draw, nor (apparently) even suspect, is that women who remain with one employer do not tend to be promoted from within, and do not, as highly paid men do, trade up by moving from company to company for higher positions carrying larger salaries. Precisely because men are larger wage earners the man's job is seen as the most important, and the woman's as "contributory" to the household income. Consequently steady employment is valued more highly than the risk taking involved in competing for more money in the endless outside searches, or taking the chance of going to one's employer with a better offer for *him* to match.

Alternative explanations are valuable to the analyst in terms of determination of target audience and warrants.

I am thus arguing that Thurow's essay is not an argument which seriously proposes alternatives (paragraph 19) but is instead an endorsement of the status quo intended to reinforce highly paid males in their current beliefs that the condition of women is only "natural," as paragraphs four and five presented.

*Thurow invokes nature as an **authorizing trope**.*

Thurow says that the problem with the statements in paragraphs four and five is that they are assertions—that no evidence is offered to support them. Then, for the rest of the essay he presents what he hopes will be taken as evidence to support them. Women, after all, have the babies, not men. Women stay home and take care of the babies, not men. This is the "Mother Nature's constant" that Gilder asserts (but leaves to Thurow the job of offering evidence for). Thurow, despite the appearance of questioning in paragraph six, agrees with Gilder totally.

Arguing for the status quo.

A point that I wish to emphasize is that argument is not always directed at affecting change. Often argument is directed *against* change, and only sometimes are those to whom the argument is directed those who *want* change. The men who constitute Thurow's target audience are happy to think that they are not "monumentally stupid or irrational" and consequently *cannot* be discriminating against women.

What does Thurow want to sell? What is his thesis? It is that the way things are is the way things must be. Who is Thurow's audience? They are those who are responsible for the way things are—men of wealth and power. What are the means employed to sell this point? The means are largely to present the appearance of a dispassionate examination of the "facts" of the economic world to show that they support the reasons offered for why things are they way they are. Thurow is not trying to make converts. He is not arguing to women that they should simply "accept their lot in life." He is, instead, preaching to the converted, but in the process of doing

Thurow preaching to the converted

it he is providing material that the converted can use to defend themselves from the constant pressure to modify the self-fulfilling current structure which is brought by those outside of the circles of wealth and power.

ARGUMENT AND THE CONVERSION EXPERIENCE

A participant in an email discussion list to which I subscribed to very recently posted the following:

> If debates aren't useful in teaching CT [Critical Thinking, the subject of the discussion list] because the focus is on winning rather than careful thinking, perhaps the Socratic method is the proper approach. Richard Paul likes to endorse such a method. Yet when we read the Socratic dialogues, almost no one learns anything. The interlocutors usually go off in a huff mad at Socrates and never change their minds. I wonder if Plato was trying to tell us something. What are the alternatives?

It occurred to me upon reading this that the question had a very particular relation to the project of this text, and to the approach to teaching writing by means of analysis rather than criticism or "response" methods. I replied to the post as follows:

The Socratic dialogue as rhetorical device rather than as philosophical vehicle

> Are not the learners those who read the dialogues? I would suggest that the implication of this is that involvement, unless one has the wisdom of S [Socrates], blunts the ability to receive the message. Those who profit most are not the participants (S. himself doesn't learn anything, but he doesn't need to), those who profit most are the "observers."

If I had the opportunity to revise this (and those of you on lists know that once you hit "send" it is unrevisable—it is instant hard copy, yours forever in exactly that form), I would not use the word "blunts," because "blunts" is metaphorically related to sharpness which, while "sharp" and "keen" are often used as metaphors for intelligence (helpful in understanding arguments) that which is sharp or keen is used to deliver, not to receive. Knives cut, penetrate, or slice, but they do not understand or receive anything. A better choice would have been "involvement . . . interferes with the ability to receive the message." I hope the relationship of this discussion to the analysis of the Thurow essay is clarified by this.

The implications of a metaphor

Thurow's intended audience is precisely "involved" in the problem, and it is precisely because of that involvement that

Thurow's argument could work with them in spite of its glaring logical deficiencies (which I hope the syllogistic analysis of why not discriminating against one's wife does not demonstrate that one does not discriminate against women makes clear).

In the so-called Socratic dialogues, the 5th century BCE Greek philosopher Socrates asks questions and is asked questions in return. The technique, as practiced by Socrates, is intended to reveal the truth by asking questions that lead to it. Or, more usually, intended to expose error.

Finding "truth" and exposing error are related, but not identical.

Typically the situation of the dialogue is that Socrates and his philosophy have been challenged by someone and Socrates proceeds, by a series of questions, to destroy the position brought to him as a challenge.

The "Socratic" method is what a great many teachers like to think they are employing when they ask students questions until they get the answer they want. Socrates, however, didn't give grades, so he had no leverage or means of bullying people until they gave him the answer that he wanted. What emerged was not supposed to be just the "right" answer, but the "right" answer which had been "there" in the head of the challenger all along and which was just waiting to be brought out.

Socrates didn't give grades.

The "interlocutors" as the email writer calls them are thus often made to look like fools by being forced through their answers to Socrates' questions to betray the positions from which they made the original challenges. Like most people who have been made fools of, they are usually not very happy about it.

In the Socratic dialogue, the interlocutor is not the target audience.

This, I believe is what the email poster had in mind when he asked "What are the alternatives," which I understand to imply that there must be a better way. I think there is, and I think that it was right in front of the poster, but he didn't notice it. The better way is the dialogue itself, which is a representation of an argument seen from the vantage point of a nonparticipant, Plato.

Plato wrote the dialogues in which Socrates is a character and the interlocutors are also characters (although, like the character Socrates, they bear the names of real historical personages). The reader of Plato's "Socratic dialogues" is the target audience. It is the reader who is to be convinced that Socrates' position is superior to that of his interlocutors.

Like Plato, the rhetorical analyst looks at arguments and "presents" them.

Consider further that the person reading Plato's account of Socrates has not publicly committed herself to any position, and so has no public investment in defending a particular position as "hers." As a result of this she is psychologically more "open," psychologically less likely to be resistant or defensive in the face of the arguments presented (or the questions asked which are intended to lead to the proper "Socratic" answer).

So is it also with the reader of Thurow. A feminist may write an outraged letter to *The New York Times* about it, but the "successful" male to whom it is targeted in defense of the status quo, need not even mention it, while feeling vindicated, deriving comfort from it, concerning his own behavior.

The Conversion Experience

Socrates is a rhetorical device used by the writer Plato in an attempt to convince his readers of the truth of the "Socratic" position, or what we now call Socratic philosophy. Meno, Euthyphro, Gorgias, and Aristophanes, regardless of whether they had real historical counterparts, are also rhetorical devices, parts of the narrative arguments by which Plato attempted to convince his audience.

What I refer to in the heading of this section as the "conversion experience" is what happens when we become convinced that there is a position which is superior to one we held earlier. My own experience is that often this happens, in effect, while we aren't watching.

Say that in January you find yourself in an argument with someone. At the time you decide to quit arguing, neither has convinced the other and (at best) you agree to disagree. Some months pass without the subject of the argument coming up again. Then in, say, September, you find yourself listening to an argument on the subject of the January argument. After listening awhile you enter the argument, but you find (if you notice) that some of the positions you are taking resemble those of the person with whom you agreed to disagree. And you may find out by the end of the argument that you have come completely over to the position you earlier rejected. I say "find out" because, if your experience is like mine, you have not been *conscious* of going through a process in which one opinion replaced another, but it would seem that you have gone through such a process nevertheless.

Written argument can do this as well. You can read an essay and find it unconvincing, but later find yourself referring to it, or parts of it, favorably. You have been through, when this happens, what I think of as the usual type of conversion experience. Very few of us, I think, when in the presence of an opposing argument, slap ourselves in the forehead and say "Oh, wow, I was completely wrong." Instead, like Socrates' interlocutors, we are likely to walk away in a huff. If we are observing an argument, however, we can avoid that personal investment, we can do what is called by members of discussion

Rhetoric and "lurking"

lists on the Internet, "lurking." We can listen without revealing ourselves until such time as we decide to jump in with some point which we consider important.

The lurking stage, and the thought processes that one goes through while in that stage, are very much like what goes on in rhetorical analysis. One attempts to understand what is going on between the people who are arguing or presenting various views. The jumping in part is something that in rhetorical analysis we don't get to, but which is the "logical" next stage. When you have seen and understood how it is done, you are prepared to do it yourself.

When you stop lurking and enter the argument you have ceased to analyze and begun to apply the tools of the rhetor.

The point of the foregoing, in terms of audience and of thesis, is that to be successful an essay does not need cause a complete conversion. It can succeed in planting an idea which later may, in memory, begin the work of the conversion.

It can succeed, like the U.S. Supreme Court justice's dissenting opinion, many years after it is written and the circumstances of the time allow it to be seen in a new way. It can succeed by simply getting a group of people who had taken something for granted previously to see that there is more than one possible view of the issue, and so on and on. The importance of the concept of target audience as that is developed in the *Glossary*, is essential. In the Socratic dialogue, that the interlocutor is not the target audience cannot be overstressed, and it is vital to remember that arguments are won by convincing people *not* to move as well as by moving people.

The subject is, as I hope I have in some way shown, almost infinitely complex. But if the analyst/writer remains aware of the questions which need to be answered in consideration of what it is that she wants to sell, to whom she wants to sell it, and by what means, she is much more likely to succeed in her writing attempts than if she does not.

Exercise 4:10. Again here my assumption is that one of the best ways to learn something is to attempt to teach it. One of the best ways of clarifying one's own understanding of something is to explain it to someone else. I have argued that sophisticated argument seldom counts on the reader simply capitulating, simply saying something like, "I give up. I was wrong. You are right." Write a five-paragraph or longer essay explaining how an argument might be constructed to produce doubt about a given subject. Do not write an essay designed to produce doubt, but write about how an essay might be constructed for that purpose.

And similarly if the analyst/writer asks of each text she encounters those same questions (what is it the writer wishes to sell, to whom, and by what means) she will soon develop a collection of modes of persuasion from which she can choose depending on her audience and what it is that she wishes to convince them of, or lead them to question, or confirm their belief in.

Every time you read an argument, you ought to try to determine why it was written in that way and not in another.

So to the reader of this text, as you proceed through the wide variety of essays which are here collected, consult the *Glossary* constantly, ask yourself constantly why did the writer choose this word instead of that, include this and exclude that, begin with the thesis, end with the thesis, or only imply the thesis, and remember finally that all written arguments come down to the same things—as Shakespeare's Hamlet said, "Words, words, words."

Every time you write something as part of an argument you ought to be able to explain why you wrote it that way and not another.

CHAPTER 5

GENERATING ARGUMENTS: TWO PARADIGMS

Thesis, target audience, Rogerian and Toulminic argument

The preceding chapters have assumed two problematics. They are, specifically, the varieties of thesis types and the potential range of target audiences. These form the bases on which the Rogerian and Toulminic arguments will be discussed. You are urged to reread the lengthy *Glossary* entry for **target audience**. Briefly, then, the analyst-now-producer of argument must determine:

1. if the thesis is overt, implied, and/or covert,

2. what reaction, among doubt, toleration, acceptance, conversion, or general or specific action, you wish to produce, and

3. if you are pursuing an immediate reaction, establishing a position for the record, or laying a foundation for future development.

STAGE ONE: DEFINE THE TARGET AUDIENCE

Your first step should be to outline the range of possible positions in relation to the subject you will be arguing about. The diagram presented in the *Glossary* is one way to approach the matter.

It represents the range of possible positions in *any* defined position on a specific subject. Try to define the extremes in relation to your subject. Remember that there may, in *fact*, in *the real world* in relationship to a particular question, be no one who actually occupies either of the two positions. The diagram is theoretical—it is intended to describe the range of *possible* opinion not simply the real world range as you know it.

You can have fun with this consideration by trying to dream up what the *most extreme* position on *any* particular question might be. I had fun, for instance, constructing the extreme for the "I will not consume another life form" position. Flowers surely die, and so also must vegetables. So how does one know when one's rice is dead? After all, if one eats it before it is dead, one is consuming seeds, which could reproduce, and is thus participating in multiple deaths. Thus, one extreme of this position would be held by people who had arrived at this conclusion and were in the process of starving themselves to death.

At the other extreme would be those people who consumed living tissue that represented to them the greatest vitality, that contained the most life. One would be a cannibal. Who consumed athletes. While they were still alive. Slightly to the left, or right, depending on which end of the diagram the extreme as assigned, would be the extreme sushi aficionado who eats her sashimi cut from the body of a living fish, or the fresh veggies nut who insists on running to the boiling water with the just picked ear of corn.

One might then proceed to define the middle, the "what" and undecided range. Then the vegans, the lacto vegans, the lacto-ovo vegans, and etc.

> Be aware that in graphic representation, two-dimensional diagrams having a right and a left and an up and a down can block understanding because of religious/political/social/economic responses to a presumed "symbolic" association with the "location" of a given idea.
>
> As "higher" and "lower" suggest value judgments, so "right" and "left" suggest ideological positions.
>
> Any "extreme" position on any question can be, and frequently is, described as "insane," or the equivalent, "fanatical."

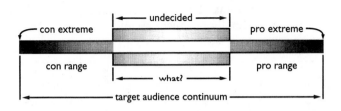

So now that you have indicated how to go about defining a range, you have to decide what it is that you want to sell. Are you trying to protect the beef cattle industry from the likes of Oprah Winfrey (who was sued by cattle raisers for saying, on air, that beef was bad for you)? Are you promoting more protein in school lunches? Do you want to shut down the veal industry because the idea of killing baby animals is repugnant?

Your next step, after having constructed the continuum, would be to consult it to see what group you would not only just "like" to convince, but who you might have some possibility of doing so.

In an ideal situation, in a world where arguments are won by reasoning from self-evident principles (see Chapter 3), you might attempt to influence everyone but those who are already in agreement with you. You could even include those who agree but who are reluctant to act on that agreement.

However, in the real world, it is unlikely, on the face of it, that the right extreme of the undecided range would respond positively to being classified with the extreme left (those at the boundary of the con classification). Consider the limited number of arguments, if indeed any arguments, which would appeal to all members of this hypothesized "target" group.

Given the range of possible positions on any given subject, the skilled rhetor is unlikely to address a large segment of the target audience spectrum.

You would then certainly be best advised to make no attempt to appeal to the extreme of the con group, and as the *Glossary* notes, may even decide to use *not* arguing to them, but deliberately insulting them, as a rhetorical tool (see the concluding paragraph of the Ivins essay in the Readings section).

Again, the principle that you need to bear in mind is that a skilled writer who is committed to furthering whatever particular sociopolitical agenda she supports writes *with a specific range of readers in mind*. Your effectiveness as a writer will be directly related to what that portion of the audience you think you can persuade would be willing to **warrant**.

Every spectrum differs from every other. Each must be defined on its own terms.

Remember also that each subject will differ from any other in the range of beliefs held by the parties to the quarrel (or "argument," in polite terms). In the case for abortion rights, for instance, *all* parties are agreed that abortion is not a good. What is at issue is at what point, if any, is it permissible to interfere in the process which finally produces a child.

Exercise 5:1. Understanding the range and complexity of target audiences is essential to the rhetor who is designing her argument for the maximum effect on the targeted group. Find an issue (perhaps one that you are personally concerned with) and describe the spectrum of opinion of that subject. Your subject could be as small as (say) "football," or as large as (say) "race," but try thinking it through to delineate and describe the full range of possible opinion.

Date as Related to Target Audience

All arguments, as Chapter 3 argued, exist in a particular historical place/time—they are in a language characteristic of a particular geographical location (country) and presented at a specific time. This may appear to be stating the obvious, but even if it is obvious it needs to be clearly laid out.

I first began to teach the 1993 Molly Ivins essay just mentioned in the same year that it was published. At that time nearly all of the five-hundred-plus people I lectured to in that year recognized the reference to "Tailhook" in the third paragraph. Roughly half recognized the J. Edgar Hoover mentioned in the first paragraph (Director of the Federal Bureau of Investigation from 1924 until his death in 1972, or 48 years). Currently less than a dozen recognize the former, and roughly the same number recognize the latter.

In order to analyze Ivins' rhetorical intentions for those references the current audience needs to have the information supplied to them that the 1993 audience had in its memory. The principle is the same as that discussed in Chapter 3 concerning the situation of the immediate audience to the 1946 "Politics and the English Language." And as the range of attitudes toward Communism differed in England in 1946 from the range of attitudes toward the former USSR and Cuba in the present-day United States, so also does the range of attitudes, and particularly their public expression, differ from 1993 to the widespread horror in response to the news of the young gay man tied to a rail fence and beaten to death in 1998.

Exercise 5:2. It is a commonplace of the "information" age that information not only wants to be free but that it multiplies beyond any possible control. Find a subject that was important to you five years ago, and imagine that you are writing about it 20 years in the future. Identify those references that you feel would need to be explained to your future audience and why you think this is likely.

Consider then, in this regard, Ivins' fourth and 13th paragraphs. In paragraph 4 she writes

> "I have nothing against gays," my mother is fond of saying, "I just wish they'd stay in the closet." But we all know by now—or should—that that state of affairs was cruel and unjust and led to terrible abuses.

Always remember that because a (target audience spectrum) population division, or category, is being talked about does not imply that it is being talked to.

Ivins, it would seem fairly clear, *is not talking to her mother*, but she is likely talking to people who share her mother's attitude.

Important here, however, is that the people who share her mother's opinion are not necessarily her mother's age. There are many people who think in the same way that their parents do, not because that is the way their parents think, but because it is somehow "right." I stress the "somehow." Typically we continue in a belief system because it has not been suggested to us that "up to date" people, "cool" people, no longer think that way.

By attributing the attitude to her mother she "dates" it. One's mother's attitudes (if they are presented in this way) are, after all, those of the previous generation, they are at least "old fashioned," and may well be regarded as completely untenable.

So when Ivins writes "we all know by now" that "all" does not include her mother (she says her mother "is" fond of saying, not "was" fond of saying). If you are one of those who share her mother's attitude you have here the opportunity to change your mind, even if you had not heretofore thought of that attitude as "cruel," or "unjust," or leading to "terrible abuses."

In paragraph 13 she writes, "I suppose some people will still feel entitled to hate gays. As the psychiatrists have been telling us, hating them seems to be a function of being afraid that you might be one yourself."

Considering that the word "phobia" means an abnormal fear (hydrophobia, or rabies, is so named because one of its symptoms is an abnormal fear of water), Ivins links hatred and fear of homosexuality without having to use the term "homophobia." It would seem clear that she is not writing to those whose feelings about homosexuality involve hatred since she cites psychiatric opinion which would likely result in vehement, if not violent, denial from those people.

What, after all, would enrage an individual who hates homosexuals more than being accused of being one? What, then, would be the point of this paragraph? I suggest that by holding the extreme up to ridicule she provides information and opportunity to those *close* to that extreme that might lead them to disassociate themselves from it.

There are conflicting conventions regarding the "age" of a belief system. "How people used to think," or how "the older generation thinks" should be compared, for instance, to the expressions "experience has taught us," and "the wisdom of the ages."

Exercise 5:3:   Describe a situation in which you write insultingly about a group of people in an attempt to influence your reader to disassociate herself from that group. Then write a paragraph of an essay that might employ such a rhetorical technique.

This argument, then, is not addressed to *all* readers/speakers of the language but to the particular subgroup that will warrant the central assumptions of the presentation of the argument. (Please note here that I did not write "the central assumptions of *the argument*"—the writer, given that she is finally not talking to people who feel as she does, has no choice but to guess at what those people to whom she is speaking will respond to, and do assume, and will warrant, which is why I wrote "of the *presentation* of the argument" rather than the beliefs of the writer of the argument.)

For the writer of argument who is a student of persuasion, as was noted in Chapter 3, there is no "general audience." In the production of argument, our variation on Toulmin's concept of the **warrant** provides an excellent tool not only for identifying another writer's target audience, but for making decisions about how to approach your own target audience. If you write, "God did not intend for us to 'tolerate' homosexuals and He says so very clearly in the Bible . . . ," you have excluded the entire range of people who do not accept the Bible as the word of God as well as those who believe that the New Testament *replaces* rather than elaborates the strictures of the Old Testament.

> How to identify the warrants of a particular argument.

Degrees of Persuasion

This moves us into a further complication related to what I referred to as "degrees of persuasion" at the beginning of this discussion. It may be your goal to move people from the right range of the opposed into the range of the undecided, and to that end you may pose questions intended, not to convince those opposed that you are right, but instead to lead them to doubt the correctness of their opposition.

We are trained into the **either/or** sort of thinking, which leads to the idea that those who are not our friends and allies are therefore our enemies. If, however, by the introduction of doubt I can prevent a group from aiding my enemy, my cause is advanced.

> Our variation on Toulmin's warrant is a valuable tool in adjusting your argument for the targeted audience.

Why this is so is not immediately apparent, but consider, say, that you are a member of a 25-person committee that is going to take a vote. Prior to the presentation of your argument, eight are in favor of the position you wish to support, 7 do not want to get involved, and 8 are opposed. If you are able to construct your argument in such a way that it can move *one* person from the opposed into the group who do not want to get involved, your position wins the vote.

In other words, to effect *change* with an argument one does not have to make converts. One needs only to introduce sufficient doubt to keep the weakest of the opposition from participating in opposing the argument (like *not* going to the polls, or abstaining).

Exercise 5.4. Using the same numbers as in the example, supply a subject about which a committee might be deliberating and describe reasons committee members might have for holding one of the four possible positions: 1) voting for, 2) voting against, 3) voting abstain, 4) not voting.

From this perspective, I hope to make the point that the rhetor particularly interested in accomplishing her sociopolitical agenda will realize that one can "win" an argument, politically speaking, without "converting" anyone. All that is necessary is to introduce doubt where there was previously (even mild) conviction.

Some arguments, in other words, are designed

> Arguments can be intended to cause doubt as well as to result in belief.

1. to drive people away from a position,

2. to attract people to a position, and/or

3. to induce those who already hold an agreeing position to hold it more tightly or to take some specific action.

Time

Finally we come to the "time" complication (as opposed to the "date" complication involving the time proximity of the availability of particular information). U.S. Supreme Court Justices who have voted with the minority often write a dissenting opinion.

> Arguments are seldom, if ever, all-or-nothing propositions.

Why? They have, after all, lost the argument—they have been unable to convince a sufficient number of their fellow justices of the correctness of their position to secure a majority vote. I suggest that they do so because they recognize that court decisions never take place outside of particular political and historical circumstances (the place/time mentioned earlier), and that these circumstances, inevitably, change. Consequently, what is a losing position today may turn out to be a winning position in the future.

The argument, if you will, is not written to convince now, but to become an item of record to solidify the position of its supporters toward that time in the future when the circumstances will allow another perspective, and in this particular application, when the membership of the court changes.

Description to Prescription (You Can't Win Them All but You Can Improve Your Odds)

I hope it is clear by now that if you have come to some conclusions about how a writer you are analyzing is trying to convince her audience of whatever her thesis is, *the techniques that have been recognized are, for the analyst, deprived of a great deal of their rhetorical appeal.* That is, when you understand how someone is trying to influence you, your ability to accept or reject that approach is improved.

It is hoped, then, that you realize the impossibility of this text (or any other) presenting "the best" way to write successful arguments, any more than, as argued in the first chapter, there is a best color for a spray can of insecticide.

Assuming that, as has been set out above, you have defined your target audience with all possible specificity, the next steps are as follows.

STAGE TWO: REFINE THE THESIS

1. Determine if there is a secondary and/or tertiary audience.

2. Determine in what circumstances your target audience will interact with the text.

   Then define what result you wish to achieve:

1. Determine if this desired result is isolated or part of a progression pointed to a specific longer term goal.

2. Determine what time frame you wish to achieve the result within.

Among the reasons for defending a losing position is that the claim the writer may establish to being consistent, and therefore dependable, may be worth more in terms of accumulating ethos than a specific victory.

The target audience is seldom a single person, but even in the event that it is, it cannot be assumed that that person will feel about and react to all things in the same way at all times. The writer needs, therefore, to consider when and how the target audience will interact with the text. If it is to a single person, is timeliness an issue? Does it require "urgent" action? Is she going to keep the text, and perhaps look at it again?

Is it possible that the recipient will send it forward to someone else, or to a group? Is it part of your strategy that if it is not responded to by the individual that you will send it forward to another individual or a group? Does the recipient know that? Would the recipient consider the text differently (more carefully, for instance) if she knew it would go forward unless she responds?

Is this going to be read in a stack of mail? In a stack of memos? As email? In the morning paper? In a professional journal? In a magazine? Will it be archived? How will it be indexed?

When and how will the audience interact with the text?

Aiming Too High

The most basic, elemental, and incorrect view of the purpose of written argument is that it is to reform the opinions of "mankind," or, humanity as we would now call it. The view assumes, in a rough way, that the writer becomes, somehow or another, possessed of the truth. Because, the truth is a good thing, what the writer finds herself impelled to do is to show the rest of the world the error of its ways in the full belief in the reasonableness of humanity and its capacity to tell truth from error.

This is the kind of thinking that led the to-be-poet Percy Shelley to publish, while an Oxford undergraduate, a tract titled *The Necessity of Atheism* in the apparent expectation that the Church of England would close down immediately. He was 19 and he was, of course, expelled. Oxford's charter, after all (and which Shelley knew well), was for the training of clergy.

Motive is always problematic.

We cannot know Shelley's motives. He may have "in fact" wished to be expelled, or he may have had other rebellions in mind. Nevertheless, the plain-spoken, the free-spoken, the "blunt," who "say what they mean, and mean what they say," to cite one of the more rhetorically and philosophically naïve commonplaces, have generally short careers as opinion makers.

Writers who simply "say what they mean and mean what they say" have short careers.

As rhetorical modes, of course, these approaches may be employed, but they are more likely to be listened to if they are delivered from positions of power [recognized ethos, respected social position, tenure, etc.] rather than from the position of an undergraduate who has just encountered the truth.

Given the ways that we interact with written language, as the previous chapters have argued, we are responsive to those positions that are, in one manner or another, not totally destructive of positions we currently occupy. The glossary's discussion of brainwashing points to a theoretical circumstance in which this principle may not hold—that is, where the arguer holds total power over the arguee—as would be the situation in a prison camp under martial law. But the person writing argument so seldom occupies this position as to render it inconsiderable (see point 2 in the discussion of Rogerian argument following).

Now, for illustration, let's assume that Shelley, as much of his later writing indicates, felt that the postulation of a supreme being was destructive of the larger happiness of humanity. Let us then further assume (which his later writing does *not* support) that his primary medium was prose as opposed to poetry. If these were the case, he might have approached the question, not as an undergraduate, but as an Oxford don, or as John Ruskin did, as a graduate publishing a long text considering alternative views. He might have approached it "**academically**," as, that is, a "**disinterested**" observer.

Had Shelley done this his views might, as a consequence of his approach, have been published and considered as "serious," and "interesting," and even "profound." He might have, as did John Ruskin, whose attitudes are so important to our present ways of thinking as to be invisible (in that they have become part of our general "givens," our overall "warrants"), have become an author of best-sellers on the subject of atheism as a necessity.

Ruskin, like the later Shelley (Shelley drowned at 39), felt that he wrote not for his time, but for the ages. The two of them could, with Whitman, have said "whether I come to my own today or in ten thousand or ten million years,/ I can cheerfully take it now, or with equal cheerfulness I can wait." I think it is probably safe to say that most of you have a somewhat more compressed agenda.

The question of the timing of the desired effect is nevertheless real. Let us consider, as mentioned earlier in this chapter, the motivations of a Supreme Court justice who writes a dissenting opinion, or better, who is chosen by those justices dissenting from the majority, and prevailing, opinion, to compose the statement of their dissent.

The argument, from some perspectives, is over. The vote has been taken. The minority, however, are fully cognizant that what they are writing relates to something with a much longer shelf-life than a single Supreme Court opinion—they are writing arguments which may in the future provide fuel for overturning the current majority opinion. The writer of the dissenting opinion has in all likelihood a shorter time frame in mind than did Whitman, but her vocabulary and citations will nevertheless be conditioned by presumptions concerning the postulated future audience.

To put it simply, I will write differently for an audience that I believe will read my words tomorrow than I will for one which is likely to read them five, or ten, or fifteen years from the present. Major portions of this text are being composed in the aftermath of Special Prosecutor Kenneth Starr's report having been submitted to Congress. I have no idea if the terminology and names associated with it will be recognizable in five years, so I must write *according to that lack of knowledge*. I must write as if the name "Starr" may be unfamiliar to my audience.

We move then to the largest generalizations that can be made about written argument. Bear in mind that arguments cannot be generated simply on the basis of *any* given generalized formulae. The formulae presented, thus, represent outlines of organizational structures from which the person constructing a written argument can choose. Moreover, these are formulae from which she can vary, on which she can improvise, and which she can incorporate to whatever extent she feels appropriate. The only limitation is that in each case her decisions should be considered in the context of the hypothetical response of the target audience.

All rhetorical goals are limited, compromised, and conditional.

TOULMINIC ARGUMENT

There are two popular paradigms for consideration and classification of argument. The first is important, for our purposes, because it proposes a methodology for the composition of argument that differs from the classical Aristotelian notion that argument is a balance among appeals to character, reason, and emotion (*Ethos*, *Logos*, and *Pathos*).

The writer should interrogate her text concerning who the intended reader is, when the response is expected, and what the desired outcome is.

Toulmin's approach proposes, as this text has throughout, that audiences are convinced according to certain conventions of evidentiary proceedings in which something less than, or at least other than, logical "proof" prevails. In the Toulminic approach the proceedings are modeled on the U.S. courtroom and the procedures for the presentation of evidence toward the specific end of establishing guilt or uncertainty.

It is essential here that you recognize that the finding of "not guilty" *is not a finding of innocence*—it is rather the finding that the evidence presented, given the *presumption* of innocence, is insufficient to *demonstrate beyond a reasonable doubt* that innocence is out of the question.

"Not guilty" does not mean "innocent" in a U.S. court of law.

The advantage to this approach, from the perspective of this text is that it frankly accepts the idea that the success of arguments is relative to the presuppositions of the audience (jury). The disadvantage is that, given the model of the courtroom, certain conditions are built in which are not the case in the world outside the courtroom, the world in which what I have called real-world argument exists.

That the courtroom is not the real world, I would hope Charles Manson, Larry Flynt, and O. J. Simpson have demonstrated. (I write aware that most of you will recognize the Manson name only in regard to Marilyn Manson, whose name derives from the original, whether his audience recognizes it or not, and that if you know Larry Flynt it is most likely as the character played by Woody Harrelson opposite Courtney Love playing Althea Gibson, Flynt's wife.) The argument we deal with here is real world argument, and that limits the usefulness of the Toulmin method. But, as the glossary indicates, it provides the pedagogy (teaching theory) of argument with a number of useful terms and concepts. The following précis outlines the essentials of the approach to familiarize the reader with the terminology of Toulminic pedagogy.

Claim   From Toulmin's perspective each argument has a claim. This term is more or less equivalent to what we have so far referred to, and complicated, in relation to the traditional notion of a thesis. What renders Toulmin's model problematic for us is that claims, outside the courtroom, are frequently not clear-cut, and are not, at the least, the typical beginning point for any but the most simplistic of arguments (A is true).

> Toulmin's claim equates to "thesis," but thesis is frequently not obvious.

Exercise 5:5.   Using either the Brady/Syfers essay in Chapter 1 or an essay of your own choosing, write five paragraphs illustrating that in real-world argument, what Toulmin calls the "claim" is problematic.

Qualifier   Again following the Toulmin categories, the "claim" may or may not be "qualified." (A is true, *except* when z, or y, or . . .), but in any case, "qualifier" is an essential term to the pedagogy.

Rebuttal   The "rebuttal" is the anticipation of a counterargument, that might be brought by the defense (if you are the prosecution) or the prosecution (if you are the defense).

Data   Data are the pieces of information offered in support of the claim. Briefly, A is true because of c, d, e, and/or f. C, d, e, and/or f constitute the "data," "support," or "back-up."

Warrant   Toulminic pedagogy uses the term "warrant" slightly differently than it has been used in the glossary and in the text in general. For Toulmin, the "warrant" amounts to the content of the unstated but assumed attitude shared between the writer and the audience.

Backing   This comprises something of a difficulty in that if a warrant *is* a warrant it does not require "backing." In Toulmin, however, "backing" is a kind of assurance offered to those who (because the warrant [Q] is "assumed") may not be clear about why it is that they believe Q and are thus potentially vulnerable to an attack on Q.

> **Exercise 5:6.** If you are having difficulty applying glossary terms to a given piece of argument writing, select three short essays from the readings and label each paragraph according to the Toulmin vocabulary presented here.

Look back at Chapter 4, particularly at Thurow's sixth paragraph. A quick read might suggest that this is a "qualification," but closer examination in the context of the remainder of the article indicates that it points back to paragraph 5, which contains, although it doesn't look like it at first view, the "claim."

> **Exercise 5:7.** Write at least a paragraph delineating what you take to be the warrants each writer hopes the reader agrees to. It will be important, however, to do so sensitively rather than by rote, bearing in mind, for instance, that the "claim" may be implied rather than stated, and that what may appear on quick reading as data offered in support of the claim, might, on more careful consideration, be better classified as part of the rebuttal.

Toulmin, as indicated, can be a valuable tool in a beginning study of argument. His paradigm is particularly important as an antidote to the notion that argument proceeds on the basis of logical constructs that we can diagram deductively and through which we can arrive at some truth.

Moreover, the approach is extremely useful as a kind of grid to overlay on a planned courtroom presentation, or committee presentation, or within a debate. It is helpful in all situations where there are rules of procedure, a defined audience, and, in some form or other, a judge or judges to pronounce when the rules have been followed and when they have not.

The practical uses of Toulminic argument

Finally, however, Toulmin will not supply us with what the second paradigm does. The Rogerian paradigm gives us a sophisticated view of the psychological importance of overcoming resistance in the progress of an argument (which ties in with an emphasis on the importance of ethos). It does so specifically as ethos involves the writer avoiding the appearance of a stake in the outcome of the argument beyond arriving at a working and temporary solution.

ROGERIAN ARGUMENT

Carl Rogers recognized two things about the resolution of conflict (which, in a large framework, is what argument seeks to accomplish). Although he never specifically put it in this way, at the base of his position are two concepts.

1. Psychological structures are essentially conservative, in the full sense of the word. We try to conserve, to "save," to "maintain" as much of the construct with which we relate to the world as we can. We seek to maintain that view by means of devices that have little to do with logic, and when they do involve logic, they involve logic used to protect that conservative position.

We tend to resist positions which constitute a direct threat to our current thinking.

2. Psychological structures must be interactive on at least two levels—the individual, and the individual in relation to a social unit. The built-in presumption here is that the psyche is not a unity. It has parts, and the relationship among these parts can break down. The individual can, in other words, be in conflict with herself (what this means is that one "part" of the construct which we call the self is in conflict with another "part," and the parts, as it were, can find themselves in a state where communication no longer occurs). And if this conflict is severe enough, the individual will no longer be able to maintain herself at a sufficient level of integrity to interact with the pertinent social unit with which it must interact to survive (family, profession, ethnicity, sexual preference, nationality).

1. Psychological structures are essentially conservative.

> **Exercise 5:8.**   The preceding paragraph is both dense and abstract. Write three or more paragraphs intended to explain the paragraph by the use of examples to someone who has not been through this text.

2. Psychological structures must be interactive.

Given this description of the psyche and its operation, one is led to the position that life, quite simply, is conflict, and the successful life is in the constant process of satisfactorily (albeit temporarily) resolving those conflicts. Argument, from this perspective, is the process by which conflict is resolved, if, and when, it is resolved.

In the anticipation of resistance to my next statement, I ask you to suspend your doubt for a long enough time to see what follows from this assumption—that there can be an "expert" who is capable of knowing, on the basis of a relatively brief interaction, more about us than we know about ourselves. (Some people find this claim outrageous, given particularly that we have spent the totality of our lives with ourselves.)

Rogers was a practicing psychotherapist. He dealt professionally with people we would now call dysfunctional, and like Freud and many other analysts, he came to conclusions about the apparently functional based on his experience with the dysfunctional.

Ethos is of primary concern for the psychoanalyst in that for the therapy she provides to have the desired outcome, the patient (client) must trust her and must trust that her activities are in the patient's (client's) best interest. The practicing analyst here has many advantages over the writer of argument. Unlike the writer of argument, she has repeat access to the target. And although both represent an investment of time, she represents an investment of both time and money, indicating that at some level the patient/client has already made the decision to trust her. That is, in the therapeutic relationship much of the resistance that the writer inevitably encounters is already overcome.

The importance of ethos in a psychological transaction

The Rogerian model suggests, however, that the writer can seek to acquire the ethos of the therapist, who is, after all, finally interested in "health," "wholeness," and, if we cannot say "happiness," we can at least say "the minimizing of unhappiness."

The Rogerian approach says, at the outset, "there is conflict here." It does not say "there is conflict here because Republicans (or Democrats), fundamentalists (or libertarians), etc., etc." are *wrong* and the only way to resolve the conflict is to isolate them or get them straightened out. Instead it says, or purports to say, that conflict is counterproductive. It says that the group in conflict resembles the condition of the dysfunctional individual. Conflict, in other words, constitutes a problem.

As Rogers' essay "Dealing With Breakdowns in Communication" (see Readings) to which you have been referred earlier approaches the matter, the vital ingredient in resolving the conflict is the ability of the disputants to put understanding before judging. Failing this, the professional, the psychotherapist, in whom the parties have invested, can suggest, and even insist on as a component of the therapy that each of the antagonists restate the other's position in terms that would be acceptable to the person whose position is being restated. The parties to a dispute, in that they have sought the help of the therapist, have implied a willingness to seek resolution of some sort.

Understanding versus judging in Rogerian argument

The Writer and the Therapist

The writer of argument, in this circumstance, has a tremendous advantage over the therapist—she may employ all of the anxiety-reducing, defense-lowering techniques in the knowledge that the parties to the conflict finally do not need to be reconciled in order for the writer to achieve her rhetorical goal. This is to say, the parties to the conflict *may very well not constitute her target audience*, or it may be that only the right or left wings of the party's membership would be a portion of the target audience. The Rogerian approach is employed as a rhetorical tool that allows the writer to present herself as a partisan to none of the conflicting positions but as a person interested in a lessening of tension, conflict, dysfunction, and in the population at large.

As I have defined the essential elements of the Rogerian approach considered as rhetorical device, they are as follows:

1. The writer presents evidence supporting the existence of a conflict, which conflict is in some way injurious to the health of the polis, of, as it were, the body politic, the "people." *The burden on the writer, here, is to establish that a resolution to the conflict is preferable to continuance of the conflict.*

2. The writer presents the positions of the major parties to the conflict in language that avoids the appearance of judgment. At this point, if it is possible to present a position in such a way that an adherent to that position would say "Yes, that is a fair statement of where we stand," all the better, but that may not be possible. Vital to the endeavor,

The therapist is committed to the client. The writer is committed to the thesis.

however, is that the presentation of the position does not reveal any overt hostility and would appear to, at the least, be trying to be "fair."

As an example, or as a pair of simultaneous examples, let us say that one of the parties to the conflict is the Ku Klux Klan, or, that it is the American Nazi Party. I can present the positions of these organizations, as it were, in ways that look "fair," in the full realization that the resolution to the conflict will not lie in finding a ground of accommodation between liberal and fascist positions. The point here is important enough to be worth spending some time on.

That position which is most satisfactory may not be the solution pleasing to the largest number.

It is sometimes assumed that the Rogerian approach automatically implies that accommodation is preferable *in any case* to a continuation of conflict, and there are aspects of the approach which could lead one to think that the position implies this. However, the "full Rogerian," as it were, does not entail this. It entails only a "fair" presentation of the positions surrounding the question at issue in an attempt to find the most satisfactory solution available according to current knowledge. The "most satisfactory" does not mean that which is pleasing to the largest number nor does it mean that which is acceptable to the least tractable.

3. The writer confesses, or implies the confession, that she has no special, or privileged information, or wisdom, or problem solving ability. Instead, she is a concerned citizen, a person trying to solve a problem in the way fairest to all parties, and that whatever position emerges as the "best solution" to the conflict, is based on limited information, limited knowledge, and because the knowledge is limited, it could become obsolete at any time given any new data.

4. Given that, the writer presents what she wants to appear, to look like, what seems to her the best position to take, at the moment. Involved, built in, is the understanding that information may emerge which will render the position untenable. It is further to be understood that if such information did emerge she would be open to it as presenting an opportunity to, by considering it, occupy a better position in relation to the question at hand.

The Rogerian, like the Socratic, expresses a willingness to come to another conclusion in the face of new knowledge.

Rogers' approach lends itself beautifully to this latter-day Socratic ploy. (Socrates was asked what penalty he would pay if, in the argument to follow, he did not emerge the victor. His charming, disarming, and ironic reply was that he would pay the penalty of the ignorant, which was to learn from the wise.)

In skeletal outline then, the elements of the Rogerian rhetorical approach are:

1. presentation of problem,
2. presentation of positions relative to the problem,
3. confession of fallibility,
4. presentation of a qualified and temporal solution in the anticipation of a correction when further data emerge.

Using the ethos of humility and concern.

The approach can be extremely powerful in its employment of the ethos of humility and concern. Further, it manifests in the depth of its presentation of conflicting positions a concerned, informed, knowledgeable, and nonpartisan intelligence interested, after all, not in one's own position, but interested in the best answer possible for all concerned.

Problems and Qualifications

What has been made here out of Carl Rogers' formulation may very well be something that he personally would have disavowed. His interest was in developing a therapeutic method which he thought might, with more funding for research, even be employed in problem solving among huge political entities like nations.

From the perspective of the post-modern rhetorician, however, his "social sciences" approach is philosophically naïve. Rogers never indicates that he had the least doubt about his own ability to be emotionally uninvolved, or, for that matter, recognized that distinguishing between **emotion** and intellect is hugely problematic. The post-modern rhetorician defines the "objectivity"—which Rogers takes for granted as actually achievable—as a rhetorical strategy.

While the Rogerian approach, at least as it has here been defined, is more important to us than the Toulminic, the Toulminic gives us the invaluable notion of the warrant with which the Rogerian does not deal. Rogers assumes that there can be a "reasonable" approach to a given subject, and that "objectivity" is possible.

To come around to an initial point of development, what Rogerian approaches recognize, that is to say, what the recognition builds into the structure of the form, is resistance to change. Rogers' words are, precisely, "The risk of being changed is one of the most frightening prospects most of us can face."

When the Rogerian approach succeeds as rhetoric it does so because it takes into account that essential "conservatism" that Rogers acknowledges, that tendency to defend our current opinions as if they were in some way bought and paid for at great personal cost and represent our integrity.

Rogers knew that most people (and perhaps all people) have, as Oscar Wilde said, the courage of the opinions of others. Wilde says, thus, that most people will reply, when asked what "they" think, with the opinions they have inherited. I would suggest that Rogers knew too that if these people are presented with the opinions of "other" others in a form where they can act toward them in a "fair" and even-handed manner, much of the threat that those opinions would otherwise represent is lessened or removed.

The Rogerian Ethos

The centrally important aspect, thus, of the Rogerian approach, is the ethos it allows the writer to asume—specifically, the ethos of the non-partisan, of that person who is outside of party, religious, racial, ethnic, or gender loyalties, who is above pettiness, who is considerate of others, and who is modest about her own abilities. Who is, in short, a peacemaker who may be accorded all of the positive emotions associated with that activity.

Where the Rogerian approach is inappropriate

As intimated above, and discussed earlier, it seems evident that there are a number of political, religious, and "racial" positions that will not accept "understanding," but that demand, instead, capitulation. If I believe that God (however defined) speaks directly to "my people" (however defined), it is unlikely that having a Rogerian argument present how and what I believe in a way acceptable to me will therefore promote harmony between me, as one of the "chosen," and those whom my "chosen" position identifies as anywhere from less important to candidates for annihilation re ethnic/genetic/racial "cleansing."

Rhetoric Is Value Neutral
From the perspective of analytic rhetoric, *all positions*, including the Rogerian, are suspect. Rhetoric, on the other hand, does not constitute, from its perspective, a position. It is in the final analysis only a methodology for persuasion. And it is equally available to *all* positions, without regard to their virtue or (to put it another way) without consideration of them as evil, relatively or not. The tools, that is to say, are available to sexism, fascism, racism, and revealed religion as well as to truth, beauty, democracy, and the "American Way."

This does not say, however, that analytic rhetoric lives outside of warrants. On the contrary its central warrant is a "faith" that, given a knowledge of the methodologies used to persuade it in any particular direction, that entity which we may think of as human consciousness will, overall, make the best decision. The assumption underlying this, the "warrant," is huge. It warrants that any position which assumes that a given group which thinks of itself as possessed of "the truth" constitutes a danger to a particular definition of "humanity." It warrants that the best system is one that presumes that all systems are concepts, and are vulnerable therefore to other concepts which increase liberty, or, to use the more politically defensible term, choice.

Given the echoes that have built up around the word "choice" in the abortion wars, this usage should be clarified. Despite Michael Jackson, and despite surgical intervention, one cannot (for the time being) alter the genetic make-up of a post-partum being. One does not, at the moment, even with surgical and hormonal intervention, have the opportunity to "choose" one's sex, or one's "race."

However, we do have a "choice" as to what membership in a given gender or "race" means. We are free, that is, to conclude that the range of differences *among* the members of one supposed "race" is larger than the differences *between* the two sets which presumably constitute separate races.

Argument that favors this position, given the principles of analytic rhetoric, is favored over argument that is based on a notion of inherent genetic superiority (whatever that might "mean") for a given group. The point, that is, from the perspective of analytic rhetoric, is that race and gender are *social constructs insofar as they are recognized and insofar as they are held to indicate significant difference.*

> Our rhetorical assumption is that knowledge of the means used to persuade will allow the informed to make the best decision. Language (hence argument) is seen as a creator of meaning.

Exercise 5:9.   After reading the Rogers essay in the Readings section of the text, outline how a Rogerian therapist might deal with a conflict between a couple, one of whom believed abortion was a woman's right and the other of whom felt it was a sin.

Exercise 5:10.   Now write an outline of an essay which uses a Rogerian argument to propose a solution to the conflict between these two positions.

The Full Rogers

The "full" compared to the "partial" Rogers

This, of course, constitutes an ideology as surely as Dr. Rogers' system does. If, however, all of this can be accepted as, as it were, the nature of the beast, there are still important things to be said about how Rogerian argument is and can be employed in writing with persuasion as its end. We have defined the characteristics of what I could call the "full Rogers." But there is the "partial Rogers" as well.

Any essay that opens with a non-rhetorical question participates in the "Rogerian."

A "partial Rogers" is any use of a single or of any combination of the previously delineated four components. The Thurow essay analyzed in Chapter 4, for instance, employs a Rogerian *frame* in that it begins with a question and ends with a "hypothetical" conclusion. What it does *not* do, given the target audience that the analysis postulates for it, is to state alternative positions in a form which would be acceptable to the holders of those positions. Indeed, regardless of how it proceeded, any essay which begins with a non-rhetorical question (something other than "How long are we going to put up with X or Y or Z atrocity, or A or B or C idiocy, etc.") opens in the manner of a Rogerian argument.

Practical Applications

What are the real-world uses of the Rogerian?

Some will, but most of you will *not* become academics, nor is it likely that many of you will, or would even want to, publish in the op-ed pages of the *New York Times*. So, other than being prepared for its techniques as a consumer of argument, of what use is a knowledge of the techniques of Rogerian argument? What advantages does it offer the ordinary mortal who may be asked, as part of her job, to write a memo, an application, a defense of X, a response to Y, or to make a case for Z?

Exercise 5:11.   Write an outline of an essay in which you respond to an assignment which asks you to recommend one of two positions on x subject (you pick the subject as if it were assigned to you). You are to make the recommendation from a vantage of "objectivity," that is, as one who has no personal interest in either position.

As always in written argument, the questions are what do you want to sell, and to whom do you want to sell it. Having determined that, the next question is, given the answers to the previous questions, what means are most likely to produce the sale. The efficacy, thus, of a Rogerian frame, will depend on the relationship the writer seeks with the targeted audience. What does the Rogerian frame offer, and who would be open to it?

I had the opportunity today to talk to a social scientist, an engineer, and a linguist, while we were waiting for a tardy committee member (a chemist) to show up. I responded to the purely social question "What have you been doing" with " I have been writing a section of my rhetoric text on Carl Rogers." All three knew who Rogers was (he died in 1991), and the social scientist asked me what he had to do with composition. Rogers, it emerged, was regarded as a theoretician of how communication takes place, rather than as someone who had presented a rhetorical tool. He was seen as a scientist, not as the creator of a theory of *persuasion*.

What seemed obvious to me was, in a way, invisible to them. They did not share my frame of reference (this book carries an email address in the hope that you all will help me where we do not share a frame of reference, or I have failed to create one). They did not share in rhetoric's **appropriation** of Rogerian theory in spite of the fact that we were sitting in a committee room preparing to discuss, and vote on subjects, in the discussion of which the ability of a given committee member to influence the others could have large and long-lasting consequences. *How* a point was presented could have a great deal to do with the way in which it was discussed. How it was defended could have a great deal to do with how the voting would turn out. And that "how" is what we have here been discussing throughout this text, under the designation of "rhetoric."

The importance of perspective in interpretation

The question to be discussed, defined, and voted on, involved the content of the "core curriculum," a term you may or may not be familiar with, but which many colleges and departments in the university regarded with huge territorial concerns. Given that x many hours would be in humanities, x many in the social sciences, and x many in the natural sciences, etc., what group was going to get what?

Like everyone in the room, I had an agenda. Mine was that I wanted the maximum possible required hours devoted to writing instruction. Knowing Rogerian technique (as indeed did three other committee members, but who had apparently never thought of it as "rhetorical"), I thought that if I could present the positions of other schools and colleges in ways that would lead their representatives to think that insistence on redefinition would seem to be quibbling (and territorial) I could preempt those presentations by presenting them in my own terms. I might not be able to discourage the engineer. But, finally, I didn't need to. If I had my vote and everyone else's, she would lose (as the lone opposing vote).

This reinforced what I had considered a vital distinction between the Rogerian method as therapy, or as truth theory, and as rhetorical device. The therapeutic approach aims at a resolution satisfactory to all parties to the therapy. If, however, I am not employed (as Rogers would have been or had been) by a *composite* of the parties to the dispute, I have no obligation to present a solution satisfactory to all parties concerned.

I can, using the same methodology, pursue my own ends, or the ends of the position I am representing. I am, in other words, *governed only by the warrants of my target audience, not the warrants of the totality of the parties to the dispute.*

Rogerian argument as therapy and as rhetorical device

Exercise 5:12. I have just presented an anecdote in an attempt to show how Rogerian rhetoric has large practical applications. Invent or narrate from experience an anecdote designed to show someone who knows nothing about Rogerian technique how it can be used to influence the outcome of a discussion.

Note: Rogers is frequently given credit (as occasionally Toulmin is) for having invented a "new" mode of argument. Much more likely is that their familiarity with the conventions of academic journal publication which call for

1. a survey of the published literature on the subject (the range of opinion possible),

2. an explanation of why the current state of the literature is not adequate to the best understanding of the subject (that there is a problem), and

3. that the writer, who, as an "academic" professional has, no personal attachment to the theory, proposes as, not the "last word," but (as she sees it) a more satisfactory position than any proposed heretofore (the temporal and qualified solution) provided Rogers with a suggestive paradigm for "civil" and "civilized," "reasonable" problem-solving discourse explain the approach.

The "academic" and the Rogerian mode are near allies.

The Thurow essay mentioned previously, for instance, although published in *The New York Times*, was written by an academic, as is the Barbara Lawrence essay, again, despite its also being published in a newspaper.

It is my hope that this text can provide you with the tools to begin or continue to develop your relationship with the language as an instrument of persuasion and as an instrument which creates, reinforces, and embodies, value. I hope that the end of this book can mark the beginning of the rest of a fruitful and rewarding life with language.

READINGS FOR ANALYSIS

INTRODUCTION

The following selection/collection of essays is in every case presented to you as an item to be approached from the perspective of the analyst. You are asked never to presume that an item has been included because it is either "a good argument," or that it represents "the appropriate way to think about a given subject." I will confess that a couple of these essays have, for me, the virtue of being fun, in addition, of course, to being rhetorically informative.

The essays represent ways in which writers attempt to persuade their targeted audiences of their theses, overt, covert, or both. It is intended always that you approach the essays with this text's three primary questions in mind, that you interrogate these essays concerning what the author is trying to sell to whom and by what means. And you are urged, as you have throughout, *not to make judgments concerning either the quality or the correctness of the positions presented except in terms of questions of who the target audience is and what that audience will warrant.* This means, of course, that at any point you can, and are encouraged to, say "I don't know how these [choose your own invective] people can think this way." But it also means that such reaction is totally inappropriate as analysis.

I have included a considerable amount of material concerning matters that could be considered "controversial." I have done so not because that which is controversial might be seen as, by definition, "interesting," but because I wish you to train yourself not to react personally to that which you are subjecting to analysis. How you react *after* you have performed the analysis is, of course, your own business. This text is designed to improve your skills as a consumer and then a producer of argument, not to instruct you in any "right way to think."

I have asked the publisher to print these essays with sufficient space in the margins to make notes. I have asked also that the paragraphs be numbered for ease in referring to them. I have deliberately placed any information concerning the author (beyond the name) and the place of original publication, *after* the study questions. (If publication data is not included with the essay, and it frequently is not, it can be found in the permissions list.) I have also been guided in my inclusion of informational notes by the simple principle that nothing that is available in a standard dictionary will be noted.

The essays are presented in alphabetical order by author. The reasoning is simple. This is not a "thematic" reader, nor is it my presumption that essays can be classified by so-called rhetorical "mode" (Ethos, Pathos, Logos). It is hoped that the arguments are mutually illuminating, and that as you become increasingly familiar with them, you can say, of essay x, "in its use of abstractions," essay x is very similar to essay y, not to mention c. In all three cases we see etc. etc. etc." So, what is needed is speedy, not thematic nor modish, access.

So use your dictionary(ies), check your encyclopedia(s), and give the essays your best analytic shot. Remember that the best analysis is one that accounts for the greatest number of the details of the text being interrogated, but that no analysis can ever be assumed to be the last word on the subject, or even "correct." I have been analyzing "Politics and the English Language" once a semester for years, and I don't think I'm anywhere near done.

Refusing Stereotypes

Donna Britt

1   Recently, I was in line at the supermarket when a voice behind me asked the cashier a routine question. Instinctively, I froze.

2   The accent was deeply, unmistakably, white Southern male. Having seen *Roots*[1] and heard Bull Connor[2] and more recently, Jesse Helms,[3] I instantly felt that the voice must belong to someone disdainful of me, a black woman.

3   But when I glanced back, the man smiled and nodded. And I knew I had no idea who he really was.

4   It reminded me of three years ago, when a number of articles appeared in the media about "Bubba." The name was used to identify all white, working-class, Southern men flexing their political muscle. I couldn't get past the name.

5   Bubba. With apologies to bright Bubbas, it conjured up someone slow-witted, reactionary, unsophisticated. I was repulsed by the smugness in characterizing an entire group by the nickname. Why, I wondered, was this deemed OK?

6   Something else has me thinking of "Bubba." It's reading the umpteenth election analysis stating that one of President Clinton's problems, as perceived by disillusioned white men, was promising to make his Cabinet "look like America."

7   If the analysis is correct, I have a question: What's wrong with a Cabinet that looks like America? That such a clearly right—even righteous—notion could seem dubious is as baffling as a "Bubba." What was wrong with searching for qualified female and minority candidates to fill jobs that traditionally had been closed to them?

8   Was it that the resulting Cabinet filled by six white men, three black men, two Latino men, two white women and a black woman—looked more like America's mixed-bag population than any previous president's?

9   That's what America looks like. It never, not from day one, looked like a collection of white men only. That's obvious. So is the fact that white men belong

---

[1] A book and then a television series purportedly tracing the history of black author Alex Haley's forebears from slavery to modernity.

[2] Birmingham, Alabama, police commissioner who authorized the use of German Shepherd dogs ("police dogs") and fire hoses against black civil rights demonstrators in 1963. He is frequently credited with aiding the civil rights movement by arousing public revulsion for his tactics. If this is accurate it constitutes an interesting example of the risks of the *ad baculum* argument when considered in a larger framework.

[3] U.S. Senator from North Carolina, "an icon of Republican conservatism" (according the *Britannica* '98 yearbook).

10   at the table. They are Americans—and a majority of the president's advisers are white men. So why resent the effort to seat other Americans, as well?

10   Most of those "others" pay taxes. They dream for their kids and themselves. They ache for love and recognition, for security and acceptance. They believe in God's promised possibilities. Like the white guys, they're great—and awful.

11   Was the "problem" the time spent looking? Choosing from outside the usual clump of candidates, beating previously unexplored bushes, takes more time than having the fruit drop in your lap from the nearest tree. A nation disgusted with "business as usual" should have been thrilled that Clinton went out of his way for something that could look as good as America.

12   Just because most people feel a psychological ease in working, playing, praying and being with those most like them doesn't always mean it's the best way to live.

13   Maybe it's time for America to start acting its age, turning its back, personally and collectively, on what's easy.

14   That means respecting our blackness or whiteness or maleness or femaleness or whatever-ness while moving beyond seeing ourselves only as that.

15   It means recognizing the complex humanity behind simple titles like "conservative" and "liberal," sharing a pie some once had all to themselves and refusing to dump anyone—including white guys at the market or in newspaper articles—into a stereotype. Easy isn't why we're here.

16   Any religion or creed worthy of the souls who believe in it says our purpose is to be more fair, more loving, and better than it is easy for us to be. Living up to "liberty and justice for all" means stretching. It means hard work.

17   Doesn't America look like she's worth it?

---

1. Highlight each question mark in Britt's article and then, after refreshing your understanding from the glossary, highlight each of those that follows a **rhetorical question**. Bear in mind here that what is "rhetorical" in this sense is not self-evident—which is to say that what is rhetorical to one group may well not be to another.

2. On the basis of the questions that you have decided that Britt approaches as "rhetorical" and those statements which are simply asserted, formulate a definition of Britt's **target audience**.

Ships in the Night

Lawrence Bush

Accord, N.Y.

1   I had only just arrived at the club when I bumped into Roger. After we had exchanged a few pleasentries, he lowered his voice and asked, "What do you think of Martha and I as a potential twosome?"

2   "That," I replied, "would be a mistake. Martha and me is more like it."

3   "You're interested in Martha?"

4   "I'm interested in clear communication."

5   "Fair enough," he agreed. "May the best man win." Then he sighed. "Here I thought we had a clear path to becoming a very unique couple."

6   "You couldn't be a very unique couple, Roger."

7   "Oh? And why is that?"

8   "Martha couldn't be a little pregnant, could she?"

9   "Say what? You think that Martha and me . . ."

10   "Martha and I."

11   "Oh." Roger blushed and set down his drink. "Gee, I didn't know."

12   "Of course you didn't," I assured him. "Most people don't."

13   " I feel very badly about this."

14   "You shouldn't say that: I feel bad. . . ."

15   "Please, don't," Roger said. "If anyone's at fault here, it's me!"

---

1. Some people need to read this piece several times before the writer's central device becomes evident. Presuming, however, that you have figured it out, present an argument re the binary that Bush is 1) defending "good" grammar, or 2) arguing that attention to grammar as opposed to common usage interferes with communication.

This piece appeared in the Op-Ed section of *The New York Times* for April 5, 1994. Lawrence Bush was identified as "an editor and a fiction writer."

Demystifying Multiculturalism

Linda Chavez

1   Multiculturalism is on the advance, everywhere from President Clinton's Cabinet to corporate boardrooms to public-school classrooms. If you believe the multiculturalists' propaganda, whites are on the verge of becoming a minority in the United States. The multiculturalists predict that this demographic shift will fundamentally change American culture—indeed destroy the very idea that America *has* a single, unified culture. They aren't taking any chances, however. They have enlisted the help of government, corporate leaders, the media, and the education establishment in waging a cultural revolution. But has America truly become a multicultural nation? And if not, will those who capitulate to these demands create a self-fulfilling prophecy?

2   At the heart of the argument is the assumption that the white population is rapidly declining in relation to the nonwhite population. A 1987 Hudson Institute report helped catapult this claim to national prominence. The study, *Workforce 2000*, estimated that by the turn of the century only 15 percent of new workers would be white males. The figure was widely interpreted to mean that whites were about to become a minority in the workplace—and in the country.

3   In fact, white males will still constitute about 45 percent—a plurality—of the workforce in the year 2000. The proportion of white men in the workforce *is* declining—it was nearly 51 percent in 1980—but primarily because the proportion of white women is growing. They will make up 39 percent of the workforce within ten years, according to government projections, up from 36 percent in 1980. Together, white men and women will account for 84 percent of all workers by 2000—hardly a minority share.

4   But the business world is behaving as if a demographic tidal wave is about to hit. A whole new industry of "diversity professionals" has emerged to help managers cope with the expected deluge of nonwhite workers. These consultants are paid as much as $10,000 a day to train managers to "value diversity," a term so ubiquitous that it has appeared in more than seven hundred articles in major newspapers in the last three years. According to Heather MacDonald in *The New Republic,* about half of Fortune 500 corporations now employ someone responsible for "diversity."

5   What precisely does valuing diversity mean? The underlying assumptions seem to be that nonwhites are so different from whites that employers must make major changes to accommodate them, and that white workers will be naturally resistant to including nonwhites in their ranks. Public-opinion polls don't bear out the latter. They show that support among whites for equal job opportunity for blacks is extraordinarily high, exceeding 90 percent as early as 1975.

As for accommodating different cultures, the problem is not culture—or race, or ethnicity—but education. Many young people, in particular, are poorly prepared for work, and the problem is most severe among those who attended inner-city schools, most of them blacks and Hispanics.

6   Nevertheless, multiculturalists insist on treating race and ethnicity as if they were synonymous with culture. They presume that skin color and national origin, which are immutable traits, determine values, mores, language, and other cultural attributes, which, of course, are learned. In the multiculturalists' world view, African Americans, Puerto Ricans, or Chinese Americans living in New York City have more in common with persons of their ancestral group living in Lagos or San Juan or Hong Kong than they do with other New Yorkers who are white. Culture becomes a fixed entity, transmitted, as it were, in the genes, rather than through experience. Thus, "Afrocentricity," a variant of multiculturalism, is "a way of being," its exponents claim. According to a leader of the Afrocentric education movement, Molefi Kete Asante, there is "one African Cultural System manifested in diversities," whether one speaks of Afro-Brazilians, Cubans, or Nigerians (or, presumably, African Americans). Exactly how this differs from the traditional racist notion that all blacks (Jews, Mexicans, Chinese, etc.) think alike is unclear. What is clear is that the multiculturalists have abandoned the ideal that all persons should be judged by the content of their character, not the color of their skin. Indeed, the multiculturalists seem to believe that a person's character is *determined* by the color of his skin and by his ancestry.

7   Such convictions lead multiculturalists to conclude that, again in the words of Asante, "[T]here is no common American culture." The logic is simple, but wrongheaded: Since Americans (or more often, their forebears) hail from many different places, each of which has its own specific culture, the argument goes, America must be multicultural. And it is becoming more so every day as new immigrants bring their cultures with them.

8   Indeed, multiculturalists hope to ride the immigrant wave to greater power and influence. They have certainly done so in education. Some 2.3 million children who cannot speak English well now attend public school, an increase of 1 million in the last seven years. Multicultural advocates cite the presence of such children to demand bilingual education and other multicultural services. The Los Angeles Unified School District alone currently offers instruction in Spanish, Armenian, Korean, Cantonese, Tagalog, Russian, and Japanese. Federal and state governments now spend literally billions of dollars on these programs.

9   Ironically, the multiculturalists' emphasis on education undercuts their argument that culture is inextricable from race or national origin. They are acutely aware just how fragile cultural identification is; why else are they so adamant about reinforcing it? Multiculturalists insist on teaching immigrant children in their native language, instructing them in the history and customs of their native land and imbuing them with reverence for their ancestral heroes, lest these youngsters be seduced by American culture. Far from losing faith in the power of assimilation, they seem to believe that without a heavy dose of multicultural indoctrination, immigrants won't be able to resist it. And they're right, though

it remains to be seen whether anything, including the multiculturalists' crude methods, will ultimately detour immigrants from the assimilation path.

10   The urge to assimilate has traditionally been overpowering in the United States, especially among the children of immigrants. Only groups that maintain strict rules against intermarriage with persons outside the group, such as Orthodox Jews and the Amish, have ever succeeded in preserving distinct, full-blown cultures within American society. (It is interesting to note that religion seems to be a more effective deterrent to full assimilation than the secular elements of culture, including language.) Although many Americans worry that Hispanic immigrants, for example, are not learning English and will therefore fail to assimilate into the American mainstream, little evidence supports the case. By the third generation in the United States, a minority of Hispanics, like other ethnic groups, speak only English and are closer to other Americans on most measures of social and economic status than they are to Hispanic immigrants. On one of the most rigorous gauges of assimilation—intermarriage—Hispanics rank high. About one-third of young third-generation Hispanics marry non-Hispanic whites, a pattern similar to that of young Asians. Even for blacks, exogamy rates, which have been quite low historically, are going up; about 3 percent of blacks now marry outside their group.

11   The impetus for multiculturalism is not coming from immigrants, but from their more affluent and assimilated native-born counterparts. The proponents are most often the elite—the best educated and most successful members of their respective racial and ethnic groups. College campuses, where the most radical displays of multiculturalism take place, are fertile recruiting grounds. Last May, for example, a group of Mexican American students at UCLA, frustrated that the university would not elevate the school's 23-year-old Chicano studies program to full department status, stormed the faculty center, breaking windows and furniture and causing half a million dollars in damage. The same month, a group of Asian American students at UC Irvine went on a hunger strike to pressure administrators into hiring more professors of Asian American studies. These were not immigrants, or even, by and large, disadvantaged students, but middle-class beneficiaries of their parents' or grandparents' successful assimilation to the American mainstream.

12   The protestors' quest had almost nothing to do with any effort to maintain their ethnic identity. For the most part, such students probably never thought of themselves as anything but American before they entered college. A recent study of minority students at the University of California at Berkeley found that most Hispanic and Asian students "discovered" their ethnic identity after they arrived on campus—when they also discovered that they were victims of systematic discrimination. As one Mexican American freshman summed it up, she was "unaware of the things that have been going on with our people, all the injustice we've suffered, how the world really is. I thought racism didn't exist and here, you know, it just comes to light." The researchers added that "students of color" had difficulty pinpointing exactly what constituted this "subtle form of the new racism. . . . There was much talk about certain facial expressions, or the way people look, and how white students take over the class and speak past you."

13   Whatever their new-found victim status, these students look amazingly like other Americans on most indices. For example, the median family income of Mexican American students at Berkeley in 1989 was $32,500, slightly above the national median for all Americans that year, $32,191; and 17 percent of those students came from families that earned more than $75,000 a year, even though they were admitted to the university under affirmative-action programs (presumably because they suffered some educational disadvantage attributed to their ethnicity).

14   Affirmative-action programs make less and less sense as discrimination diminished in this society—which it indisputably has—and as minorities improve their economic status. Racial and ethnic identity, too, might wane if there weren't such aggressive efforts to ensure that this not happen. The multiculturalists know they risk losing their constituency if young blacks, Hispanics, Asians, and others don't maintain strong racial and ethnic affiliations. Younger generations must be *trained* to think of themselves as members of oppressed minority groups entitled to special treatment. And the government provides both the incentives and the money to ensure that this happens. Meanwhile, the main beneficiaries are the multicultural professionals, who often earn exorbitant incomes peddling identity.

15   One particularly egregious example occurred in the District of Columbia last fall. The school system paid $250,000 to a husband-and-wife consultant team to produce an Afrocentric study guide to be used in a single public elementary school. Controversy erupted after the two spent three years and produced only a five-page outline. Although the husband had previously taught at Howard University, the wife's chief credential was a master's degree from an unaccredited "university" which she and her husband had founded. When the *Washington Post* criticized the school superintendent for his handling of the affair, he called a press conference to defend the couple, who promptly claimed they were the victims of a racist vendetta.

16   D.C. students rank lowest in the nation in math and fourth-lowest in verbal achievement; one can only wonder what $250,000 in tutoring at one school might have done. Instead, the students were treated to bulletin boards in the classrooms proclaiming on their behalf: "We are the sons and daughters of The Most High. We are the princes and princesses of African kings and queens. We are the descendants of our black ancestors. We are black and we are proud." This incident is not unique. Thousands of consultants with little or no real expertise sell feel-good programs to school systems across the nation.

17   Multiculturalism is not a grassroots movement. It was created, nurtured, and expanded through government policy. Without the expenditure of vast sums of public money, it would wither away and die. That is not to say that ethnic communities would disappear from the American scene or the groups would not retain some attachment to their ancestral roots. American assimilation has always entailed some give and take, and American culture has been enriched by what individual groups brought to it. The distinguishing characteristic of American culture is its ability to incorporate so many disparate groups, creating a new

whole from the many parts. What could be more American, for example, than jazz and film, two distinctive art forms created, respectively, by blacks and immigrant Jews but which all Americans think of as their own? But in the past, government—especially public schools—saw it as a duty to try to bring newcomers into the fold by teaching them English, by introducing them to the great American heroes as their own, by instilling respect for American institutions. Lately, we have nearly reversed course, treating each group, new and old, as if what is most important is to preserve its separate identity and space.

18   It is easy to blame the ideologues and radicals who are pushing the disuniting of America, to use Arthur Schlesinger's phrase, but the real culprits are those who provide multiculturalists the money and the access to press their cause. Without the acquiescence of policy-makers and ordinary citizens, multiculturalism would be no threat. Unfortunately, most major institutions have little stomach for resisting the multicultural impulse—and many seem eager to comply with whatever demands the multiculturalists make. Americans should have learned by now that policy matters. We have only to look at the failure of our welfare and crime policies to know that providing perverse incentives can change the way individuals behave—for the worse. Who is to say that if we pour enough money into dividing Americans we won't succeed?

---

1. Restricting yourself to paragraph 1 of the essay as a *base* for analysis, examine the writer's use of pronouns throughout. How, finally, would the analyst define the "we" that is implied as being other than the "they"?
2. On the basis of the foregoing analysis make an argument supporting a particular **definition** of the article's thesis.
3. Compare this article's use of **statistics** as support data with that of another article, the Thurow piece in Chapter 4, for instance.

Linda Chavez is the author of the 1991 *Out of the Barrio,* and has held a number of fellowships and directorships of institutes and centers. The article first appeared in the *National Review* on February 21, 1994.

The Prescriptive Tradition

David Crystal

Prescriptivism

1   In its most general sense, prescriptivism is the view that one variety of language has an inherently higher value than others, and that this ought to be imposed on the whole of the speech community. The view is propounded especially in relation to grammar and vocabulary, and frequently with reference to pronunciation. The variety which is favoured, in this account, is usually a version of the "standard" written language, especially as encountered in literature, or in the formal spoken language which most closely reflects this style. Adherents to this variety are said to speak or write "correctly"; deviations from it are said to be "incorrect."

2   All the main European languages have been studied prescriptively, especially in the 18th century approach to the writing of grammars and dictionaries. The aims of these early grammarians were threefold; (a) they wanted to codify the principles of their languages, to show that there was a system beneath the apparent chaos of usage, (b) they wanted a means of settling disputes over usage, (c) they wanted to point out what they felt to be common errors, in order to "improve" the language. The authoritarian nature of the approach is best characterized by its reliance on "rules" of grammar. Some usages are "prescribed," to be learnt and followed accurately; others are "proscribed," to be avoided. In this early period, there were no half-measures: usage was either right or wrong, and it was the task of the grammarian not simply to record alternatives, but to pronounce judgment upon them.

3   These attitudes are still with us, and they motivate a widespread concern that linguistic standards should be maintained. Nevertheless, there is an alternative point of view that is concerned less with "standards" than with the *facts* of linguistic usage. This approach is summarized in the statement that is the task of the grammarian to *describe*, not *prescribe*—to record the facts of linguistic diversity, and not to attempt the impossible tasks of evaluating language variation or halting language change. In the second half of the 18th century, we already find advocates of this view, such as Joseph Priestley, whose *Rudiments of English Grammar* (1761) insists that "the custom of speaking is the original and only just standard of any language." Linguistic issues, it is argued, cannot be solved by logic and legislation. And this view has become the tenet of the modern linguistic approach to grammatical analysis.

4   In our own time, the opposition between "descriptivists" and "prescriptivists" has often become extreme, with both sides painting unreal pictures of the other. Descriptive grammarians have been presented as people who do not care about standards, because of the way they see all forms of usage as equally valid. Prescriptive grammarians have been presented as blend adherents to a historical tradition. The opposition has even been presented in quasi-political terms—of radical liberalism vs elitist conservatism.

5   If these stereotypes are abandoned, we can see that both approaches are important, and have more in common than is often realized—involving a mutual interest in such matters as acceptability, ambiguity, and intelligibility. The descriptive approach is essential because it is the only way in which the competing claims of different standards can be reconciled: when we know the facts of language use, we are in a better position to avoid the idiosyncrasies of private opinions, and to make realistic recommendations about teaching or style. The prescriptive approach provides a focus for the sense of linguistic values which everyone possesses, and which ultimately forms part of our view of social structure, and of our own place within it. After 200 years of dispute, it is perhaps sanguine to expect any immediate rapport to be achieved, but there are some grounds for optimism, now that sociolinguists are beginning to look more seriously at prescriptivism in the context of explaining linguistic attitudes, uses, and beliefs.

The Academies

6   Some countries have felt that the best way to look after a language is to place it in the care of an academy. In Italy, the *Accadémia della Crusca* was founded as early as 1582, with the object of purifying the Italian language. In France, in 1635, Cardinal Richelieu established the *Académie française*, which set the pattern for many subsequent bodies. The statues of the *Académie* define as its principal function:

> to labour with all possible care and diligence to give definite rules to our language, and to render it pure, eloquent, and capable of treating the arts and sciences.

The 40 academicians were drawn from the ranks of the church, nobility, and military—a bias which continues to the present day. The *Académie*'s first dictionary appeared in 1694.

7   Several other academies were founded in the 18th and 19th centuries. The Spanish Academy was founded in 1713 by Philip V, and within 200 years corresponding bodies had been set up in most South American Spanish countries. The Swedish Academy was founded in 1786; the Hungarian in 1830. There are three Arabic academies, in Syria, Iraq, and Egypt. The Hebrew Language Academy was set up more recently, in 1953.

8   In England, a proposal for an academy was made in the 17th century, with the support of such men as John Dryden and Daniel Defoe. In Defoe's view, the reputation of the members of this academy

would be enough to make them the allowed judges of style and language; and no author would have the impudence to coin without their authority . . . There should be no more occasion to search for derivations and constructions, and it would be as a criminal then to coin words as money.

In 1712, Jonathan Swift presented his *Proposal for Correcting, Improving and Ascertaining the English Tongue,* in which he complains to the Lord Treasurer of England, the Earl of Oxford, that

> our language is extremely imperfect; that its daily improvements are by no means in proportion to its daily corruptions; that the pretenders to polish and refine it have chiefly multiplied abuses and absurdities; and that in many instances it offends against every part of grammar.

His academy would "fix our language for ever," for,

> I am of the opinion, it is better a language should not be wholly perfect, than it should be perpetually changing.

The idea received a great deal of support at the time, but nothing was done. And in due course, opposition to the notion grew. It became evident that the French and Italian academies had been unsuccessful in stopping the course of language change. Dr. Johnson, in the Preface to his *Dictionary,* is under no illusion about the futility of an academy, especially in England, where he finds "the spirit of English liberty" contrary to the whole idea:

> When we see men grow old and die at a certain time one after another, century after century, we laugh at the elixir that promises to prolong life to a thousand years; and with equal justice may the lexicographer be derided, who being able to produce no example of a nation that has preserved their words and phrases from mutability, shall imagine that his deictionary can emblem his language, and secure it from corruption, and decay, that it is in his power to change sublunary nature, or clear the world at once from folly, vanity, and affectation.

From time to time, the idea of an English Academy continues to be voiced, but the response has never be enthusiastic. A similar proposal in the USA was also rejected. By contrast, since the 18th century, there has been an increasing flow of individual grammars, dictionaries, and manuals of style in all parts of the English-speaking world.

Language Change

9   The phenomenon of language change probably attracts more public notice and criticism than any other linguistic issue. There is a widely held belief that change must mean deterioration and decay. Older people observe the casual speech of the young, and conclude that standards have fallen markedly. They place the blame in various quarters—most often in the schools, where patterns of language education have changed a great deal in recent years, but also in state public

broadcasting institutions, where any deviations from traditional norms provide an immediate focus of attack by conservative, linguistically sensitive listeners. The concern can even reach national proportions, as in the widespread reaction in Europe against what is thought of as the "American" English invasion.

Unfounded Pessimism

10   It is understandable that many people dislike change, but most of the criticism of linguistic change is misconceived. It is widely felt that the contemporary language illustrates the problem at its worst, but this belief is shared by every generation. Moreover, many of the usage issues recur across generations: several of the English controversies which are the focus of current attention can be found in the books and magazines of the 18th and 19th centuries—the debate over *it's me* and *very unique*, for example. In *The Queen's English* (1863), Henry Alford, the Dean of Canterbury, lists a large number of usage issues which worried his contemporaries, and gave them cause to think that the language was rapidly decaying. Most are still with us, with the language not obviously affected. In the mid-19th century, it was predicted that British and American English would be mutually unintelligible within 100 years!

11   There are indeed cases where linguistic change can lead to problems of unintelligibility, ambiguity, and social division. If change is too rapid, there can be major communication problems, as in contemporary Papua New Guinea—a point which needs to be considered in connection with the field of language planning. But as a rule, the parts of language which are changing at any given time are tiny, in comparison to the vast, unchanging areas of language. Indeed, it is because change is so infrequent that it is so distinctive and noticeable. Some degree of caution and concern is therefore always desirable, in the interests of maintaining precise and efficient communication; but there are no grounds for the extreme pessimism and conservatism which is so often encountered—and which in English is often summed up in such slogans as "Let us preserve the tongue that Shakespeare spoke."

The Inevitability of Change

12   For the most part, language changes because society changes. To stop or control the one requires that we stop or control the other—a task which can succeed to only a very limited extent. Language change is inevitable and rarely predictable, and those who try to plan a language's future waste their time if they think otherwise—time which would be better spent in devising fresh ways of enabling society to cope with the new linguistic forms that accompany each generation. These days, there is in fact a growing recognition of the need to develop a greater linguistic awareness and tolerance of change, especially in a multi-ethnic society. This requires, among other things, that schools have the knowledge and resources to teach a common standard, while recognizing the existence and value of linguistic diversity. Such policies provide a constructive alternative to the emotional attacks which are so commonly made against the

development of new words, meanings, pronunciations, and grammatical constructions. But before these policies can be implemented, it is necessary to develop a proper understanding of the inevitability and consequences of linguistic change.

13   Some people go a stage further, and see change in language as a progression from a simple to a complex state—a view which was common as a consequence of 19th-century evolutionary thinking. But there is no evidence for this view. Languages do not develop, progress, decay, evolve, or act according to any of the metaphors which imply a specific endpoint and level of excellence. They simply change, as society changes. If a language dies out, it does so because its status alters in society, as other cultures and languages take over its role: it does not die because it has "got too old," or "becomes too complicated," as is sometimes maintained. Nor, when languages change, do they move in a predetermined direction. Some are losing inflections; some are gaining them. Some are moving to an order where the verb precedes the object; others to an order where the object precedes the verb. Some languages are losing vowels and gaining consonants; others are doing the opposite. If metaphors must be used to talk about language change, one of the best is that of a system holding itself in a state of equilibrium, while changes take place within it; another is that of the tide, which always and inevitably changes, but never progresses, while it ebbs and flows.

---

1. Highlight each sentence in paragraphs 1–3 that use the **passive voice**. After having read the entire article, offer an explanation for Crystal's use of the passive.
2. **History** is often used to reinforce a concept rather than to discredit it. Discuss how Crystal's use of the historical is intended to function differently.
3. In what ways can Crystal's essay be seen as **Rogerian**?
4. Understanding the essay as an argument, what is Crystal's **thesis**?

Is This a Dagger Which I See Before Me?
No, Congressman, It's Korea

Barney Frank

1   Sometimes the First Amendment can be aggravating. Ten years of legislating dissuades me from allowing legislators to tell adults what to write or say. But then I read about our soft Middle Eastern underbelly being menaced by a radical Shiite dagger. Or I am threatened by the spectacle of Central American dominoes hurtling through our window of vulnerability. And I fantasize about how pleasant it would be to ban all metaphors from political discussions.

2   Metaphors can be fun. My favorite budget debate on the House floor was the one in 1982 when an anguished Republican insisted that the Democrats "stop milking this dead horse." (In a spirit of conciliation, one Democrat advised him to return "not to carry all his spilt milk in one basket.") But few metaphor users can meet this standard.

3   People claim they use metaphors to advance understanding, by explaining complex or obscure phenomena in terms of simple and familiar ones. They don't. What they usually do is to become so enamored of a simplistic figure of speech that they substitute it for reality, and consequently discuss issues in a distorted and mechanistic fashion.

4   Foreign policy is especially vulnerable to this displacement of complex reality by metaphoric simple-mindedness. Physical shapes of countries lead otherwise sensible people to discuss international events in the terms 1-year-olds use when assembling geographic jigsaw puzzles.

5   Take soft underbellies. People who worry about being attacked from the south, or who would like to attack other people from their south, tend to be "underbelly" fetishists. Winston Churchill drove Allied war planners to distraction 40 years ago by opposing a crosschannel invasion in favor of a Mediterranean attack on the "Axis'" soft underbelly. Finally, someone seems to have gotten across the point that southern France is, in fact, no softer than northern France. Crocodiles and turtles have hard backs and soft underbellies. Countries do not. They have northern and southern borders, neither of which is necessarily more vulnerable than the other.

6   But the fact that it is distinctly unhelpful does not present this metaphor from remaining in use. A recent *Post* story quoted an Indonesian general as justifying an attack on Timor as necessary to stave off "a Marxist threat to our soft underbelly." I understand why Indonesians shudder at the thought of a bristly-bearded Karl Marx approaching their underbellies. But this has nothing to do with oppressing East Timor.

7   Another physical metaphor popular in foreign affairs is the country-as-weapon. I have grown up being told that Korea is essential to our security because it is pointed like a dagger at the back of Japan. First of all, I doubt very much that countries have fronts or backs. And if Japan does have a back, it seems unduly ethnocentric for us to decide that this is the part nearest Asia. But metaphor-mongers understand the value of making them graphic. Underbellies must always be soft, and threats always aimed at one's rear, except of course when they are aimed at one's heart (see box).

8   The popular current variant of the "they're coming up behind us" metaphor is the one which warns of the Marxist danger in our Central American back yard. Confirming the suspicion of Central Americans that we regard them as not just an appendage, but as a rear appendage, hardly seems the best way to inspire their confidence in our intentions. But it apparently sounds more ominous to conjure up Castroites and Sandinistas capturing our back yard than it would be to warn of them infesting our lawn, or infiltrating our side porch.

9   To return to Korea, it is relevant that Korea is near Japan. It is wholly irrelevant that it is roughly dagger shaped. Unless levitation is far more advanced in the East than I realize, the danger of Korea's being stuck into Japan seems negligible.

10   This does not mean that we should ignore Korea, nor cease our effort to protect it from any invasion from its north. It does not mean that because of its shape, people have greatly overrated its threat to Japan. Historically of course, the threat has been the other way—from Japan to Korea. And as to Korea's use as a communist weapon against Japan, given communist control of all of China, the extra threat Korea presents would not have been seen as significant if that country were round or flat instead of lumpily pointed.

11   Speaking of lumpiness, recently there has been division in the metaphor camp about how best to describe Korea. William Manchester's biography of MacArthur refers to it as a "lumpy phallus." In the Victorian era, deciding whether Korea was dagger or a phallus would have meant determining whether Japan preferred death to dishonor. In our time, it probably means we will soon be told about the prophylactic role assigned to the Seventh Fleet.

12   And then of course we have the dominoes. It is undeniable that events in one country can have a profound effect on its neighbors. It is demonstrably untrue that the "fall" of any one nation automatically or even probably means the "fall" of all of its neighbors. (Apparently, countries, unlike dominoes, can fall in several directions at once.) Either the automaticity of the domino theory is wrong, or Thailand and Malaysia have been secretly communist since the late '70s. Incidentally, the domino theory is at its most impressive when it describes the impact of an island nation on its neighbors across the water. Presumably this variant is the domino wave effect.

13   Domestic policy also suffers from metaphor distortion by people who tire of complexity. A popular argument against the need for concern about the distribution of our national income is the argument that a rising tide lifts all boats. This means that an increase in the overall GNP will make everyone better off, so that government need not concern itself with how particular segments fare.

'To Borrow a Phrase'

Daggers can be at your front as well as your back. A sampling from reports in this newspaper over the past few years shows the dagger aimed at the heart may be anything from a nation-state to a hamburger stand:

- Aug. 23, 1977: A report in *The Post* says Israelis see a fully independent state controlled by Palestinians as a "dagger pointed at the heart of Israel."
- Dec. 12, 1977: A broadcast by Saudi Arabia's official radio says that is little hope for peace in the Mideast "as long as Israeli occupation of Arab territory and Jerusalem continues. . . . This occupation is a dagger stuck in the heart of the Arab nation. . . ."
- April 9, 1979: A *Post* story on the "Sagebrush rebellion" says some federal officials consider the movement "a dagger aimed at the heart of the Bureau of Land Management."
- Sept. 9, 1979: The Soviets say in an English-language broadcast beamed to the United States that the American naval base at Guantanamo is a "dagger pointed at the heart of the young republic" of Cuba.
- Sept. 12, 1979: An Annapolis resident, testifying before the city council on proposal to put a hamburger dispensary in his neighborhood says, "Put a McDonalds's here and you will place a dagger in the heart of Hillsmere."
- Oct. 2, 1979: Sen. Edward Zorinsky (D-Neb.) says, "Let's face it, 2,000 to 3,000 Soviet combat troops in Cuba is, to borrow a phrase, a thorn in our side, not a dagger in our hearts."
- Sept. 18, 1980: The Ethiopian government in a letter to President Carter describes a recent agreement between the United States and Somalia on U.S. military access as "a dagger poised at the heart of Ethiopia."
- Nov. 2, 1981: Israeli Foreign Minister Yitzhak Shamir, discussing a list of Saudi peace proposals says each is a "poisoned dagger thrust into the heart of Israel's existence."
- March 23, 1983: President Reagan describes a Democratic budget proposal as "a dagger aimed straight at the heart of America's rebuilding program."

14   As many Republicans like to point out, one of the first to use this metaphor was John Kennedy, who said a number of profound and useful things. This was not one of them. People are not boats. The economy is not a tide. And an increase in GNP may occur in a way that leaves some people no better off than they were, while others find their condition worsening. It would be possible to combat this metaphor on its own terms by pointing out that a rising tide is not great news to people who are on tiptoes in the water. It would be better to stop using it, and to recognize that concern for economic equity requires a good deal more than simply pumping up the GNP.

15   Then we have the comforting metaphor that suggests that government can be made efficient as easily as a sponge is made drier. This one assumes that government spending consists of two elements of different consistencies: socially useful, or hard spending; and socially wasteful, or soft spending. Thus you can make government efficient by simply compressing the whole, so that the softer

substance—fat, water, or something less pleasant is squeezed out, leaving a mass of hard stuff—bone, muscle, etc., behind.

16   This is often the justification for across-the-board cuts in government programs. Unfortunately, the metaphor is dead wrong. There is little correlation between the social usefulness of programs and their ability to survive massive cutbacks. To meet the metaphor on its own terms, what is socially soft is often politically hard, and vice versa. Squeeze the budget like a sponge and you may well victimize poor children while wealthy farmers remain unscathed. The hard way to cut out wasteful spending is to identify it, and work to get the political support necessary to remove it. It's much easier to pretend by use of a convenient metaphor that simply reducing the total will automatically leave a more efficient mass behind.

17   Fortunately, for all my discomfort, the First Amendment endures. I am resigned to continuing to live my life among camels putting their noses into tents; lawyers sliding down slippery slopes; and cancers spreading in unlikely ways across the landscape or on what is known as the body politic. But the next time I hear a colleague on the Foreign Affairs Committee ask "Is this a dagger which I see before me?" I think I will say, "No Congressman, it's Korea."

---

1. After reading the essay very carefully mark each instance of **hyperbole,** and then with another color or method of notation, each statement you take to be **ironic.**
2. At what point does it become undeniable that the essay is using humor?
3. If you did not know Frank's political affiliation, could you determine it from the essay? How?
4. How briefly can you state Frank's **thesis?**
5. How concisely can you define Frank's **target audience?**
6. Frank's essay is filled with sexual implications (see particularly paragraph 11). Does Frank being an "out" homosexual influence your analysis of his rhetorical strategy?

This essay was first printed in the *Washington Post* in 1988.

A Liberalism of Heart and Spine

Henry Louis Gates, Jr.

1   Gunmen burst into a Bahai church in a South African township, line up the few white (Iranian) members of the congregation and shoot them dead. The Bahai religion holds that all races are one, and the Azanian People's Liberation Army, which apparently dispatched the killers, explained that it wanted to send a clear message against the mixing of races.

2   In fact, the Azanian movement has been profoundly shaped by European racial thinking, as you might expect a group that borrows its names from an invented place of barbarism in Evelyn Waugh's satiric novel *Black Mischief.* The truth is, the Azanians' abjuration of "race mixing" has nothing to do with indigenous local traditions and everything to do with the logic of apartheid.

3   "One million Arabs are not worth a Jewish fingernail," Rabbi Yaacov Perrin said in a funeral eulogy for Dr. Baruch Goldstein before a thousand sympathizers. The phrase reflects a perverse misreading of a passage from Exodus. But we have heard this voice before. It is the voice of messianic hatred. We hear it from the Balkans to the Bantustans; we hear it from Hezbollah and from Kach. We hear it in the streets of Bensonhurst.

4   And, of course, we hear it from some who profess to be addressing the misery of black America. "Never will I say I am not an anti-Semite," said Khalid Abdul Muhammad of the Nation of Islam. "I pray that God will kill my enemy and take him off the face of the planet Earth." He is peddling tape recordings of his speeches under the suggestive title "No Love for the Other Side."

5   And so it goes, with the victimized bidding to be victimizers. That suffering ennobles is a lie, an old lie that has been exposed countless times, yet has proved surprisingly durable.

6   Messianic hatred is scarcely the province of the privileged classes. David Duke draws his support from the least affluent and most anxious of white Southerners. Similarly, if calculating demagogues find inviting prey in black America, our immediate circumstances make this unsurprising. That nearly half of African American children live in poverty is one scandal; another is simply that this fact has become an acceptable feature of our social landscape, as unremarkable as crab grass. No love for the other side?

7   Yet if profoundly antimodern creeds like these continue to grow, perhaps liberalism—that political tradition of individual liberty that harks back at least to the Enlightenment—must shoulder some blame.

8   For too long, liberalism has grown accustomed to excusing itself from other people's problems. Genital mutilation in Africa? Don't ask us to arbitrate among the mores of other cultures. Human rights abuses in China? Are we really in a

position to judge? Deference to the autonomy of other beliefs, other values, other cultures has become an easy alibi for moral isolationism. When we need action, we get handwringing. When we need forthrightness, we get equivocation.

9   What we have is a rhetoric of relativism. But let's call such "moral relativism" by its real name: moral indifference. And let's admit how finite are our vaunted moral sympathies, here in the comfortable West.

10   According to recent reports, perhaps 100,000 people have died in recent ethnic conflicts that have raged through tiny Burundi. Could any type of intervention have helped? Maybe not. But that isn't the point. The point is that nobody is asking. Not enough love for the other side. Meanwhile, the tragedy of Bosnia took on the look of the Kitty Genovese syndrome on a global scale.

11   We need a liberalism that has confidence in its own insights, a liberalism possessed of clarity as well as compassion. To creeds that prate of sacred fingernails, as the rabbi did, of "no love for the other side," of the sins of mixing ethnic or racial categories, we must juxtapose a muscular humanism. A humanism that is without arrogance and is unafraid to assert itself, its hard-won moral knowledge. One that neither shuns religious devotion nor mistakes itself for a religion. One that has courage as well as conviction.

12   There is something of a paradox here. The most heinous of deeds have always been committed in the name of future generations, of an awaiting utopia. The nature of these evils could not be concealed if they were committed in the name of our own interests in the here and now, but utopianism wraps them in the garb of virtuous "sacrifice." Accordingly, it is its stoutly anti-utopian aspect— its capacity for self-doubt—that liberalism has claimed as a moral advantage.

13   But the capacity to entertain uncertainly needn't entail Hamlet-like paralysis. It merely promotes a willingness to revise our beliefs in the light of experience, to extend respect to those we do not agree with. Is it, after all, unreasonable to be suspicious of Westerners who are exercised over female circumcision but whose eyes glaze over when the same women are merely facing starvation?

14   The Azanian, the West Bank fanatic, the American demagogue march to a single drum. There has been much talk about the politics of identity—a politics that has a collective identity as its core. One is to assert oneself in the political arena as a woman, a homosexual, a Jew, a person of color.

15   But while the conversation about it may seem recent, the phenomenon itself is age-old. The politics of identity starts with the assertion of a collective allegiance. It says: This is who we are, make room for us, accommodate our special needs, confer recognition upon what is distinctive about us. It is about the priority of difference, and while it is not, by itself, undesirable, it is—by itself— dangerously inadequate.

16   By contrast, what I'm calling humanism starts not with the possession of identity, but with the capacity to *identify with*. It asks what we have in common with others, while acknowledging the diversity among ourselves. It is about the promise of a shared humanity.

17   In short, the challenge is to move from a politics of identity to a politics of identification. It was this conversion that Malcolm X underwent toward the end of his life. If Minister Farrakhan, a brilliant, charismatic man, undergoes a

similar conversion, he will earn place in the annals of our time. If not, he will just be another in a long line of racial demagogues, joining Father Coughlin, Gerald L. K. Smith, and the like.

18   A politics of identification doesn't enjoin us to ignore or devalue our collective identities. For it's only by exploring the multiplicity of human life in culture that we can come to terms with the commonalities that cement communitas. It is only by this route that we can move a little closer to what the poet Robert Hayden, himself a Bahai, conjured up when he urged us to "renew the vision of a human world where godliness / is possible and man / is neither god, nigger, honkey, wop, nor kike / but man / permitted to be man." We may be anti-utopian, but we have dreams, too.

---

1. Mark those statements that are undefended **assertions** in paragraphs 1–5 of this essay. **Note:** Gate's first paragraph contains no assertions. Each of its statements is subject to verification.
2. Is Gates presenting this as an **argument from authority?**
3. If so, who would be the **audience targeted** to accept the authority?
4. If not, what **warrants** does Gates expect the **targeted audience** to accept?
5. Mark and characterize each of Gates' uses of "we" in terms of his targeted audience.

When this essay was published in the *New York Times* Gates chaired the Afro-American Studies program at Harvard University.

Too Early in the Game for Karen

Ellen Goodman

Boston

1   The Karen O'Connor story began on a basketball court in Illinois and ended in the Supreme Court in Washington.

2   It began looking like a simple enough tale about boys and girls and basketball, and ended looking like a case study in mental gymnastics.

3   The star of this legal sporting event was 4' 11" tall and 11 years old when she wanted to try out for the boys' team at school instead of the girls' team. Karen's reasons were the obvious ones: the boys' team was better and she was good enough to make it.

4   But the school kept her out of tryouts, and off the team, because she was a girl.

5   The way Karen and her parents figured it, this was an out-and-out case of discrimination, just the sort of thing banned by the 14th Amendment. So they sued.

6   The school, on the other hand, figured it differently. It said that single-sex teams didn't discriminate: they gave girls a separate but equal chance to participate in sports, just the sort of thing encouraged by Title IX. And so they defended.

7   Well, the case dribbled up the legal system. Karen's offense won in the lower court. The school's defense won on appeal. Finally, last week, the Supreme Court left intact the appellate court ruling. For the moment, at least, single-sex teams are both legal and constitutional. But what is most intriguing to me isn't written on the scoreboard. It's the way the case walked the balance beam of equal opportunity.

8   On one side we had Karen, who wanted to be treated as an individual. She wanted her talents judged against all comers, male or female. That is, unquestionably, one definition of equal opportunity.

9   On the other side we had the school officials, who wanted all girls to have an equal chance with all boys, an equal chance to play team ball and learn sports skills. That is another definition of equal opportunity.

10   These two notions don't necessarily conflict. But in real life, they can.

11   If the Supreme Court had ruled that all team sports had to be integrated at every school level, the end result might have been technically "fair," but disastrous. The best players would have won the varsity letters, the chance to play team sports, the chance to play at all. But at this point in history, those players would have been overwhelmingly male.

12   A few talented girls like Karen might have benefited from this "opportunity," but the majority would have ended up on the sidelines.

13   As Jennifer Nupp of the Women's Equity Action League, puts it, "Letting in one girl here or there doesn't really help the overall picture of women in sports."

Equal opportunity for the individual can even retard equal opportunity for the group.

14   If I were choosing a model for women in sports, it wouldn't be the match between Billie Jean King and Bobby Riggs. It would be the gradual and permanent development of women's team tennis into an exciting and competitive sport of its own.

15   In that same vein, Title IX has generally been implemented in a way that provides women with separate but equal (or less unequal) equipment, money, coaching, teamwork in sports like basketball.

16   But there is still this quandary: siphoning off the stars, the Karens, into boys' teams hurts the goal of building better girls' teams. But preventing the stars, the Karens, from playing on boys' teams hurts their own personal goals.

17   The conflict between the 14th Amendment and Title IX in sports, between methods to achieve equal opportunities for an individual or for a group, is likely to be raised again. It's a real one. But I don't think it will last forever.

18   At the moment Karen herself is playing on a coed community team and a girl's school team. But as girls are encouraged to play sports, the Karens won't be such exceptions. The teams may integrate more completely at her age, or the skills of the average girl may sharpen enough to challenge the best.

19   Karen was just caught in the gap. She took a free throw at the Supreme Court and she missed. Her aim was good, but her timing was off.

---

1. Goodman's title immediately engages a **metaphor,** "game," which forms a basis for the **metaphoric** play of the rest of the essay. Define "the game" as Goodman uses it in the title, and then present at least three related **metaphors** from the essay.
2. Aside from their being different activities, how else does balance beam differ from, say, split rings? How does this interact with Goodman's argument?
3. What does "timing" have to do with a "free throw"? Giving the writer the benefit of the doubt, as the analyst must do, how might Goodman be employing this apparent anomaly?

A Proposal to Abolish Grading

Paul Goodman

1   Let half a dozen of the prestigious Universities—Chicago, Stanford, the Ivy League—abolish grading, and use testing only and entirely for pedagogic purposes as teachers see fit.

2   Anyone who knows the frantic temper of the present schools will understand the transvaluation of values that would be effected by this modest innovation. For most of the students, the competitive grade has come to be the essence. The naive teacher points to the beauty of the subject and the ingenuity of the research; the shrewd student asks if he is responsible for that on the final exam.

3   Let me at once dispose of an objection whose unanimity is quite fascinating. I think that the great majority of professors agree that grading hinders teaching and creates a bad spirit, going as far as cheating and plagiarizing. I have before me the collection of essays, *Examining in Harvard College*, and this is the consensus. It is uniformly asserted, however, that the grading is inevitable; for how else will the graduate schools, the foundations, the corporations *know* whom to accept, reward, hire? How will the talent scouts know whom to tap?

4   By testing the applicants, of course, according to the specific task-requirements of the inducting institution, just as applicants for the Civil Service or for licenses in medicine, law, and architecture are tested. Why should Harvard professors do the testing *for* corporations and graduate schools?

5   The objection is ludicrous. Dean Whitla, of the Harvard Office of Tests, points out that the scholastic-aptitude and achievement tests used for *admission* to Harvard are a superexcellent index for all-around Harvard performance, better than high-school grades or particular Harvard course-grades. Presumably, these college-entrance tests are tailored for what Harvard and similar institutions want. By the same logic, would not an employer do far better to apply his own job-aptitude test rather than to rely on the vagaries of Harvard section-men? Indeed, I doubt that many employers bother to look at such grades; they are more likely to be interested merely in the fact of a Harvard diploma, whatever that connotes to them. The grades have most of their weight with the graduate schools—here, as elsewhere, the system runs mainly for its own sake.

6   It is really necessary to remind our academics of the ancient history of Examination. In the medieval university, the whole point of the grueling trial of the candidate was whether or not to accept him as a peer. His disputation and lecture for the Master's was just that, a masterpiece to enter the guild. It was not to make comparative evaluations. It was not to weed out and select for an extramural licensor or employer. It was certainly not to pit one young fellow against another in an ugly competition. My philosophic impression is that the

medievals thought they knew what a good job of work was and that we are competitive because we do not know. But the more status is achieved by largely irrelevant competitive evaluation, the less will we ever know.

7   (Of course, our American examinations never did have this purely guild orientation, just as our faculties have rarely had absolute autonomy; the examining was to satisfy Overseers, Elders, distant Regents—and they as paternal superiors have always doted on giving grades, rather than accepting peers. But I submit that this set-up itself makes it impossible for the student to *become* a master, to *have* grown up, and to commence on his own. He will always be making an A or B for some overseer. And in the present atmosphere, he will always be climbing on his friend's neck.)

8   Perhaps the chief objectors to abolishing grading would be the students and their parents. The parents should be simply disregarded; their anxiety has done enough damage already. For the students, it seems to me that a primary duty of the university is to deprive them of their props, their dependence on extrinsic valuation and motivation, and to force them to confront the difficult enterprise itself and finally lose themselves in it.

9   A miserable effect of grading is to nullify the various uses of testing. Testing, for both student and teacher, is a means of structuring, and also of finding out what is blank or wrong and what has been assimilated and can be taken for granted. Review—including high-pressure review—is a means of bringing together the fragments, so that there are flashes of synoptic insight.

10   There are several good reasons for testing, and kinds of test. But if the aim is to discover weakness, what is the point of down-grading and punishing it, and thereby inviting the student to conceal his weakness, by faking and bulling, if not cheating? The natural conclusion of synthesis is the insight itself, not a grade for having had it. For the important purpose of placement, if one can establish in the student the belief that one is testing *not* to grade and make invidious comparisons but for his own advantage, the student should normally seek his own level, where he is challenged and yet capable, rather than trying to get by. If the student dares to accept himself as he is, a teacher's grade is a crude instrument compared with a student's self-awareness. But it is rare in our universities that students are encouraged to notice objectively their vast confusion. Unlike Socrates, our teachers rely on power-drives rather than shame and ingenuous idealism.

11   Many students are lazy, so teachers try to goad or threaten them by grading. In the long run this must do more harm than good. Laziness is a character-defense. It may be a way of avoiding learning, in order to protect the conceit that one is already perfect (deeper, the despair that one *never* can be). It may be a way of avoiding just the risk of failing and being down-graded. Sometimes it is a way of politely saying, "I won't." But since it is the authoritarian grown-up demands that have created such attitudes in the first place, why repeat the trauma? There comes a time when we must treat people as adult, laziness and all. It is one thing courageously to fire a do-nothing out of your class; it is quite another thing to evaluate him with a lordly F.

12   Most important of all, it is often obvious that balking in doing the work, especially among bright young people who get to great universities, means exactly

what it says: The work does not suit me, not this subject, or not at this time, or not in this school, or not in school altogether. The student might not be bookish; he might be school-tired; perhaps his development ought now to take another direction. Yet unfortunately, if such a student is intelligent and is not sure of himself, he *can* be bullied into passing, and this obscures everything. My hunch is that I am describing a common situation. What a grim waste of young life and teacherly effort! Such a student will retain nothing of what he has "passed" in. Sometimes he must get mononucleosis to tell his story and be believed.

13   And ironically, the converse is also probably commonly true. A student flunks and is mechanically weeded out, who is really ready and eager to learn in a scholastic setting, but he has not quite caught on. A good teacher can recognize the situation, but the computer wreaks its will.

---

1. I have asserted a number of times in this text that an **argument** must be considered in relationship to its historical circumstances. Goodman's essay was first published in 1964, some 36 years before this writing. Go carefully through the essay and mark those sections which you think "date" it, that is, make it a document of the 1960s, but not of the turn of the century.
2. After completing the previous question, try to define Goodman's **targeted audience** at the time of his writing. Consider especially, at the outset, paragraph 3. Mark each time Goodman asks a question. How would you characterize his use of this device?

Goodman died at the age of 61 in 1972. This essay is from his book *Compulsory Miseducation* published in 1964. Goodman was a college professor. He is best known for his book *Growing Up Absurd*. See preservenet.com/theory.Goodman.html for a downloadable collection of his articles.

Language and Control

Gopac (Newt Gingrich)

1   As you know, one of the key points in the Gopac [instructional tapes] is that "language matters." As we mail tapes to candidates, and use them in training sessions across the country, we hear a plaintive plea: "I wish I could speak like Newt."

2   That takes years of practice. But we believe that you can have a significant impact on your campaign if we help a little. That is why we have created this list of words and phrases.

3   This list is prepared so that you might have a directory of words to use in writing literature and letters, in preparing speeches, and in producing material for the electronic media. The words and phrases are powerful. Read them. Memorize as many as possible. And remember that, like any tool, these words will not help if they are not used.

OPTIMISTIC POSITIVE GOVERNING WORDS

4   Use the list below to help define your campaign and your vision of public service. These words can help give extra power to your message.

common sense	*help*	*principle(d)*
courage	*liberty*	*pristine*
crusade	*light*	*pro-environment*
dream	*moral*	*prosperity*
duty	*movement*	*reform*
empower(ment)	*passionate*	*rights*
fair	*peace*	*strength*
family	*pioneer*	*truth*
freedom	*precious*	*vision*
hard work	*pride*	*workfare*

CONTRASTING WORDS

5   Often we search hard for words to define our opponents. Sometimes we are hesitant to use contrast. These are powerful words that can create a clear and

easily understood contrast. Apply these to the opponent, his record, proposals and party.

anti-child	*disgrace*	*red tape*
anti-flag	*excuses*	*self-serving*
betray	*failure*	*sensationalists*
bizarre	*greed*	*shallow*
cheat	*hypocrisy*	*shame*
collapse	*incompetent*	*sick*
corruption	*liberal*	*status quo*
crisis	*lie*	*steal*
decay	*machine*	*taxes*
deeper	*obsolete*	*they/them*
destroy	*pathetic*	*traitors*
devour	*radical*	*welfare*

---

1. Highlight each of the pronouns in the excerpt and write an analysis of the presumed relationship between the first person plural pronouns and the second person pronouns. What is the difference between the way the first person plural is used before the second list as opposed to earlier in the excerpt?
2. There are no third person pronouns. What is used instead, and why might Gingrich have used it?

The above is an excerpt from "Language: A Key Mechanism of Control" published in *Harper's Magazine* in November of 1990 from a pamphlet sent to Republican candidates running in the 1990 elections. The pamphlet was developed by "Gopac" (which presumably is an acronym for GOP [Grand Old Party] PAC [political action committee]), which was headed by then-House Republican Whip, Newt Gingrich.

Curbing the Sexploitation Industry

Tipper Gore

1   I can't even count the times in the last three years, since I began to express my concern about violence and sexuality in rock music, that I have been called a prude, a censor, a music hater, even a book burner. So let me be perfectly clear: I detest censorship. I'm not advocating censorship but rather a candid and vigorous debate about the dangers posed for our children by what I call the "sexploitation industry."

2   We don't need to put a childproof cap on the world, but we do need to remind the nation that children live in it, too, and deserve respect and sensitive treatment.

3   When I launched this campaign in 1985 I went to the source of the problem, sharing my concerns and proposals with the entertainment industry. Many producers were sympathetic. Some cooperated with my efforts. But others have been overly hostile, accusing me of censorship and suggesting, unfairly, that my motives are political. This resistance and hostility has convinced me of the need for a two-pronged campaign, with equal effort from the entertainment industry and concerned parents. Entertainment producers must take the first step, by labeling sexually explicit material.

4   But the industry cannot be expected to solve the problem on its own. Parents should encourage producers to cooperate and praise them when they do. Producers need to know that parents are aware of the issue and are reading their advisory labels. Above all, they need to know that somebody out there cares, that the community at large is not apathetic about the deep and lasting damage being done to our children.

5   What's at issue is not the occasional sexy rock lyric. What troubles—indeed, outrages—me is far more vicious: a celebration of the most gruesome violence, coupled with the explicit message that sado-masochism is the essence of sex. We're surrounded by examples—in rock lyrics, on television, at the movies and in rental videos. One major TV network recently aired a preview of a soap opera rape scene during a morning game show.

6   The newest craze in horror movies is something called the "teen slasher" film, and it typically depicts the killing, torture and sexual mutilation of women in sickening detail. Several rock groups now simulate sexual torture and murder during live performances. Others titillate youthful audiences with strippers confined in cages on stage and with half-naked dancers, who often act out sex with band members. Sexual brutality has become the common currency of America's youth culture and with it the pervasive degradation of women.

7   Why is this graphic violence dangerous? It's especially damaging for young children because they lack the moral judgment of adults. Many children are only dimly aware of the consequences of their actions, and, as parents know, they are excellent mimics. They often imitate violence they see on TV, without necessarily understanding what they are doing or what the consequences might be. One 5-year-old boy from Boston recently got up from watching a teen-slasher film and stabbed a 2-year-old girl with a butcher knife. He didn't mean to kill her (and luckily he did not). He was just imitating the man in the video.

8   Nor does the danger end as children grow older. National health officials tell us that children younger than teenagers are apt to react to excessive violence with suicide, satanism, drug and alcohol abuse. Even grown-ups are not immune. One series of studies by researchers at the University of Wisconsin found that men exposed to films in which women are beaten, butchered, maimed and raped were significantly desensitized to the violence. Not only did they express less sympathy for the victims, they even approved of lesser penalties in hypothetical rape trials.

9   Sado-masochistic pornography is a kind of poison. Like most poisons, it probably cannot be totally eliminated, but it certainly could be labeled for what it is and be kept away from those who are most vulnerable. The largest record companies have agreed to this—in principle at least. In November 1985, the Recording Industry Association of America adopted my proposal to alert parents by having producers either put warning labels on records with explicitly sexual lyrics or display the lyrics on the outside of the record jackets. Since then, some companies have complied in good faith, although others have not complied at all.

10   This is where we parents must step in. We must let the industry know we're angry. We must press for uniform voluntary compliance with labeling guidelines. And we must take an active interest at home in what our children are watching and listening to. After all, we can hardly expect that the labels or printed lyrics alone will discourage young consumers.

11   Some parents may want to write to the record companies. Others can give their support to groups like the Parent Teacher Association, which have endorsed the labeling idea. All of us can use our purchasing power. We have more power than we think, and we must use it. For the sake of our children, we simply can't afford to slip back into apathy.

12   My concern for the health and welfare of children has nothing to do with politics: It is addressed to conservatives and liberals alike. Some civil libertarians believe it is wrong even to raise these questions—just as some conservatives believe that the Government should police popular American culture. I reject both these views. I have no desire to restrain artists or cast a "chill" over popular culture. But I believe parents have First Amendment rights, too.

13   The fate of the family, the dignity of women, the mental health of children—these concerns belong to everyone. We must protect our children with choice, not censorship. Let's start working in our communities to forge a moral consensus for the 1990's. Children need our help, and we must summon the courage to examine the culture that shapes their lives.

1. Try to define to whom Gore is speaking when she writes "we" and "our."
2. What is assumed as given in the last sentence of paragraph 1?
3. After having identified this given, examine how it is intended to work with the examples which begin at the end of paragraph 5. What sort of argument is being presented in paragraph 8?
4. Mark each item in the essay you would identify as a cliché. How do you think these are being used rhetorically?

This piece, published in the *New York Times* in 1988, is particularly rhetorically interesting in contrast to the counter essay by Frank Zappa, which is the last piece in the Readings section. This is a selection from Gore's 1987 book *Raising PG Kids in an X-Rated World*, which is currently out of print. Reputedly the Parents' Music Resource Center, of which Gore was cofounder, has now taken Rap music as its subject of concern.

Everything Spoken Here

Paul Greenburg

1   They're breaking out all over, the language wars. The century just ending was dominated by ideology. You could tell by the world wars, concentration camps and general hatefulness.

2   Now that the world has grown sick of ideology, the next battleground may be culture and its clearest carrier: language. Once again, what should be man's highest achievement—ideas, language, art, culture—is being transformed into a source of contention rather than enlightenment.

3   There is apparently nothing noble and liberating that our species cannot transform into something base and hateful. Note these items from the summer's news of the linguistically weird:

4   In Algeria, Arabic has been declared the only official language. All government offices, public and private businesses, and political parties will have to use Arabic in all their correspondence and deliberations. Naturally, the Berbers, who have their own language, are protesting. As for French, which many Algerians speak, it's out, too. It's a piquant turn of events at a time when the Academie Française in Paris is fighting a rear-guard action against the pervasive power of English.

5   Algeria provides only the latest example of how Arab civilization, the most tolerant and advanced in the world when Europe was still in the Dark Ages, continues to restrict itself.

6   It's no coincidence that the most vibrant of cultures tend to be the most open, welcome and willing to learn from others. And yet the notion persists that a language or culture can be advanced by suppressing others. Strange. Using the force of law to impose one's own language on others is a confession of weakness, not a sign of strength. Call it the Quebec Syndrome.

7   Nor is this country safe from language wars. Most of us are caught between the devil of English First (and maybe only) and the deep blue sea of multiculturalism, which would splinter the single, civil culture that holds us together. Each extreme produces its own nutty extravagances:

8   A postal clerk who speaks Spanish dares answer a question posed to her in that language and winds up in a heap of trouble. In a separate but equal seizure of linguistic correctness, a federal judge in Alabama has told that state to stop giving its exam for driver's licenses only in English. Why? Because that practice has a "disparate impact" on immigrants who speak another language. Well, sure, I reckon it would—like not being able to read STOP in English. Talk about a disparate, to say desperate, impact.

9   What we have here are two more examples of the death of common sense in American law and civilization. Why make a federal case out of a simple conversation in Spanish or, for that matter, in French or Italian or Chinese or Tex-Mex?

10   And instead of forcing Alabama to translate its driver's exam into 120 different languages (and the traffic signs, too?) why not, in all good will and hospitality, offer an English course for immigrants built around how to pass the driver's license exam? Talk about an incentive to learn the language.

11   If there is a single, one-sentence guide to creating a civic culture that embraces us all, and at the same time respects all our ethnic origins, it might be: Don't be a damfool.

12   Instead, we're seeing echoes of the kind of hysteria that swept the country at the beginning of the century.

13   The object then and now should be the same: To respect the intimate culture of others while joining with them in one and the same civic culture—and language. Of course English should be the national language, but making it the official one could reduce it to a provocation.

14   I think of how as a child I left my Yiddish-speaking home every weekday morning to go to Creswell Elementary School in Shreveport, La., where the lingua franca was American—or, to be more exact, Southron. The infinite varieties of American—please, let's not confuse it with English—ranged from the black dialect I heard down on Texas Avenue to the occasional touch of Cajun for lagniappe. Then there was the daily dose of Hebrew after school. And the smattering of Arabic from the Lebanese families with shops on the same block as my father's. It didn't seem confusing so much as inviting, and each language and culture had its place. And everybody was American.

15   How strange that we're now so puzzled and frightened by the old American balance of diversity and unity. The whole process of *E Pluribus Unum* is simple—and not so simple. Somehow the common civic culture absorbs the best, or at least most useful or amusing, aspects of all the quite different cultures. Until there comes a time when no Fourth of July concert is complete without a stirring rendition of Tchaikovsky's 1812 Overture, that paean to the Russian national spirit. Go explain. But it feels right. America absorbs, learns, adapts, grows, embraces, and becomes more . . . American.

16   We did it before, and we'll do it again. Just think of the civic culture as a kind of July the Fourth Pops Concert down by the river in Little Rock, or a sing-along with the Boston Pops on the Esplanade. All of us are there making harmony, all beating time to Sousa or Bernstein, all of us firmly committed to jazz, baseball and the Constitution of the United States. And then we all return to our own families, homes, churches, communities. We are *both* diverse and united, and whole-hearted in both those callings. And we enjoy our differences. Or at least we do when we're not being damfools.

---

1. What similarities do you see between the approaches of Greenburg and Molly Ivins?
2. Do their approaches to argument share anything with Tipper Gore's piece?
3. Where do you find the most concise statement of Greenburg's **thesis**?
4. What is his primary rhetorical tool?
5. What is the rhetorical purpose of the roughly six-paragraph "introduction" Greenburg employs?

In Defense of the Animals

Meg Greenfield

1   I might as well come right out with it. Contrary to some of my most cherished prejudices, the animal-rights people have begun to get to me. I think that in some part of what they say they are right.

2   I never thought it would come to this. As distinct from the old-style animal rescue, protection, and shelter organizations, the more aggressive newcomers, with their "liberation," of laboratory animals and periodic championship of the claims of animal well-being over human well-being when a choice must be made, have earned a reputation in the world I live in as fanatics and just plain kooks. And even with my own recently (relatively) raised consciousness, there remains a good deal in both their critique and their prescription for the virtuous life that I reject, being not just a practicing carnivore, a wearer of shoe leather, and so forth, but also a supporter of certain indisputably agonizing procedures visited upon innocent animals in the furtherance of human welfare, especially experiments undertaken to improve human health.

3   So, viewed from the pure position, I am probably only marginally better than the worst of my kind, if that: I don't buy the complete "speciesist" analysis or even the fundamental language of animal "rights" and continue to find a large part of what is done in the name of that cause harmful and extreme. But I also think, patronizing as it must sound, that the zealots are required early on in any movement if it is to succeed in altering the sensibility of the leaden masses, such as me. Eventually they get your attention. And eventually you at least feel obliged to weigh their arguments and think about whether there may not be something there.

4   It is true that this end has often been achieved—as in my case—by means of vivid, cringe-inducing photographs, not by an appeal to reason or values so much as by an assault on squeamishness. From the famous 1970s photo of the newly skinned baby seal to the videos of animals being raised in the most dark, miserable, stunting environment as they are readied for their life's sole fulfillment as frozen patties and cutlets, these sights have had their effect. But we live in a world where the animal protein we eat comes discreetly prebutchered and prepacked so the original beast and his slaughtering are remote from our consideration, just as our furs come on coat hangers in salons, not on their original proprietors; and I see nothing wrong with our having to contemplate the often unsettling reality of how we came by the animal products we make use of. Then we can choose what we want to do.

5   The objection to our being confronted with these dramatic, disturbing pictures is first that they tend to provoke a misplaced, uncritical, and highly emotional

concern for animal life at the direct expense of a more suitable concern for human suffering. What goes into the animals' account, the reasoning goes, necessarily comes out of ours. But I think it is possible to remain stalwart in your view that the human claim comes first and in your acceptance of the use of animals for human betterment and *still* to believe that there are some human interests that should not take precedence. For we have become far too self-indulgent, hardened, careless, and cruel in the pain we routinely inflict upon these creatures for the most frivolous, unworthy purposes. And I also think that the more justifiable purposes, such as medical research, are shamelessly used as cover for other activities that are wanton.

6   For instance, not all of the painful and crippling experimentation that is undertaken in the lab is being conducted for the sake of medical knowledge or other purposes related to basic human well-being and health. Much of it is being conducted for the sake of superrefinements in the cosmetic and other frill industries, the noble goal being to contrive yet another fragrance or hair tint or commercially competitive variation on all the daft, fizzy, multicolored "personal care" products for the medicine cabinet and dressing table, a firmer-holding hair spray, that sort of thing. In other words, the conscripted, immobilized rabbits and other terrified creatures, who have been locked in boxes from the neck down, only their heads on view, are being sprayed in the eyes with different burning, stinging substances for the sake of adding to our already obscene store of luxuries and utterly superfluous vanity items.

7   Oddly, we tend to be very sentimental about animals in their idealized, fictional form and largely indifferent to them in realms where our lives actually touch. From time immemorial, humans have romantically attributed to animals their own sensibilities—from Balaam's biblical ass who providently could speak and who got his owner out of harm's way right down to Lassie and the other Hollywood pups who would invariably tip off the good guys that the bad guys were up to something. So we simulate phony cross-species kinship, pretty well down in the cuteness of it all—Mickey and Minnie and Porky—and ignore, if we don't actually countenance, the brutish things done in the name of Almighty Hair Spray.

8   This strikes me as decadent. My problem is that it also causes me to reach a position that is, on its face, philosophically vulnerable, if not absurd—the muddled, middling, inconsistent place where finally you are saying it's all right to kill them for some purposes, but not to hurt them gratuitously in doing it or to make them suffer horribly for one's own trivial whims.

9   I would feel more humiliated to have fetched up on this exposed rock, if I didn't suspect I had so much company. When you see pictures of people laboriously trying to clean the Exxon gunk off of sea otters even knowing that they will only be able to help out a very few, you see this same outlook in action. And I think it *can* be defended. For to me the biggest cop-out is the one that says that if you don't buy the whole absolutist, extreme position it is pointless and even hypocritical to concern yourself with lesser mercies and ameliorations. The pressure of the animal-protection groups has already had some impact in

improving the way various creatures are treated by researchers, trainers, and food producers. There is much more in this vein to be done. We are talking about rejecting wanton, pointless cruelty here. The position may be philosophically absurd, but the outcome is the right one.

---

1. Considering the **target audience spectrum** in relationship to the question of "animal rights," what segment do you find Greenfield targeting?
2. Greenfield characterizes herself as in a transitional state in regard to her opinions. What might be the rhetorical purpose of introducing the **personal** in this way?
3. Is it useful to use **Rogerian** terminology to discuss this essay? Is there some sense in which it begins with a question?

Greenfield is a Pulitzer Prize winner for her editorial work with the *Washington Post*. This column was published in *Newsweek* in 1989.

Giving Things Names

S. I. and Alan R. Hayakawa

1   The figure below shows eight objects, let us say animals, four large and four small, a different four with round heads with another four with square heads, and still another four with curly tails and another four with straight tails. These animals, let us say, are scampering about your village, but since at first they are of no importance to you, you ignore them. You do not even give them a name.

2   One day, however, you discover that the little ones eat up your grain, while the big ones do not. A differentiation sets itself up, and, abstracting the common characteristics of A, B, C, D, you decide to call these *gogo*; E, F, G, and H you decide to call *gigi*. You chase away the *gogo*, but leave the *gigi* alone. Your neighbor, however, has had a different experience; he finds that those with square heads bite, while those with round heads do not. Abstracting the common characteristics of B, D, F, and H, he calls them *daba*, and A, C, E, and G, he calls *dobo*. Still another neighbor discovers, on the other hand, that those with curly tails kill snakes, while those with straight tails do not. He differentiates them, abstracting still another set of common characteristics: A, B, E, and F are *busa*, while C, D, G, and H are *busana*.

3   Now imagine that the three of you are together when E runs by. You say, "There goes the *gigi*"; your first neighbor says, "There goes the *dobi*"; your other neighbor says, "There goes the *busa*." Here, immediately, a great controversy arises. What is it *really*, a gigi, a dobo, or a busa? What is its *right name*? You are quarreling violently when along comes a fourth person from another village who calls it a *muglock*, an edible animal, as opposed to *uglock*, an inedible animal—which doesn't help matters a bit.

4   Of course, the question, "What is it *really*?" "What is its *right name*?" is a nonsense question. By a nonsense question is meant one that is not capable of being answered. Things can have "right names " only if there is a necessary

connection between symbols and things symbolized, and we have seen that there is not. That is to say, in the light of your interest in protecting your grain, it may be necessary for you to distinguish the animal E as a *gigi*; your neighbor, who doesn't like to be bitten, finds it practical to distinguish it as a *dobo*: your other neighbor, who likes to see snakes killed, distinguishes it as a *busa*. What we call things and where we draw the line between one class of things and another depend upon the interests we have and the purposes of the classification. For example, animals are classified in one way by the meat industry, in a different way by the leather industry, in another different way by the fur industry, and in a still different way by the biologist. None of these classifications is any more final than any of the others; each of them is useful for its purpose.

5   This holds, of course, regarding everything we perceive. A table "is" a table to us, because we can understand its relationship to our conduct and interests; we eat at it, work on it, lay things on it. But to a person living in a culture where no tables are used, it may be a very strong stool, a small platform, or a meaningless structure. If our culture and upbringing were different, that is to say, our world would not even look the same to us.

6   Many of us, for example, cannot distinguish between pickerel, pike, salmon, smelt, perch, crappie, halibut, and mackerel; we say that they are "just fish, and I don't like fish." To a seafood connoisseur, however, these distinctions are real, since they mean the difference to him between one kind of a good meal, a very different kind of good meal, or a poor meal. To a zoologist, who has other and more general ends in view, even finer distinctions assume great importance. When we hear the statement, then, "This fish is a specimen of pompano, *Trachinotus carolinus*," we accept this as being "true," even if we don't care, not because that is its "right name," but because that is how it is *classified* in the most complete and most general system of classification that people scientifically interested in fish have evolved.

7   When we name something, then, we are classifying. *The individual object or event we are naming, of course, has no name and belongs to no class until we put it in one.* To illustrate again, suppose that we were to give the extensional meaning of the word "Korean." We would have to point to all "Koreans" living at a particular moment and say, "The word 'Korean' denotes at the present moment these persons: $A_1, A_2, A_3, \ldots A_n$." Now, let us say, a child, whom we shall designate as Z, is born among these "Koreans." *The extensional meaning of the word "Korean," determined prior to the existence of Z, does not include* Z. Z is a new individual belonging to no classification, since all classifications were made without taking Z into account. Why, then, is Z also a "Korean"? *Because we say so.* And, saying so—fixing the classification—we have determined to a considerable extent future attitudes toward Z. For example, Z will always have certain rights in Korea; in other nations he will be regarded as an "alien" and will be subject to laws applicable to "aliens."

8   In matters of "race" and "nationality," the way in which classifications work is especially apparent. For example, I am by birth a "Canadian," by "race" a "Japanese," and am now an "American." Although I was legally admitted to the United States on a Canadian passport as a "non-quota immigrant," I was unable to apply for American citizenship until after 1952. Until 1965, American

immigration law used classifications based on "nationality" and on "race." A Canadian entering the United States as a permanent resident had no trouble getting in, unless he happened to be of Oriental extraction, in which case his "nationality" became irrelevant and he was classified by "race." If the quota for his "race"—for example, Japanese—was filled (and it often was), and if he could not get himself classified as a non-quota immigrant, he was not able to get in at all. (Since 1965, race and national origin have been replaced with an emphasis on "family reunification" as the basis for American immigration law, and race is no longer explicitly mentioned.) Are all these classifications "real"? Of course they are, *and the effect that each of them has upon what he may or may not do constitutes their "reality."*

9 I have spent my entire life, except for short visits abroad, in Canada and the United States. I speak Japanese haltingly, with a child's vocabulary and an American accent; I do not read or write it. Nevertheless, because classifications seem to have a kind of hypnotic power over some people, I am occasionally credited with (or accused of) having an "Oriental mind." Since Buddha, Confucius, General Tojo, Mao Tse-tung, Pandit Nehru, Pajiv Gandhi, and the proprietor of the Golden Pheasant Chop Suey House all have "Oriental minds," it is difficult to know whether to feel complimented or insulted.

10 When is a person "black"? By the definition once widely accepted in the United States, any person with even a small amount of "Negro blood"—that is, whose parents or ancestors were classified as "Negroes"—is "black." *It would be exactly as justifiable to say that any person with even a small amount of "white blood" is "white."* Why say one rather than the other? Because the former system of classification *suits the convenience of those making the classification.* (The classification of blacks and other minorities in this country has often suited the convenience of whites.) Classification is not a matter of identifying "essences." It is simply a reflection of social convenience or necessity—and different necessities are always producing different classifications.

11 There are few complexities about classifications at the level of dogs and cats, knives and forks, cigarettes and candy, but when it comes to classifications at high levels of abstraction, for example, those describing conduct, social institutions, philosophical and moral problems, serious difficulties occur. When one person kills another, is it an act of murder, an act of temporary insanity, an act of homicide, an accident, or an act of heroism? As soon as the process of classification is completed, our attitudes and our conduct are, to a considerable degree, determined. We hang the murderer, we treat the insane, we absolve the victim of circumstance, we pin a medal on the hero.

The Blocked Mind

12 We need not concern ourselves here with the injustices done to "Jews," "Roman Catholics," "Republicans," "redheads," "chorus girls," "sailors," "Southerners," "Yankees," and so on, by snap judgments or, as it is better to call them, fixed reactions. "Snap judgments" suggests that such errors can be avoided by thinking more slowly; this, of course, is not the case, for some people think very slowly

with no better results. What we are concerned with is the way in which we block the development of our own minds by automatic reactions.

13   In the grip of such reactions, some people may say, "A Jew's a Jew. There's no getting around that"—confusing the denoted, extensional Jew with the fictitious "Jew" inside their heads. Such persons, the reader will have observed, can usually be made to admit, on being reminded of certain "Jews" whom they admire—perhaps Albert Einstein, Sandy Koufax, Jascha Heifetz, Benny Goodman, Woody Allen, Henry Kissinger, or Kitty Dukakis—that "there are exceptions, of course." They have been compelled by experience, that is to say, to take cognizance of at least a few of the multitude of Jews who do not fit their preconceptions. At this point, however, they continue triumphantly, "But exceptions only prove the rule?"[1]—which is another way of saying, "Facts don't count."

14   People who "think" in this way may identify some of their best friends as "Jewish"; but to explain this they may say, "I don't think of them as Jews at all. They're just friends." In other words, the fictitious "Jew" inside their heads remains unchanged *in spite of their experience.*

15   People like this may be said to be impervious to new information. They continue to vote Republican or Democratic, no matter what the Republicans or Democrats do. They continue to object to socialists, no matter what the socialists propose. They continue to object to socialists, no matter what the socialists propose. They continue to regard mothers as sacred, no matter who the mother. A woman who had been given up on both by physicians and psychiatrists as hopelessly insane was being considered by a committee whose task it was to decide whether or not she should be committed to an asylum. One member of the committee doggedly refused to vote for commitment. "Gentlemen," he said in tones of deepest reverence, "you must remember that this woman is, after all, a mother." Similarly, some people continue to hate Protestants or Catholics, no matter which Protestant or Catholic. Ignoring characteristics left out in the process of classification, they overlook—when the term Republican is applied to the party of Abraham Lincoln, the party of Warren Harding, the party of Richard Nixon, and the party of Ronald Reagan—the rather important differences among them.

Cow₁ Is Not Cow₂

16   How do we prevent ourselves from getting into such intellectual blind alleys, or, finding we are in one, how do we get out again? One way is to remember that practically all statements in ordinary conversation, debate, and public controversy taking the form "Republicans are Republicans," "Business is business," "Boys will be boys," "Woman drivers are woman drivers," and so on, are *not true.* Let us put one of these blanket statements back into a context in life.

---

[1] This extraordinarily fatuous saying originally meant, "The exception tests the rule "—*Exceptio probat regulum.* This older meaning of the word "prove" survives in such an expression as "automobile proving ground."

> "I don't think we should go through with this deal, Bill. Is it altogether fair to the railroad company?"

> "Aw, forget it! *Business is business,* after all."

17   Such an assertion, although it looks like a "simple statement of fact," is not simple and is not a statement of fact. The first "business" *denotes* the transaction under discussion; the second "business" invokes the *connotations* of the word. The sentence is a *directive,* saying, "Let us treat this transaction with complete disregard for considerations other than profit, as the word 'business' suggests." Similarly, when a father tries to excuse the mischief done by his sons, he says, "Boys will be boys"; in other words, "Let us regard the actions of my sons with that indulgent amusement customarily extended toward those whom we call "boys," though the angry neighbor will say, of course, "Boys, my eye! They're little hoodlums; that's what they are!" Such assertions are not informative statements but directives directing us to classify the object or event under discussion in given ways, in order that we may feel or act as suggested by the terms of the classification.

18   There is a simple technique for preventing such directives from having their harmful effect on our thinking. It is the suggestion made by Korzybski that we add "index numbers " to our terms, thus: $Englishman_1$, $Englishman_2$, . . . ; cow_1, cow_2, cow_3 . . . ; $communist_1$, $communist_2$, $communist_3$. The terms of the classification tell us what the individuals in that class have in common; *the index numbers remind us of the characteristics left out.* A rule can then be formulated as a general guide in all our thinking and reading: police $officer_1$ *is not* police $officer_2$; mother-in-law_1 *is not* mother-in-law_2, and so on. This rule, if remembered, prevents us from confusing levels of abstraction and forces us to consider the facts on those occasions when we might otherwise find ourselves leaping to conclusions which we may later have cause to regret.

"Truth"

19   Many semantic problems are, ultimately, problems of classification and nomenclature. Take, for example, the extensive debate over abortion. To opponents of legalized abortion, the unborn entity within a woman's womb is a "baby." Because abortion foes *want* to end abortion, they insist that the "baby" *is* a human being with its own legal rights and that therefore "*abortion is murder.*" They call themselves "pro-life" to emphasize their position. Those who *want* individual women to be able to choose whether or not to end a pregnancy call that same unborn entity a "fetus" and insist that the "fetus" *is not* a viable human being capable of living on its own, and claim that a woman has a "right" to make such a choice. Partisans of either side have accused the other of "perverting the meanings of words " and of "not being able to understand plain English."

20   The decision finally rests not upon appeals to past authority, but upon *what society wants.* In the case *Roe v. Wade,* the Supreme Court found that a "right"—specifically, a right to privacy—permits women to make a private, medical decision

before a certain stage of pregnancy. If society again wants doctors prosecuted for performing abortions, as they often were before 1973, it will obtain a new decision from Congress or the Supreme Court that abortion "is" murder or that the unborn entity "is" a human being. Either way, society will ultimately get the decision it collectively wants, even if it must wait until the present members of the Supreme Court are dead and an entirely new court is appointed. When the desired decision is handed down, people will say, "Truth has triumphed." *Society, in short, regards as "true" those systems of classification that produce the desired results.*

21   The scientific test of "truth," like the social test, is strictly practical, except for the fact that the "desired results" are more severely limited. The results desired by society may be irrational, superstitious, selfish, or humane, but the results desired by scientists are only that our systems of classification produce predictable results. Classifications, as amply indicated already, determine our attitudes and behavior toward the object or event classified. When lightning was classified as "evidence of divine wrath," no courses of action other than prayer were suggested to prevent one's being struck by lightning. But after Benjamin Franklin classified it as "electricity," a measure of control over it was achieved by the invention of the lightning rod. Certain physical disorders were formerly classified as "demonic possession," and this suggested that we "drive the demons out" by whatever spells or incantations we could think of. The results were uncertain. But when those disorders were classified as "bacillus infections," courses of action were suggested that led to more predictable results. Science seeks only the *most generally useful* systems of classification; these it regards for the time being, until more useful classifications are invented, as "true."

---

1. Notice particularly the two sentences that open paragraph 4. What is the rhetorical function of the phrase "Of course"?
2. As the Hayakawas present this essay is it an **argument from authority**?
3. In paragraph 5 "of course" is used again, preceding a very large **claim** that nothing we perceive has a "right" name. And that **claim** is broadened by the statement in the same paragraph that culture and upbringing go so far as to determine how the world "looks," or what we see when we look at a thing. If the second use of "of course" similar to the first?
4. Is the "appearance" **claim** supported in the same way that the "right" name **claim** is?
5. In paragraph 8 Hayakawa puts the word "race" in quotes. Why?
6. In the same paragraph notice the word "real." Does real here mean what it meant in relation to names?
7. There is a good deal of humor in this essay. Find three examples of it (e.g., paragraph 12) and offer an explanation of its rhetorical function.

Despite what might appear to be the "liberality" of his linguistics, S. I. Hayakawa was the control-bringing president of San Francisco State from 1968 to 1973, and later a one-term Republican senator. *Language in Thought and Action*, from which this essay was taken, is often held up as a model of clear **expository** writing. It is here presented, "of course," as argument.

When Nice People Burn Books

Nat Hentoff

1   It happened one splendid Sunday morning in a church. Not Jerry Falwell's Baptist sanctuary in Lynchburg, Virginia, but rather the First Unitarian Church in Baltimore. On October 4, 1981, midway through the 11 A.M. service, pernicious ideas were burned at the altar.

2   As reported by Frank P. L. Somerville, religion editor of *The Baltimore Sun*, "Centuries of Jewish, Christian, Islamic, and Hindu writings were 'expurgated' because of sections described as 'sexist.'

3   "Touched off by a candle and consumed in a pot on a table in front of the altar were slips of paper containing 'patriarchal' excerpts from Martin Luther, Thomas Aquinas, the Koran, St. Augustine, St. Ambrose, St. John Chrysostom, the Hindu Code of Manu V, an anonymous Chinese author, and the Old Testament." Also hurled into the purifying fire were works by Kierkegaard and Karl Barth.

4   The congregation was much exalted: "As the last flame died in the pot, and the organ pealed, there was applause," Somerville wrote.

5   I reported this news of the singed holy spirit to a group of American Civil Liberties Union members in California, and one woman was furious. At me.

6   We did the same thing at our church two Sundays ago," she said. "And long past time, too. Don't you understand it's just symbolic?"

7   I told this ACLU member that when the school board in Drake, North Dakota, threw thirty-four copies of Kurt Vonnegut's *Slaughterhouse Five* into the furnace in 1973, it wasn't because the school was low on fuel. That burning was symbolic, too. Indeed, the two pyres—in North Dakota and in Baltimore—were witnessing to the same lack of faith in the free exchange of ideas.

8   What an inspiring homily for the children attending services at a liberated church: They now know that the way to handle ideas they don't like is to set them on fire.

9   The stirring ceremony in Baltimore is just one more illustration that the spirit of the First Amendment is not being savaged only by malign forces of the Right, whether private or governmental. Campaigns to purge school libraries, for example, have been conducted by feminists as well as by Phyllis Schlafly. Yet, most liberal watchdogs of our freedom remain fixed on the Right as the enemy of free expression.

10   For a salubrious change, therefore, let us look at what is happening to freedom of speech and press in certain enclaves—some colleges, for instance—where the New Right has no clout at all. Does the pulse of the First Amendment beat more vigorously in these places than where the Yahoos are?

11   Well, consider what happened when Eldridge Cleaver came to Madison, Wisconsin, last October to savor the exhilarating openness of dialogue at the University of Wisconsin. Cleaver's soul is no longer on ice; it's throbbing instead with a religious conviction that is currently connected financially, and presumably theologically, to the Reverend Sun Myung Moon's Unification Church. In Madison, Cleaver never got to talk about his pilgrim's progress from the Black Panthers to the wondrously ecumenical Moonies. In the Humanities Building— Humanities—several hundred students and others outraged by Cleaver's apostasy shouted, stamped their feet, chanted "Sieg Heil," and otherwise prevented him from being heard.

12   After ninety minutes of the din, Cleaver wrote on the blackboard, "I regret that the totalitarians have deprived us of our constitutional rights to free assembly and free speech. Down with communism. Long live democracy."

13   And, raising a clenched fist while blowing kisses with his free hand, Cleaver left. Cleaver says he'll try to speak again, but he doesn't know when.

14   The University of Wisconsin administration, through Dean of Students Paul Ginsberg, deplored the behavior of the campus totalitarians of the Left, and there was a fiercely denunciatory editorial in *The Madison Capital Times*: "These people lack even the most primitive appreciation of the Bill of Rights."

15   It did occur to me, however, that if Eldridge Cleaver had not abandoned his secularist rage at the American Leviathan and had come to Madison as the still burning spear of black radicalism, the result might have been quite different if he had been shouted down that night by young apostles of the New Right. That would have made news around the country, and there would have been collectively signed letters to *The New York Review of Books* and *The Nation* warning of the prowling dangers to free speech in the land. But since Cleaver has long since taken up with bad companions, there is not much concern among those who used to raise bail for him as to whether he gets to speak freely or not.

16   A few years ago, William F. Buckley Jr., invited to be commencement speaker at Vassar, was told by student groups that he not only would be shouted down if he came but might also suffer some contusions. All too few liberal members of the Vassar faculty tried to educate their students about the purpose of a university, and indeed a good many faculty members joined in the protests against Buckley's coming. He finally decided not to appear because, he told me, he didn't want to spoil the day for the parents. I saw no letters on behalf of Buckley's free-speech rights in any of the usual liberal forums for such concerns. After all, he had not only taken up with bad companions; he was an original bad companion.

17   During the current academic year, there were dismaying developments concerning freedom for bad ideas in the college press. The managing editor of *The Daily Lobo*, the University of New Mexico's student newspaper, claimed in an editorial that Scholastic Aptitude Test scores show minority students to be academically inferior. Rather than rebut his facile misinterpretation of what those scores actually show—that class, not race, affects the results—black students and their sympathizers invaded the newspaper's office.

18   The managing editor prudently resigned, but the protesters were not satisfied. They wanted the head of the editor. The brave Student Publications Board

temporarily suspended her, although the chairman of the journalism department had claimed the suspension was a violation of her First Amendment rights. She was finally given her job back, pending a formal hearing, but she decided to quit. The uproar had not abated, and who knew what would happen at her formal hearing before the Student Publications Board?

19   When it was all over, the chairman of the journalism department observed that the confrontation had actually reinforced respect for First Amendment rights on the University of New Mexico campus because infuriated students now knew they couldn't successfully insist on the firing of an editor because of what had been published.

20   What about the resignations? Oh, they were free-will offerings.

21   I subscribe to most of the journalism reviews around the country, but I saw no offer of support to those two beleaguered student editors in New Mexico from professional journalists who invoke the First Amendment at almost any public opportunity.

22   Then there was a free-speech war at Kent State University, as summarized in the November 12, 1982, issue of *National On-Campus Report*. Five student groups at Kent State are vigorously attempting to get the editor of the student newspaper fired. They are: "gay students, black students, the undergraduate and graduate student governments, and a progressive student alliance."

23   Not a reactionary among them. Most are probably deeply concerned with the savaging of the free press in Chile, Uruguay, Guatemala, South Africa, and other such places.

24   What had this editor at Kent State done to win the enmity of so humanistic a grand alliance? He had written an editorial that said that a gay student group should not have access to student-fee money to sponsor a Hallowe'en dance. Ah, but how had he gone about making his point?

25   "In opening statements," says the *National On-Campus Report*, "He employed words like 'queer' and 'nigger' to show that prejudice against any group is undesirable." Just like Lenny Bruce. Lenny, walking on stage in a club, peering into the audience, and asking, "Any spics here tonight? Any kikes? Any niggers?"

26   Do you think Lenny Bruce could get many college bookings today? Or write a column for a college newspaper?

27   In any case, the rest of the editorial went on to claim that the proper use of student fees was for educational, not social, activities. The editor was not singling out the Kent Gay/Lesbian Foundation. He was opposed to any student organization using those fees for dances.

28   Never mind. He had used impermissible words. Queer. Nigger. And those five influential cadres of students are after his head. The editor says that university officials have assured him, however, that he is protected at Kent State by the First Amendment. If that proves to be the case, those five student groups will surely move to terminate, if not defenestrate, those university officials.

29   It is difficult to be a disciple of James Madison on campus these days. Take the case of Phyllis Schlafly and Wabash College. The college is a small, well-regarded liberal arts institution in Crawfordsville, Indiana. In the spring of 1981,

the college was riven with discord. Some fifty members of the ninety-odd faculty and staff wrote a stiff letter to the Wabash Lecture Series Committee, which had displayed the exceedingly poor taste to invite Schlafly to speak on campus the next year.

30   The faculty protesters complained that having the Sweetheart of the Right near the Wabash River would be "unfortunate and inappropriate." The dread Schlafly is "an ERA opponent . . . a far-right attorney who travels the country, being highly paid to tell women to stay at home fulfilling traditional roles while sending their sons off to war."

31   Furthermore, the authors wrote, "The point of view she represents is that of an ever-decreasing minority of American women and men, and is based in sexist mythology which promulgates beliefs inconsistent with those held by liberally educated persons, and this does not merit a forum at Wabash College under the sponsorship of our Lecture Series."

32   This is an intriguing document by people steeped in the traditions of academic freedom. One of the ways of deciding who gets invited to a campus is the speaker's popularity. If the speaker appeals only to a "decreasing minority of American women and men," she's not worth the fee. So much for Dorothy Day, were she still with us.

33   And heaven forfend that anyone be invited whose beliefs are "inconsistent with those held by liberally educated persons." Mirror, mirror on the wall.

34   But do not get the wrong idea about these protesting faculty members: "We subscribe," they emphasized, "to the principles of free speech and free association, of course."

35   All the same, "it does not enhance our image as an all-male college to endorse a well-known sexist by inviting her to speak on our campus." If Phyllis Schlafly is invited nonetheless, "we intend not to participate in any of the activities surrounding Ms. Schlafly's visit and will urge others to do the same."

36   The moral of the story: If you don't like certain ideas, boycott them.

37   The lecture committee responded to the fifty deeply offended faculty members in a most unkind way. The committee told the signers that "William Buckley would endorse your petition. No institution of higher learning, he told us on a visit here, should allow to be heard on its campus any position that it regards as detrimental or 'untrue.'"

38   "Apparently," the committee went on, "error is to be refuted not by rational persuasion, but by censorship."

39   Phyllis Schlafly did come to Wabash and she generated a great deal of discussion—most of it against her views—among members of the all-male student body. However, some of the wounded faculty took a long time to recover.

40   One of them, a tenured professor, took aside at a social gathering the wife of a member of the lecture committee that had invited Schlafly. Both were in the same feminist group on campus.

41   The professor cleared her throat, and said to the other woman, "You are going to leave him, aren't you?"

42   "My husband? Why should I leave him?"

43   "Really, how can you stay married to someone who invited Phyllis Schlafly to this campus?"

44   And really, should such a man even be allowed visitation rights with the children?

45   Then there is the Ku Klux Klan. As Klan members have learned in recent months, both in Boston and in Washington, their First Amendment right peaceably to assemble—let alone actually to speak their minds—can only be exercised if they are prepared to be punched in the mouth. Klan members get the same reception that Martin Luther King Jr. and his associates used to receive in Bull Conner's Birmingham.

46   As all right-thinking people know, however, the First Amendment isn't just for anybody. That presumably is why the administration of the University of Cincinnati has refused this year to allow the KKK to appear on campus. Bill Wilkerson, the Imperial Wizard of the particular Klan faction that has been barred from the University of Cincinnati, says he's going to sue on First Amendment grounds.

47   Aside from the ACLU's, how many *amicus* briefs do you think the Imperial Wizard is likely to get from liberal organizations devoted to academic freedom?

---

1. The incident in paragraph 1 happened in one place and, therefore, did not happen *everywhere else.* Given this, why does Hentoff tell his readers a specific place that it did not happen?
2. Of paragraphs 2 and 3, one sentence is Hentoff's. Given that it is impossible to "hurl" a slip of paper, what sort of rhetorical device are we seeing here?
3. In paragraph 7, Hentoff uses the word "faith." Can an argument be made that he is playing on the word's religious associations?
4. Elaborate on what Hentoff may have in mind with the phrase "singed holy spirit" in paragraph 5 and "stirring ceremony" in paragraph 9.

Nat Hentoff writes regularly for *The Village Voice* and other politically interested magazines. He is probably best known as a tireless defender of the First Amendment. His *The First Freedom: The Tumultuous History of Free Speech in America* was published in 1980.

The Gettysburg Address[1]

Gilbert Highet

Fourscore and seven years ago our fathers brought forth on this continent, a new nation, conceived in Liberty, and dedicated to the proposition that all men are created equal.

Now we are engaged in a great civil war, testing whether that nation or any nation so conceived and so dedicated, can long endure. We are met on a great battle-field of that war. We have come to dedicate a portion of that field, as a final resting place for those who here gave their lives that that nation might live. It is altogether fitting and proper that we should do this.

But, in a larger sense, we can not dedicate—we can not consecrate—we can not hallow—this ground. The brave men, living and dead, who struggled here, have consecrated it, far above our poor power to add or detract. The world will little note, nor long remember, what we say here, but it can never forget what they did here. It is for us the living, rather, to be dedicated here to the unfinished work which they who fought here have thus far so nobly advanced. It is rather for us to be here dedicated to the great task remaining before us—that from these honored dead we take increased devotion to that cause for which they gave the last full measure of devotion—that we here highly resolve that these dead shall not have died in vain—that this nation, under God, shall have a new birth of freedom—and that government of the people, by the people, for the people, shall not perish from the earth.

Fourscore and seven years ago . . .

1   These five words stand at the entrance to the best-known monument of American prose, one of the finest utterances in the entire language, and surely one of the greatest speeches in all history. Greatness is like granite: it is molded in fire, and it lasts for many centuries.

2   Fourscore and seven years ago. . . . It is strange to think that President Lincoln was looking back to the 4th of July 1776, and that he and his speech are now further removed from us than he himself was from George Washington and the Declaration of Independence.

3   Fourscore and seven years before the Gettysburg Address, a small group of patriots signed the Declaration. Fourscore and seven years after the Gettysburg Address, it was the year 1950, and that date is already receding rapidly into our troubled, adventurous, and valiant past.

4   Inadequately prepared and at first scarcely realized in its full importance, the dedication of the graveyard at Gettysburg was one of the supreme moments of

---

[1] This essay is treated at length in Chapter 2.

American history. The battle itself had been a turning point of the war. On the 4th of July 1863, General Meade repelled Lee's invasion of Pennsylvania. Although he did not follow up his victory, he had broken one of the most formidable aggressive enterprises of the Confederate armies. Losses were heavy on both sides. Thousands of dead were left on the field, and thousands of wounded died in the hot days following the battle. At first, their burial was more or less haphazard; but thoughtful men gradually came to feel that an adequate burying place and memorial were required. These were established by an interstate commission that autumn, and the finest speaker in the North was invited to dedicate them. This was the scholar and statesman Edward Everett of Harvard. He made a good speech—which is still extant: not at all academic, it is full of close strategic analysis and deep historical understanding.

5   Lincoln was not invited to speak, at first. Although people knew him as an effective debater, they were not sure whether he was capable of making a serious speech on such a solemn occasion. But one of the impressive things about Lincoln's career is that he constantly strove to grow. He was anxious to appear on that occasion and to say something worthy of it. (Also, it has been suggested, he was anxious to remove the impression that he did not know how to behave properly—an impression which had been strengthened by a shocking story about his clowning on the battlefield of Antietam the previous year.) Therefore when he was invited he took considerable care with his speech. He drafted rather more than half of it in the White House before leaving, finished it in the hotel at Gettysburg the night before the ceremony (not in the train, as sometimes reported), and wrote out a fair copy next morning.

6   There are many accounts of the day itself, 19 November 1863. There are many descriptions of Lincoln, all showing the same curious blend of grandeur and awkwardness, or lack of dignity, or—it would be best to call it humility. In the procession he rode horseback: a tall lean man in a high plug hat, straddling a short horse, with his feet too near the ground. He arrived before the chief speaker, and had to wait patiently for half an hour or more. His own speech came right at the end of a long and exhausting ceremony, lasted less than three minutes, and made little impression on the audience. In part this was because they were tired, in part because (as eyewitnesses said) he ended almost before they knew he had begun, and in part because he did not speak the Address, but read it, very slowly, in a thin high voice, with a marked Kentucky accent, pronouncing "to" as "toe" and dropping his final R's.

7   Some people of course were alert enough to be impressed. Everett congratulated him at once. But most of the newspapers paid little attention to the speech, and some sneered at it. *The Patriot and Union* of Harrisburg wrote, "We pass over the silly remarks of the President; for the credit of the nation we are willing . . . that they shall no more be repeated or thought of"; and the *London Times* said, "The ceremony was rendered ludicrous by some of the sallies of that poor President Lincoln," calling his remarks "dull and commonplace." The first commendation of the Address came in a single sentence of the *Chicago Tribune*, and the first discriminating and detailed praise of it appeared in the *Springfield Republican*, the *Providence Journal* and the *Philadelphia Bulletin*. However,

three weeks after the ceremony and then again the following spring, the editor of *Harper's Weekly* published a sincere and thorough eulogy of the Address, and soon it was attaining recognition as a masterpiece.

8   At the time, Lincoln could not care much about the reception of his words. He was exhausted and ill. In the train back to Washington, he lay down with a wet towel on his head. He had caught smallpox. At that moment he was incubating it, and he was stricken down soon after he reentered the White House. Fortunately it was a mild attack, and it evoked one of his best jokes: he told his visitors, "At last I have something I can give to everybody."

9   He had more than that to give to everybody. He was a unique person, far greater than most people realize until they read his life with care. The wisdom of his policy, the sources of his statesmanship— these were things too complex to be discussed in a brief essay. But we can say something about the Gettysburg Address as a work of art.

10   A work of art. Yes: for Lincoln was a literary artist, trained both by others and by himself. The textbooks he used as a boy were full of difficult exercises and skillful devices in formal rhetoric, stressing the qualities he practiced in his own speaking: antithesis, parallelism, and verbal harmony. Then he read and reread many admirable models of thought and expression: the King James Bible, the essays of Bacon, the best plays of Shakespeare. His favorites were *Hamlet, Lear, Macbeth, Richard III,* and *Henry IV,* which he had read dozens of times. He loved reading aloud, too, and spent hours reading poetry to his friends. (He told his partner Herndon that he preferred getting the sense of any document by reading it aloud.) Therefore, his serious speeches are important parts of the long and noble classic tradition of oratory which begins in Greece, runs through Rome to the modern world, and is still capable (if we do not neglect it) of producing masterpieces.

11   The first proof of this is that the Gettysburg Address is full of quotations— or rather of adaptations—which give it strength. It is partly religious, partly (in the highest sense) political: therefore it is interwoven with memories of the Bible and memories of American history. The first and the last words are Biblical cadences. Normally Lincoln did not say "Fourscore" when he meant eighty; but on this solemn occasion he recalled the important dates in the Bible—such as the age of Abraham when his first son was born to him, and he was "Fourscore and six years old."[2] Similarly he did not say there was a chance that democracy might die out: he recalled the somber phrasing of the Book of Job—where Bildad speaks of the destruction of one who shall vanish without a trace, and says that "his branch shall be cut off; his remembrance shall perish from the earth."[3] Then again, the famous descriptions of our State as "government of the people, by the people, for the people" was adumbrated by Daniel Webster in 1830 (he spoke of "the people's government, made for the people, made by the people,

---

2 Genesis 16:16.

3 Job 18:16-17.

and answerable to the people") and then elaborated in 1854 by the abolitionist Theodore Parker (as "government of all the people, by all the people, for all the people"). There is good reason to think that Lincoln took the important phrase "Under God" (which he interpolated at the last moment) from Weems, the biographer of Washington; and we know that it had been used at least once by Washington himself.

12   Analyzing the Address further, we find that it is based on a native theme or group of themes. The subject is—how can we put it so as not to disfigure it?— the subject is the kinship of life and death, that mysterious linkage which we see sometimes as the physical succession of birth and death in our world, sometimes as the contrast, which is perhaps a unity, between death and immortality. The first sentence is concerned with birth:

> Our fathers brought forth a new nation, conceived in liberty.

13   The final phrase but one expresses the hope that

> this nation, under God, shall have a *new birth* of freedom.

14   And the last phrase of all speaks of continuing life as the triumph over death. Again and again throughout the speech, this mystical contrast and kinship reappear: "those who *gave their lives* that that nation might *live*," "the brave men *living* and *dead*," and so in the central assertion that the dead have already consecrated their own burial place, while "it is for us, the *living*, rather to be dedicated . . . to the great task remaining." The Gettysburg Address is a prose poem; it belongs to the same world as the great elegies, and the adagios of Beethoven.

15   Its structure, however, is that of a skillfully contrived speech. The oratorical pattern is perfectly clear. Lincoln describes the occasion, dedicates the ground, and then draws a larger conclusion by calling on his hearers to dedicate themselves to the preservation of the Union. But within that, we can trace his constant use of at least two important rhetorical devices.

16   The first of these is *antithesis*: opposition, contrast. The speech is full of it. Listen:

> The world will little *note*
> nor long *remember*   what *we say* here
> but it can never *forget*   what *they did* here.

17   And so in nearly every sentence: "brave men, living and dead"; "to add or detract." There is the antithesis of the Founding Fathers and the men of Lincoln's own time:

> Our fathers *brought forth* a new nation. . . .
>
> Now *we* are . . . testing whether that nation . . . can long *endure*.

18   And there is the more terrible antithesis of those who have already died and those who still live to do their duty. Now, antithesis is the figure of contrast and conflict. Lincoln was speaking in the midst of a great civil war.

19   The other important pattern is different. It is technically called tricolon—the division of an idea into three harmonious parts, usually of increasing power. The most famous phrase of the Address is a tricolon:

> government of the people
> by the people
> and   for the people.

20   The most solemn sentence is a tricolon:

> we cannot dedicate
> we cannot consecrate
> we cannot hallow this ground.

21   And above all, the last sentence (which has sometimes been criticized as too complex) is essentially two parallel phrases, with a tricolon growing out of the second and then producing another tricolon: a trunk, three branches, and a cluster of flowers. Lincoln says that it is for his hearers to be dedicated to the great task remaining before them. Then he goes on,

> that from these honored dead

—apparently he means "in such a way that from these honored dead"—

> we take increased devotion to that cause.

22   Next, he restates this more briefly:

> that we here highly resolve . . .

23   And now the actual resolution follows, in three parts of growing intensity:

> that these dead shall not have died in vain
> that this nation, under God, shall have a new birth of freedom

and that (one more tricolon)

> government of the people
> by the people
> and   for the people
> shall not perish from the earth.

24   Now, the tricolon is the figure which, through division, emphasizes basic harmony and unity. Lincoln used antithesis because he was speaking to a people at war. He used the tricolon because he was hoping, planning, praying for peace.

25   No one thinks that when he was drafting the Gettysburg Address, Lincoln deliberately looked up these quotations and consciously chose these particular patterns of thought. No, he chose the theme. From its development and from the emotional tone of the entire occasion, all the rest followed, or grew—by that marvelous process of choice and rejection which is essential to artistic creation. It does not spoil such a work of art to analyze it as closely as we have done; it is altogether fitting and proper that we should do this: for it helps us to penetrate more deeply into the rich meaning of the Gettysburg Address, and it allows us the very rare privilege of watching the workings of a great man's mind.

A Person Paper on Purity in Language

William Satire (alias Douglas R. Hofstadter) (September, 1983)

1   It's high time someone blew the whistle on all the silly prattle about revamping our language to suit the purposes of certain political fanatics. You know what I'm talking about—those who accuse speakers of English of what they call "racism." This awkward neologism, constructed by analogy with the well-established term "sexism," does not sit well in the ears, if I may mix my metaphors. But let us grant that in our society there may be injustices here and there in the treatment of either race from time to time, and let us even grant these people their terms "racism" and "racist." How valid, however, are the claims of the self-proclaimed "black libbers," or "negrists"—those who would radically change our language in order to"liberate" us poor dupes from its supposed racist bias?

2   Most of the clamor, as you certainly know by now, revolves around the age-old usage of the noun "white" and words built from it, such as *chairwhite, mailwhite, repairwhite, clergywhite, middlewhite, Frenchwhite, forewhite, whitepower, whiteslaughter, oneupwhiteship, straw white, whitehandle,* and so on. The negrists claim that using the word "white," either on its own or as a component, to talk about *all* the members of the human species is somehow degrading to blacks and reinforces racism. Therefore the libbers propose that we substitute "person" everywhere where "white" now occurs. Sensitive speakers of our secretary tongue of course find this preposterous. There is great beauty to a phrase such as "All whites are created equal." Our forebosses who framed the Declaration of Independence well understood the poetry of our language. Think how ugly it would be to say "All persons are created equal," or "All whites and blacks are created equal." Besides, as any schoolwhitey can tell you, such phrases are redundant. In most contexts, it is self-evident when "white" is being used in an inclusive sense, in which case it subsumes members of the darker race just as much as fairskins.

3   There is nothing denigrating to black people in being subsumed under the rubric "white"—no more than under the rubric "person." After all, white is a mixture of all the colors of the rainbow, including black. Used exclusively, the word "white" has no connotations whatsoever of race. Yet many people are hung up on this point. A prime example is Abraham Moses, one of the more vocal spokeswhites for making such a shift. For years, Niss Moses, authoroon of the well-known negrist tracts *A Handbook of Nonracist Writing* and *Words and Blacks,* has had nothing better to do than go around the country making speeches advocating the downfall of "racist language" that ble objects to. But when you analyze bler objections, you find they all fall apart at the seams. Niss

Moses says that words like "chairwhite" suggest to people—most especially impressionable young whiteys and blackeys—that all chairwhites belong to the white race. How absurd! It is quite obvious, for instance, that the chairwhite of the League of Black Voters is going to be a black, not a white. Nobody need think twice about it. As a matter of fact, the suffix "white" is usually not pronounced with a long 'i' as in the noun "white," but like "wit," as in the terms *saleswhite, freshwhite, penwhiteship, first basewhite,* and so on. It's just a simple and useful component in building race-neutral words.

4   But Niss Moses would have you sit up and start hollering "Racism!" In fact, Niss Moses sees evidence of racism under every stone. Ble has written a famous article, in which ble vehemently objects to the immortal and poetic words of the first white on the moon, Captain Nellie Strongarm. If you will recall, whis words were:"One small step for a white, a giant step for whitekind." This noble sentiment is anything but racist; it is simply a celebration of a glorious moment in the history of White.

5   Another of Niss Moses' shrill objections is to the age-old differentiation of whites from blacks by the third-person pronouns "whe" and "ble." Ble promotes an absurd notion: that what we really need in English is a single pronoun covering *both* races. Numerous suggestions have been made, such as "pe," "tey," and others. These are all repugnant to the nature of the English language, as the average white in the street will testify, even if whe has no linguistic training whatsoever. Then there are advocates of usages such as "whe or ble," "whis or bler," and so forth. This makes for monstrosities such as the sentence "When the next President takes office, whe or ble will have to choose whis or bler cabinet with great care, for whe or ble would not want to offend any minorities." Contrast this with the spare elegance of the normal way of putting it, and there is no question which way we ought to speak. There are, of course, some yapping black libbers who advocate writing "bl/whe" everywhere, which, aside from looking terrible, has no reasonable pronunciation. Shall we say "blooey" all the time when we simply mean "whe"? Who wants to sound like a white with a chronic sneeze?

*   *

6   One of the more hilarious suggestions made by the squawkers for this point of view is to abandon the natural distinction along racial lines, and to replace it with a highly unnatural one along sexual lines. One such suggestion—emanating, no doubt, from the mind of a madwhite—would have us say "he" for male whites (and blacks) and "she" for female whites (and blacks). Can you imagine the outrage with which sensible folk of either sex would greet this "modest proposal"?

7   Another suggestion is that the plural pronoun "they" be used in place of the inclusive "whe." This would turn the charming proverb "Whe who laughs last, laughs best" into the bizarre concoction "They who laughs last, laughs best." As if anyone in whis right mind could have thought that the original proverb applied only to the white race! No, we don't need a new pronoun to "liberate" our minds. That's the lazy white's way of solving the pseudo-problem of racism.

In any case, it's ungrammatical. The pronoun "they" is a plural pronoun, and it grates on the civilized ear to hear it used to denote only one person. Such a usage, if adopted, would merely promote illiteracy and accelerate the already scandalously rapid nosedive of the average intelligence level in our society.

8   Niss Moses would have us totally revamp the English language to suit bler purposes. If, for instance, we are to substitute "person" for "white," where are we to stop? If we were to follow Niss Moses' ideas to their logical conclusion, we would have to conclude that ble would like to see small blackeys and whiteys playing the game of "Hangperson" and reading the story of "Snow Person and the Seven Dwarfs." And would ble have us rewrite history to say, "Don't shoot until you see the *persons* of their eyes!"? Will pundits and politicians henceforth issue *person* papers? Will we now have egg yolks and egg *persons*? And pledge allegiance to the good old Red, *Person*, and Blue? Will we sing, "I'm dreaming of a *person* Christmas"? Say of a frightened white, "Whe's *person* as a sheet!"? Lament the increase of *person*-collar crime? Thrill to the chirping of bob*persons* in our gardens? Ask a friend to *person* the table while we go visit the *persons'* room? Come off it, Niss Moses—don't personwash our language!

9   What conceivable harm is there in such beloved phrases as "No white is an island," "Dog is white's best friend," or "White's inhumanity to white"? Who would revise such classic book titles as Bronob Jacowski's *The Ascent of White* of Eric Steeple Bell's *Whites of Mathematics*? Did the poet who wrote "The best-laid plans of mice and whites gang aft agley" believe that blacks' plans gang *ne'er* agley? Surely not! Such phrases are simply metaphors; everyone can see beyond that. Whe who interprets them as reinforcing racism must have a perverse desire to feel oppressed.

10   "Personhandling" the language is a habit that not only Niss Moses but quite a few others have taken up recently. For instance, Nrs. Delilah Buford has urged that we drop the useful distinction between "Niss " and "Nrs." (which, as everybody know, is pronounced "Nissiz," the reason for which nobody knows!). Bler argument is that there is no need for the public to know whether a black is employed or not. *Need* is, of course, not the point. Ble conveniently sidesteps the fact that there is a *tradition* in our society of calling unemployed blacks "Niss" and employed blacks "Nrs." Most blacks—in fact, the vast majority—prefer it that way. They *want* the world to know what their employment status is, and for good reason. Unemployed blacks want prospective employers to know they are available, without having to ask embarrassing questions. Likewise, employed blacks are proud of having found a job, and wish to let the world know they are employed. This distinction provides a sense of security to all involved, in that everyone knows where ble fits into the scheme of things.

11   But Nrs. Buford refuses to recognize this simple truth. Instead, ble shiftily turns the arguments into one about whites, asking why it is that whites are universally addressed as "Master," without any differentiation between employed and unemployed ones. The answer, of course, is that in Anerica and other Northern societies, we set little store by the employment status of whites. Nrs. Buford can do little to change that reality, for it seems to be tied to innate biological differences between whites and blacks. Many white-years of research, in fact,

have gone into trying to understand why it is that employment status matters so much to blacks, yet relatively little whites. It is true that both races have a longer life expectancy if employed, but of course people often do not act so as to maximize their life expectancy. So far, it remains a mystery. In any case, whites and blacks clearly have different constitutional inclinations, and different goals in life. And so I say, *Vive na différence!*

*   *

12   As for Nrs. Buford's suggestion that both "Niss" and "Nrs." be unified into the single form of address "Ns." (supposed to rhyme with "fizz"), all I have to say is, it is arbitrary and clearly a thousand years ahead of its time. Mind you, this "Ns." is an abbreviation concocted out of thin air: it stands for absolutely nothing. Who ever heard of such toying with language? And while we're on this subject, have you yet run across the recently founded *Ns.* Magazine, dedicated to the concerns of the "liberated black"? It's sure to attract the attention of a trendy band of black airheads for a little while, but serious blacks surely will see through its thin veneer of slick, glossy Madison Avenue approaches to life.

13   Nrs. Buford also finds it insultingly asymmetric that when a black is employed by a white, ble changes bler firmly name to whis firmly name. But what's so bad about that? Every firm's core consists of a boss (whis job is to make sure long-term policies are well charted out) and a secretary (bler job is to keep corporate affairs running smoothly on a day-to-day basis). They are both equally important and vital to the firm's success. No one disputes this. Beyond them there may of course be other firmly members. Now it's quite obvious that all members of a given firm should bear the same firmly name—otherwise, what are you going to call the firm's products? And since it would be nonsense for the boss to change whis name, it falls to the secretary to change bler name. Logic, not racism, dictates this simple convention.

14   What puzzles me the most is when people cut off their noses to spite their faces. Such is the case with the time-honored colored suffixes "oon" and "roon," found in familiar words such as *ambassadroon, stewardoon,* and *sculptroon.* Most blacks find it natural and sensible to add those suffixes onto nouns such as "aviator" or "waiter." A black who flies an airplane may proudly proclaim, "I'm an aviatroon!" But it would sound silly, if not ridiculous, for a black to say of blerself, "I work as a waiter." On the other hand, who could object to my saying that the lively Ticely Cyson is a great actroon, or that the hilarious Quill Bosby is a great comedioon? You guessed it—authoroons such as Niss Mildred Hempsley and Nrs. Charles White, both of whom angrily reject the appellation "authoroon," deep though its roots are in our language. Nrs. White, perhaps one of the finest poetoons of our day, for some reason insists on being known as a "poet." It leads one to wonder, is Nrs. White *ashamed* of being black, perhaps? I should hope not. White needs Black, and Black needs White, and neither race should feel ashamed.

15   Some extreme negrists object to being treated with politeness and courtesy by whites. For example, they reject the traditional notion of "Negroes first," preferring to open doors for themselves, claiming that having doors opened for

them suggests implicitly that society considers them inferior. Well, would they have it the other way? Would these incorrigible grousers prefer to open doors for whites? What do blacks want?

*   *

16   Another unlikely word has recently become a subject of controversy: "blackey." This is, of course, the ordinary term for black children (including teen-agers), and by affectionate extension it is often applied to older blacks. Yet, incredible though it seems, many blacks—even teen-age blackeys—now claim to have had their "consciousness raised," and are voguishly skittish about being called "blackeys." Yet it's as old as the hills for blacks employed in the same office to refer to themselves as "the office blackeys." And for their superior to call them "my blackeys" helps make the ambiance more relaxed and comfy for all. It's hardly the mortal insult that libbers claim it to be. Fortunately, most blacks are sensible people and realize that mere words do not demean; they know it's how they are *used* that counts. Most of the time, calling a black—especially an older black—a "blackey" is a thoughtful way of complimenting bler, making bler feel young, fresh, and hirable again. Lord knows, I certainly wouldn't object if someone told me that I looked whiteyish these days!

17   Many young blackeys go through a stage of wishing they had been born white. Perhaps this is due to popular television shows like *Superwhite* and *Batwhite*, but it doesn't really matter. It is perfectly normal and healthy. Many of our most successful blacks were once tomwhiteys and feel no shame about it. Why should they? Frankly, I think tomwhiteys are often the cutest little blackeys—but that's just my opinion. In any case, Niss Moses (once again) raises a ruckus on this score, asking why we don't have a corresponding word for young whiteys who play blackeys' games and generally manifest a desire to be black. Well, Niss Moses, if this were a common phenomenon, we most assuredly *would* have such a word, but it just happens not to be. Who can say why? But given that tomwhiteyes are a dime a dozen, it's nice to have a word for them. The lesson is that White must learn to fit language to reality; White cannot manipulate the world by manipulating mere words. An elementary lesson, to be sure, but for some reason Niss Moses and others of bler ilk resist learning it.

18   Shifting from the ridiculous to the sublime, let us consider the Holy Bible. The Good Book is of course the source of some of the most beautiful language and profound imagery to be found anywhere. And who is the central character of the Bible? I am sure I need hardly remind you; it is God. As everyone knows, Whe is male and white, and that is an indisputable fact. But have you heard the latest joke promulgated by tasteless negrists? It is said that one of them died and went to Heaven and then returned. What did ble report? "I have seen God, and guess what? Ble's female!" Can anyone say that this is not blasphemy of the highest order? It just goes to show that some people will stoop to any depths in order to shock, I have shared this "joke" with a number of friends of mine (including several blacks, by the way), and, to a white, they have agreed that it sickens them to the core to see Our Lord so shabbily mocked. Some things are just in bad taste, and there are no two ways about it. It is scum like this who are responsible for some of the great problems in our society today, I am sorry to say.

*   *

19   Well, all of this is just another skirmish in the age-old Battle of the Races, I guess, and we shouldn't take it too seriously. I am reminded of words spoken by the great British philosopher Alfred West Malehead in whis commencement address to my *alma secretaria*, the University of North Virginia: "To enrich the language of whites is, certainly, to enlarge the range of their ideas." I agree with this admirable sentiment wholeheartedly. I would merely point out to the overzealous that there are some extravagant notions about language that should be recognized for what they are: cheap attempts to let dogmatic, narrow minds enforce their views on the speakers lucky enough to have inherited the richest, most beautiful and flexible language on earth, a language whose traditions run back through the centuries to such deathless poets as Milton, Shakespeare, Wordsworth, Keats, Walt Whitwhite, and so many others . . . Our language owes an incalculable debt to these whites for their clarity of vision and expression, and if the shallow minds of bandwagon-jumping negrists succeed in destroying this precious heritage for all whites of good will, that will be, without any doubt, a truly female day in the history of Northern White.

Post Scriptum

20   Perhaps this piece shocks you. It is meant to. The entire point of it is to use something that we find shocking as leverage to illustrate the fact that something that we usually close our eyes to is also very shocking. The most effective way I know to do so is to develop an extended analogy with something known as shocking and reprehensible. Racism is that thing, in this case. I am happy with this piece, despite—but also because of—its shock value. I think it makes its point better than any factual article could. As a friend of mine said,"It makes you so uncomfortable that you can't ignore it." I admit that rereading it makes even me, the author, uncomfortable!

21   Numerous friends have warned me that in publishing this piece I am taking a serious risk of earning myself a reputation as a terrible racist. I guess I cannot truly believe that anyone would see this piece that way. To misperceive it this way would be like calling someone a vicious racist for telling other people "The word 'nigger' is extremely offensive." If *allusions* to racism, especially for the purpose of satirizing racism and its cousins, are confused with racism itself, then I think it is time to stop writing.

22   Some people have asked me if to write this piece, I simply took a genuine William Safire column (appearing weekly in the *New York Times Magazine* under the title "On Language") and "fiddled" with it. That is far from the truth. For years I have collected examples of sexist language, and in order to produce this piece, I dipped into this collection, selected some of the choicest, and ordered them very carefully. "Translating" them into this alternate world was sometimes

extremely difficult, and some words took weeks. The hardest terms of all, surprisingly enough, were "Niss," "Nrs.," and "Ns.," even though "Master" came immediately. The piece itself is not based on any particular article by William Safire, but Safire has without doubt been one of the most vocal opponents of nonsexist language reforms, and therefore merits being safired upon.

23   Interestingly, Master Safire has recently spoken out on sexism in whis column (August 5, 1984). Lamenting the inaccuracy of writing either "Mrs. Ferraro" or "Miss Ferraro" to designate the Democratic vice-presidential candidate whose husband's name is "Zaccaro," whe writes:

> It breaks my heart to suggest this, but the time has come for *Ms.* We are no longer faced with a theory, but a condition. It is unacceptable for journalists to dictate to a candidate that she call herself *Miss* or else use her married name; it is equally unacceptable for a candidate to demand that newspapers print a blatant inaccuracy by applying a married honorific to a maiden name.

How disappointing it is when someone finally winds up doing the right thing but for the wrong reasons! In Safire's case, this shift was entirely for journalistic rather than humanistic reasons! It's as if Safire wished that women had never entered the political ring, so that the Grand Old Conventions of English—good enough for our grandfathers—would never have had to be challenged. How heartless of women! How heartbreaking the toll on our beautiful language!

---

1. When you read this piece for the first time (and it requires several readings), highlight every term that is unusual. What is it that is unusual about the last sentence of the first paragraph?
2. How long did it take you to figure out what sort of substitutions Hofstadter is making?
3. Paragraphs 3 and 4 complicate the matter even more by problematizing what are, for us, gendered pronouns. Make a chart identifying the "translated" references for "Niss," "whis," bler," etc.
4. Notice that Hofstadter waits until paragraph 12 to say anything that would clarify his use of "secretary tongue" in paragraph 2. Why do you think he does this?

Hofstadter is a regular columnist for *Scientific American*, where his column was intended, says the editor of that journal, to present "a bridge between the scientific and the literary viewpoints." Hofstadter himself comments that he had been offered "a unique opportunity to say anything I wanted to say to a vast, ready-made audience in a prestigious context." From our perspective this means that the **audience** for whom Hofstader writes can be counted on to put more effort into reading what he writes than the columnist who writes for a daily newspaper can expect.

Gays' Parade a Useful Exercise

Molly Ivins

1   Well, the gay folks had a fine march in Washington, D.C., but I think they missed a couple of bets. Jack Gordon suggests that they should have had a ceremony thanking the feds for naming that fine building right there on Pennsylvania Avenue after one of their own. That's the J. Edgar Hoover Building.[1]

2   Speaking of whom, there was a great example of why we don't want to force gays to stay in the closet.

3   And I would have liked to see a banner reading "Ban Heterosexuals from the Military—Remember Tailhook." I trust you all took a look at the charming little report on that incident.[2]

4   I suspect that finally ventilating all the myths and misconceptions about gays is a useful exercise, even for those who should prefer not to think about them. "I have nothing against gays," my mother is fond of saying, "I just wish they'd stay in the closet." But we all know by now—or should—that that state of affairs was cruel and unjust and led to terrible abuses.

5   Of all the odd misperceptions current about homosexuality, perhaps the oddest is that it is a choice, that people choose to be homosexual.

6   That strikes me as so patently silly. Did any of us who are straight choose to be heterosexual? When? For heaven's sakes, how can anyone believe that people choose to be homosexual? "I think it would be a lot of fun to be called 'queer' and 'sissy' for the rest of my life, so I think I'll be gay."

7   Last time I checked, the experts were still leaning toward the view that homosexuality is multicausational (isn't that a dandy word?). Most gay people I know believe they were literally born that way, that it's like being left-handed or brown-eyed. But in at least some cases, there is apparently some developmental influence as well.

8   The best description I ever heard of sexual orientation came from Dr. John Money of Johns Hopkins University, who used to draw it on a horizontal scale going from 1 to 10, with 1 being completely homosexual and 10 being completely

---

[1] J. Edgar Hoover was director of the FBI for 48 years. It has been suggested that Hoover's dedication to looking for "Reds" and his attempt to break Martin Luther King rather than pursuing organized crime was the result of organized crime's knowledge of his being a transvestite and a homosexual.

[2] "Tailhook" refers to a 1991 Las Vegas convention of aircraft carrier pilots and personnel after which the U.S. Navy severed its ties with the organization in the wake of accusations of sexual assault, public lewdness, and the use of government vehicles in the transportation of prostitutes, all with the knowledge and tacit consent of military leaders.

heterosexual. Money says that very few people are either 1 or 10 and about as few are at 5 (totally bisexual). Most of us fall into a clump ranging from about 6 to 8, while there's a smaller clump of homosexuals ranging from about 4 to 2.

9   Because homosexuality occurs in many species of animals and because it has appeared in all human cultures throughout history, we must conclude that it is what statisticians call a "normal aberrant" (and isn't that a dandy phrase?).

10   I saw a letter to the editor last week declaring that homosexuality is a symptom of the decadence and decline of civilization and that it didn't exist among primitive people such as American Indians. *Au contraire*, as we say in Lubbock. Aside from the insult to Indians, there were indeed gay Indians before the white man came, and at least in the Plains tribes, they were regarded as sort of endearingly special.

11   As a matter of law, I do not see that we have any choice but to seek to ensure that gays have full civil rights. They are citizens; as Jesse Jackson said Sunday, no one gives them a break on April 15. They serve honorably in the military, ban or no ban.

12   It has been my observation that some gay people are absolutely wonderful human beings, and some are complete you-know-whats, and most are somewhere in between. Depressingly like heterosexuals. So I suggest we all grow up and get over our small-town prejudices. (I can never remember whether it was "Queers wear red on Friday" or "green on Thursday." Didn't we grow up with some silly ideas?) In our fair land, no one can force us to be tolerant. But neither can prejudice be allowed to keep people out of jobs for which they are qualified.

13   I suppose some people will continue to feel entitled to hate gays. As the psychiatrists have been telling us, hating them seems to be a function of being afraid that you might be one yourself.

---

1. Highlight the words in the text that indicate her **level of diction**.
2. What rhetorical purpose does Ivins use her mother for?
3. Write a **target audience** consideration of what you think is going on in her last paragraph. While this does not constitute *invective*, how might it be related to its rhetorical use.

Molly Ivins is a Texan who writes frequently for the *Nation* and other national magazines of political opinion. The cover of her book *Molly Ivins Can't Say That, Can She?* carries a picture of the author with her boots up on the desk. And she's smiling.

Junk and the First Amendment

Susan Jacoby

1   It is no news that many women are defecting from the ranks of civil libertarians on the issue of obscenity. The conviction of Larry Flynt, publisher of *Hustler* magazine—before his metamorphosis into a born-again Christian—was greeted with unabashed feminist approval. Harry Rheems, the unknown actor who was convicted by a Memphis jury for conspiring to distribute the movie *Deep Throat*, has carried on his legal battles with almost no support from women who ordinarily regard themselves as supporters of the First Amendment. Feminist writers and scholars have even discussed the possibility of making common cause against pornography with adversaries of the women's movement—including opponents of the equal rights amendment and "right-to-life" forces.

2   All of this is deeply disturbing to a woman writer who believes, as I always have and still do, in an absolute interpretation of the First Amendment. Nothing in Larry Flynt's garbage convinces me that the late Justice Hugo L. Black was wrong in his opinion that "the Federal Government is without any power whatsoever under the Constitution to put any type of burden on free speech and expression of ideas of any kind (as distinguished from conduct)." Many women I like and respect tell me I am wrong; I cannot remember having become involved in so many heated discussions of a public issue since the end of the Vietnam War. A feminist writer described my views as those of a "First Amendment junkie."

3   Many feminist arguments for controls on pornography carry the implicit conviction that porn books, magazines, and movies pose a greater threat to women than similarly repulsive exercises of free speech pose to other offended groups. This conviction has, of course, been shared by everyone—regardless of race, creed, or sex—who has ever argued in favor of abridging the First Amendment. It is the argument used by some Jews who have withdrawn their support from the American Civil Liberties Union because it has defended the right of American Nazis to march through a community inhabited by survivors of Hitler's concentration camps.

4   If feminists want to argue that the protection of the Constitution should not be extended to *any* particularly odious or threatening form of speech, they have a reasonable argument (although I don't agree with it). But it is ridiculous to suggest that the porn shops on 42nd Street are more disgusting to women than a march of neo-Nazis is to survivors of the extermination camps.

5   The arguments over pornography also blur the vital distinction between expression of ideas and conduct. When I say I believe unreservedly in the First

Amendment, someone always comes back at me with the issue of "kiddie porn." But kiddie porn is not a First Amendment issue. It is an issue of the abuse of power—the power adults have over children—and not of obscenity. Parents and promoters have no more right to use their children to make porn movies than they do to send them to work in coal mines. The responsible adults should be prosecuted, just as adults who use children for back-breaking farm labor should be prosecuted.

6   Susan Brownmiller, in *Against Our Will: Men, Women and Rape,* has described pornography as "the undiluted essence of antifemale propaganda." I think this is a fair description of some types of pornography, especially of the brutish subspecies that equates sex with death and portrays women primarily as objects of violence.

7   The equation of sex and violence, personified by some glossy rock record album covers as well as by *Hustler,* has fed the illusion that censorship of pornography can be conducted on a more rational basis than other types of censorship. Are all pictures of naked women obscene? Clearly not, says a friend. A Renoir nude is art, she says, and *Hustler* is trash. "Any reasonable person" knows that.

8   But what about something between art and trash—something, say, along the lines of *Playboy* or *Penthouse* magazines? I asked five women for their reactions to one picture in Penthouse and got responses that ranged from "lovely" and "sensuous" to "revolting" and "demeaning." Feminists, like everyone else, seldom have rational reasons for their preferences in erotica. Like members of juries, they tend to disagree when confronted with something that falls short of 100 percent vulgarity.

9   In any case, feminists will not be the arbiters of good taste if it becomes easier to harass, prosecute, and convict people on obscenity charges. Most of the people who want to censor girlie magazines are equally opposed to open discussion of issues that are of vital concern to women: rape, abortion, menstruation, contraception, lesbianism—in fact, the entire range of sexual experience from a women's viewpoint.

10   Feminist writers and editors and filmmakers have limited financial resources: Confronted by a determined prosecutor, Hugh Hefner will fare better than Susan Brownmiller. Would the Memphis jurors who convicted Harry Rheems for his role in *Deep Throat* be inclined to take a more positive view of paintings of the female genitalia done by sensitive feminist artists? *Ms.* magazine has printed color reproductions of some of those art works; *Ms.* is already banned from a number of high school libraries because someone considers it threatening and/or obscene.

11   Feminists who want to censor what they regard as harmful pornography have essentially the same motivation as other would be censors: They want to use the power of the state to accomplish what they have been unable to achieve in the marketplace of ideas and images. The impulse to censor places no faith in the possibilities of democratic persuasion.

12   It isn't easy to persuade certain men that they have better uses for $1.95 each month than to spend it on a copy of *Hustler*? Well, then, give the men no choice in the matter.

13   I believe there is also a connection between the impulse toward censorship on the part of people who used to consider themselves civil libertarians and a more general desire to shift responsibility from individuals to institutions. When I saw the movie *Looking for Mr. Goodbar*, I was stunned by its series of visual images equating sex and violence, coupled with what seems to me the mindless message (a distortion of the fine Judith Rossner novel) that casual sex equals death. When I came out of the movie, I was even more shocked to see parents standing in line with children between the ages of ten and fourteen.

14   I simply don't know why a parent would take a child to see such a movie, any more than I understand why people feel they can't turn off a television set their child is watching. Whenever I say that, my friends tell me I don't know how it is because I don't have children. True, but I do have parents. When I was a child, they did turn off the TV. They didn't expect the Federal Communications Commission to do their job for them.

15   I am a First Amendment junkie. You can't OD on the First Amendment, because free speech is its own best antidote.

---

1. This essay bases its arguments on a distinction between "expression" and "conduct," the "possibilities of democratic persuasion" in the "marketplace of ideas and images," and parental control. Discuss her presentation of each of these items in terms of the **target audience** she is trying to reach. Be sure to supply textual evidence in support of your hypotheses.
2. In paragraph 9 Jacoby writes, "[feminists], like everyone else, seldom have rational reasons for their preferences in erotica." What would a "rational reason" for such a preference be? What sort of argument is Jacoby presenting here?

This essay was first published in January of 1978 in the *New York Times* op-ed section as "Hers." Subsequent higher court decisions reversed both the Flynt and the Rheems cases.

'Gender Bender' Ads: Same Old Sexism

Jean Kilbourne

1   Two new "gender bender" TV commercials, in which women leer at men as they drink sodas or drive cars, have led to so much hoopla that you'd think women were mugging men on Madison Avenue. Some people feel these turnabout ads are fair play; others see hypocrisy in women objectifying men while complaining about being sex objects themselves.

2   In one of the commercials, women office workers gather to watch a construction worker doff his shirt to quaff a Diet Coke. Just why he has to get undressed to enjoy his drink is unclear. In the second ad, two women make suggestive comments about men who use flashy automobiles as substitutes for virility. Eventually, the women are impressed by a hunk in an economical Hyundai.

3   Despite all the hubbub, though, these ads are neither fair play nor hypocrisy. In fact, they aren't even turnabouts, despite their literal switching of gender roles.

4   For one thing, these two ads are more about marketing than about men. Remember, these are isolated examples in a sea of commercials that use women as sex objects to sell everything from shampoo to champagne. As consumers of advertising, we are used to seeing women's bodies displayed, discussed, disrobed. When a man's body is used in this way, it comes as a shock. This, of course, is the point for advertisers who wish to break through the 1,500 ads to which the average American is exposed daily.

5   Also, despite their apparent role reversals, these ads are intended less to liberate women than to comfort men. The Diet Coke commercial makes men less self-conscious about using a diet product—a product that might be considered "feminine." The Hyundai commercial reassures men that they can drive a less expensive car and still have sex appeal. In this homophobic society, the presence of women on-screen also assures male viewers that users of these products are straight. But, either way, women are cast in a supporting role.

6   This suggests another way these ads practice the same old sexism: they presume a male audience. When a woman is presented as a sex object in a commercial, no on-screen audience is necessary. The voyeur is on the other side of the screen: the man watching her on television. These gender-bender ads are no different. The women in them continue to be women observed by men.

7   In any event, these ads in no way portray or reflect the real world. Women rarely gather to ogle men's bodies, while the reverse is commonplace. And when real women talk about men, they are more likely to discuss their behavior out of bed: their capacity for intimacy, their willingness or reluctance to share domestic chores and childrearing, their kindness or cruelty. Contrary to some men's

fears, a woman trying to impress other women is more likely to boast about her mate's status than his penis size, his bonds rather than his buns.

8   This is objectification too, of course, but of a very different kind. The sad truth about the Hyundai ad is that in real life most women would be more impressed by the luxurious car.

9   Most importantly, there is no danger for men in the gender-bender ads, while objectified women are always at risk. In the Diet Coke ad, for instance, the women are physically separated from the shirtless man. He is the one in control. His body is powerful, not passive. Imagine a true role reversal of this ad: a group of businessmen gather to leer at a beautiful woman worker on her break, who removes her shirt before drinking her Diet Coke. This scene would be frightening, not funny, as the Diet Coke ad is. And why is the Diet Coke ad funny? Because we know it doesn't describe any truth.

10   But suppose the men in these two commercials are being objectified. So what? "Reverse sexism" is as moronic a concept as "reverse racism." When men objectify women, they do so in a culture in which women are constantly objectified and in which there are consequences—from economic discrimination to violence—to that objectification. For men, though, there are no such consequences. Men are not likely to be raped, harassed or beaten (at least not by women). Men do not perform various daily rituals to protect themselves from sexual assault, whereas women do. How many men are frightened to be alone with a woman in an elevator? How many men cross the street when a group of women approach?

11   What would a true "gender bender" ad look like? As background, consider an ad that ran a year or so ago in several women's magazines:

> Your breasts may be too big, too saggy, too pert, too flat, too full, too far apart, too close together, too A-cup, too lopsided, too jiggly, too pale, too padded, too pointy, too pendulous, or just two mosquito bites. But with Dep styling products, at least you can have your hair the way you want it. Make the most of what you've got.

12   This ad was not considered newsworthy. But think about the reaction if a jeans company ran the following, imaginary ad somewhere:

> Your penis may be too small, too droopy, too limp, too lopsided, too narrow, too fat, too jiggly, too hairy, too pale, too red, too pointy, too blunt, or just two inches. But at least you can have a great pair of jeans. Make the most of what you've got.

13   This is a true gender-bender ad. But, on Madison Avenue and in society in general, such treatment of men is unthinkable.

---

1. Hypothesize concerning why the writer ended rather than began with her last three paragraphs.
2. Kilbourne's article is largely concerned with advertising's **target audience**. How would you define Kilbourne's **target audience** and why.
3. If you were not familiar with the concept of "**objectifying**" as some feminists define the term, would it be possible to define it by the end of the essay?

You are Liberal, You Strongly Favor Gay Rights

Charles Krauthammer

1 You are liberal. You strongly favor gay rights. You also have young children. Are you indifferent to their ultimate sexual orientation, or do you wish them to grow up to be heterosexual? You can be honest. This is a secret ballot.

2   One probably needs a secret ballot because, given the level of intimidation in the gay rights debate, to publicly express a preference for heterosexuality is to open oneself up to charges of bigotry and narrow-mindedness. Why the preference for heterosexuality? For some parents, it is a matter of morality or religion. For others it is a question of aesthetics. For still others, like me, the reasons are utilitarian. We want happiness for our kids. Life is hard enough. Gay life is particularly hard. One wishes to minimize, to the extent that one can, the burdens one's children will have to bear.

3   To put it somewhat differently, parents have many wishes for their children. That they should grow up strong and healthy. That they should have satisfying careers. And the most ancient and common wish that they should marry and have children and a happy family life. For these last wishes heterosexuality is an overwhelming advantage. It is natural, therefore, that just as parents have the inclination and right to wish to influence the development of a child's character, they have the inclination and right to try to influence a child's sexual orientation. Gay advocates argue, however, that such influence is an illusion. Sexual orientation, they claim, is biologically fated and thus is entirely impervious to environmental influence. Unfortunately, E. L. Pattullo, former director of Harvard's Center for the Behavioral Sciences, recently pointed out in *Commentary* magazine, the scientific evidence does not support such a claim. It is odd, moreover, that those most fervent for multicultural curricula and sensitivity training on the theory that society can influence how children learn to hate, now protest that society has no influence on how children learn to love.

4   How is it that one's character, moral sense, capacity for empathy and compassion can all be shaped by education—they must be or we wouldn't be expending vast amounts of effort in schools to teach these things—but the object of one's affections is fixed by some genetic command?

5   On the other hand, if sexual orientation, like character, is affected by environment. I come to what *New Republic* editor Andrew Sullivan has called (critically) the "moderate" position on gay rights. The moderate position advocates tolerance and attempts to grant as much civic equality to homosexuals as possible—but not to the point of sending societal and pedagogic messages that homosexuality is but one of many lifestyles about which society is indifferent.

6   The "moderate" insists on the right to a cultural and educational environment that conveys, without disrespect but without apology, a societal preference

for heterosexuality in the same way that, for example, society can without disrespect express a preference for two-parent over one-parent families or biological parenthood over surrogacy.

7   There is nothing here to imply intolerance. It is, for example, the duty of any parent to accept, embrace, and love a child who is homosexual. But many parents feel it equally their duty to try to raise a child in such a way as to reduce the chances for such an outcome. It is perfectly legitimate, therefore, for parents in Queens, N.Y., to have revolted against a school administration that offered *Heather has Two Mommies* and *Daddy's Roommate* as suggested reading for first graders. It is one thing to teach children that homosexuals must be treated with respect. It is quite another to teach that there is nothing to choose between homosexual and heterosexual life. If gay rights were just a demand for 'freedom,' there would have been no Queens revolt (which brought down the chancellor of the New York City public school system) and little debate about gay rights. There is, after all no great constituency for sodomy laws. But one need only read the manifesto issued by last weekend's Gay and Lesbian March on Washington to see how much sentimental and anachronistic is the view that gay rights today is about 'freedom.' "We demand," it reads, "inclusion of Lesbian, Gay, Bisexual, and Transgender studies in multicultural curricula." And "full and equal inclusion of Lesbians, Gays, Bisexuals and Transgendered people in the educational system." And "that the definition of family include the full diversity of all family structures."

8   Freedom—the ability to conduct private acts without harassment or molestation—of course. But the homosexual movement demands much more: not toleration but public legitimation of homosexuality—through such public institutions as gay marriage and gay school curricula—as the moral equivalent of heterosexuality.

9   Now that is a very tall ideological order, a demand, in fact, to reorder a nation's social and moral structures. And most Americans are not prepared to accept that, though fewer will say that for fear of being vilified as homophobics. They respect freedom of private conduct, but will not accept demands for the public legitimization of a lifestyle that they would never in good conscience wish upon their children.

---

1. What is the rhetorical function of the last sentence of Krauthammer's first paragraph?
2. In paragraph 3, what **questions are begged** by the term "pointed out?" Why does Krauthammer introduce that sentence with the word "unfortunately?"
3. Consider the relationship between Ivin's paragraphs 8 and 9 and Krauthammer's third paragraph. What **authorizing trope** is being invoked in both cases?
4. In paragraph 8, consider whether incest is a "private act." If it is not, how would Krauthammer define "private act?"
5. Would you consider civil right legislation concerning racism "a demand to reorder a nation's social and moral structure?" What bearing might this have on Krauthammer's argument in terms of who he has **targeted** as his audience?

Krauthammer is a Pulitzer Prize winner as a syndicated columnist.

An Even Exchange

Karla Kuban

1   At first glance, Taos, N.M., seemed to be heaven on earth. I moved there be-cause it's beautiful: celery-sage-covered mesas, peach orchards, verdant pastures, mountain meadows full of clematis and fairy slippers, howling coyotes, the Rio Grande abundant with cutthroat trout.

2   My third week there I ran into a friend at the post office, and we walked next door to Dori's for coffee. When he warned me I should be careful in Taos—lock my bike, bolt my doors, don't walk alone at night—I was surprised. For all its beauty, he said, raising an eyebrow, Taos was a dark little place.

3   Taos has three major cultural communities—Pueblo Indian, Hispanic, and Anglo—and has a high unemployment rate, 15 percent. When I went to the post office, our postal clerk handed my bundled mail to me. "Look at that," he said, glancing at a *Taos News* headline: "Teen Receives Skull Fracture in Fight on Bent Street." I had seen many headlines like it describing stabbing deaths, rapes, assaults with crowbars, and other violent crimes. "That's sad," he continued. "That's sorry."

4   In 1997 Taos County police dispatchers received more than 16,000 calls. Nineteen local police officers, 13 New Mexico State Police officers and 18 Taos County sheriff's department officers serve a county of 28,000 inhabitants.

5   The newspaper had been reporting a peeping Tom for months, and a man was finally arrested. I learned he was one of the crew workers in my yard. He had knocked on my door and asked for my key so he could repair the balcony over the weekend while I was out of town. "How did you know I was going out of town?" I asked. He said he forgot.

6   A female friend and I went out for breakfast. I told her I was feeling unsafe. She pulled a .38 special out of her backpack and laid it on the table. I didn't feel that unsafe, I told her. Get one, she said. I couldn't. I was terrified of guns.

7   As I was riding my horse on a back road, four boys in a low rider pulled up, jeering and launching beer bottles over their car. The one on the passenger side, a kid, maybe 12, told me they could make me get off my horse and go with them. He pointed a finger at me and pulled the trigger. Blam, he mouthed.

8   I knew that violence was rarely random and without warning. Yet, at night, alone in my house, I began to worry. I could get a dog. I could take a course in self-defense.

9   I asked another friend whether I should buy a gun. He had one, he said. His former wife carried a short-barrelled .357 in her purse. Almost every woman he knew in Taos carried a gun.

10   At the post office I saw the kid from the low rider who had fired his finger at me. He was with a tiny woman who might have been his mother, and I was unafraid of him there. As he walked by I grabbed his arm. Hello, I said through clenched teeth. He stared vacantly into my eyes. He didn't ask, How do I know you; never mind, Did I scare you? I wanted to slap him for pointing a finger at me and pretending to shoot.

11   While crime around the country was decreasing, I realized I had chosen to live in a place where I felt more fearful than I ever had. I had made the wrong decision in moving there.

12   I want to the Wild West Trading Company, where Mike asked, "May I help you?" I filled out the Brady Bill form in case, down the road, he could help me.

13   A friend called to tell me that at 3 A.M. she woke to gunshots under her window, and when police arrived they found six bullet holes in the adobe wall of her house.

14   A few weeks later I went back to the gun store and saw Mike. I looked at several kinds of guns and within an hour I brought my new .357 home, three-fingering it gingerly by the butt of the stock as if it were dirty business, contaminated or unsanitary, the way I might have lifted a dead mouse by its tail and tossed it into the garbage.

15   Considering that my father is a gun collector and that I grew up with Remington, Ruger and Merkel rifles, Super Blackhawk .44 magnums, a Colt pistol, and a Mossberg shotgun, to name a few, you would think I'd rest easy with a gun in my bedside drawer. But I knew that if someone broke into my house and I pulled out my gun, I had to shoot to kill. If I couldn't, I might die. Everything falls under headings: safety and fear, tranquility and distress, darkness and light. Our every move is defined by antipodal forces. A gun's components bear contradictions: coldness and heat, pull giving way to push, a deafening blast followed by silence. My fear had shifted. In buying a gun I had exchanged one fear for another, perhaps even elevated it. But I could live with that.

---

1. Can this essay be classified as a *meditation*?
2. What is Kuban's **thesis**?
3. Who is Kuban's **target audience**?
4. What do you think is the rhetorical purpose of the continual mentioning of pistol caliber and type (.38 special, short-barrelled .357, etc.)
5. What is the "Brady Bill form"?

Kuban is a novelist.

Four-Letter Words Can Hurt You

Barbara Lawrence

1   Why should any words be called obscene? Don't they all describe natural human functions? Am I trying to tell them, my students demand, that the "strong,
earthy, gut-honest"—or, if they are fans of Norman Mailer, the "rich, liberating,
existential"—language they use to describe sexual activity isn't preferable to
"phony-sounding middle-class words like 'intercourse' and 'copulate'?" "Cop
You Late!" they say with fancy inflections and gagging grimaces. "Now what is
that supposed to mean?"

2   Well, what is it supposed to mean? Any why indeed should one group of
words describing human functions and human organs be acceptable in ordinary
conversation and another, describing presumably the same organs and functions,
be tabooed—so much so, in fact, that some of these words still cannot appear
in print in many parts of the English-speaking world.

3   The argument that these taboos exist only because of "sexual hangups"
(middle-class, middle-age, feminist), or even that they are a result of class
oppression (the contempt of the Norman conquerors for the language of their
Anglo-Saxon serfs), ignores a much more likely explanation, it seems to me, and
that is the sources and functions of the words themselves.

4   The best known of the tabooed sexual verbs, for example, comes from the
German *ficken*, meaning "to strike"; combined, according to Partridge's etymo-
logical dictionary *Origins*, with the Latin sexual verb *futuere*; associated in turn
with the Latin *fustis*, "a staff or cudgel"; the Celtic *buc*, "a point, hence to
pierce"; the Gaelic *batair*, "a cudgeller"; the Early Irish *baulaim*, "I strike"; and
so forth. It is one of what etymologists sometimes call "the sadistic group of
words for the man's part in copulation."

5   The brutality of this word, then, and its equivalents ("screw," "bang," etc.)
is not an illusion of the middle class or a crochet of Women's Liberation. In their
origins and imagery these words carry undeniably painful, if not sadistic, implications, the object of which is almost always female. Consider, for example,
what a "screw" actually does to the wood it penetrates; what a painful, even
mutilating, activity this kind of analogy suggests. "Screw" is particularly interesting in this context, since the noun, according to Partridge, comes from words
meaning "groove," "nut," "ditch," "breeding sow," "scrofula," and "swelling,"
while the verb, besides its explicit imagery, has antecedent associations to "write
on," "scratch," "scarify," and so forth—a revealing fusion of a mechanical or
painful action with an obviously denigrated object.

6   Not all obscene words, of course, are as implicitly sadistic or denigrating to women as these, but all that I know seem to serve a similar purpose: to reduce the human organism (especially the female organism) and human functions (especially the sexual and procreative) to their least organic, most mechanical dimension; to substitute a trivializing or deforming resemblance for the complex human reality of what is being described.

7   Tabooed male descriptives, when they are not openly denigrating to women, often serve to divorce a male organ or function from any significant interaction with the female. Take the word "testes," for example, suggesting "witnesses" (from the Latin *testis*) to the sexual and procreative strengths of the male organ; and the obscene counterpart of this word, which suggests little more than a mechanical shape. Compare almost any of the "rich," "liberating" sexual verbs, so fashionable today among male writers, with that much-derived Latin word "copulate" ("to bind or join together") or even that Anglo-Saxon phrase (which seems to have had no trouble surviving the Norman Conquest) "make love."

8   How arrogantly self-involved the tabooed words seem in comparison to either of the other terms, and how contemptuous of the female partner. Understandably so, of course, if she is only a "skirt," a "broad," a "chick," a "pussycat," or a "piece." If she is, in other words no more than her skirt, or what her skirt conceals; no more than a breeder, or the broadest part of her; no more than a piece of a human being or a "piece of tail."

9   The most severely tabooed of the female descriptives, incidentally, are those like a "piece of tail." Which suggest (either explicitly or through antecedents) that there is no significant difference between the female channel through which we are all conceived and born and the anal outlet common to both sexes—a distinction that pornographers have always enjoyed obscuring.

10   This effort to deny women their biological identity, their individuality, their humanness, is such an important aspect of obscene language that one can only marvel at how seldom, in a era preoccupied with definitions of obscenity, this fact is brought to our attention. One problem, of course, is that many of the people in the best position to do this (critics, teachers, writers) are so reluctant today to admit that they are angered or shocked by obscenity. Bored, maybe, unimpressed, aesthetically displeased, but—no matter how brutal or denigrating the material—never angered, never shocked.

11   And yet how eloquently angered, how piously shocked many of these same people become if denigrating language is used about any minority group other than women; if the obscenities are racial or ethnic, that is, rather than sexual. Words like "coon," "kike," "spic," "wop," after all, deform identity, deny individuality and humanness in almost exactly the same way that sexual vulgarisms and obscenities do.

12   No one that I know, least of all my students, would fail to question the values of a society whose literature and entertainment rested heavily on racial or ethnic pejoratives. Are the values of a society whose literature and entertainment rest as heavily as ours on sexual pejoratives any less questionable?

1. What is the rhetorical function of Lawrence's students?
2. How are they characterized?
3. Define the word "tabooed."
4. In what parts of the English speaking world were "these words" forbidden? (The essay was first published in 1973.)
5. Consider what a screw "actually" does to the wood it penetrates. Why would one use a screw in preference to, say a nail or glue?
6. What kind of argument is involved with calling something "undeniable?"
7. See **etymology, argument from.** In contemporary usage is the word Lawrence claims derives from the German "ficken" exclusively descriptive of male action?
8. How is Lawrence defining "ordinary conversation"?

This often anthologized essay first appeared in the Op-Ed section of the *New York Times* on September 27 of 1973 and later in *Redbook*.

The Case for Torture

Michael Levin

1   It is generally assumed that torture is impermissible, a throwback to a more brutal age. Enlightened societies reject it outright, and regimes suspected of using it risk the wrath of the United States.

2   I believe this attitude is unwise. There are situations in which torture is not merely permissible but morally mandatory. Moreover, these situations are moving from the realm of imagination to fact.

3   Suppose a terrorist has hidden an atomic bomb on Manhattan Island which will detonate at noon on July 4 unless . . . (here follow the usual demands for money and release of his friends from jail). Suppose, further, that he is caught at 10 A.M. of the fateful day, but—preferring death to failure—won't disclose where the bomb is. What do we do? If we follow due process—wait for his lawyer, arraign him—millions of people will die. If the only way to save those lives is to subject the terrorist to the most excruciating possible pain, what grounds can there be for not doing so? I suggest there are none. In any case, I ask you to face the question with an open mind.

4   Torturing the terrorist is unconstitutional? Probably. But millions of lives surely outweigh constitutionality. Torture is barbaric? Mass murder is far more barbaric. Indeed, letting millions of innocents die in deference to one who flaunts his guilt is moral cowardice, an unwillingness to dirty one's hands. If *you* caught the terrorist, could you sleep nights knowing that millions died because you couldn't bring yourself to apply the electrodes?

5   Once you concede that torture is justified in extreme cases, you have admitted that the decision to use torture is a matter of balancing innocent lives against the means needed to save them. You must now face more realistic cases involving more modest numbers. Someone plants a bomb on a jumbo jet. He alone can disarm it, and his demands cannot be met (or if they can, we refuse to set a precedent by yielding to his threats). Surely we can, we must, do anything to the extortionist to save the passengers. How can we tell 300, or 100, or 10 people who never asked to be put in danger, "I'm sorry, you'll have to die in agony, we just couldn't bring ourselves to. . . ."

6   Here are the results of an informal poll about a third, hypothetical, case. Suppose a terrorist group kidnapped a newborn baby from a hospital. I asked four mothers if they would approve of torturing kidnappers if that were necessary to get their own newborns back. All said yes, the most "liberal" adding that she would administer it herself.

7   I am not advocating torture as punishment. Punishment is addressed to deeds irrevocably past. Rather, I am advocating torture as an acceptable measure for

preventing future evils. So understood, it is far less objectionable than many extant punishments. Opponents of the death penalty, for example, are forever insisting that executing a murderer will not bring back his victim (as if the purpose of capital punishment were supposed to be resurrection, not deterrence or retribution). But torture, in the cases described, is intended not to bring anyone back but to keep innocents from being dispatched. The most powerful argument against using torture as a punishment or to secure confessions is that such practices disregard the rights of the individual. Well, if the individual is all that important—and he is—it is correspondingly important to protect the rights of individuals threatened by terrorists. If life is so valuable that it must never be taken, the lives of the innocents must be saved even at the price of hurting the one who endangers them.

8   Better precedents for torture are assassination and preemptive attack. No Allied leader would have flinched at assassinating Hitler, had that been possible. (The Allies did assassinate Heydrich.) Americans would be angered to learn that Roosevelt could have had Hitler killed in 1943—thereby shortening the war and saving millions of lives—but refused on moral grounds. Similarly, if nation A learns that nation B is about to launch an unprovoked attack, A has a right to save itself by destroying B's military capability first. In the same way, if the police can by torture save those who would otherwise die at the hands of kidnappers or terrorists, they must.

9   There is an important difference between terrorists and their victims that should mute talk of the terrorists' "rights." The terrorist's victims are at risk unintentionally, not having asked to be endangered. But the terrorist knowingly initiated his actions. Unlike his victims, he volunteered for the risks of his deed. By threatening to kill for profit or idealism, he renounces civilized standards, and he can have no complaint if civilization tries to thwart him by whatever means necessary.

10   Just as torture is justified only to save lives (not extort confessions or recantations), it is justifiably administered only to those *known* to hold innocent lives in their hands. Ah, but how can the authorities ever be sure they have the right malefactor? Isn't there a danger of error and abuse? Won't We turn into Them?

11   Questions like these are disingenuous in a world in which terrorists proclaim themselves and perform for television. The name of their game is public recognition. After all, you can't very well intimidate a government into releasing your freedom fighters unless you announce that it is your group that has seized its embassy. "Clear guilt" is difficult to define, but when 40 million people see a group of masked gunmen seize an airplane on the evening news, there is not much question about who the perpetrators are. There will be hard cases where the situation is murkier. Nonetheless, a line demarcating the legitimate use of torture can be drawn. Torture only the obviously guilty, and only for the sake of saving innocents, and the line between Us and Them will remain clear.

12   There is little danger that the Western democracies will lose their way if they choose to inflict pain as one way of preserving order. Paralysis in the face of evil

is the greater danger. Some day soon a terrorist will threaten tens of thousands of lives, and torture will be the only way to save them. We had better start thinking about this.

---

1. Who is "I"? How does Levin go about establishing his **ethos** in this essay?
2. Who is "we," and does "we" stand in a consistent relationship to "you"?
3. Go through the essay and highlight each **absolute**. Consider these in terms of **target audience** and **warrants**.
4. What is the rhetorical function of the word "liberal" in paragraph 6?

At the time this article was published (*Newsweek*, 1982), Levin was a professor of philosophy at the City College of New York.

Of Whales and Wisdom

Robert McNally

1   Always we have sought after wisdom. The urge itself never changes, but the site of the search often does. Sometimes we turn to the stars, sometimes to cast monkey bones, sometimes to messiahs or gurus or ayatollahs. Lately we're looking to the sea. The wisdom of the ages, it is being said, resides in the whales and dolphins.

2   Once I listened to a woman who had swum with a beluga, an experience she found "a little like falling in love." The swim aroused in her a sense of "a crack in the cosmic egg, a tunnel of experience that scratched a genetic memory." She came away "a fuller human being, not so arrogant."

3   She is hardly alone. People go "gaga" at the sight of dolphins, and cries of seraphic transport rise at the close approach of a great whale. This is not pretense; there is something very real here. On the open sea no sight equals the coming of the dolphins. "If you yourself can withhold three cheers at beholding these vivacious fish," Melville wrote of the dolphins, "then heaven help ye; the spirit of godly gamesomeness is not in ye."

4   But there's something more going on these days. It began largely with John Lilly and his books and articles on cetaceans. Lilly holds that cetaceans are every bit as high on the evolutionary scale as humans, and perhaps even higher. Lilly maintains that dolphins, because of their large and well-developed brains, are more intelligent than humans. They are also wiser and happier. They live freely and joyfully, without inhibitions about sex or elimination, without anxiety or tension. And cetaceans are transcendentally accomplished; they daily achieve religious heights a human mystic rarely can reach in a whole lifetime.

5   There is an empirical issue here: Do the facts bear out Lilly's view or not? No categorical answer is available, simply because few facts are known. We know little about cetaceans' mental processes and communication; we know less about the social life of these animals in the wild.

6   Yet the empirical question is only part of the issue, and perhaps the less important part; the heart of the matter is philosophical. The image of the wise and happy dolphin has developed along with that curious assemblage of ideas and groups called the human-potential movement, whose purpose it is to raise our consciousness unto the New Age. The movement springs from a dissatisfaction with the bourgeois mentality. The typical middle-class American is seen as uptight, status-conscious, money-grubbing and sexually boring: These characteristics lead to prostate trouble, heart disease, child and alcohol abuse, and protofascism. The New Age will arise with people who are loose, laid-back, flowing, sexually experimental, and able to be-in-the-moment. The cetaceans, so the New

Age spokesmen intimate, have already hit upon this natural wisdom. They are what we should become.

7   This view of the Old Bourgeois versus the New Age as the whole spectrum of conscious and intelligent experience is incredibly presumptuous. Instead of seeing dolphins as different and unique, we narcissistically require them to be what we wish ourselves to be. We're not looking at the cetaceans; we're holding up a mirror to ourselves.

8   The New Age view of cetaceans is not new. It is merely the anthropocentrism of the ages in contemporary jargon. From the time of our earliest myths of special creation, we have seen ourselves as set apart from other animals. We are lord and master; the others are our servants and underlings. Darwin overturned this comfortably lordly world by showing that the human species is just like all the rest, the product of time and natural selection—but the point never quite sank in. Evolution, which is in fact chaotic and purposeless, we understood as a biological drive for perfection culminating in humankind. Thus, we have taken our need for primacy and under-pinned it with Darwinian theory instead of religion. Humans are in the driver's seat, whether it was God or natural selection that put us there.

9   The New Age view of cetaceans is a contemporary variation on this theme. We are at the top: cetaceans are our equals: therefore, cetaceans must be like us. Our high status remains assured; we must only share it.

10   This self-deceiving solution erodes the real challenge: to understand other species as others, not as lesser creatures but as different beings. We have only a fragmentary understanding of the other animals; the discovery of some language ability in chimpanzees and gorillas shows how little we really know, how much more we have to learn. And much of that learning should focus on the cetaceans, because of their apparent intelligence, their beauty and grace, and especially because of the godly gamesomeness they inspire. They deserve to be understood on their own terms, not in an anthropocentric miscasting as the carriers of our current fantasy of salvation.

---

1. One way to think about this essay is in terms of its approach to hierarchies as these pertain to anthropocentrism. Who makes up the **target audience** for this essay (consider particularly the presentation in paragraph 8).
2. Paragraphs 1 and 6 contain lists. Examine and explain how McNally uses these series lists rhetorically.
3. Discuss the use of **passive voice** and **absolutes** in paragraph 1.

Sierra, where this piece was originally published in 1980, is the bulletin of the Sierra Club, an organization devoted to issues of environmental preservation. You may find interesting that in July of 1999, data were released indicating that dolphins frequently kill their own young and engage in what has been called "serial killing" of porpoises for no apparent reason. Although this characterization is in itself anthropocentric, this behavior makes the dolphin one of very few mammals that kill, apparently, for fun.

English Belongs to Everybody

Robert MacNeil

1   This is a time of widespread anxiety about the language. Some Americans fear that English will be engulfed or diluted by Spanish and want to make it the official language. There is anxiety about a crisis of illiteracy, or a crisis of semiliteracy among high school, even college, graduates.

2   Anxiety, however, may have a perverse side effect: experts who wish to "save" the language may only discourage pleasure in it. Some are good-humored and tolerant of change, others intolerant and snobbish. Language reinforces feelings of social superiority or inferiority; it creates insiders and outsiders; it is a prop to vanity or a source of anxiety, and on both emotions the language snobs play. Yet the changes and the errors that irritate them are no different in kind from those which have shaped our language for centuries. As Hugh Kenner wrote of certain British critics in *The Sinking Island*, "They took note of language only when it annoyed them." Such people are killjoys: they turn others away from an interest in the language, inhibit their use of it, and turn pleasure off.

3   Change is inevitable in a living language and is responsible for much of the vitality of English; it has prospered and grown because it was able to accept and absorb change.

4   As people evolve and do new things, their language will evolve too. They will find ways to describe the new things and their changed perspective will give them new ways of talking about the old things. For example, electric light switches created a brilliant metaphor for the oldest of human experiences, being *turned on* or *turned off*. To language conservatives those expressions still have a slangy, low ring to them; to others they are vivid, fresh-minted currency, very spendable, very "with it."

5   That tolerance for change represents not only the dynamism of the English-speaking peoples since the Elizabethans, but their deeply rooted ideas of freedom as well. This was the idea of the Danish scholar Otto Jespersen, one of the great authorities on English. Writing in 1905, Jespersen said in his *Growth and Structure of the English Language*:

> The French language is like the stiff French garden of Louis XIV, while the English is like an English park, which is laid out seemingly without any definite plan, and in which you are allowed to walk everywhere according to your own fancy without having to fear a stern keeper enforcing rigorous regulations. The English language would not have been what it is if the English had not been for centuries great respecters of the liberties of each individual and if everybody had not been free to strike out new paths for himself.

6   I like that idea and do not think it just coincidence. Consider that the same cultural soil, the Celtic-Roman-Saxon-Danish-Norman amalgam, which produced the English language also nourished the great principles of freedom and rights of man in the modern world. The first shoots sprang up in England and they grew stronger in America. Churchill called them "the joint inheritance of the English-speaking world." At the very core of those principles are popular consent and resistance to arbitrary authority; both are fundamental characteristics of our language. The English-speaking peoples have defeated all efforts to build fences around their language, to defer to an academy on what was permissible English and what not. They'll decide for themselves, thanks just the same.

7   Nothing better expresses resistance to arbitrary authority than the persistence of what grammarians have denounced for centuries as "errors." In the common speech of English-speaking peoples—Americans, Englishmen, Canadians, Australians, New Zealanders, and others—these usages persist, despite rising literacy and wider education. We hear them every day:

> Double negative: "I don't want none of that."
> Double comparative: "Don't make that any more heavier!"
> Wrong verb: "Will you learn me to read?"

8   These "errors" have been with us for at least four hundred years, because you can find each of them in Shakespeare.

> Double negative: In *Hamlet*, the King says:
>
> Nor what he spake, though it lack'd form a little,
> Was not like madness.
>
> Double comparative: In *Othello*, the Duke says:
>
> Yet opinion . . . throws a more safer voice on you.
>
> Wrong verb: In *Othello*, Desdemona says:
>
> My life and education both do learn me how to respect you.

9   I find it very interesting that these forms will not go away and lie down. They were vigorous and acceptable in Shakespeare's time; they are far more vigorous today, although not acceptable as standard English. Regarded as error by grammarians, they are nevertheless in daily use all over the world by a hundred times the number of people who lived in Shakespeare's England.

10   It fascinates me that *axe*, meaning "ask," so common in black American English, is standard in Chaucer in all forms—*axe, axen, axed*: "and *axed* him if Troilus were there." Was that transmitted across six hundred years or simply reinvented?

11   English grew without a formal grammar. After the enormous creativity of Shakespeare and the other Elizabethans, seventeenth- and eighteenth-century critics thought the language was a mess, like an overgrown garden. They weeded it by imposing grammatical rules derived from tidier languages, chiefly Latin, whose precision and predictability they trusted. For three centuries, with some slippage here and there, their rules have held. Educators taught them and written English

conformed. Today, English-language newspapers, magazines, and books every-where broadly agree that correct English obeys these rules. Yet the wild varieties continue to threaten the garden of cultivated English and, by their numbers, ac-tually dominate everyday usage.

12   Nonstandard English formerly knew its place in the social order. Characters in fiction were allowed to speak it occasionally. Hemingway believed that Amer-ican literature really did not begin until Mark Twain, who outraged critics by reproducing the vernacular of characters like Huck Finn. Newspapers still clean up the grammar when they quote the ungrammatical, including politicians. The printed word, like Victorian morality, has often constituted a conspiracy of respectability.

13   People who spoke grammatically could be excused the illusion that their writ held sway, perhaps the way the Normans thought that French had con-quered the language of the vanquished Anglo-Saxons. A generation ago, people who considered themselves educated and well-spoken might have had only glancing contact with nonstandard English, usually in a well-understood class, regional, or rural context.

14   It fascinates me how differently we all speak in different circumstances. We have levels of formality, as in our clothing. There are very formal occasions, of-ten requiring written English: the job application or the letter to the editor—the dark-suit, serious-tie language, with everything pressed and the lint brushed off. There is our less formal out-in-the-world language—a more comfortable suit, but still respectable. There is language for close friends in the evenings, on week-ends—blue-jeans-and-sweat-shirt language, when it's good to get the tie off. There is family language, even more relaxed, full of grammatical short cuts, fam-ily slang, echoes of old jokes that have become intimate shorthand—the lan-guage of pajamas and uncombed hair. Finally, there is the language with no clothes on; the talk of couples—murmurs, sighs, grunts—language at its least self-conscious, open, vulnerable, and primitive.

15   Broadcasting has democratized the publication of language, often at its most informal, even undressed. Now the ears of the educated cannot escape the lan-guage of the masses. It surrounds them on the news, weather, sports, commer-cials, and the ever-proliferating talk and call-in shows.

16   This wider dissemination of popular speech may easily give purists the idea that the language is suddenly going to hell in this generation, and may explain the new paranoia about it.

17   It might also be argued that more Americans hear more correct, even beau-tiful, English on television than was ever heard before. Through television more models of good usage reach more American homes than was ever possible in other times. Television gives them lots of colloquial English, too, some awful, some creative, but this is not new.

18   Hidden in this is a simple fact: our language is not the special private prop-erty of the language police, or grammarians, or teachers, or even great writers. The genius of English is that it has always been the tongue of the common peo-ple, literate or not.

19   English belongs to everybody: the funny turn of phrase that pops into the mind of a farmer telling a story; or the traveling salesman's dirty joke; or the teenager saying, "Gag me with a spoon"; or the pop lyric—all contribute, are all as valid as the tortured image of the academic, or the line the poet sweats over for a week.

20   Through our collective language sense, some may be thought beautiful and some ugly, some may live and some may die; but it is all English and it belongs to everyone—to those of us who wish to be careful with it and those who don't care.

1. Consider this essay in terms of the appeal to **tradition**. How does MacNeil present his evidence to counter that argument?
2. Highlight each instance of the plant and garden **metaphor** as MacNeil develops it, and discuss its rhetorical implications.
3. In what ways does this essay attempt to persuade by invoking **authority**, or perhaps better, authorities?

Olympics of Mediocrity Can Fight Racism

Jeff Millar

1   Welcome, Mr. Prez, to Houston for your Tuesday night ESPN colloquium on sports and race.

2   African-Americans are likely to express concern at the disparity between the numbers of black athletes playing the games and the much smaller proportion of blacks who are coaches or run the front offices. It is one of the principal indicators African-Americans offer of the prevalence of racism in the sports industry.

3   Some African-Americans hold it is racist to say that blacks are "better at sports than whites" because there derives from this racist belief a racist corollary: Genetic black physical superiority implies genetic black intellectual inferiority.

4   To follow one's intellectual curiosity in this direction—why are 80 percent of their players in the NBA of African lineage; why are athletes of African lineage the world's elite of sprint and most distance running—is to walk chin-first into taboo.

5   In the *New Yorker* magazine last year, Malcolm Gladwell, a Canadian of African lineage and a track star when he was in high school, published an article titled "The Sports Taboo" and did just that.

6   Gladwell had identified the issue as semantic: People use the word "different" when they should be using a word of more precision used by geneticists and statisticians: "variance."

7   Gladwell find parallels in studies of the math skills of adolescent boys and girls. There is consistently more variance in boys: more girls than boys in the statistical middle; more boys than girls in the top percentiles of math skill; and more boys than girls at the bottom. Variance, says Gladwell, occurs "in almost every conceivable area of gender difference" where one might say that "averages" are similar.

8   Gladwell cites DNA studies of African tribes which suggest that in the African population there is more genetic variation than in all of the rest of the world put together. "If everyone were wiped out except the Africans," he wrote, "almost all the human genetic diversity would be preserved. . . . So you can expect groups of Africans to be more variable in respect to almost anything that has a genetic component."

9   In athletics, suggests Gladwell, whites are like girls and blacks are like boys—there are fewer blacks at the middle than there at the outer percentiles of very good and very bad.

10   If it is wider African genetic variance and the learned helplessness of white athletes that feeds a racist belief that blacks are "better at sports" and the racist

corollary of "the spectacle of black athleticism" begetting "a highly public image of black retardation" (Gladwell quoting a University of Texas scholar), then what is to be done as correction?

11   The media could take substantially more interest in examples of African genetic variance at its upper end as it manifests in things in addition to athletics. The local sportscasters send remote crews to the homes of black kids when they announce at which school they're going to play their college ball. How about going to the home of a black kid when he announces which offer he's accepted of the several big-name universities which are competing to give him a full academic ride?

12   If we could see the statistical and genetic truth given flesh, then perhaps white racists might be persuaded that filling full the athletic vessel does not mean draining the intellectual vessel.

13   What seems called for is an international anti-Olympics among the bottommost variants of all races, myth-smashing, once-and-for-all proof that the *average* black guy can't jump any higher than the *average* white guy.

14   I don't see, though, NBC paying very much for the right to telecast this.

15   So it's bully-pulpit time, Mr. President. You have a budget chain or two to yank. Maybe you can nudge PBS.

---

1. Paragraphs 5–10 of Millar's essay invoke another essay by Malcolm Gladwell. How does Millar treat the issue of **authority** in these paragraphs?

2. Compare Millar's use of an "outside" source to Talbert's later in the readings.

3. Paragraph 13 introduces the "international anti-olympics" that he says would prove "once and for all" that the "*average* black guy can't jump any higher than the *average* white guy." The "occasion" of this essay was Clinton's participation in the ESPN colloquium on sports and race in Houston with which the essay opens. It closes again addressing Clinton. Examine these four paragraphs (the first and the closing three) and decide what rhetorical function they are intended to fulfill. See **overheard argument** specifically.

4. Getting an anti-olympics on PBS is Millar's **overt thesis**. But, as with "Why I Want a Wife," could that **thesis** serve another purpose?

Millar was film critic for the *Houston Chronicle* and is co-author of the comic strips "Tank MacNamara" and "Second Chances." He receives email at jeff.millar@chron.com.

Stop Your Sniveling: Take It Like a Woman

Jacquelyn Mitchard

1   "I'm not exactly throwing up," says my 8-year-son. "But I feel as though I might start throwing up if I move too quickly."

2   I looked him over.

3   "I know you don't feel well," I told him. "I believe you. But you must take it like a woman."

4   When I tell my three sons this, it drives them nuts. Yes, they're pretty used to gender equality. Yes, they know that a woman can drive a big truck and raise a big family alone.

5   But they have this idea that when I say such things, I'm trying to insult them. And you know that I'm not.

6   Some people think that because I complain about the ways of men, I don't like men.

7   But I do. I do. I'm the sister of a great man, and I hope someday to fall wildly in love with one. As the mother of three sons, I'm heavily invested in testosterone futures.

8   I like men, and I don't like cheap malebashing. I don't like the little calendars and gift books that make fun by suggesting all men are selfish and spoiled and can't express their feelings. In fact, I know men so able to express their feelings that they can go on expressing them even after others in the room have fallen asleep. But the sickness thing . . . well, the way men react to illness. It's got to be stopped.

9   I don't mean serious illness. I don't mean paralysis, Lyme disease or shingles. I mean kind of achy and sniffly. I mean a little south of the way a person feels before work on a morning when her 10-month-old is teething.

10   If you are a woman, you have to take it like a woman. You have to grit your teeth, go to work, do spinning class, then do a seventh-grade book report on *Remembrance of Things Past*. If you don't, other women will jeer at you and call you a weakling.

11   If you are a man, though, and you have these same symptoms, you can sleep. You can sleep until *Oprah* is over. If you have a child, you can let him live on HoHos for 24 hours and no one will disrespect you.

12   That's why there are all those one-liners: Women have three speeds—low, medium and high. Men have two speeds—on and off.

13   There's this movement I now think of as Sick Man Walking. A few weeks ago, I saw my brother performing it. It looks kind of like what you do on a NordicTrack but without the arms.

14   "Why are you doing this?" I asked him.

15   "I can't move my head or legs too much," he told me.

16   "Why don't you take some aspirins?"

17   "I don't think I could swallow aspirins. . . ."

18   Since he is my sibling, and not a regular person, I was able to suggest, "Then why don't you stick them up your nose?"

19   Just yesterday, while researching this column, I decided to compare notes with a male buddy. Here was the question: Before you decide to cancel plans because of illness, what do you ask yourself?

20   His No. 1 question: "Do I have enough energy?"

21   Mine: "Can I focus my eyes?"

22   Now, I know this is sort of a stereotype. I'm not trying to be a macho girl here. But these are actual examples taken from real-life cases involving healthy adult men, many of whom participate in team sports and have had psychotherapy.

23   True, I have never had to build a building or fight a war while coping with illness.

24   But I've had to write stories. Keep appointments. Go out on dates with men who were expressing their feelings. Care for children, including children who were blowing beets.[1]

25   Now, you know this situation is bad and wrong. However, there is still time to rescue the current generation of men-in-training. People commonly blame doting mothers for the way men behave when they are ill. But I think mothers get a bad rap here. I think all those books about the nature of men and the nature of women have it pegged wrong.

26   I think that, contrary to popular opinion, men pay so much attention to their own feelings that they might really be the ones who could, you know, press the red button if they happened to have a sinus infection on the day World War III started.

27   But we can help. And we must. Repeat after me. "Take it like a woman."

---

1. Mitchard is playing on the cliché "take it like a man" in an essay that invokes gender difference throughout. Like Frank and Ivins she uses humor to allow her to discuss material that some members of her audience might otherwise find offensive. And like Frank and Ivins, a good deal of the humor lies in her level of diction. Highlight examples of this and compare her and Ivins' use of the **vernacular**.
2. Who is "we" in this essay?
3. How does Mitchard achieve and sustain an association between men and children?
4. Who is her **target audience?**
5. As with Millar and Syfers, Mitchard's **overt thesis** can be argued to be a rhetorical device in itself in the communication of her implied thesis. What argument can be made to support this position?

Mitchard invites email from her readers at *mitch@mailbag.com*.

---

[1] In response to my email inquiry, Mitchard defined "blowing beets" as "blowing chunks," or throwing up.

Do Patterns Exist in Nature?

Richard Nilsen

1   The human mind has an astonishing proclivity for finding patterns. It is our greatest talent, perhaps a defining one.

2   Take any large string of events, items or tendencies, and the brain will organize them and throw a story around them, creating order even where none exists.

3   Consider the night sky, for instance, a rattling jostle of burning pinpoints. We find in that chaos the images of bears and serpents, lions and bulls. Even those who no longer can find the shape of a great bear can spot the Big Dipper. The outline seems drawn in the sky with stars, yet the constellations have no actual existence outside the order-creating human mind.

4   Our own lives—which are a complex tangle of events, conflicting emotions and motives—are too prodigal to fit into a single coherent narrative, even the size of a Russian novel. Yet we do so all the time, creating a sense of self as if we were writing autobiographies and giving our lives a narrative shape that makes them meaningful to us.

5   We usually believe the narrative version of our lives actually exists. Yet all of us could write an entirely different story by stringing events together with a different emphasis.

6   The question always arises: Are the patterns actually there in life and nature, or do we create them in our heads and cast them like a net over reality?

7   The issue is central to a new movie by first-time filmmaker Darren Aronofsky called *Pi*. In the film, a misfit math genius is searching for the mathematical organizing principle of the cosmos.

8   His working hypotheses are simple:
"One: Mathematics is the language of nature.
"Two: Everything around us can be represented and understood through numbers.
"Three: If you graph the numbers of any system, patterns emerge.
"Therefore: There are patterns everywhere in nature."

9   The movie's protagonist nearly drives himself nuts with his search until he cannot bear his own obsession anymore.

10   But the film also questions in a roundabout way whether the patterns exist or not.

11   When different number series—each 216 digits long—seem to be important, an older colleague warns our hero that, once you begin looking for a pattern, it seems to be everywhere.

12   It's like when you buy a yellow Volkswagen and suddenly every other car on the road is immediately a yellow VW. Nothing has changed but your perception.

13   Mathematicians find patterns in nature, yet math itself is purely self-referential. It can only describe itself.

14   As mathematician/philosopher Bertrand Russell put it: "Mathematics may be defined as the subject in which we never know what we are talking about nor whether what we are saying is true."

15   In other words, "one plus one equals two" is no different from saying "a whale is not a fish." You have only spoken within a closed system. "A whale is not a fish" tells us nothing about whales but a lot about our language.

16   It is a description of linguistic categories, not an observational statement about existence. Biology can be organized as a system of knowledge to make the sentence false—indeed, at other times in history a whale was a fish.

17   "One plus one" likewise describes the system in which the equation is true.

18   It is possible to cast other patterns over reality. For instance, artists understand perfectly well how "one plus one equals three."

19   That is, there is the one thing, the other thing, and then the two together: one sock, the other sock, and the pair of socks. That is three things.

20   In art, we constantly put one object up against another object and observe the interaction between them. In that sense, one plus one can equal three.

21   When mathematicians say that numbers describe the world, they are speaking metaphorically. Numbers do not, in fact, describe the world. The patterns of numbers seem to mimic the patterns we discern in nature and bear an analogical relation to them.

22   The fact that this seems to happen so often may be little more than the yellow VW effect.

23   For experience is large and contains multitudes, even infinities. In any very large set, patterns can be found.

24   That is the trick behind numerology. If the name Ronald Wilson Reagan can be turned numerologically into the symbol for Satan, well, looked at another way, it can be turned into a recipe for Cobb salad. All it takes is a system ingenious enough to do it.

25   Even by its own terms, mathematics has trouble describing the world. Some of the most common patterns in nature, for instance, defy mathematical definition and can only be described by numbers that are not, in fact, numbers.

26   This is true from the double helix of DNA through the knobbly whorls on a pine cone and up through the spiral arms of a galactic nebula.

27   Pi, for instance, was first defined as the fraction 22/7 but even Pythagoras recognized that the ratio was not precise. Pi, it turns out, is an irrational number—in other words, a number that cannot be written as a number, a decimal of infinite extent.

28   There are others, equally important. Phi, which describes the decimal reduction of the golden section. It is also an irrational number.

29   To the Greeks, the golden section was the ratio "AB is to BC as BC is to AC." It also generates the Fibonacci series and is said to define how nature makes spirals.

30   Look at the end of a whelk shell, they say, or the longitudinal section of a nautilus shell, and you will see the Fibonacci series in action.

31   Yet it is not actually true. When you look at whelks, you find spirals that approximate in different degrees of accuracy the Fibonacci series, but never ever, except in the ideal world of math, hit it dead on.

32   Nature is varied; math is precise.

33   Our hero in the film believes in the Fibonacci spiral: "My new hypothesis: If we're built from spirals while living in a giant spiral, then is it possible that everything we put our hands to is infused with the spiral?"

34   He begins to sound more and more paranoid.

35   And paranoia has been defined as a belief in a hidden order behind the visible.

36   Paranoia and idealism thus are siblings.

37   There seems to be hard wiring in the human brain that makes us cast patterns over the world. That hard wiring seems to bring forth what Carl Jung called archetypes, that is, the narrative patterns our brains spin out and the shape we then jigger all of actual experience into.

38   And when forced to choose between the coherent pattern and the incoherent reality, we always choose the pattern. Perhaps we could not live otherwise.

---

1. Is this a **Rogerian** argument, or usefully considered as a member of the family of such arguments?

2. Highlight all of the analogies in Nilsen's argument. Do you find any kind of pattern in them?

3. Notice Nilsen's use of works like "appears," "seems," and "perhaps." How does this usage fit with his **thesis**?

4. How do you think Nilsen would respond to the argument that he himself is imposing a pattern on the process of human understanding?

O'Connor's Limbo[1]

Philip Nobile

1   At the close of a long academic career contemplating the earth and its inhabitants, an eminent British naturalist was asked what attribute he would ascribe to God, the author of creation. "A fondness for beetles" the old man replied, referring to the oddity that beetles comprise more than one-quarter of all animal species. If that question were posed today, a modern naturalist might reply, "a fondness for miscarriage." In fact, three out of 10 conceptions end prematurely, often without any recognition of their arrival or departure.

2   But John Cardinal O'Connor, the anti-rubber rosarian, and former Vietnam war lover, prayed only to stop man-made abortions last Saturday during a march on a midtown abortion clinic with a band of well opiated Catholics. Surrounded by more bodyguards than Christ had on Palm Sunday, O'Connor still guarded the dirty secret that God is the All Mighty Abortionist.

3   Evidence for this natural (i.e., God-given) avalanche of miscarriages was first reported four years ago in the *New England Journal of Medicine*. The news about the huge volume of early and invisible miscarriages was only a one-day story in the press, but metaphysically the *NEJM* article was a blockbuster, perhaps as threatening to the Christian creed as Copernicus's discovery that the earth revolved around the sun, and not the other way around, as the Catholic Church had mistakenly taught for centuries.

4   How so? The most influential "proof" for the existence of God is the argument from design: Only a Supreme Being, contend theists who have not read Darwin or Stephen Jay Gould, could have made a world as wondrously complex as our own. Yet now we learn He has fashioned creation so that about one third of His likenesses die in the womb. We are not talking about beetles, but millions and millions of human souls swept away in cosmic oblivion.

5   Catholic philosophers have always buried natural evils—monsoons, earthquakes, famines—in mumbojumbo about God's writing straight with crooked lines. But nature's abominable rate of spontaneous abortions suggests the existence of a Fawlty Designer—if there is any design at all.

6   The fate of dead fetuses is a headscratcher for theology, too. Forget demonic possession, the Blessed Mother's hymen, and the Third Secret of Fatima. The destiny of miscarried and aborted souls is the greatest unsolved mystery of Christianity, a doctrinal embarrassment that haunts the credibility of the church, as if any remained after Voltaire, and mocks its role as defender of the unborn.

---

[1] Research: Ronnie Sarig.

7   Although the pope in Rome and the cardinal on Madison Avenue believe that fetuses are full-blown folks from the split-second of conception and have equated abortion with the Holocaust, they fail to mention that the church has shortchanged the never-born in eternity. According to Catholic tradition, the souls of dead fetuses, stained by original sin, are excluded from heaven. This closed-door policy goes back to Jesus's tough saying: "Unless a man be born again of water and the holy spirit, he cannot enter the kingdom of heaven" (John 3:5). Instead, these undocumented alien spirits proceed to limbo, an ethereal Club Med supposedly located on the rim of heaven. Imagined as a place of "natural happiness," it is marred only by sad feelings about missing the company of God. "Its lamentations are not the shrieks of pain, but hopeless sighs," Dante wrote in *The Divine Comedy*. Yet the church has not spoken infallibly: limbo is merely pious legend like the Shroud of Turin.

8   Inevitably, the primitive church looked for some loop-holes in the gospel's exclusionary attitude. First, it did not seem fair that the prophets of the Old Testament were barred from the eternal promised land. Second, converts who had yet to be baptized were being martyred like flies. Thus the church stretched the concept of baptism to account for these hardship cases. Clever theologians came up with "baptism of desire" for the Jewish prophets and for all good people who, by accidents of history, never heard Jesus's warning about being born again. "Baptism of blood" was devised to cover prospective converts who were boiled or roasted for the faith.

9   But the unborn were not as lucky. The church could not figure out how to save their tainted souls or, failing that, where to bunk them in eternity. A heartless Augustine cast them into the fires of hell, but a more sympathetic Aquinas leaned toward limbo. In 1794, Pius VI issued the encyclical *Auctorem Fidei* asserting that the aborted did not go to hell after all. Although Pius VI referred to limbo by name, he did not declare its existence certain. Showing zero interest, the Vatican has said nothing about limbo in the past 200 years.

10   Unappreciated in life, unwelcome in death; where do the unborn discards finally come to rest? I asked John Cardinal O'Connor's right-hand theologian about their ultimate destination. "God knows," replied Monsignor William J. Smith, "God knows." This untidy theology puts prolife Catholics in a ridiculous position. Consider the pastoral disaster involved in telling the faithful that God made millions of unbaptizable "babies" solely to condemn them to suffer his loss forever. This is why prelate-zealots like Cardinal O'Connor never get around to sermonizing on the horrible implications of limbo. They would rather not remind the laity that the aborted, whom the cardinal regards as "holy innocents," are neither holy enough nor innocent enough for salvation. Nor are mothers informed that they will never met their miscarried little ones in heaven.

11   Hoping to save the church from this theological cul-de-sac, a few liberal theologians have speculated that aborted souls will be ransomed at the end of time when limbo merges with heaven. But the Vatican denounced this wishful unorthodox thinking in 1958 as "lacking solid foundation." And despite the obvious appeal of opening heaven to the lodgers of limbo, even this move has a major design flaw. It would mean that God has predestined the salvation of millions of beings.

12 Furthermore, if limbo and heaven eventually dock up, then human-induced abortion loses its moral and tragic sting. The living ought to envy the grateful aborted. We who have been born must face devilish temptations like group sex, cocaine, and tax cheating that severely reduce the chance to be saved. Who among us, if allowed to choose, would not have gladly skipped this brief vale of tears, a grain of sand on the beach of eternity, for an express trip to God's kingdom? *Sub species aeternitatis*, abortion is a no-win issue for prolife Christians who dare to pose as catchers in the womb.

---

1. It can be argued that the closing paragraph of Nobile's essay, like Ivins' essay, is designed to make a particular group of people angry. How could deliberately making any group angry contribute to a persuasive purpose (this is not a **rhetorical question**)?
2. How does Nobile define "natural"?
3. Karl Marx defined religion as "the opium of the common people." How is Nobile's allusion to this in his third paragraph intended to function rhetorically? Does Nobile's shifting among levels of diction involve **invective**?
4. Does Nobile's fifth paragraph involve an unstated **either/or**?
5. How does Nobile distinguish between abortion and miscarriage?
6. Who is Nobile's **target audience**?

Politics and the English Language[1]

George Orwell

1   Most people who bother with the matter at all would admit that the English language is in a bad way, but it is generally assumed that we cannot by conscious action do anything about it. Our civilization is decadent and our language—so the argument runs—must inevitably share in the general collapse. It follows that any struggle against the abuse of language is a sentimental archaism, like preferring candles to electric light or hansom cabs to aeroplanes. Underneath this lies the half-conscious belief that language is a natural growth and not an instrument which we shape for our own purposes.

2   Now, it is clear that the decline of a language must ultimately have political and economic causes: it is not due simply to the bad influence of this or that individual writer. But an effect can become a cause, reinforcing the original cause and producing the same effect in an intensified form, and so on indefinitely. A man may take to drink because he feels himself to be a failure, and then fail all the more completely because he drinks. It is rather the same thing that is happening to the English language. It becomes ugly and inaccurate because our thoughts are foolish, but the slovenliness of our language makes it easier for us to have foolish thoughts. The point is that the process is reversible. Modern English, especially written English, is full of bad habits which spread by imitation and which can be avoided if one is willing to take the necessary trouble. If one gets rid of these habits one can think more clearly, and to think clearly is a necessary first step towards political regeneration: so that the fight against bad English is not frivolous and is not the exclusive concern of professional writers. I will come back to this presently, and I hope that by that time the meaning of what I have said here will have become clearer. Meanwhile, here are five specimens of the English language as it is now habitually written.

3   These five passages have not been picked out because they are especially bad—I could have quoted far worse if I had chosen—but because they illustrate various of the mental vices from which we now suffer. They are a little below the average, but are fairly representative samples. I number them so that I can refer back to them when necessary.

> (1) I am not, indeed, sure whether it is not true to say that the Milton who once seemed not unlike a seventeenth-century Shelley had not become, out of an experience ever more bitter in each year, more alien [sic] to the founder of that Jesuit sect which nothing could induce him to tolerate.

> Professor Harold Laski (Essay in *Freedom of Expression*)

---

[1] This essay is discussed at length in Chapter 3.

(2) Above all, we cannot play ducks and drakes with a native battery of idioms which prescribes such egregious collocations of vocables as the basic *put up with* for *tolerate* or *put at a loss* for *bewilder*.

Professor Lancelot Hogben (*Interglossa*)

(3) On the one side we have the free personality: by definition it is not neurotic, for it has neither conflict nor dream. Its desires, such as they are, are transparent, for they are just what institutional approval keeps in the forefront of consciousness; another institutional pattern would alter their number and intensity; there is little in them that is natural, irreducible, or culturally dangerous. But on the other side, the social bond itself is nothing but the mutual reflection of these self-secure integrities. Recall the definition of love. Is not this the very picture of a small academic? Where is there a place in this hall of mirrors for either personality or fraternity?

Essay on psychology in politics (New York)

(4) All the "best people" from the gentlemen's clubs, and all the frantic fascist captains, united in common hatred of Socialism and bestial horror of the rising tide of the mass revolutionary movement, have turned to acts of provocation, to foul incendiarism, to medieval legends of poisoned wells, to legalize their own destruction of proletarian organizations, and rouse the agitated petty-bourgeoisie to chauvinistic fervour on behalf of the fight against the revolutionary way out of the crisis.

Communist pamphlet

(5) If a new spirit is to be infused into this old country, there is one thorny and contentious reform which must be tackled, and that is the humanization and galvanization of the B.B.C. Timidity here will bespeak canker and atrophy of the soul. The heart of Britain may be sound and of strong beat, for instance, but the British lion's roar at present is like that of Bottom in Shakespeare's *Midsummer Night's Dream*—as gentle as any sucking dove. A virile new Britain cannot continue indefinitely to be traduced in the eyes or rather ears, of the world by the effete languors of Langham Place, brazenly masquerading as "standard English." When the Voice of Britain is heard at nine o'clock, better far and infinitely less ludicrous to hear aitches honestly dropped than the present priggish, inflated, inhibited, school-ma'amish arch braying of blameless bashful mewing maidens!

Letter in *Tribune*

4   Each of these passages has faults of its own, but, quite apart from avoidable ugliness, two qualities are common to all of them. The first is staleness of imagery; the other is lack of precision. The writer either has a meaning and cannot express it, or he inadvertently says something else, or he is almost indifferent as to whether his words mean anything or not. This mixture of vagueness and sheer incompetence is the most marked characteristic of modern English prose, and especially of any kind of political writing. As soon as certain topics are raised, the concrete melts into the abstract and no one seems able to think of turns of speech that are not hackneyed: prose consists less and less of *words* chosen for the sake of their meaning, and more and more of *phrases* tacked

together like the sections of a prefabricated hen house. I list below, with notes and examples, various of the tricks by means of which the work of prose-construction is habitually dodged:

5   **Dying Metaphors.**   A newly invented metaphor assists thought by evoking a visual image, while on the other hand a metaphor which is technically "dead " (e.g., *iron resolution*) has in effect reverted to being an ordinary word and can generally be used without loss of vividness. But in between these two classes there is a huge dump of worn-out metaphors which have lost all evocative power and are merely used because they save people the trouble of inventing phrases for themselves. Examples are: *Ring the changes on, take up the cudgels for, toe the line, ride roughshod over, stand shoulder to shoulder with, play into the hands of, no axe to grind, grist to the mill, fishing in troubled waters, on the order of the day, Achilles' heel, swan song, hotbed.* Many of these are used without knowledge of their meaning (what is a "rift," for instance?), and incompatible metaphors are frequently mixed, a sure sign that the writer is not interested in what he is saying. Some metaphors now current have been twisted out of their original meaning without those who use them even being aware of the fact. For example, *toe* the line is sometimes written *tow* the line. Another example is the *hammer and the anvil* now always used with the implication that the anvil gets the worst of it. In real life it is always the anvil that breaks the hammer, never the other way about: a writer who stopped to think what he was saying would be aware of this, and would avoid perverting the original phrase.

6   **Operators or Verbal False Limbs.**   These save the trouble of picking out appropriate verbs and nouns, and at the same time pad each sentence with extra syllables which give it an appearance of symmetry. Characteristic phrases are *render inoperative, militate against, make contact with, be subjected to, give rise to, give grounds for, have the effect of, play a leading part (role) in, making itself felt, take effect, exhibit a tendency to, serve the purpose of,* etc., etc. The keynote is the elimination of simple verbs. Instead of being a single word, such as *break, stop, spoil, mend, kill,* a verb becomes a *phrase,* made up of a noun or adjective tacked on to some general-purpose verb such as *prove, serve, form, play, render.* In addition, the passive voice is wherever possible used in preference to the active, and noun constructions are used instead of gerunds (*by examination of* instead of *by examining*). The range of verbs is further cut down by means of the *-ize* and *de-* formations, and the banal statements are given an appearance of profundity by means of the *not un-* formation. Simple conjunctions and prepositions are replaced by such phrases as *with respect to, having regard to, the fact that, by dint of, in view of, in the interests of, on the hypothesis that*; and the ends of sentences are saved from anticlimax by such resounding common-places as *greatly to be desired, cannot be left out of account, a development to be expected in the near future, deserving of serious consideration, brought to a satisfactory conclusion,* and so on and so forth.

7   **Pretentious Diction.**   Words like *phenomenon, element, individual (as noun), objective, categorical, effective, virtual, basic, primary, promote, constitute, exhibit, exploit, utilize, eliminate, liquidate,* are used to dress up simple

statements and give an air of scientific impartiality to biased judgments. Adjectives like *epoch-making, epic, historic, unforgettable, triumphant, age-old, inevitable, inexorable, veritable*, are used to dignify the sordid processes of international politics, while writing that aims at glorifying war usually takes on an archaic colour, its characteristic words being: *realm, throne, chariot, mailed fist, trident, sword, shield, buckler, banner, jackboot, clarion*. Foreign words and expressions such as *cul de sac, ancien régime, deus ex machina, mutatis mutandis, status quo, gleichshaltung, weltanshauung*, are used to give an air of culture and elegance. Except for the useful abbreviations *i.e., e.g.,* and *etc.,* there is no real need for any of the hundreds of foreign phrases now current in English. Bad writers, and especially scientific, political and sociological writers, are nearly always haunted by the notion that Latin or Greek words are grander than Saxon ones, and unnecessary words like *expedite, ameliorate, predict, extraneous, deracinated, clandestine, subaqueous* and hundreds of others constantly gain ground from their Anglo-Saxon opposite numbers.[2] The Jargon peculiar to Marxist writing (*hyena, hangman, cannibal, petty bourgeois, these gentry, lacquey, flunky, mad dog, White Guard*, etc.) consists largely of words and phrases translated from Russian, German or French; but the normal way of coining a new word is to use a Latin or Greek root with the appropriate affix and, where necessary, the -ize formation. It is often easier to make up words of this kind (*deregionalize, impermissible, extramarital, nonfragmentary*, and so forth) than to think up the English words that will cover one's meaning. The result, in general, is an increase in slovenliness and vagueness.

8   **Meaningless Words.**   In certain kinds of writing, particularly in art criticism and literary criticism, it is normal to come across long passages which are almost completely lacking in meaning.[3] Words like *romantic, plastic, values, human, dead, sentimental, natural, vitality*, as used in art criticism, are strictly meaningless, in the sense that they not only do not point to any discoverable object, but are hardly ever expected to do so by the reader. When one critic writes, "The outstanding feature of Mr. X's work is its living quality," while another writes, "The immediately striking thing about Mr. X's work is its peculiar deadness," the reader accepts this as a simple difference of opinion. If words like *black* and *white* were involved, instead of the jargon words *dead* and *living*, he would see at once that language was being used in an improper way. Many political words are similarly abused. The word *Fascism* has now no meaning except in so far as it signifies "something not desirable." The words *democracy*,

---

[2] An interesting illustration of this is the way in which the English flower names which were in use till very recently are being ousted by Greek ones, snapdragon becoming antirrhinum, forget-me-not becoming myosotis, etc. It is hard to see any practical reason for this change of fashion: it is probably due to an instinctive turning away from the more homely word and a vague feeling that the Greek word is scientific.

[3] Example: "Comfort's catholicity of perception and image, strangely Whitmanesque in range, almost the exact opposite in aesthetic compulsion, continues to evoke that trembling atmospheric accumulative hinting at a cruel, an inexorably serene timelessness. . . . Wrey Gardiner scores by aiming at simple bull's-eyes with precision. Only they are not so simple, and through this contented sadness runs more than the surface bittersweet of resignation." (*Poetry Quarterly*)

socialism, freedom, patriotic, realistic, justice, have each of them several different meanings which cannot be reconciled with one another. In the case of a word like *democracy,* not only is there no agreed definition, but the attempt to make one is resisted from all sides. It is almost universally felt that when we call a country democratic we are praising it: consequently the defenders of every kind of régime claim that it is a democracy, and fear that they might have to stop using the word if it were tied down to any one meaning. Words of this kind are often used in a consciously dishonest way. That is, the person who uses them has his own private definition, but allows his hearer to think he means something quite different. Statements like *Marshal Petain was a true patriot, The Soviet Press is the freest in the world, The Catholic Church is opposed to persecution,* are almost always made with intent to deceive. Other words used in variable meanings, in most cases more or less dishonestly, are: *class, totalitarian, science, progressive, reactionary, bourgeois, equality.*

9   Now that I have made this catalogue of swindles and perversions, let me give another example of the kind of writing that they lead to. This time it must of its nature be an imaginary one. I am going to translate a passage of good English into modern English of the worst sort. Here is a well-known verse from *Ecclesiastes:*

> I returned and saw under the sun, that the race is not to the swift, nor the battle to the strong, neither yet bread to the wise, nor yet riches to men of understanding, nor yet favor to men of skill; but time and chance happeneth to them all.

Here it is in modern English:

> Objective consideration of contemporary phenomena compels the conclusion that success or failure in competitive activities exhibits no tendency to be commensurate with innate capacity, but that a considerable element of the unpredictable must invariably be taken into account.

10   This is a parody, but not a very gross one. Exhibit (3), above, for instance, contains several patches of the same kind of English. It will be seen that I have not made a full translation. The beginning and ending of the sentence follow the original meaning fairly closely, but in the middle the concrete illustrations—race, battle, bread—dissolve into the vague phrase "success or failure in competitive activities." This had to be so, because no modern writer of the kind I am discussing—no one capable of using phrases like "objective consideration of contemporary phenomena"—would ever tabulate his thoughts in that precise and detailed way. The whole tendency of modern prose is away from concreteness. Now analyze these two sentences a little more closely. The first contains forty-nine words but only sixty syllables, and all its words are those of everyday life. The second contains thirty-eight words of ninety syllables: eighteen of its words are from Latin roots, and one from Greek. The first sentence contains six vivid images, and only one phrase ("time and chance") that could be called vague. The second contains not a single fresh, arresting phrase, and in spite of its ninety syllables it gives only a shortened version of the meaning contained in

the first. Yet without a doubt it is the second kind of sentence that is gaining ground in modern English. I do not want to exaggerate. This kind of writing is not yet universal, and outcrops of simplicity will occur here and there in the worst-written page. Still, if you or I were told to write a few lines on the uncertainty of human fortunes, we should probably come much nearer to my imaginary sentence than to the one from *Ecclesiastes*.

11   As I have tried to show, modern writing at its worst does not consist in picking out words for the sake of their meaning and inventing images in order to make the meaning clearer. It consists in gumming together long strips of words which have already been set in order by someone else, and making the results presentable by sheer humbug. The attraction of this way of writing is that it is easy. It is easier—even quicker, once you have the habit—to say *In my opinion it is not an unjustifiable assumption that* than to say *I think*. If you use ready-made phrases, you not only don't have to hunt for words; you also don't have to bother with the rhythms of your sentences, since these phrases are generally so arranged as to be more or less euphonious. When you are composing in a hurry—when you are dictating to a stenographer, for instance, or making a public speech—it is natural to fall into a pretentious, Latinized style. Tags like a *consideration which we should do well to bear in mind* or a *conclusion to which all of us would readily assent* will save many a sentence from coming down with a bump. By using stale metaphors, similes and idioms, you save much mental effort, at the cost of leaving your meaning vague, not only for your reader but for yourself. This is the significance of mixed metaphors. The sole aim of a metaphor is to call up a visual image. When these images clash— as in *The Fascist octopus has sung its swan song, the jackboot is thrown into the melting pot*—it can be taken as certain that the writer is not seeing a mental image of the objects he is naming; in other words he is not really thinking. Look again at the examples I gave at the beginning of this essay. Professor Laski (1) uses five negatives in fifty-three words. One of these is superfluous, making nonsense of the whole passage, and in addition there is the slip *alien* for *akin*, making further nonsense, and several avoidable pieces of clumsiness which increase the general vagueness. Professor Hobgen (2) plays ducks and drakes with a battery which is able to write prescriptions, and, while disapproving of the every day phrase put up with, is unwilling to look egregious up in the dictionary and see what it means; (3), if one takes an uncharitable attitude towards it, is simply meaningless: probably one could work out its intended meaning by reading the whole of the article in which it occurs. In (4), the writer knows more or less what he wants to say, but an accumulation of stale phrases chokes him like tea leaves blocking a sink. In (5), words and meaning have almost parted company. People who write in this manner usually have a general emotional meaning—they dislike one thing and want to express solidarity with another—but they are not interested in the detail of what they are saying. A scrupulous writer, in every sentence that he writes, will ask himself at least four questions, thus: What am I trying to say? What words will express it? What image or idiom will make it clearer? Is this image fresh enough to have an effect? And he will probably ask himself two more: Could I put it more shortly?

Have I said anything that is avoidably ugly? But you are not obliged to go to all this trouble. You can shirk it by simply throwing your mind open and letting the ready-made phrases come crowding in. They will construct your sentences for you—even think your thoughts for you, to a certain extent—and at need they will perform the important service of partially concealing your meaning even from yourself. It is at this point that the special connection between politics and the debasement of language becomes clear.

12   In our time it is broadly true that political writing is bad writing. Where it is not true, it will generally be found that the writer is some kind of rebel, expressing his private opinions and not a "party line." Orthodoxy, of whatever colour, seems to demand a lifeless, imitative style. The political dialects to be found in pamphlets, leading articles, manifests, White Papers and the speeches of under-secretaries do, of course, vary from party to party, but they are all alike in that one almost never finds in them a fresh, vivid, home-made turn of speech. When one watches some tired hack on the platform mechanically repeating the familiar phrase—*bestial atrocities, iron heel, bloodstained tyranny, free peoples of the world, stand shoulder to shoulder*—one often has a curious feeling that one is not watching a live human being but some kind of dummy: a feeling which suddenly becomes stronger at moments when the light catches the speaker's spectacles and turns them into blank discs which seem to have no eyes behind them. And this is not altogether fanciful. A speaker who uses that kind of phraseology has gone some distance towards turning himself into a machine. The appropriate noises are coming out of his larynx, but his brain is not involved as it would be if he were choosing his words for himself. If the speech he is making is one that he is accustomed to make over and over again, he may be almost unconscious of what he is saying, as one is when one utters the responses in church. And this reduced state of consciousness, if not indispensable, is at any rate favorable to political conformity.

13   In our time, political speech and writing are largely the defence of the indefensible. Things like the continuance of British rule in India, the Russian purges and deportations, the dropping of the atom bombs on Japan, can indeed be defended, but only by arguments which are too brutal for most people to face, and which do not square with the professed aims of political parties. Thus political language has to consist largely of euphemism, question-begging and sheer cloudy vagueness. Defenseless villages are bombarded from the air, the inhabitants driven out into the countryside, the cattle machine-gunned, the huts set on fire with incendiary bullets: this is called *pacification*. Millions of peasants are robbed of their farms and set trudging along the roads with no more than they can carry: this is called *transfer of population* or *rectification of frontiers*. People are imprisoned for years without trial, or shot in the back of the neck or sent to die of scurvy in Arctic lumber camps: this is called *elimination of unreliable elements*. Such phraseology is needed if one wants to name things without calling up mental pictures of them. Consider for instance some comfortable English professor defending Russian totalitarianism. He cannot say outright, "I believe in killing off your opponents when you can get good results by doing so." Probably, therefore, he will say something like this:

While freely conceding that the Soviet regime exhibits certain features which the humanitarian may be inclined to deplore, we must, I think, agree that a certain curtailment of the right to political opposition is an unavoidable concomitant of transitional periods, and that the rigours which the Russian people have been called upon to undergo have been amply justified in the sphere of concrete achievement.

14   The inflated style is itself a kind of euphemism. A mass of Latin words falls upon the facts like soft snow, blurring the outlines and covering up all the details. The great enemy of clear language is insincerity. When there is a gap between one's real and one's declared aims, one turns as it were instinctively to long words and exhausted idioms, like a cuttlefish squirting out ink. In our age there is no such thing as "keeping out of politics." All issues are political issues, and politics itself is a mass of lies, evasions, folly, hatred and schizophrenia. When the general atmosphere is bad, language must suffer. I should expect to find—this is a guess which I have not sufficient knowledge to verify—that the German, Russian and Italian languages have all deteriorated in the last ten or fifteen years, as a result of dictatorship.

15   But if thought corrupts language, language can also corrupt thought. A bad usage can spread by tradition and imitation, even among people who should and do know better. The debased language that I have been discussing is in some ways very convenient. Phrases like *a not unjustifiable assumption, leaves much to be desired, would serve no good purpose, a consideration which we should do well to bear in mind,* are a continuous temptation, a packet of aspirins always at one's elbow. Look back through this essay, and for certain you will find that I have again and again committed the very faults I am protesting against. By this morning's post I have received a pamphlet dealing with conditions in Germany. The author tells me that he "felt impelled" to write it. I open it at random, and here is almost the first sentence that I see: "[The Allies] have an opportunity not only of achieving a radical transformation of Germany's social and political structure in such a way as to avoid a nationalistic reaction in Germany itself, but at the same time of laying the foundations of a co-operative and unified Europe." You see, he "feels impelled" to write—feels, presumably, that he has something new to say—and yet his words, like cavalry horses answering the bugle, group themselves automatically into the familiar dreary pattern. This invasion of one's mind by ready-made phrases (*lay the foundations, achieve a radical transformation*) can only be prevented if one is constantly on guard against them, and every such phrase anesthetizes a portion of one's brain.

16   I said earlier that the decadence of our language is probably curable. Those who deny this would argue, if they produced an argument at all, that language merely reflects existing social conditions, and that we cannot influence its development by any direct tinkering with words and constructions. So far as the general tone or spirit of a language goes, this may be true, but it is not true in detail. Silly words and expressions have often disappeared, not through any evolutionary process but owing to the conscious action of a minority. Two recent examples were *explore every avenue* and *leave no stone unturned,* which were killed by the jeers of a few journalists. There is a long list of fly-blown metaphors

which could similarly be got rid of if enough people would interest themselves in the job; and it should also be possible to laugh the not un- formation out of existence,[4] to reduce the amount of Latin and Greek in the average sentence, to drive out foreign phrases and strayed scientific words, and, in general, to make pretentiousness unfashionable. But all these are minor points. The defence of the English language implies more than this, and perhaps it is best to start by saying what it does not imply.

17   To begin with it has nothing to do with archaism, with the salvaging of obsolete words and turns of speech, or with the setting up of a "standard English" which must never be departed from. On the contrary, it is especially concerned with the scrapping of every word or idiom which has outworn its usefulness. It has nothing to do with correct grammar and syntax, which are of no importance so long as one makes one's meaning clear, or with the avoidance of Americanisms, or with having what is called a "good prose style." On the other hand, it is not concerned with fake simplicity and the attempt to make written English colloquial. Nor does it even imply in every case preferring the Saxon word to the Latin one, though it does imply using the fewest and shortest words that will cover one's meaning. What is above all needed is to let the meaning choose the word, and not the other way about. In prose, the worst thing one can do with words is to surrender to them. When you think of a concrete object, you think wordlessly, and then, if you want to describe the thing you have been visualizing you probably hunt about till you find the exact words that seem to fit it. When you think of something abstract you are more inclined to use words from the start, and unless you make a conscious effort to prevent it, the existing dialect will come rushing in and do the job for you, at the expense of blurring or even changing your meaning. Probably it is better to put off using words as long as possible and get one's meaning as clear as one can through pictures or sensations. Afterwards one can choose—not simply accept—the phrase that will best cover the meaning, and then switch round and decide what impression one's words are likely to make on another person. This last effort of the mind cuts out all stale or mixed images, all prefabricated phrases, needless repetitions, and humbug and vagueness generally. But one can often be in doubt about the effect of a word or a phrase, and one needs rules that one can rely on when instinct fails. I think the following rules will cover most cases:

(i) Never use a metaphor, simile or other figure of speech which you are used to seeing in print.

(ii) Never use a long word where a short one will do.

(iii) If it is possible to cut a word out, always cut it out.

(iv) Never use the passive when you can use the active.

(v) Never use a foreign phrase, a scientific word or a jargon word if you can think of an everyday English equivalent.

(vi) Break any of these rules sooner than say anything outright barbarous.

---

[4] One can cure oneself of the not un- formation by memorizing this sentence: A not unblack dog was chasing a not unsmall rabbit across a not ungreen field.

18   These rules sound elementary, and so they are, but they demand a deep change of attitude in anyone who has grown used to writing in the style now fashionable. One could keep all of them and still write bad English, but one could not write the kind of stuff that I quoted in those five specimens at the beginning of this article.

19   I have not here been considering the literary use of language, but merely language as an instrument for expressing and not for concealing or preventing thought. Stuart Chase and others have come near to claiming that all abstract words are meaningless, and have used this as a pretext for advocating a kind of political quietism. Since you don't know what Fascism is, how can you struggle against Fascism? One need not swallow such absurdities as this, but one ought to recognize that the present political chaos is connected with the decay of language, and that one can probably bring about some improvement by starting at the verbal end. If you simplify your English, you are freed from the worst follies of orthodoxy. You cannot speak any of the necessary dialects, and when you make a stupid remark its stupidity will be obvious, even to yourself. Political language—and with variations this is true of all political parties, from Conservatives to Anarchists is designed to make lies sound truthful and murder respectable, and to give an appearance of solidity to pure wind. One cannot change this all in a moment, but one can at least change one's own habits, and from time to time one can even, if one jeers loudly enough, send some worn-out and useless phrase—some jackboot, Achilles' heel, hotbed, melting pot, acid test, veritable inferno or other lump of verbal refuse—into the dustbin where it belongs.

A Pyrrhic Victory

Anna Quindlen

1   Pop quiz: A 16-year-old is appropriately treated at a school clinic after he is advised that the reason it feels as if he is going to die when he urinates is because he has a sexually transmitted disease. Told that condoms could have protected him from infection, he asks for some. A nurse tells him to wait while she looks for his name on the list of students whose parents have confidentially requested that their sons and daughters not receive them.

2   The student replies: (a) "No problem"; (b) "Hmmm—an interesting way to balance the reproductive health of adolescents and the rights of parents'; (c) Nothing. He sidles out of the office and not long afterward gets a whopping case of chlamydia.

3   Condoms, condoms, condoms. As those who oppose condom distribution in the schools gloated over an appellate court decision that said the program violated parents' rights, Alwyn Cohall, the pediatrician who oversees several school-based clinics in New York, quoted Yogi Berra. "It's déja vu all over again," said Dr. Cohall, who has to clean up the messes made when sexually active kids don't use condoms. And he wasn't smiling.

4   Over the last two years the Board of Education has wasted time better spent on instructional issues giving and receiving lectures on latex. The opt-out provision its members are now likely to adopt is the "let me see if you're on the list, dear" scenario outlined above, and if you think it might have a chilling effect on a young man too self-conscious to ask for Trojans in a drugstore, then you get an A in adolescent psychology.

5   You get extra credit if you figure that being on the list will be scant protection against disease if the young man has sex anyhow. "A victory for parents," some have called the provision. But is it Pyrrhic?

6   Dr. Cohall, a champion of condom distribution, agrees that it is best if teenagers abstain from sexual activity and talk to their parents about issues of sex, morality, and health. But he also notes that in 1992 his three high school clinics saw around 150 cases of sexually transmitted diseases like condyloma, chlamydia, and the better-known gonorrhea and syphilis.

7   He has a 16-year-old in the hospital right now who got AIDS from her second sexual partner. And he recalls a girl who broke her leg jumping out an apartment window because her mother found her birth control pills, seized her by the throat, and said, according to the kid, "I brought you into the world; I can take you out of it."

8   Don't you just love those little mother-daughter sex talks?

9   He also knows that at the heart of the balancing act between keeping kids healthy and keeping parents involved there has always been a covert place in which many opponents of condom distribution really settle. It's called Fantasyland.

10   You could see that in the response to the rather mild commercials on condom use and abstinence that the Department of Health and Human Services unveiled this week. The general secretary of the National Conference of Catholic Bishops immediately said the ads "promote promiscuity" and the networks should reject them. At the same time, ABC said it would not run the spots during its prime-time "family-oriented" programs.

11   So foolish. ABC's own *Roseanne* has been far more candid about sexuality than any of the new government public-service spots. And what could be a better way to foment conversation with the children of the video age than a television advertisement? Right there in your living room you have a goad to the kind of discussion that opponents of condom distribution have always argued is the purview of parents. And you put the ads on late at night? Do we really want to talk with our kids? Or do we just want to talk about talking to them?

12   The Board of Education could do a great good if it found ways to truly foster parent-child communication in all things, not just matters sexual. But instead its members argue about condoms. This isn't really about condoms, of course, but about control and the shock of adolescent sexuality and the difficulty parents have communicating with their kids and a deep and understandable yearning for simpler times.

13   While we yearn and argue, Dr. Cohall visits his 16-year-old AIDS patient. Her parents' involvement may someday consist of visiting the cemetery. Imagine how they'd feel if they put her on the no-condom list, then put her in the hospital, then put her in the ground. Some victory.

---

1. If we consider Quindlen's "pop quiz" in terms of its rhetorical intent, would it be useful to think of it as a sort of **rhetorical question?**
2. Highlight each instance of Quindlen's use of the teacher/student relationship as rhetorical device. What does the use of this device imply in terms of Quindlen's hoped for interaction with her **target audience?**
3. Based on the evidence of the text, attempt to define what Quindlen thinks about "parental involvement."
4. In paragraph 11, Quindlen writes the two word sentence, "So foolish." Based on this and instances like it, who do you think Quindlen's **target audience** is, and of what does she want to convince it?

When It All Started

William Raspberry

1   It all started in the late 1960's, says William Kilpatrick of Boston College, when we stripped education of its moral component.

2   The "it," of course, is the despicable behavior of our children. They are self-centered, self-indulgent and short-sighted. They are loyal to nothing, feel entitled to everything, and are forever crying about what someone—a teacher, a group, or "the system"—has done to them. Their moral standards, if one dares call them that, are of the most elastic sort.

3   How could such wonderful parents as ourselves have produced such awful offspring? Kilpatrick, a professor of education, tries to tell us in his new book, *Why Johnny Can't Tell Right from Wrong: Moral Illiteracy and the Case for Character Education.*

4   He said the idea for the book came to him when the subject of the Ten Commandments came up in class and he decided to have his students recite them so he could list them on the board. They couldn't.

5   "It wasn't that individuals couldn't think of them all," he told a reporter for the *Boston Globe.* "The whole class working together to come up with the complete list couldn't do it."

6   He saw that episode as proof of what he came to call "moral illiteracy"—the failure of schools to teach, and of students to learn, the eternal verities. I see it in simpler terms: the Ten Commandments are such a mixture of ethics and overlapping religious proscriptions that it's hard to remember them all—even while violating them.

7   My guess is that Professor Kilpatrick and the *Globe* reporter couldn't have named all 10 before they got embarrassed and went and looked them up—and that you can't either. Try it, and you'll see what I mean.

8   But what of Kilpatrick's central point: that the cause of our downhill slide is the neglect of moral teachings in our schoolrooms?

9   The schools are as likely a culprit as any. I don't doubt that it was a serious mistake to abandon moral and ethical instruction (as opposed to instruction about morals and ethics). But it's not our only mistake, and a case could be made for any of a number of starting points for our—that is, our children's—awfulness. It all started (we could argue) with Ronald Reagan's conservatives and their condonation of the economics of greed. How can our children be modest and compassionate when they have been taught by their national leadership that rich is good and poverty the just reward of sloth?

10   It all started with the liberal idea that how we feel is more important than what we do. Feeling is inherently individual, and to focus on how we feel is to

free ourself of concern for others (except insofar as looking after others makes us feel good about ourselves). The path from feeling to self-indulgence is short and smooth. You can get there—our children got there—without even thinking about it.

11   It all started with co-ed dorms. In the old days (our days) we were not left to our own impulsive devices. There were rules and structures and expectations that kept us from doing what everybody knew we were dying to do. The rules and expectations have changed utterly (can you imagine members of your high school class being urged by teachers and public officials to practice "safe sex"?). And the structures that used to save us the necessity of the hard choice (I'd love to, Bob, but where?) have been replaced by co-ed dorms.

12   It all started with right-on-red. The rules used to have clear and consistent meaning. Things were good or bad, right or wrong. Green meant "go," red meant "stop." Now everything is confused and conditional. Red means "stop, but if the street is relatively clear, or if you have confidence in your car's acceleration, go ahead and turn right."

13   The upshot is just what you'd expect. More and more people are merely almost stopping on red, and frightening numbers are going straight through on red. And the practice is not limited to driving. For growing numbers of people, all rules are marked with asterisks that tempt us (tempt our children) to stretch the limits to the breaking point.

14   It all started with the notion (first recorded in the Garden of Eden) that anything that's forbidden is, on that account, more desirable. But don't blame poor Adam and Eve.

15   It all started with Satan.

---

1. Go through the essay with a highlighter and mark every instance of an **absolute**. Does this tell you anything about how Raspberry is using them?
2. Raspberry calls the Ten Commandments a "mixture of ethics and overlapping religious proscription." What commandments do you think he would cite as examples of proscription?
3. If you could name the Ten Commandments what does that demonstrate about your relation to Raspberry's **target audience**?
4. Where does Raspberry directly address the reader with what rhetorical intent?
5. Using a different colored highlighter, go through the essay and mark every pronoun. What is Raspberry doing with the "us"? in paragraph 13?
6. Why is it not possible for the careful reader to believe that Raspberry believes that it "all started with Satan"? To stay within the confines of that religious narrative, where did Satan come from (remember that the title says "when " it all started, not "where")?
7. If the **thesis** of "When It All Started" is **implied** (like the thesis of "Why I Want a Wife), what is that thesis? How shortly can you state it?

This editorial appeared in January of 1993 by-lined to William Raspberry "a syndicated columnist based in Washington, D.C." under the headline "Trouble started with right-on-red, co-ed dorms and rules with asterisks." Raspberry won a Pulitzer Prize for commentary in 1994.

The Bible Says

Carl T. Rowan

1   Years ago a country preacher in Tennessee warned me that "even the devil can quote the Bible."

2   Sure enough, we've got politicians here who are quoting the Bible to justify a lot of cruelty and discrimination.

3   Senate Majority Leader Trent Lott, R-Miss., has not only declared that homosexuals are sinners, he says they manifest a sickness "like alcohol and sex addiction" and need help.

4   House Majority Leader Dick Armey, R-Irving, was quick to defend Lott, citing a passage from I Corinthians 6 that says, "Neither fornicators nor idolators, nor adulterers, nor effeminate . . . shall inherit the kingdom of God."

5   Lott and Armey probably will be heartened when I tell them that a more specific passage is in Leviticus 20:13, where God says to Moses: "If a man also lie with mankind, as he lieth with a woman, both of them have committed an abomination; they shall surely be put to death. . . ."

6   It is interesting that the bashers of homosexuals will take that literally but will overlook God also saying to Moses: "And the man that committeth adultery with *another* man's wife, *even he* that committeth adultery with his neighbor's wife, the adulterer and the adulteress shall surely be put to death."

7   Armey and Lott talk as though they are making the Bible the bedrock of public policy in America. Lott, for example, leads a Senate move to deny the confirmation of James Hormel to be ambassador to Luxembourg because Hormel is a self-declared homosexual.

8   If they really intend to take the Bible literally, not only will they have to make fornication a capital offense, they will have to ask every nominee for anything whether he or she has ever committed adultery. By those biblical standards they could clean out a majority of both the House and Senate.

9   "I do abide by the Bible," Armey said in explaining his rejection of homosexuals. I wonder if he abides by Leviticus 11, in which God tells Moses that the people must not eat pork or rabbit or shrimp or lobster, or anything in the seas and rivers that does not have fins and scales?

10   "Whatsoever hath no fins nor scales in the water *shall* be an abomination to you," Leviticus says.

11   I've known preachers who would not take Leviticus seriously but would argue that the Bible (Genesis 10) shows that God put a curse on Noah's son Ham, and doomed all his descendants to be servants. And black skins are, in the reading of some racists, a sign of that curse.

12   The Bible is a remarkable book, subject to interpretations that justify deeds
that are Christlike and acts that are inhuman. But it does not enlighten us on
the question whether homosexuality is a disease or a form of sexuality that was
imposed by the Creator.

13   One thing I'm sure of: We face calamity as a nation if our Congress is ever
dominated by the passions of members who push their special interpretations of
what the Bible says.

14   We have some clear constitutional prohibitions against this, and we ought
to reject early those who, in the name of God, cast the first and last stones.

---

1. Rowan never uses the word, nor does he cite it from the Bible, but I would
   suggest that his major argument is the **implication** that using a portion of the
   Bible to justify a particular policy and ignoring other parts of it, constitutes
   hypocrisy. Compare the way that Rowan deals with the Bible as a guide to
   value to the way Raspberry approaches it.
2. What is the **either/or** Rowan puts forward in paragraph 12? Do you think it
   is intended to suggest a re**definition** of the question?
3. What are the "clear constitutional prohibitions" Rowan refers to?
4. Can any comparisons be drawn between Rowan's attitude toward the constitution in relationship to religious texts and Hentoff's? To put the question
   slightly differently, do either or both of them treat the Constitution with the
   deference usually accorded by believers to their particular religious text (The
   Old Testament, the Quran, the Book of Mormon, etc.).

Rowan is a syndicated columnist based in Washington, D.C.

Dealing with Breakdowns in Communication

Carl Rogers

1   It may seem curious that a person whose whole professional effort is devoted to psychotherapy should be interested in problems of communication. What relationship is there between providing therapeutic help to individuals with emotional maladjustments and the concern of this conference with obstacles to communication? Actually the relationship is very close indeed. The whole task of psychotherapy is the task of dealing with a failure in communication. The emotionally maladjusted person, the "neurotic," is in difficulty first because communication within himself has broken down, and second because as a result of this his communication with others has been damaged. If this sounds somewhat strange, then let me put it in other terms. In the "neurotic" individual, parts of himself which have been termed unconscious, or repressed, or denied to awareness, become blocked off so that they no longer communicate themselves to the conscious or managing part of himself. As long as this is true, there are distortions in the way he communicates himself to others, and so he suffers both within himself, and in his interpersonal relations. The task of psychotherapy is to help the person achieve, through a special relationship with a therapist, good communication within himself. Once this is achieved he can communicate more freely and more effectively with others. We may say then that psychotherapy is good communication, within and between men. We may also turn that statement around and it will still be true. Good communication, free communication, within or between men, is always therapeutic.

2   It is, then, from a background of experience with communication in counseling and psychotherapy that I want to present here two ideas. I wish to state what I believe is one of the major factors in blocking or impeding communication, and then I wish to present what in our experience has proven to be a very important way of improving or facilitating communication.

3   I would like to propose, as an hypothesis for consideration, that the major barrier to mutual interpersonal communication is our very natural tendency to judge, to evaluate, to approve or disapprove, the statement of the other person, or the other group. Let me illustrate my meaning with some very simple examples. As you leave the meeting tonight, one of the statements you are likely to hear is, "I didn't like that man's talk." Now what do you respond? Almost invariably your reply will be either approval or disapproval of the attitude expressed. Either you respond, "I didn't either. I thought it was terrible," or else you tend to reply, "Oh, I thought it was really good." In other words, your primary reaction is to evaluate what has just been said to you, to evaluate it from your point of view, your own frame of reference.

4   Or take another example. Suppose I say with some feeling, "I think the Republicans are behaving in ways that show a lot of good sound sense these days," what is the response that arises in your mind as you listen? The overwhelming likelihood is that it will be evaluative. You will find yourself agreeing, or disagreeing, or making some judgment about me such as "He must be a conservative," or "He seems solid in his thinking." Or let us take an illustration from the international scene. Russia says vehemently, "The treaty with Japan is a war plot on the part of the United States." We rise as one person to say "That's a lie!"

5   This last illustration brings in another element connected with my hypothesis. Although the tendency to make evaluations is common in almost all interchange of language, it is very much heightened in those situations where feelings and emotions are deeply involved. So the stronger our feelings, the more likely it is that there will be no mutual element in the communication. There will be just two ideas, two feelings, two judgments, missing each other in psychological space. I'm sure you recognize this from your own experience. When you have not been emotionally involved yourself, and have listened to a heated discussion, you often go away thinking, "Well, they actually weren't talking about the same thing." And they were not. Each was making a judgment, an evaluation, from his own frame of reference. There was really nothing which could be called communication in any genuine sense. This tendency to react to any emotionally meaningful statement by forming an evaluation of it from our own point of view, is, I repeat, the major barrier to interpersonal communication.

6   But is there any way of solving this problem, of avoiding this barrier? I feel that we are making exciting progress toward this goal and I would like to present it as simply as I can. Real communication occurs, and this evaluative tendency is avoided, when we listen with understanding. What does that mean? It means *to see the expressed idea and attitude from the other person's point of view, to sense how it feels to him to achieve his frame of reference in regard to the thing he is talking about.*

7   Stated so briefly, this may sound absurdly simple, but it is not. It is an approach which we have found extremely potent in the field of psychotherapy. It is the most effective agent we know for altering the basic personality structure of an individual, and improving his relationships and his communications with others. If I can listen to what he can tell me, if I can understand how it seems to him, if I can see its personal meaning for him, if I can sense the emotional flavor which it has for him, then I will be releasing potent forces of change in him. If I can really understand how he hates his father, or hates the university, or hates communists—if I can catch the flavor of his fear of insanity, or his fear of atom bombs, or of Russia—it will be of the greatest help to him in altering those very hatreds and fears, and in establishing realistic and harmonious relationships with the very people and situations toward which he has felt hatred and fear. We know from our research that such empathic understanding—understanding with a person, not about him—is such an effective approach that it can bring about major changes in personality.

8   Some of you may be feeling that you listen well to people, and that you have never seen such results. The chances are very great indeed that your listening has

not been of the type I have described. Fortunately I can suggest a little laboratory experiment which you can try to test the quality of your understanding. The next time you get into an argument with your wife, or your friend, or with a small group of friends, just stop the discussion for a moment and for an experiment, institute this rule. "Each person can speak up for himself only after he has first restated the ideas and feelings of the previous speaker accurately, and to that speaker's satisfaction." You see what this would mean. It would simply mean that before presenting your own point of view, it would be necessary for you to really achieve the other speaker's frame of reference—to understand his thoughts and feelings so well that you could summarize them for him. Sounds simple doesn't it? But if you try you will discover it one of the most difficult things you have ever tried to do. However, once you have been able to see the other's point of view, your own comments will have to be drastically revised. You will also find the emotion going out of the discussion, the differences being reduced, and those differences which remain being of a rational and understandable sort.

9   Can you imagine what this kind of an approach would mean if it were projected into larger areas? What would happen to a labor-management dispute if it was conducted in such a way that labor, without necessarily agreeing, could accurately state management's point of view in a way that management could accept, and management, without approving labor's stand, could state labor's case in a way that labor agreed was accurate? It would mean that real communication was established, and one could practically guarantee that some reasonable solution would be reached.

10   If then this way of approach is an effective avenue to good communication and good relationships, as I am quite sure you will agree if you try the experiment I have mentioned, why is it not more widely tried and used? I will try to list the difficulties which keep it from being utilized.

11   In the first place it takes courage, a quality which is not too widespread. I am indebted to Dr. S. I. Hayakawa, the semanticist, for pointing out that to carry on psychotherapy in this fashion is to take a very real risk, and that courage is required. If you really understand another person in this way, if you are willing to enter his private world and see the way life appears to him, without any attempt to make evaluative judgments, you run the risk of being changed yourself. You might see it his way, you might find yourself influenced in your attitudes or your personality. The risk of being changed is one of the most frightening prospects most of us can face. If I enter, as fully as I am able, into the private world of a neurotic or psychotic individual, isn't there a risk that I might become lost in that world? Most of us are afraid to take that risk. Or if we had a Russian communist speaker here tonight, or Senator Joe McCarthy, how many of us would dare to try to see the world from each of these points of view? The great majority of us could not *listen*; we would find ourselves compelled to *evaluate*, because listening would seem too dangerous. So the first requirement is courage, and we do not always have it.

12   But there is a second obstacle. It is just when emotions are strongest that it is most difficult to achieve the frame of reference of the other person or group.

Yet it is the time the attitude is most needed, if communication is to be established. We have not found this to be an insuperable obstacle in our experience in psychotherapy. A third party, who is able to lay aside his own feelings and evaluations, can assist greatly by listening with understanding to each person or group and clarifying the views and attitudes each holds. We have found this very effective in small groups in which contradictory or antagonistic attitudes exist. When the parties to a dispute realize that they are being understood, that someone sees how the situation seems to them, the statements grow less exaggerated and less defensive, and it is no longer necessary to maintain the attitude, "I am 100% right and you are 100% wrong." The influence of such an understanding catalyst in the group permits the members to come closer and closer to the objective truth involved in the relationship. In this way mutual communication is established and some type of agreement becomes much more possible. So we may say that though heightened emotions make it much more difficult to understand *with* an opponent, our experience makes it clear that a neutral, understanding, catalyst type of leader or therapist can overcome this obstacle in a small group.

13   This last phrase, however, suggests another obstacle to utilizing the approach I have described. Thus far all our experience has been with small face-to-face groups—groups exhibiting industrial tensions, religious tensions, racial tensions, and therapy groups in which many personal tensions are present. In these small groups our experience, confined by a limited amount of research, shows that this basic approach leads to improved communication, to greater acceptance of others and by others, and to attitudes which are more positive and more problem-solving in nature. There is a decrease in defensiveness, in exaggerated statements, in evaluative and critical behavior. But these findings are from small groups. What about trying to achieve understanding between larger groups that are geographically remote? Or between face-to-face groups who are not speaking for themselves, but simply as representatives of others, like the delegates at Kaesong? Frankly we do not know the answers to these questions. I believe the situation might be put this way. As social scientists we have a tentative test-tube solution of the problem of breakdown in communication. But to confirm the validity of this test-tube solution, and to adapt it to the enormous problems of communication-breakdown between classes, groups, and nations, would involve additional funds, much more research, and creative thinking of a high order.

14   Even with our present limited knowledge we can see some steps which might be taken, even in large groups, to increase the amount of listening with, and to decrease the amount of evaluation about. To be imaginative for a moment, let us suppose that a therapeutically oriented international group went to the Russian leaders and said, "We want to achieve a genuine understanding of your views and even more important, of your attitudes and feelings, toward the United States. We will summarize and resummarize these views and feelings if necessary, until you agree that our description represents the situation as it seems to you." Then suppose they did the same thing with the leaders in our own country. If they then gave the widest possible distribution to these two

views, with the feelings clearly described but not expressed in name-calling, might not the effect be very great? It would not guarantee the type of understanding I have been describing, but it would make it much more possible. We can understand the feelings of a person who hates us much more readily when his attitudes are accurately described to us by a neutral third party, than we can when he is shaking his fist at us.

15   But even to describe such a first step is to suggest another obstacle to this approach of understanding. Our civilization does not yet have enough faith in the social sciences to utilize their findings. The opposite is true of the physical sciences. During the war when a test-tube solution was found to the problem of synthetic rubber, millions of dollars and an army of talent was turned loose on the problem of using that finding. If synthetic rubber could be made in milligrams, it could and would be made in the thousands of tons. And it was. But in the social science realm, if a way is found of facilitating communication and mutual understanding in small groups, there is no guarantee that the finding will be utilized. It may be a generation or more before the money and the brains will be turned loose to exploit that finding.

16   In closing, I would like to summarize this small-scale solution to the problem of barriers in communication, and to point out certain of its characteristics.

17   I have said that our research and experience to date would make it appear that breakdowns in communication, and the evaluative tendency which is the major barrier to communication, can be avoided. The solution is provided by creating a situation in which each of the different parties come to understand the other from the other's point of view. This has been achieved, in practice, even when feelings run high, by the influence of a person who is willing to understand each point of view empathically, and who thus acts as a catalyst to precipitate further understanding.

18   This procedure has important characteristics. It can be initiated by one party, without waiting for the other to be ready. It can even be initiated by a neutral third person, providing he can gain a minimum of cooperation from one of the parties.

19   This procedure can deal with the insincerities, the defensive exaggerations, the lies, the "false fronts" which characterize almost every failure in communication. These defensive distortions drop away with astonishing speed as people find that the only intent is to understand, not judge.

20   This approach leads steadily and rapidly toward the discovery of the truth, toward a realistic appraisal of the objective barriers to communication. The dropping of some defensiveness by one party leads to further dropping of defensiveness by the other party, and truth is thus approached.

21   This procedure gradually achieves mutual communication. Mutual communication tends to be pointed toward solving a problem rather than toward attacking a person or group. It leads to a situation in which I see how the problem appears to you, as well as to me, and you see how it appears to me, as well as to you. Thus accurately and realistically defined, the problem is almost certain to yield to intelligent attack, or if it is in part insoluble, it will be comfortably accepted as such.

22   This then appears to be a test-tube solution to the breakdown of communication as it occurs in small groups. Can we take this small scale answer, investigate it further, refine it, develop it and apply it to the tragic and well-nigh fatal failures of communication which threaten the very existence of our modern world? It seems to me that this is a possibility and a challenge which we should explore.

---

1. Go through the essay and highlight each word that describes Rogers' "hypothesis for consideration" as **tentative** rather than **definitive**.
2. With a different highlighting color, go through the essay and mark each passage that contains some sort of **truth claim** (in the third sentence, the word "Actually," for instance).
3. Is it useful to use our definitions of Rogerian argument to analyze Roger's argument?
4. Is there anything in the essay to make you think that Rogers would think that composition theory has **appropriated** his theory?

Carl Rogers, who died in 1987, was a psychotherapist. He gave us the concept of the Rogerian argument, for a discussion of which see Chapter 5 and the Glossary.

Metaphors: Live, Dead, and Silly

Roger Sale

1   I may only be betraying my own ignorance, but the way metaphor usually is taught seems to invite my students to think of it as an ornament to their style, an effect achieved in poetry but not really necessary for any decent, hard-working plain style. As a result, most students seem unaware of the way metaphor pervades even the plainest and most hard-working of styles, and is the dominant feature of almost all our speech. Students seem to feel that metaphor is something they can "use" or not "use" as they wish, and so when they decide to use metaphors, they become wildly self-conscious and liable to cliché. When asked, they speak of metaphor as something different from a simile. "The moon was a ghostly galleon tossed upon stormy seas," they have learned, is a metaphor, and "My love is like a red, red rose" is a simile. Their examples, as I say, come from poems; metaphors are what you learn about in English classes, nowhere else.

2   The definition of metaphor most students have carried with them from English class to English class, however, can serve a wider purpose than it usually does. A metaphor is a comparison in which one thing is said to be another thing, as opposed to a simile, which is a comparison in which one thing is said to be like another thing. The distinction may have its purpose, but a moment's reflection will show that when one thing is said to be another thing, that does not mean that it in fact is that other thing but only that it is like that thing; metaphors and similes do exactly the same thing. When I say, in the first sentence of this paragraph, that students "have carried" a definition of metaphor from class to class, I do not mean that this carrying is literally the same carrying one might do if the subject were a ball of twine, but only that what students do with their definition of metaphor is like what they might do with a ball of twine. The word "carry" is a metaphor here, then. Look at the words "show" and "do" in the third sentence of this paragraph. These are obviously not felt as metaphors, yet they obviously are not meant to be taken literally; a moment's reflection cannot "show," a metaphor cannot "do" or be "felt" except metaphorically.

3   You can take almost any passage and treat it like the pictures in which you try to find the hidden animals. How many metaphors can you find in the following:

> Sure, I see Joe Fisher every morning. He comes in after class, scrounges around until he finds someone with a dime, buys his coffee and then he parks himself off in the corner. Within five minutes the son-of-a-bitch is holding court with a bunch of women. It's incredible. He sits back, pounds his spoon

on the table, blows smoke down their throat, looks bored, yet somehow he manages it and so as to seem the biggest thing in their world. I've seen girls who wouldn't give me the time of day and to whom I've been princely treat him like some guru. It's as though he digs some language or tunes in on some obscure wave length made just for Joe Fisher and women.

4   Without stretching the idea of metaphor very much, I count nineteen: scrounges, parks, son-of-a-bitch, holding court, bunch, incredible, pounds, blows smoke down their throats, manages, biggest thing, world, seen, give me the time of day, princely, guru, digs some language, tunes in on some wave length, obscure, made. And that doesn't count those that are like metaphors, even if one doesn't want to call them that: every morning, someone with a dime, within five minutes, all, treat. Within a hundred words Joe Fisher is a rodent, a car, a male offspring of a female dog, a king, a stage director, a wise man, a mystic, a favored child of nature for whom things are "made."

5   Granted that an unprepared speech in conversation has the highest metaphorical density of any language we use, the game can be played even in conversations where everything is short bursts, with newspapers, with dialogue in movies. Our sense of the world involves us so constantly and completely in metaphors that there is little exaggeration in saying that all our speech and writing approaches metaphor; for example, you can hear many people who don't know what a metaphor is make one out of "literally" when they say, "He literally brought the house down," by which, of course, it is not to be understood that that is what he literally did.

6   Given the way metaphors pervade our speech, a few statements are perhaps in order. A metaphor is a kind of lie or untruth: something is said to be something that it is not. "He parks himself in the corner" compares Joe to an automobile. Unpacking the metaphor, we can say, "Joe is like an automobile in the way he finds his place of rest," or, simply, "Joe is an automobile," or, "Joe is an automobile in this respect." We cannot, nor do we want to, say, "An automobile is Joe." If a metaphor were not a metaphor, it would be an identity and therefore reversible, as in "Sunrise is the beginning of day" and "The beginning of day is sunrise." There is a kind of magic in our key verb "to be," such that it cannot only make equalities and definitions but can state or imply likenesses between two things that aren't each other and do not, in most respects, resemble each other, like Joe and an automobile. Likewise, metaphors are not capable of replacing each other; "Joe parks himself in the corner" is okay, and so is "The car parks hard," but "Joe parks hard" won't do. All this is perhaps elementary enough, but it can have consequences that are not always easy to determine, so it is best to get the elementary things straight. One of the basic tasks of intelligent living is to understand the extent to which certain statements which use some form of "to be " are statements of identity: "God is . . . ," "My country is . . . ," "You are. . . ." Most really important statements about the human condition or the nature of the universe are of the form "X is Y" and if "You are the promised kiss of springtime" is only a rather pretty and confused pile-up of metaphors, what are we to say of "God is the Father Almighty"? In any event, we must see that though many metaphors do not take the grammatical form of

"X is Y," all metaphors can be transformed into statements of that pattern and often can best be understood and evaluated when this transformation is made. This is especially true when the metaphor lies in a verb—"Joe scrounged," "Joe parked," "Joe held court"—and the fact that the statement is metaphorical is apt to pass unnoticed. It is often possible to examine the implications of one's own statements by taking all the metaphors and turning them into the "X is Y" form, and quite often writers gain a much better grip on their writing when they practice doing this. If nothing else, to take a paragraph of one's own writing and to unpack and rephrase all its metaphors is to see what a strange and wonderful instrument the language is and how much control it is possible to exert over one's use of it. Here, for instance, is a paragraph with some rather interesting metaphors that its author probably was unaware he was using:

> In Sherwood Anderson's "I Want to Know Why," only one of the characters is described in depth. Here we see a boy whose entire life has but one goal, to be a trainer or a jockey. His dreams are the dreams of a young boy, not those of a grown man. Hopping freights, exploring strange places, living only for his moments at the stables and the track—these are described so vividly the reader can feel them. The boy's life centers around the track, and as long as this is so, the boy's world is secure. The races are always there, along with the parade of new colts. The boy depends heavily on the horses for this way of life.

7   Let's again list the metaphors: in depth, see, entire life, dreams, grown man, hopping freights, exploring strange places, moments, feel, centers around, world, secure, always there, parade, depends heavily, way of life. What I want to look at especially are those which are so much a part of the way we speak that the metaphorical quality of the phrase is not easy to see. First, though, a word about "centered around," which must be the commonest mixed metaphor in the present use of the language. A mixed metaphor is not simply two consecutive metaphors; "That man is a snake, a rat" is simply a change of metaphor. A mixed metaphor is an absurdity that arises when someone is not aware that he is using a metaphor: "We pulverized them into sending up the white flag" is such a mix, because to pulverize something is to leave it in no condition to send up white flags; "The foundation of his position must flounder" is mixed because, of the many wonderful things metaphorical foundations can do, floundering is not one. The term "centered around" is, in this sense, self-contradictory, because to center on something is to be, metaphorically, at the one point incapable of motion—around, through, by, or any other way. What happens, of course, is that people forget that "to center" is a metaphor in itself and so demands a preposition appropriate to the action of centering.

8   Mixed metaphors, however, are really an interesting sidelight, and most writers learn early to avoid them. More important are the metaphors in this paragraph that silently construct this writer's "world": in depth, world, secure. The questions raised by metaphors of depth and shallowness really ask us who we think we are and how we see others. The writer here says that only the boy in this story "is described in depth." One way of stating the curiosity of the problem is to point out that almost certainly this writer means that the boy is

the only character described "at length." Surely, "in depth" and "at length" should not mean the same thing, but the fact that they do tells us something. Most studies that are carried on in depth are carried on longer than other studies, but whatever else is implied by "in depth" is seldom made clear. Presumably, to be deep is not to be shallow, and a study in depth would explore the deeps, the profundities, the complexities, of a person or a problem. Presumably, also, one could carry on at great length, that is, for a long time, about a problem and never explore its depths. The difficulty is that no one will ever confess this, because if an analysis that takes five minutes is not deep, no one expected it could be, but an analysis that takes far longer ought to be far deeper. So it is that we presume, or let others presume for us, that length makes depth. It is possible, though in our world it is not allowed to be possible, that someone can be deep about someone else in a single sentence, and it is not only possible but likely that most people can go on at length about a problem without every being deep. As long as length and depth are allowed to measure the same things, however, no one is apt to find this out, and the confusion of metaphorical reality can only be a really long and deep confusion.

9   Now, "world," that most fashionable of metaphors. "The boy's world is secure," says the passage; professional football or fashion or Henry Orient or youth or marijuana or almost everything else one can name is said to have its own "world," or "sphere" (it used to be only a "niche"). In James Baldwin's world, in the world of Harlem, in the modern world, in my world, and each time the metaphor is used the implication grows stronger that each item that has a world is isolated from everything else in creation. "This is my Father's world," says the hymn, but that is not the way the term is used now; the metaphor says that it is not all of us, or the physical body known as the earth, but some small segment thereof, that is its world. If someone tells me that I do not live in his world, he implies that the gap between my world and his is so great that I cannot possibly know what his life is like. It is as though there were no common inheritance of humanity, of a Western tradition, of American life, that is shared; each lives in his own world, each peers out onto a universe of strangers, each finds his own world made up of himself and a few other like-minded people. I have spoken as though the classroom were a separate world, and have constantly deplored the fact that the metaphor may speak truly. It is a common metaphor, and if what it implies is true, then it is hard to know how we are going to get along in "the world."

10   Finally, "secure" and "security." My dictionary does not really think that the word as it is used in this sentence is metaphorical any longer: "The boy's world is secure," and "secure" here means "free from or not exposed to danger." What is interesting here is the way in which the term so often is used in a context that implies transience, fragility, and danger. The writer here says: "The boy's life centers around the track, and as long as this is so, the boy's world is secure." We know, thus, that the security is temporary. It is a word most often used by or about people who do not feel in the least safe; or, it may be said, people who live in their own "world" tend to use the word "secure" but seldom feel as the word or metaphor implies they do. Here are some common usages:

I don't ever feel very secure when called upon to speak. [Here "secure" means comfortable or relaxed.]

She needs more security than he will ever be able to give her. [Here "Security" means steadiness.]

If he gets the best job, he will feel secure. [Here "security" almost means valuable.]

The moment he gets outside the security of the classroom, he fumbles and feels lost. [Here "security" means protection.]

11   What we have here is a spectrum of meanings for "secure," no one clearly literal or metaphorical, no one quite like any of the others, so that the word has a solidity of tone but no solidity of meaning. Such a word is harder to use than "in depth" or "world" when what one needs is a sense that the word is a metaphor. The word "security," like the word "real," can be used well only by someone who is fully aware of its different shadings and nuances. It is a word that has come to prominence precisely because what it describes or implies is so seldom felt, and the word often seems like a cry for help from someone who knows there is no help. "If he gets that job he will feel secure" is a harmless enough sentence, but the "he" it describes is no fun to contemplate at all, for any "he" that needs this or that job to feel secure is quite obviously never going to feel secure, no matter what job he gets. "She needs more security than he will ever be able to give her" means "She must marry a rock, nothing else will save her." "I don't ever feel secure when called upon to speak" means, really, "I don't ever feel secure." As a result, though "secure" and "security" themselves are not, in the strict sense, metaphors as used most of the time, they can be used as a means of avoiding a gnawing sense of pathos, loneliness, and insecurity when their potential meanings are clear to both user and reader or listener.

12   I have concentrated on the three words discussed above because they were the ones the paragraph offered, and I have done so only to show the kind of awareness about metaphor that any concentrated thought about writing can provoke. Three other words would call for a quite different discussion but not for a different awareness. Metaphor is how we live because it is the way we relate what we see to what we know: this is like that. The only sentences we can construct that are really without metaphors are those we construct just to prove we can do it. Care in the use of metaphor is tantamount to careful writing; sloppiness in the use of metaphor is the same thing as sloppy writing. The best and only way I know to become aware of this is to perform exercises like those I've been doing in the last few pages. Take something you have written that you are rather proud of, or maybe just something that seems all right but from which you don't see how to go on. List its metaphors, unpack a few of the obvious ones, then a few of the hidden ones that may or may not seem like metaphors to you. All of a sudden, instead of being a great writer or a drudge, you are aware of yourself for what, most importantly, you are—a user of words.

---

1. Both Sale and Lawrence speak as teachers. Are there comparisons that can be made between the way they "use" their relationship to their students rhetorically?

2. Compare what might be described as Sale's "attitude" toward his students with Lawrence's.
3. What comparisons can be drawn between Sale's "listing" in paragraph 3 and Orwell's use of the same device?
4. Are there other comparisons that can be drawn between Orwell's and Sale's essays?
5. Compare Sale's treatment of mixed metaphor in paragraph 8 with Barney Frank's.

Feminists and the Clinton Question

Gloria Steinem

1   If all the sexual allegations now swirling around the White House turn out to be true, President Clinton may be a candidate for sex addiction therapy. But feminists will still have been right to resist pressure by the right wing and the media to call for his resignation or impeachment. The pressure came from another case of the double standard.

2   For one thing, if the President had behaved with comparable insensitivity toward environmentalists, and at the same time remained their most crucial champion and bulwark against an anti-environmental Congress, would they be expected to desert him? I don't think so. If President Clinton were as vital to preserving freedom of speech as he is to preserving reproductive freedom, would journalists be condemned as "inconsistent" for refusing to suggest he resign? Forget it.

3   For another, there was and is a difference between the accusations against Mr. Clinton and those against Bob Packwood and Clarence Thomas, between the experiences reported by Kathleen Willey and Anita Hill. Commentators might stop puzzling over the President's favorable poll ratings, especially among women, if they understood the common-sense guideline to sexual behavior that came out of the women's movement 30 years ago: no means no; yes means yes.

4   It's the basis of sexual harassment law. It also explains why the media's obsession with sex qua sex is offensive to some, titillating to many, and beside the point to almost everybody. Like most feminists, most Americans become concerned about sexual behavior when someone's will has been violated; that is, when "no" hasn't been accepted as an answer.

5   Let's look at what seem to be the most damaging allegations, those made by Kathleen Willey. Not only was she Mr. Clinton's political supporter, but she is also old enough to be Monica Lewinsky's mother, a better media spokeswoman for herself than Paula Jones, and a survivor of family tragedy, struggling to pay her dead husband's debts.

6   If any of the other women had tried to sell their stories to a celebrity tell-all book publisher, as Ms. Willey did, you might be even more skeptical about their motives. But with her, you think, "Well, she needs the money."

7   For the sake of argument here, I'm also believing all the women, at least until we know more. I noticed that CNN polls taken right after Ms. Willey's interview on "60 Minutes" showed that more Americans believed her than President Clinton.

8   Nonetheless, the President's approval ratings have remained high. Why? The truth is that even if the allegations are true, the President is not guilty of sexual

harassment. He is accused of having made a gross, dumb and reckless pass at a supporter during a low point in her life. She pushed him away, she said, and it never happened again. In other words, President Clinton took "no" for an answer.

9   In her original story, Paula Jones essentially said the same thing. She went to then-Governor Clinton's hotel room, where she said he asked her to perform oral sex and even dropped his trousers. She refused, and even she claims that he said something like, "Well, I don't want to make you do anything you don't want to do."

10   Her lawyers now allege that as a result of the incident Ms. Jones described, she was slighted in her job as a state clerical employee and even suffered long-lasting psychological damage. But there appears to be little evidence to support those accusations. As with the allegations in Ms. Willey's case, Mr. Clinton seems to have made a clumsy sexual pass, then accepted rejection.

11   This is very different from the cases of Clarence Thomas and Bob Packwood. According to Anita Hill and a number of Mr. Packwood's former employees, the offensive behavior was repeated for years, despite constant "no's." It also occurred in the regular workplace of these women, where it could not be avoided.

12   The women who worked for Mr. Packwood described a man who groped and lunged at them. Ms. Hill accused Clarence Thomas of regularly and graphically describing sexual practices and pornography. In both cases, the women said they had to go to work every day, never knowing what sexual humiliation would await them—just the kind of "hostile environment" that sexual harassment law was intended to reduce.

13   As reported, Monica Lewinsky's case illustrates the rest of the equation: "Yes means yes." Whatever it was, her relationship with President Clinton has never been called unwelcome, coerced or other than something she sought. The power imbalance between them increased the index of suspicion, but there is no evidence to suggest that Ms. Lewinsky's will was violated; quite the contrary. In fact, her subpoena in the Paula Jones case should have been quashed. Welcome sexual behavior is about as relevant to sexual harassment as borrowing a car is to stealing one.

14   The real violators of Ms. Lewinsky's will were Linda Tripp, who taped their talks, the F.B.I. agents who questioned her without a lawyer and Kenneth Starr, the independent prosecutor who seems intent on tailoring the former intern's testimony.

15   What if President Clinton lied under oath about some or all of the above? According to polls, many Americans assume he did. There seems to be sympathy for keeping private sexual behavior private. Perhaps we have a responsibility to make it O.K. for politicians to tell the truth—providing they are respectful of "no means no; yes means yes"—and still be able to enter high office, including the Presidency.

16   Until then, we will disqualify energy and talent the country needs—as we are doing right now.

---

1. In her second paragraph Steinem makes two **analogies** to illustrate what she calls "another case of the double standard." What is the "double standard" to which she refers?

2. In her analogies she uses the phrase "if the President had behaved with comparable insensitivity." What would constitute such behavior in these two cases?
3. In her fourth paragraph Steinem proposes three categories of response to what she calls "the media's obsession with sex qua sex." Are these categories overlapping? If so, how is this intended to function rhetorically?
4. Speculate on Steinem's rhetorical intentions for the analogy she uses to close paragraph 13.
5. What assumptions lie behind the last sentence of paragraph 15 (from another perspective, what **questions are begged**)? What does this say about Steinem's **target audience?**

Goria Steinem has been a Playboy bunny, is a founder of the National Women's Political Caucus; and she is the founding and continuing editor of *Ms. Magazine.*

The Abortion Clinic Shootings: Why?

Randall A. Terry

1   As the nation heard with sorrow the news of the deplorable shooting spree at abortion facilities in Brookline,[1] the question is asked: Why? Why this sudden rise of violence in this arena?

2   I have been intricately involved in the antiabortion movement for more than a decade. I have led thousands of people in peaceful antiabortion activism via Operation Rescue. Hence, I enjoy a perspective few have. So I submit these answers to the question "Why?"

3   Enemies of the babies and the antiabortion movement will argue that the conviction that abortion is murder, and the call to take nonviolent direct action to save children from death, inevitably leads to the use of lethal force. This argument is ludicrous—unless one is prepared to argue that Gandhi's nonviolent civil disobedience in India during the 1930s led to the murder of British officials; or that Dr. Martin Luther King's nonviolent civil disobedience led to the violent actions that accompanied the civil rights movement in the United States during the 1960s.

4   So why, then, this recent violent outburst? Law enforcement officials need look no further than *Roe v. Wade*; abortion providers need look no further than their own instruments of death; and Congress and the president need look no further than the Freedom of Access to Clinic Entrances Act to understand the roots of the shootings.

5   The Supreme Court's attempt to overthrow Law (capital "L") in order to legalize and legitimize murder has led to the inevitable—a disregard of or contempt for law. I say the court's attempt, for the court can no more overturn Law and legalize murder than it can overturn the law of gravity. God's immutable commandment "Thou shalt not murder" has forever made murder illegal. The court's lawlessness is breeding lawlessness. The court cannot betray the foundation of law and civilization—the Ten Commandments—and then expect a people to act "lawful" and "civilized."

6   Let us look at the abortion industry itself. Abortion is murder. And just as segregation and the accompanying violence possess the seeds for further violence, likewise it appears that the Law of sowing and reaping is being visited upon the abortion industry. A society cannot expect to tear 35 million innocent babies from their mothers' wombs without reaping horrifying consequences.

---

[1] On December 30, 1994, a gunman opened fire at two Massachusetts abortion clinics killing two people and wounding several others.

Was it perhaps inevitable that the violent abortion industry should itself reap a portion of what it has so flagrantly and callously sown?

7   Now to Congress and the judiciary. Similar to the civil rights activists, antiabortion activists have often been brutalized at the hands of police and then subjected to vulgar injustices in sundry courts of law. Add to this the Freedom of Access to Clinic Entrances Act, which turns peaceful antiabortion activists into federal felons and perhaps one can understand the frustration and anger that is growing in Americans.

8   The abortion industry can partly blame itself for the recent shootings. It clamored for harsh treatment of peaceful antiabortion activists, and it usually got it. Now it has to deal with an emerging violent fringe. John F. Kennedy stated, "Those who make peaceful revolution impossible will make violent revolution inevitable." One would think the prochoice crowd would belatedly heed the late president's warning, but they haven't. They're urging an all too political Justice Department to launch a witch hunt into the lives of peaceful antiabortion activists and leaders. Make no mistake—what the pro-choice people want is to pressure law enforcement and the courts to intimidate anyone who condemns abortion as murder. Their recent public relations scam is to blame all antiabortion people for the shootings. And they will not be content until they have crushed all dissent against abortion. We must not allow them to cause us to cower in silence.

9   To those who support the recent shootings or herald John Salvi as a hero, I ask you: Has God authorized one person to be policeman, judge, jury, and executioner? Is it logical to leap from nonviolent life-saving activities to lethal force? Read your history! Remember the principles of Calvin, Knox, and Cromwell concerning lower magistrates. Are you likening John Salvi and Co. to Knox or Cromwell? Are you calling for revolution? Please consider these questions before calling someone who walks into a clinic and starts randomly shooting people a hero.

10   So what can be done to curtail this trend? First, the Freedom of Access to Clinic entrances Act should be repealed immediately. This oppressive law is an outrage. The crushing weight of the federal government punishing peaceful protesters is the kind of thing we would expect in Communist China against political dissidents.

11   Second, the courts must stop abusing antiabortion activists. We must be accorded the same tolerance and leniency that every politically correct protester receives nationwide, i.e., small fines, two days in jail, charges dismissed, etc.

12   Finally, and this is most urgent, child killing must be brought to an immediate end. Whether the Supreme Court declares the personhood and inalienable right to life of preborn children or the Constitution is amended or the president signs an emancipation proclamation for children or Congress outlaws abortion outright, we must bring a swift end to the murder of innocent children.

---

1. Terry's rhetorical approach is highly dependent on **definition**. Note that in paragraph 3 he refers first to "the babies" and then to saving "children from

death." Who would **warrant** this terminology, and how does it define his **target audience?**

2. Paragraph 5 is almost a festival of exercises in definition. Show how Terry gets from "law" to "Law" to "illegal."
3. Is "Thou shalt not murder" the form of the commandment you are familiar with? What rhetorical purpose would explain Terry's rendering it thus?
4. Rhetorically how would you explain Terry's departing from standard grammar in the last sentence of paragraph 5 ("lawful" and "civilized")?

Randall Terry is the founder of Operation Rescue.

How to Convince a Reluctant Scientist

John Timpane

At the end of reasons comes persuasion.
—Ludwig Wittgenstein, *On Certainty*

1   At the end of every successful argument, no matter how weighty the evidence or powerful the reasoning, the beholder performs a nonrational act: the leap to acceptance. It may be short—one may feel pushed—but a leap it always is.

2   What makes a scientific argument persuasive? Granted, there is no one nation called "science" but a panoply of tribes with their respective handicrafts. A cosmologist might nod, and a chemical engineer squirm, when someone argues that the unobserved *must* exist for the observed to make sense. Certain branches of physics absolutely demand reproducibility—but an anthropologist may get only one chance to live amid the !Kung.

3   There are some basic persuaders, more or less familiar, more or less honored. Robert K. Merton's five elements of scientific endeavor—originality, detachment, universality, skepticism and public accessibility—all play a role. If results and methods follow the rules we know, and if we find the candor and testability we expect, we are at least nearer to feeling well disposed. Yet in the sciences as elsewhere, conviction involves other forces, both reason and nonreason.

4   Our sense of what connects, what fits, what ramifies, can often move us to acceptance. Results that bear little connection to existing work will persuade little. But if study A forges connections between studies B, K, and S, or if it newly illuminates an established fact, a tiny epiphany can happen.

5   Or a massive one. Sir Isaac Newton's audience was impressed when he derived his laws of physics from observations made by Galileo—but overwhelmed when he then showed that the moon, planets and stars obeyed these same principles. It did not escape the notice of James D. Watson and Francis Crick that their proposed structure for DNA helped to explain the copying mechanism of the genetic material. Ramification may work also from without. If we realize the argument we have just heard is supported by independent evidence, our personal paradigms may start to budge. Some scientists initially resisted John Ostrom's argument that the ancestors of modern birds were ground-dwelling theropods. But when we watch a hawk hop after a desert rat, we are not far from the awkward leap of *Archaeopteryx*.

6   To be persuasive, then, you can be only so original. Total originality, to the point at which no one else speaks your language, may cripple your argument's progress in the world (as happened initially to Thomas Young's wave theory of

light). Call it the Law of Obviousness: better to be a half-step ahead and understood than a whole step and ignored.

* * *

7   Prestige sells, too. Freeman Dyson has noted the "profound consequences" of status in the sciences. A famous team at a famous institution backed by famous money is a hard combination to resist. Even harder is the status that comes with large projects. Almost irresistible is the assent of prestigious colleagues or superiors.

8   Publicity, for better or worse, begets prestige. Scientists today—of necessity—are veritable master organists at the great keyboards of the media. Going public spurs debate, encourages verification, attracts funds. Today, when there is more science than ever before, a number of scientists see no alternative to invoking the hosanna and the gee whiz.

9   Many scientists believe arguments they have never read or heard, simply because most of their peers believe. As Thomas S. Kuhn writes, "There is no standard higher than the assent of the relevant community. The transfer of allegiance from one paradigm to another is a conversion experience that cannot be forced."

10   And sometimes the sheer beauty of a demonstration can render an argument compelling. Einstein's special theory of relativity gained acceptance not only by its power to explain observed phenomena but also by the elegance of the equation $E = mc^2$. Cell biologists wax rhapsodic over Erkki Ruoslahti's experiments showing that a certain molecule, called an integrin, mediates the adhesion of cells to the protein fibronectin. Ruoslahti's work was of such beauty that other cell biologists found it extremely and immediately persuasive.

* * *

11   Much of what makes a scientific argument convincing, in the end, has to do with things other than science. By saying so, we do not impugn or undermine the sciences so much as we recognize their humanity. Some postmodernist thinkers—those, for example, who practice the collection of methods called deconstruction—believe that the important role of the nonrational in the sciences is a scandal, when in fact that role is fairly familiar to anyone who actually does a science for a living.

12   Besides, such conceptual issues cease to have much importance past the lab door, which opens into a world of different priorities. In the workplace, scientists have utter faith in the reality of the world and in themselves. They have to. (Otherwise, their experiments, and perhaps they, may turn to tar.) The order of things, furthermore, pressures them to treat all data, especially their own, with thorough skepticism. After all, these pragmatic, naive, realist skeptics must eventually submit their findings to another entity in which they trust—the candid, bruising machinery of peer review.

13   How, then, does the history of science unfold? According to reason, drawn by the ineluctable, magnetic pull of truth? Or by bursts, gaps, sudden nonrational disjunctions? Perhaps the latter amounts to the former, since the aggregate of

thousands of nonrational moments—when individual scientists are persuaded, convinced, converted—adds up to a progress of sorts. Conversion happens when a piece falls into place and renders the whole puzzle new. Often the new vision is so powerful that our decision to accept may seem hardly a decision at all. Yet a decision it always is. Precisely because they are not rational, such leaps—from final ice floe to riverbank—are wonderfully, deeply human.

---

1. Explain the relationship between paragraph 2 and what I refer to as an **authorizing trope**, the **argument from science**.
2. Who is Ludwig Wittgenstein?
3. The metaphor is "tribes with respective handicrafts." The comparison is between a social science and physics. What **questions are being begged** here? Is there any sort of **accommodation** going on in this paragraph (2)?
4. According to Timpane, does science yield truth?
5. How does Timpane deal with another of the **authorizing tropes**, the **argument from reason**? See especially his last paragraph.

Advice for the Anti-Smokers:
Take a Message from Garcia

Abigail Trafford

1   Long ago, I used to smoke. I was a student in Paris and I never went out without a red package of Royales and my black cigarette holder. I smoked over an espresso in the afternoon after class. I smoked over a glass of *anis* late at night.

2   I smoked because it was a prop along with long hair and poetry, a symbol of coming of age, of living on the edge. It was a year when students at the Sorbonne gathered and marched in protest. It was a year on my own, a time of hope, a celebration of freedom, symbolized by plumes of cigarette smoke.

3   I smoked for the same reasons my daughters and I and millions of Americans reveled in the music of the Grateful Dead and now mourn the sad end of Jerry Garcia. The Grateful Dead is about attitude, image, and lifestyle, and Jerry Garcia was the rock existentialist whose sound communicated across generations.

4   His music was about independence and staking out your own turf and finding a comfortable personality. And so were my cigarettes. I smoked, in the words of the Grateful Dead, because *"All the years combine. . . . In the end there's just a song comes cryin' up the night."* An ashtray of half-smoked Royales. The black cigarette holder on the table. The empty glass. Paris in the sixties. *"It seems like all this life was just a dream. Stella blue. Stella blue."*

5   By contrast with such images of adventure and poetry, President Clinton's new crackdown on teenage smoking is going to be a tough sell. It focuses on health, but in fact is a direct intervention in the rites of passage for many teenagers.

6   The medical reasons against smoking are indisputable, and Garcia's death last week at age fifty-three gave the president a dramatic example of the consequences of unhealthy living. Captain Trips smoked three packs of cigarettes a day, lived off junk food, took all kinds of drugs and became a heroin addict, dying ignominiously in a rehab center where he was being treated for a relapse. President Clinton warned: "Young people should say: 'I'm not going to die that way.'"

7   But if the anti-smoking forces are to be successful, they must take a page from the Grateful Dead on how to reach the hearts and minds of young people. So far, do-not-smoke campaigns aimed at teenagers have largely missed the mark. It doesn't work to tell them to just say no.

8   Yet public health messages are generally written like commandments of medical virtue: Don't smoke, don't drink (too much), don't eat (too much), don't drive (too fast, without a seat belt), don't take illegal drugs, don't accept rides from strangers, don't have sex (before you're ready, before you know how to use a condom, before you're in a monogamous relationship, before you're married).

9   But as every parent knows, the forbidden fruit is the tastiest to young people. "Teenagers tend to rebel as a routine. The best way to get teenagers to do something is to tell them not to do it," says George D. Lundberg, editor of the *Journal of the American Medical Association.*

10   Compare the negative public health messages with the songs of the Grateful Dead. The group did not gloss over the fatal realities of growing up, but it talked about them in a way that struck a chord and made young people listen: *"What in the world ever became of sweet Jane. She lost her sparkle, you know she isn't the same. Livin' on reds, vitamin C, and cocaine. All a friend can say is 'Ain't it a shame.'"*

11   For the most part, the Grateful Dead was about optimism. It gave fans a good feeling now, not a promise of better hearts or lungs in middle age. As the song goes: *"Dear Mr. Fantasy play us a tune. Something to make us all feel happy. Do anything to take us out of this gloom. Sing a song, play guitar, make us happy."*

12   To succeed, a cultural revolution that takes away smoking has to replace it with *"something to make us all feel happy . . . [and] take us out of this gloom."*

13   Unfortunately, cigarette advertisers have been more successful than anti-smoking forces when it comes to taking the basics of the Grateful Dead message. Billboards advertising cigarettes promise virility, power, sexuality, a message that smoking is an escape from the unbearable feelings of growing up.

14   The challenge of the president's attack on tobacco is to take the message away from the advertisers and turn it around so that young people will understand that their transition from teenager to adult—their demand to be recognized as an individual—does not depend on smoking. In fact, their lives depend on making this cultural shift.

15   After Paris, I gave up smoking. Luckily, I never learned to inhale properly, which is the key to not getting addicted. Unlike most smokers, I was able to quit without a second thought.

16   Yet I never forgot my Paris days or the symbolism of a package of Royales. As the song goes, smoking had been for me *"A box of rain [that] will ease the pain, and Love will see you through."*

---

1. Trafford's first three paragraphs begin with the same word. Why?
2. Paragraph 3 makes a simple **assertion** concerning why "my daughters and I and millions of Americans," "reveled" in the music of the Grateful Dead. What does this tell you about her **target audience**?
3. What are the implications of the phrase "but in fact" in paragraph 5? This essay was written in 1995. Do teenagers (did teenagers) find Paris, espresso, and cigarette holders manifestations of "independence" and what is "comfortable"?
4. With whom is paragraph 7's "just say no" associated? What does it suggest about the **target audience**?
5. Is paragraph 9 an **argument from authority**? Is it implied that therefore teenagers should be urged *to* smoke?
6. What is Trafford's **thesis**, and to whom is she arguing? Can useful rhetorical comparisons be made between this piece and the R. J. Reynolds piece?

Give Children the Vote

Vita Wallace

1   I first became interested in children's rights two years ago, when I learned that several states had passed laws prohibiting high school dropouts from getting driver's licenses. I was outraged, because I believe that children should not be forced to go to school or be penalized if they choose not to, a choice that is certainly the most sensible course for some people.

2   I am what is called a home schooler. I have never been to school, having always learned at home and in the world around me. Home schooling is absolutely legal, yet as a home schooler, I have had to defend what I consider to be my right to be educated in the ways that make the most sense to me, and so all along I have felt sympathy with people who insist on making choices about how they want to be educated, even if that means choosing not to finish high school. Now this choice is in jeopardy.

3   Since first learning about the discriminatory laws preventing high school dropouts from getting driver's licenses that have been passed by some state legislatures, I have done a lot of constitutional and historical research that has convinced me that children of all ages must be given the same power to elect their representatives that adults have, or they will continue to be unfairly treated and punished for exercising the few legal options they now have, such as dropping out of high school.

4   Most people, including children themselves, probably don't realize that children are the most regulated people in the United States. In addition to all the laws affecting adults, including tax laws, children must comply with school attendance laws, child labor laws, and alcohol and cigarette laws. They are denied driver's licenses because of their age, regardless of the dropout issue; they are victims of widespread child abuse; and they are blatantly discriminated against everywhere they go, in libraries, restaurants, and movie theaters. They have no way to protect themselves: Usually they cannot hire lawyers or bring cases to court without a guardian, and they are not allowed to vote.

5   The child labor and compulsory schooling laws were passed by well-meaning people to protect children from exploitation. Child labor laws keep children from being forced to work, and compulsory schooling allows all children to get an education. But the abolition of slavery in 1865 didn't end the exploitation of black people. They needed the right to vote and the ability to bring lawsuits against their employers. Children need those rights too. Without them, laws that force children to go to school and generally do not allow them to work may be necessary to prevent exploitation, but they also take away children's rights as citizens to life, liberty, and the pursuit of happiness. In my case, the

compulsory education laws severely limited my right to pursue the work that is important to me (which is surely what "the pursuit of happiness" referred to in the Declaration of Independence).

6   I am sixteen now, still not old enough to vote. Like all children, then, the only way I can fight for children's rights is by using my freedom of speech to try to convince adults to fight with me. While I am grateful that I have the right to speak my mind, I believe that it is a grave injustice to deny young people the most effective tool they could have to bring about change in a democracy. For this reason, I suggest that the right of citizens under 18 to vote not be denied or abridged on account of age.

7   Many people argue that it would be dangerous to let loose on society a large group of new voters who might not vote sensibly. They mean that children might not vote for the right candidates. The essence of democracy, however, is letting people vote for the wrong candidates. Democratic society has its risks, but we must gamble on the reasonableness of all our citizens, because it is less dangerous than gambling on the reasonableness of a few. That is why we chose to be a democracy instead of a dictatorship in the first place.

8   As it is, only 36 to 40 percent of adults who are eligible to vote actually vote in nonpresidential years, and about 25 percent of the population is under 18. As you can see, our representatives are elected by a very small percentage of our citizens. That means that although they are responsible *for* all of us, they are responsible *to* only a few of us. Politicians usually do all they can to keep that few happy, because both voters and politicians are selfish, and a politician's reelection depends on the well-being of the voters. Large segments of society that are not likely or not allowed to vote are either ignored or treated badly because of this system. It would be too much to expect the few always to vote in the interests of the many. Under these circumstances, surely the more people who vote the better, especially if they are of both sexes and of all races, classes, and ages.

9   People also claim that children are irresponsible. Most of the teenagers who act irresponsibly do so simply because they are not allowed to solve their problems in any way that would be considered responsible—through the courts or legislature. They fall back on sabotage of the system because they are not allowed to work within it.

10   Some people believe that children would vote the way their parents tell them to, which would, in effect, give parents more votes. Similarly, when the Nineteenth Amendment was passed in 1920, giving women the vote, many people thought women would vote the way their husbands did. Now women are so independent that the idea of women voting on command seems absurd. The Nineteenth Amendment was a large part of the process that produced their independence. I think a similar and equally desirable result would follow if children were allowed to vote. They are naturally curious, and most are interested in the electoral process and the results of the elections even though they are not allowed to vote. Lacking world-weary cynicism, they see, perhaps even more clearly than their elders, what is going on in their neighborhoods and what is in the news.

11   Suffragist Belle Case La Follette's comment that if women were allowed to vote there would be a lot more dinner-table discussion of politics is as true of children today. More debate would take place not only in the home but among children and adults everywhere. Adults would also benefit if politics were talked about in libraries, churches, stores, laundromats, and other places where children gather.

12   People may argue that politicians would pander to children if they could vote, promising for instance that free ice cream would be distributed every day. But if kids were duped, they would not be duped for long. Children don't like to be treated condescendingly.

13   Even now, adults try to manipulate children all the time in glitzy TV ads or, for example, in the supposedly educational pamphlets that nuclear power advocates pass out in school science classes. Political candidates speak at schools, addressing auditoriums full of captive students. In fact, schools should be no more or less political than workplaces. Children are already exposed to many different opinions, and they would likely be exposed to even more if they could vote. The point is that with the vote, they would be better able to fight such manipulation, not only because they would have the power to do so but because they would have added reason to educate themselves on the issues.

14   What I suggest is that children be allowed to grow into their own right to vote at whatever rate suits them individually. They should not be forced to vote, as adults are not, but neither should they be hindered from voting if they believe themselves capable, as old people are not hindered.

15   As for the ability to read and write, that should never be used as a criterion for eligibility, since we have already learned from painful past experience that literacy tests can be manipulated to ensure discrimination. In any case, very few illiterate adults vote, and probably very few children would want to vote as long as they couldn't read or write. But I firmly believe that, whether they are literate or not, the vast majority of children would not attempt to vote before they are ready. Interest follows hand in hand with readiness, something that is easy to see as a home schooler but that is perhaps not so clear to many people in this society where, ironically, children are continually taught things when they are not ready, and so are not interested. Yet when they are interested, as in the case of voting, they're told they are not yet ready. I think I would not have voted until I was eight or nine, but perhaps if I had known I could vote I would have taken an interest sooner.

16   Legally, it would be possible to drop the voting-age requirements. In the Constitution, the states are given all powers to set qualifications for voters except as they defy the equal protection clause of the Fourteenth Amendment, in which case Congress has the power to enforce it. If it were proved that age requirements "abridge the privileges or immunities of citizens of the United States" (which in my opinion they do, since people born in the United States or to U.S. citizens are citizens from the moment they are born), and if the states could not come up with a "compelling interest" argument to justify a limit at a particular age, which Justices Potter Stewart, Warren Burger, and Harry Blackmun agreed

they could not in *Oregon v. Mitchell* (the Supreme Court case challenging the 1970 amendment to the Voting Rights Act that gave 18-year-olds the vote), then age requirements would be unconstitutional. But it is not necessary that they be unconstitutional for the states to drop them. It is within the power of the states to do that, and I believe that we must start this movement at the state level. According to *Oregon v. Mitchell*, Congress cannot change the qualifications for voting in state elections except by constitutional amendment, which is why the Twenty-sixth Amendment setting the voting age at eighteen was necessary. It is very unlikely that an amendment would pass unless several states had tried eliminating the age requirement and had good results. The experience of Georgia and Kentucky, which lowered their age limits to eighteen, helped to pass the Twenty-sixth Amendment in 1971.

17   Already in our country's history several oppressed groups have been able to convince the unoppressed to free them. Children, who do not have the power to change their situation, must now convince the adults who do to allow them that power.

---

1. In paragraph 6 Wallace reveals her age, and that she is one of those referred to as "they" in the preceding. How is this intended to function rhetorically? Think specifically in terms of **ethos**.
2. It might be useful in dealing with this essay to look back at the Thurow argument for why it is that husbands do not (indeed could not) discriminate against women. Try to take Wallace's arguments and express them as **syllogisms**. Look particularly at paragraph 8 in this regard. Try to write the **syllogism** that concludes "Therefore, the more people who vote, the better." This of course involves **definition** in large ways.
3. Does paragraph 9 contain an **argument** or an **assertion**? Remember that an **argument** needs to have three terms, but only one statement preceding the conclusion (**enthymeme**).
4. If you decide that it is an argument, try to write out the full form of the **syllogism**, including, that is, what the **enthymeme** leaves out.

This essay was published in *The Nation* in 1991. "Childhood," it has been suggested, like any other classification, or definition, was invented, not discovered. Children, it has been seriously argued, before the 19th century, were regarded as small people. They were not "innocent," but merely ignorant, as each of us is to one extent or another. One way to look at Wallace's argument is that it says that age, sex, race, or (continue the list as you like) are not in *themselves* sufficient reason for discrimination. That is to say, the criteria for enfranchisement should not be based on any of these utterly arbitrary measures. This is not the same as to say that there should be no criteria—it is to say that specific sorts of classifications should not qualify as criteria. *The Nation* likes a good contest, and publication of this piece constituted a test of the **slippery slope** of "Hell, if we let women vote, next thing it's gonna be kids." Where will it all end, thus, is a non-question. What is a question is how are we to define criteria.

When the Lie Is So Big

Frank Zappa

The following is an edited version of the testimony of Frank Zappa before the Senate Commerce Committee on Record Labeling in September of 1985. Francis Vincent Zappa was a musician, a performer, a satirist, a composer and arranger, and a social activist. The main body of the text presented here is taken from the written statement submitted to the committee before the testimony was delivered. It has been edited by the insertion of selected material Zappa added at the hearing itself. That material will be indicated by being enclosed in square brackets.

1   [The first thing I would like to do, because I know there is some foreign press involved here and they might not understand what the issue is about, one of the things the issue is about is the First Amendment to the Constitution, and it is short and I would like to read it so they will understand. It says:

> Congress shall make no law respecting the an establishment of religion or prohibiting the free exercise thereof, or abridging the freedom of speech or of the press, or the right of the people peaceably to assemble and to petition the government for a redress of grievances.

That is for reference.]

2   These are my personal observations and opinions. They are addressed to the PMRC[1] as well as this committee. I speak on behalf of no group or professional organization.

3   The PMRC proposal is an ill-conceived piece of non-sense which fails to deliver any real benefits to children, infringes the civil liberties of people who are not children, and promises to keep the courts busy for years dealing with interpretational and enforcemental problems inherent in the proposal's design.

4   It is my understanding that, in law, First Amendment issues are decided with a preference for the least restrictive alternative. In this context, the PMRC's demands are the equivalent of treating dandruff by decapitation.

5   No one has forced Mrs. Baker or Mrs. Gore[2] to bring Prince or Sheena Easton into their homes. Thanks to the Constitution, they are free to buy other forms of music for their children. Apparently they insist on purchasing the work of contemporary recording artists in order to support a personal illusion of

---

[1] PMRC is the acronym of the Parent's Music Resource Center.

[2] The reference is to the wives of Senators Baker and Gore, both "Founders" of the PMRC.

aerobic sophistication. Ladies, please be advised: the $8.98 purchase price does not entitle you to a kiss on the foot from the composer or performer in exchange for a spin on the family Victrola.[3]

6   Taken as a whole, the complete list of PMRC Demands reads like an instruction manual for some sinister kind of toilet training program to housebreak all composers and performers because of the lyrics of a few. Ladies, how dare you?

7   The ladies' shame must be shared by the bosses at the major labels who, through the RIAA[4] chose to bargain away the rights of composers, performers, and retailers in order to pass H.R. 2911, The Blank Tape Tax, a private tax levied by an industry on consumers for the benefit of a select group within that industry.

8   Is this a consumer issue? You bet it is. The major record labels need to have H.R. 2911 whiz through a few committees before anybody smells a rat. One of them is chaired by Senator Thurmond. Is it a coincidence that Mrs. Thurmond is affiliated with the PMRC.

9   I can't say she's a member because the PMRC has no members. Their secretary told me on the phone last Friday that the PMRC has no members . . . only founders. I asked how many other D.C. wives are non-members of an organization that raises money by mail, has a tax exempt status, and seems intent on running the Constitution of the United States through the family paper-shredder. I asked her if it was a cult. Finally she said she couldn't give me an answer and that she had to call their lawyer.

10   While the wife of the Secretary of the Treasury recites "Gonna drive my love inside you," and Senator Gore's wife talks about "bondage" and "oral sex at gunpoint" on the CBS Evening News, people in high places work on a tax bill that is so ridiculous the only way to sneak it through is to keep the public's mind on something else: "Porn Rock."

11   The PMRC practices a curious double standard with these fervent recitations. Thanks to them, helpless young children all over America get to hear about oral sex at gunpoint on network TV several nights a week. Is there a secret FCC dispensation here? What sort of end justifies *these* means? PTA parents should keep an eye on these ladies if that's their idea of "good taste."

12   Is the basic issue morality? Is it mental health? Is it an issue at all? The PMRC has created a lot of confusion with the improper comparisons between song lyrics, videos, record packaging, radio broadcasting, and live performances. These are all different mediums, and the people who work in them have a right to conduct their business without trade-restraining legislation whipped up like an instant pudding by The Wives of Big Brother.

13   Is it proper that the husband of a PMRC nonmember/founder/person sits on any committee considering business pertaining to the blank tape tax or his wife's

---

[3] A Victrola is a record player, the hugely popular product of R.C.A. Victor, and so named by them. "Victrola" became a generic term for a record player in the same way that we derive the word "fridge" from "Frigidaire," and "Kleenex" for facial tissue.

[4] RIAA is the acronym of the Recording Industry Association of America.

lobbying organization? Can any committee thus constituted find facts in a fair and unbiased manner? This committee has three [that we know about: Senator Danforth, Senator Packwood, and Senator Gore. For some reason they seem to feel there is no conflict of interest involved]. A minor conflict of interest?

14   The PMRC promotes their program as a harmless type of consumer information service providing "guideline" which will assist baffled parents in the determination of the "suitability" of records listened to by "very young children." The methods they propose have several unfortunate side effects, not the least of which is the reduction of all American music, recorded and live, to the intellectual level of a Saturday morning cartoon show.

15   Teenagers with $8.98 in their pocket might go into a record store alone, but "very young children" do not. Usually there is a parent in attendance. The $8.98 is in the parent's pocket. The parent can always suggest that the $8.98 be spent on a book.

16   If the parent is afraid to let the child read a book, perhaps the $8.98 can be spent on recordings of instrumental music. Why not bring jazz or classical music into your home instead of Blackie Lawless or Madonna? Great music with no words at all is available to anyone with sense enough to look beyond this week's platinum-selling fashion plate.

17   Children in the "vulnerable" age bracket have a natural love for music. If, as a parent, you believe they should be exposed to something more uplifting than "Sugar Walls," support Music Appreciation programs in schools. Why haven't you considered your child's need for consumer information? Music Appreciation costs very little compared to sports expenditures. Your children have a right to know that something besides pop music exists.

18   It is unfortunate that the PMRC would rather dispense governmentally sanitized Heavy Metal Music than something more "uplifting." Is this an indication of the PMRC's personal taste, or just another manifestation of the low priority this administration has placed on Education for the Arts in America? The answer, of course, is neither. You can't distract people from thinking about an unfair tax by talking about Music Appreciation. For that you need sex . . . and lots of it.

19   Because of the subjective nature of the PMRC ratings, it is impossible to guarantee that some sort of "despised concept" won't sneak through, tucked away in new slang or the overstressed pronunciation of an otherwise innocent word. If the goal here is total verbal/moral safety, there is only one way to achieve it: watch no TV, read no books, see no movies, listen to only instrumental music, or buy no music at all.

20   The establishment of a rating system, voluntary or otherwise, opens the door to an endless parade of Moral Quality Control Programs based on "Things Certain Christians Don't Like." What if the next bunch of Washington Wives demands a large yellow "J" on all material written or performed by Jews in order to save helpless children from exposure to "concealed Zionist doctrine"?

21   Record ratings are frequently compared to film ratings. Apart from the quantitative difference, there is another that is more important: people who act in films are hired to "pretend." No matter how the film is rated, it won't hurt

them personally. Since many musicians write and perform their own material and stand by it as their art (whether you like it or not), an imposed rating will stigmatize them as individuals. How long before composers and performers are told to wear a festive little PMRC armband with their Scarlet Letter on it?

22   The PMRC rating system restrains trade in one specified musical field: Rock. No ratings have been requested for Comedy records or Country Music. Is there anyone in the PMRC who can differentiate infallibly between Rock and Country Music? Artists in both fields cross stylist lines. Some artists include comedy material. If an album is part Rock, part Country, part Comedy, what sort of label would it get? Shouldn't the ladies be warning everyone that inside those Country albums with the American flags, the big trucks, and the atomic pompadours there lurks a fascinating variety of songs about sex, violence, and the devil, recorded in a way that lets you hear every word, sung for you by people who have been to prison and are proud of it.

23   If enacted, the PMRC program would have the effect of protectionist legislation for the Country Music Industry, providing more security for cowboys than it does for children. One major retail outlet has already informed the Capitol Records sales staff that it would not purchase or display an album with any kind of sticker on it.

24   Another chain with outlets in shopping malls has been told by the landlord that if it racked "hard-rated albums" they would lose their lease. That opens up an awful lot of shelf space for somebody. Could it be that a certain Senatorial husband and wife team from Tennessee sees this as an "affirmative action program" to benefit the suffering multitudes in Nashville?

25   Is the PMRC attempting to save future generations from SEX ITSELF? The type, the amount, and the timing of sexual information given to a child should be determined by the parents, not by people who are involved in a tax scheme cover-up.

26   The PMRC has concocted a Mythical Beast, and compounds the chicanery by demanding "consumer guidelines" to keep it from inviting your children inside its sugar walls. Is the next step the adoption of a "PMRC National Legal Age For Comprehension of Vaginal Arousal"? Many people in this room would gladly support such legislation, but, before they start drafting their bill, I urge them to consider these facts:

1. There is no conclusive scientific evidence to support the claim that exposure to any sort of music will cause the listener to commit a crime or damn his soul to hell.

2. Masturbation is not illegal. If it is not illegal to do it, why should it be illegal to sing about it?

3. No medical evidence of hairy palms, warts, or blindness has been linked to masturbation or vaginal arousal, nor has it been proved that hearing references to either topic turns the listener into a social liability.

4. Enforcement of anti-masturbatory legislation could prove costly and time consuming.

5. There is not enough prison space to hold all the children who do it.

The PMRC's proposal is most offensive in its moral tone. It seeks to enforce a set of implied religious values on its victims. Iran has a religious government. Good for them. I like having the capitol of the United States in Washington, DC, in spite of recent efforts to move it to Lynchburg, VA.[5]

27   Fundamentalism is not a state religion. The PMRC's request for labels regarding sexually explicit lyrics, violence, drugs, alcohol, and especially occult content reads like a catalog of phenomena abhorrent to practitioners of that faith. How a person worships is a private matter, and should not be inflicted upon or exploited by others. Understanding the leanings of this organization, I think it is fair to wonder if their rating system will eventually be extended to inform parents as to whether a musical group has homosexuals in it. Will the PMRC permit musical groups to exist, but only if gay members don't sing, and are not depicted on the album cover?

28   The PMRC has demanded that record companies "re-evaluate" the contracts of those groups who do things on stage that *they* find offensive. I remind the PMRC that groups are composed of individuals. If one guy wiggles too much, does the whole band get an "X"? If the group gets dropped from the label as a result of this re-evaluation process, do the other guys in the group who weren't wiggling get to sue the guy who wiggled because he ruined their careers? Do the founders of this tax exempt organization with no members plan to indemnify record companies for any losses incurred from unfavorably decided breach of contract suits, or is there a PMRC secret agent in the Justice Department?

29   Should individual musicians be rated? If so, who is to determine if the guitar player is a "X," the vocalist is a "D/A" or the drummer is a "V"? If the base player (or his Senator) belongs to a religious group that dances around with poisonous snakes, does he get an "O"? What if he has an earring in one ear, wears an Italian horn around his neck, sings about his astrological sign, practices yoga, reads the Caballa, or owns a rosary? Will his "occult content" go into an old CoIntelPro computer, emerging later as a "fact" to determine if he qualifies for a home-owner loan? Will they tell you this is necessary to protect the folks next door from the possibility of "devil-worship" lyrics creeping through the wall?

30   What hazards await the unfortunate retailer who accidentally sells an "O" rated record to somebody's little Johnny? Nobody in Washington seemed to care when Christian terrorists bombed abortion clinics in the name of Jesus. Will you care when the "Friends of The Wives of Big Brother" blow up the shopping mall?

31   The PMRC wants ratings to start as of the date of their enactment. That leaves the current crop of "objectionable material" untouched. What will be the status of recordings from that Golden Era to censorship? Do they become collector's items . . . or will another "fair and unbiased committee" order them destroyed in a public ceremony?

32   Bad facts make bad law, and people who write bad laws are, in my opinion, more dangerous than songwriters who celebrate sexuality. Freedom of Speech, Freedom of Religious Thought, and the Right to Due Process for composers,

---

[5] Consult the first paragraph of Nat Hentoff's "When Nice People Burn Books" in this volume in reference to the significance of Lynchburg.

performers, and retailers are imperiled if the PMRC and the major labels consummate this nasty bargain.

33   Are we expected to give up Article One so the big guys can collect an extra dollar one every blank tape and 10 to 25% on tape recorders? What's going on here? Do *we* get to vote on this tax? There's an awful lot of smoke pouring out of the legislative machinery used by the PMRC to inflate this issue. Try not to inhale it.[6] Those responsible for the vandalism should pay for the damage by voluntarily rating themselves. If they refuse, perhaps the voters could assist in awarding the Congressional "X," the Congressional "D/A," the Congressional "V," and the Congressional "O." Just like the ladies say: these ratings are necessary to protect our children. I hope it is not too late to put them where they really belong.

34   [I think that this whole matter has gotten completely blown out of proportion, and I agree with Senator Exon that there is a very dubious reason for having this event. I also agree with Senator Exon that you should not be wasting time on stuff like this, because from the beginning I have sensed that it is somebody's hobby project.

35   Now, I have done a number of interviews on television. People keep saying, can you not take a few steps in their direction, can you not sympathize, can you not empathize? I do more than that at this point. I have got an idea for a way to stop all of this stuff and a way to give parents what they really want, which is information, accurate information as to what is inside the album, without providing a stigma for the musicians who have played on the album or the people who sing it or the people who wrote it. And I think that if you listen carefully to this idea that it might just get by all of the constitutional problems and everything else.

36   As far as I am concerned I have no objection to having all of the lyrics placed on the album routinely, all the time. But there is a little problem. Record companies do not own the right automatically to take these lyrics, because they are owned by a publishing company.

37   So, just as all the rest of the PMRC proposals would cost money, this would cost money too, because the record companies would need—they should not be forced to bear the cost, the extra expenditure to the publisher to print those lyrics.

38   If you consider that the public needs to be warned about the contents of the records, what better way to do it than to let them see exactly what the songs say? That way you do not have to put any kind of subjective rating on the record. You do not have to call it R, X, D/A, anything. You can read it for yourself.

39   But in order for it to work properly, the lyrics should be on a uniform kind of sheet. Maybe even the Government could print those sheets. Maybe it should even be paid for by the Government, if the Government is interested in making sure that people have consumer information in this regard.

---

[6] It should be noted that this admonition was delivered well before Bill Clinton's admission to smoking marijuana, but not to inhaling.

40   And you also have to realize that if a person buys the record and takes it out of the store, once it is out of the store you can't return it if you read the lyrics at home and decide that little Johnny is not supposed to have it.

41   I think that that should at least be considered, and the idea of imposing these ratings on live concerts, on the albums, asking record companies to re-evaluate or drop or violate contracts they already have with artists should be thrown out.

42   That is all I have to say.]

---

1. Both the RJ Reynolds ad, "I'm One," that this book begins with and Zappa's testimony, with which the book closes, occur in highly charged political circumstances, and both warn against government interference in choices which, it is argued in each case, should be personal. Can you make a rhetorical case for them both being intended to be "overheard"?

2. Write a short essay in which you offer an explanation for Zappa's direct and insulting treatment of the very people it would seem, on first look, that he hopes to persuade. Consider your answer to question one when you answer this.

3. In using the phrase "the Wives of Big Brother" Zappa directly invokes Orwell's *1984*. From your study of "Politics and the English Language" would you be able to make a case for a useful comparison of the rhetoric of this essay and Orwell's?

Frank Zappa died in 1993 of prostate cancer. He was 53. He is survived by his wife, Gail, and his children, Ahmet, Diva, Dweezil, and Moon. Anyone interested in the work of this prolific and well loved icon of the music world is urged to visit www.zappa.com.

ACKNOWLEDGMENTS

26 "Why I Want a Wife" by Judy Brady as appeared in *MS Magazine,* December 1979. Reprinted by permission of the author.

113 "Why Woman Are Paid Less than Men" by Lester Thurow from *THE NEW YORK TIMES,* March 8, 1981. Copyright © 1981 by The New York Times Co.

167 "It's Wrong to Lump People Into Senseless Categories" by Donna Britt as appeared in *HOUSTON CHRONICLE,* November 29, 1994. Copyright © 1994, The Washington Post Writers Group. Reprinted with permission.

169 "Ships in the Night" by Lawrence Bush from *THE NEW YORK TIMES,* Op-Ed, April 5, 1994. Copyright © 1994 by the New York Times Co. Reprinted by permission.

171 "Demystifying Multiculturalism" by Linda Chavez from *NATIONAL REVIEW,* February 21, 1994, pp. 26-32. Copyright © 1994 by National Review, Inc., 215 Lexington Avenue, New York, NY 10016. Reprinted by permission.

177 "The Prescriptive Tradition" from *THE CAMBRIDGE ENCYCLOPEDIA OF LANGUAGE,* 2nd Edition by David Crystal. Reprinted with the permission of Cambridge University Press.

183 "Is This a Dagger Which I See Before Me? No Congressman, It's Korea" by Barney Frank as appeared in *THE WASHINGTON POST,* July 27, 1988. Reprinted by permission of the author.

187 "A Liberalism of Heart & Shine" by Henry Louis Gates, Jr. from *THE NEW YORK TIMES,* Op-Ed, March 27, 1994. Copyright © 1994 by the New York Times Co. Reprinted by permission.

191 "Too Early in the Game for Karen" by Ellen Goodman from *THE WASHINGTON POST,* January 10, 1981. Copyright © 1981, The Boston Globe Newspaper Co./Washington Post Writers Group. Reprinted with permission.

193 "A Proposal to Abolish Grading" by Paul Goodman from *COMPULSORY MISEDUCATION.* Reprinted by permission of Sally Goodman.

197 From "Newt Gingrich" by Gopac in *HARPER'S Magazine,* November 1990.

199 "Curbing the Sexploitation Industry" by Tipper Gore from *THE NEW YORK TIMES,* March 14, 1988. Copyright © 1988 by the New York Times Co. Reprinted by permission.

203 "Everything Spoken Here" by Paul Greenberg as appeared in the *FT. WORTH STAR TELEGRAM,* July 12, 1998. Reprinted by permission of Paul Greenberg, Editorial Page Editor of the Arkansas Democrat-Gazette and a syndicated columnist.

205 "In Defense of Animals" by Meg Greenfield originally appeared in *NEWSWEEK,* April 17, 1989.

209 Chapter 11 from *LANGUAGE IN THOUGHT AND ACTION,* Fifth Edition by S. J. Hayakawa and Alan R. Hayakawa, copyright © 1990 by Harcourt, Inc., reprinted by permission of the publisher.

215 "When Nice People Burn Books" by Nat Hentoff as appeared in *THE PROGRESSIVE,* February 1983. Reprinted by permission of the author.

221 "The Gettysburg Address" by Gilbert Highet. Copyright © 1954 by Gilbert Highet. Reprinted by permisison of Curtis Brown, Ltd.

227 From *METAMAGICAL THEMAS: QUESTING FOR THE ESSENCE OF MIND* by Douglas Hofstadter. Copyright © 1985 by Basic Books, Inc. Reprinted by permission of Basic Books, a member of Perseus Books, L.L.C.

235 "Gays Parade a Useful Exercise" by Molly Ivins as appeared in the *HOUSTON CHRONICLE,* April 28, 1993.

237 "A First Amendment Junkie" by Susan Jacoby. Copyright © 1978 by Susan Jacoby. Originally appeared in *THE NEW YORK TIMES.* Reprinted by permission of Georges Borchardt, Inc., for the author.

241 "'Gender Bender' Ads: Same Old Sexism" by Jean Kilbourne from *THE NEW YORK TIMES,* May 15, 1994. Reprinted by permission of the author.

243 "You Are Liberal, You Strongly Favor Gay Rights" by Charles Krauthammer from *THE NEW REPUBLIC,* June 6, 1981. Reprinted by permission of The New Republic, © 1981, The New Republic, Inc.